Evidence-Based Treatment
of Personality Dysfunction

Evidence-Based Treatment of Personality Dysfunction
Principles, Methods, and Processes

Edited by

Jeffrey J. Magnavita

American Psychological Association

Washington, DC

Published by
American Psychological Association
750 First Street, NE
Washington, DC 20002
www.apa.org

To order
APA Order Department
P.O. Box 92984
Washington, DC 20090-2984
Tel: (800) 374-2721; Direct: (202) 336-5510
Fax: (202) 336-5502; TDD/TTY: (202) 336-6123
Online: www.apa.org/books/
E-mail: order@apa.org

In the U.K., Europe, Africa, and the Middle East, copies may be ordered from
American Psychological Association
3 Henrietta Street
Covent Garden, London
WC2E 8LU England

Typeset in Goudy by Circle Graphics, Inc., Columbia, MD

Printer: Maple-Vail, York, PA
Cover Designer: Minker Design, Sarasota, FL

The opinions and statements published are the responsibility of the authors, and such opinions and statements do not necessarily represent the policies of the American Psychological Association.

Library of Congress Cataloging-in-Publication Data

Evidence-based treatment of personality dysfunction : principles, methods, and processes / edited by Jeffrey J. Magnavita.
     p. cm.
  Includes bibliographical references and index.
  ISBN-13: 978-1-4338-0747-3 (print)
  ISBN-10: 1-4338-0747-5 (print)
  ISBN-13: 978-1-4338-0748-0 (electronic)
  ISBN-10: 1-4338-0748-3 (electronic)
1. Personality disorders—Patients—Treatment. I. Magnavita, Jeffrey J.

  RC554.E94 2010
  616.85'8106—dc22
                              2009039872

British Library Cataloguing-in-Publication Data

A CIP record is available from the British Library.

Printed in the United States of America
First Edition

CONTENTS

CONTRIBUTORS

Allan A. Abbass, MD, FRCPC, Centre for Emotions and Health, Dalhousie University, Halifax, Nova Scotia, Canada

Jack C. Anchin, PhD, Department of Psychology, University at Buffalo—SUNY, Buffalo, NY

Louis G. Castonguay, PhD, Department of Psychology, Pennsylvania State University, University Park

Kenneth L. Critchfield, PhD, Utah Neuropsychiatric Institute and Department of Psychology, University of Utah, Salt Lake City

Prudence F. Cuper, MA, Department of Psychology, Duke University, Durham, NC

Catherine Eubanks-Carter, PhD, Brief Psychotherapy Research Program, Beth Israel Medical Center, New York, NY

Jay L. Lebow, PhD, ABPP, The Family Institute at Northwestern University, Evanston, IL

W. John Livesley, MD, PhD, Department of Psychiatry, University of British Columbia Vancouver, British Columbia, Canada

Jeffrey J. Magnavita, PhD, ABPP, Glastonbury Psychological Associates, P.C. Clinical Affiliate Staff, Department of Psychiatry Hartford Hospital, Unified Psychotherapy Project, Glastonbury, CT

Stanley B. Messer, PhD, Graduate School of Applied and Professional Psychology, Rutgers University, Piscataway, NJ

J. Christopher Muran, PhD, Derner Institute for Advanced Psychological Studies, Adelphi University, Garden City, NY; Brief Psychotherapy Research Program, Beth Israel Medical Center, New York, NY

Aaron L. Pincus, PhD, Department of Psychology, Pennsylvania State University, University Park

Clive J. Robins, PhD, ABPP, ACT, Department of Psychiatry and Behavioral Sciences, Duke University Medical Center, Durham, NC

M. Zachary Rosenthal, PhD, Department of Psychiatry and Behavioral Sciences, Duke University Medical Center, Durham, NC

Jeremy D. Safran, PhD, Department of Psychology, New School for Social Research, New York, NY; Brief Psychotherapy Research Program, Beth Israel Medical Center, New York, NY

William B. Stiles, PhD, Department of Psychology, Miami University, Oxford, OH

Stephen Strack, PhD, United States Department of Veterans Affairs, Los Angeles, CA; Fuller Graduate School of Psychology, Pasadena, CA

Amanda A. Uliaszek, MS, Northwestern University, Evanston, IL

PREFACE

The treatment of personality disorders—or, more broadly, personality dysfunction—is a rapidly evolving focus of contemporary mental health practice. The study of personality, which fell out of favor for a period in academic psychology and now is in resurgence, remains a useful construct for clinicians and clinical researchers. Personality offers a tool that helps clinicians organize complex interrelated sets of phenomena in a manner that allows for optimal clinical strategizing. Most contemporary theorists and clinical scientists view personality as a complex system that has self-organizing qualities and, although prone to chaos, also has discernable patterns for which tools of science and pattern recognition can be used. Many of these ways of using pattern recognition are presented by the authors in this volume, who have considerable clinical and research experience and have been able to distill and refine these in a manner that will be of great benefit to clinical practitioners.

This volume was conceived during a period of critical transition for clinical science and practice. The need for clinical services has never seemed greater in contemporary time than since the return of the veterans after World War II. The demands of contemporary society and the need to adjust to rapid global changes, economic stressors, technological change, climate change, population shifts, and cultural blending is stressing many members of society beyond their ability to cope and adapt. Personality dysfunction seems ubiquitous and can be seen taking its toll at every level of society. We live in a time where those tasked with leading our major institutions have shown levels of deviant behavior that previously seemed unimaginable to those who entrusted them to safeguard society. Social, political, economic, and global stressors have trickled down to families who must adapt to ever-decreasing resources and institutional safeguards.

Clinicians are under siege as well. We are asked to provide assistance to increasingly more difficult conditions with greater pressure to get results in a cost-effective manner. The cost of personality disorders to society is enormous, and yet there is little in the way of political will to identify and address these conditions. There still remains a stigma and a denial of the problem in regard to clinical mental health treatment. Unfortunately, personality disorders, although they likely have some genetic underpinnings, are transferred from generation to generation via the multigenerational transmission process. These patterns of dysfunction are transmitted through a variety of mechanisms, including not only child abuse and neglect but also poverty, discrimination, marginalization, and social factors.

Clinicians need to base their best practices on the most current research available to them to maximize their treatment impact; however, the available evidence for clinicians is not so readily accessible. The sources of evidence that are required to provide an evidence-based practice are not so easy to find. Complicated treatment decisions require lines of evidence from multiple sources that for many clinicians are beyond their resources to efficiently find. This volume was conceived as a way for those who are at the forefront of theory, research, and practice to distill what is most important from the extant evidence base. Clearly, a volume of this size can never present all the information a clinician needs to know, but the authors in this volume did their best to bring together the evidence they think is critical to guide practice. Each contributor worked diligently within stringent space constraints to offer readers the best that he or she could find in the evidence and show how it can be used to optimize treatment. It was truly a pleasure and a labor of love to work with such an esteemed group of clinical scientists, and I hope readers will share our excitement about what can be done in the hands of a compassionate clinician who is using the best evidence available to enhance personality adaptation and functioning at all levels in our society.

ACKNOWLEDGMENTS

A work of this magnitude takes a village of scholars, researchers, clini-cians, theorists, and, most of all, people who are suffering and seek our under-standing and assistance. I want to express my gratitude to what I consider to be seminal organizations in the advancement of psychotherapy that have been important to my development and that are made up of some of the most intel-lectually challenging and passionate individuals one could ever know. First, I would like to thank all the individuals from the Divisions of Psychotherapy and Clinical Psychology of the American Psychological Association who have supported my development over many decades, allowing me to test my ideas out in safe and supportive venues. I am also indebted to the Society of Psy-chotherapy Exploration and Integration, whose members have allowed me to present my work to those I consider to be the most informed leaders in psy-chotherapy and who have at times disagreed with but ultimately respected my drive toward unification of psychotherapy. I also am indebted to the Society for Psychotherapy Research, which has provided me with an opportunity to interact and befriend many of the leading psychotherapy researchers in the world. Many of the individuals whom I am thanking spent their scarce time discussing some issues vital to this volume and the field. I am also thankful for the Society for the Study of Personality Disorders and the researchers who publish a stream of vital empirical evidence related to the topic of treating personality dysfunction. Finally, the last organization that has been a home for my work is the International Association of Experiential Dynamic Therapy, of which I am delighted to be a founding member and which is devoted to presenting its members' work internationally via video. I have tremendous respect for the cofounders who bravely present their work for others to see and thus allow their essential vulnerability to be revealed in a way needed to advance clinical science.

Evidence-Based Treatment of Personality Dysfunction

1

THEORY AND PRACTICE OF EVIDENCE ABOUT TREATMENT OF PERSONALITY DYSFUNCTION

JEFFREY J. MAGNAVITA AND WILLIAM B. STILES

At one time or another, virtually all mental health clinicians are faced in the consulting room with individuals and families who test their skills, patience, and endurance. Many of these individuals enter treatment with complaints of symptoms such as anxiety, depression, problems with emotional regulation, relational difficulties, substance use disorders, and a range of other concerns that indicate they are having trouble coping and functioning at their optimal level in their families, workplaces, and communities (Magnavita, 2005). Often, after first-line treatment interventions for Axis I disorders have been tried, and when treatment response is poor, the clinician hypothesizes that problems with the patient's personality functioning might be compromising treatment. At this juncture, many clinicians feel at a loss for how to proceed, and often the treatment ends with less than satisfactory results.

All too often, even well-trained clinicians prefer to refer difficult or treatment-refractory patients to other specialists, who likely administer a range of psychopharmacologic agents, use alternative treatments, and then become frustrated themselves. Some clinicians feel they do not have an adequate conceptual understanding of the personality system and how it operates or why dysfunctional personality patterns endure. Even worse, many clinicians allow difficult patients to slip away from treatment while breathing a sigh of relief, justifying their difficulty engaging the patient by saying to themselves "The patient wasn't motivated," "He was untreatable," "She was beyond my ability level," and making similar rationalizations.

Although some patients with more severe personality dysfunction may be beyond a particular clinician's competence, letting such patients slip away means that the opportunity to refer a patient to a colleague with the skills and training to handle the level of challenge was lost when the patient may have been ripe for change. A missed opportunity to treat someone who is ready to change can have a multigenerational impact in that dysfunctional behavior patterns may be passed on to successive generations of that individual's family. Such a missed opportunity may occur when there is a lack of understanding about the existing treatment approaches that have some evidentiary basis in the accumulated research findings and clinical wisdom.

The treatment of personality dysfunction is a relatively new specialty. Although characterological disorders were the target of much early 20th-century psychoanalytic treatment, it was not until the 1980s, when the field focused on systematic diagnostics for personality disorders, that new treatment strategies were developed and researched. Since then, the treatment of personality dysfunction has advanced rapidly. However, relative to the scope of the problem, there is little research to guide the treatment. Personality dysfunction challenges clinicians with its heterogeneity, which requires a spectrum of treatment formats, methods, and conceptual tools. Another important issue that drives the evidence-based movement in the mental health profession is patients' and consumers' rights to receive the best care available. Clinicians face many challenges, one of which is keeping abreast of the latest developments. Unfortunately, there is often a major delay between the development of effective methods and their adoption by clinical practitioners.

PATIENTS HAVE THE RIGHT TO EFFECTIVE TREATMENT

In an editorial, Oldham (2007) echoed a question asked earlier by Klerman (1990) concerning a case of a patient with severe depression who had been receiving psychotherapy for 7 months without medication: "How are we doing developing an evidence base concerning the efficacy of psychotherapy, often longer term, for severe and disabling personality disorders that either stand alone or co-occur with depression or other axis I conditions?" (p. 1465). This question was one of the motivations for this volume. There is often a significant gap between the publication of research and dissemination of results that are applicable to clinical practice, leaving clinicians without a base of evidence on which to make informed treatment decisions and to help them decide how to approach each case in an individualized manner. The evidence-based movement in the fields of mental health and medicine is an attempt to resolve this transmission process and thus attempts to put at the fingertips of clinicians the latest relevant research.

EVOLUTION OF THE EVIDENCE-BASED TREATMENT MOVEMENT

The treatment of clinical syndromes and personality dysfunction historically has varied from clinician to clinician on the basis of the unique education and training that each clinician has received. Psychoanalysts' patients received psychoanalytic treatment, behaviorally inclined therapists' patients were apt to receive cognitive behavior therapy, and so forth. Beginning in the 1980s, when the integrative treatment movement was spawned, however, differential treatment selection became a realistic option. Clinicians became more comfortable offering multiple modalities and integrative forms of treatment that sought to draw on the most potent aspects and methods and drawn from various schools. Of course, researchers could not separately assess each of the blended theories and techniques. Hundreds of schools of psychotherapy existed, and subjecting each of them—much less all of the blends—to experimental assessment was beyond the realm of reason and expense. Various approaches became dominant as each school struggled for attention and funding. Often, the market for new techniques drove the field as clinicians hungry for effective methods sought out innovators who offered new methods and techniques. During the last two decades of the 20th century the field of mental health was in a state of massive growth and chaos. Many in the field saw the need to ground the plethora of approaches on the foundation of observations and sound science; thus, the *empirically based movement* was spawned. This movement has had a profound influence on the shape of the field and the practice of clinical treatment of mental disorders. Another trend that was also highly influential, though in some cases controversial, was the *empirically supported treatment (EST) movement*.

EMPIRICALLY SUPPORTED TREATMENT

The EST movement was initiated by the American Psychological Association's (APA's) Division 12 (Society of Clinical Psychology), when a task force issued a report urging the field to identify and disseminate research findings to guide clinical practice (APA, 2005). EST is based on evidence from randomized clinical trials (RCTs) of treatment approaches. For an approach to qualify, it had to meet certain criteria in regard to the design and number of RCTs completed. Approaches were rated and published in EST lists that were available to consumers, insurance companies, and clinicians (e.g., Chambless et al., 1998).

As a guide for clinical practice, however, "the work on ESTs has proved quite controversial for a variety of reasons" (Stewart & Chambless, 2007, p. 269). Some clinicians have criticized EST because they believe that certain forms of psychotherapy are more amenable to this type of research protocol. Others have criticized what they see as an undervaluing of other forms of evidence, such as clinical expertise and experience in decision making. Smith (2009) "challenge[d] the validity of the technological model of therapy on which it is based" (p. 34). He argued that the concerns people bring to psychotherapists cannot be understood as separate components of the person and that psychotherapy requires engagement with the person more broadly.

In much of clinical medicine RCTs are considered the scientific gold standard. The RCT is a statistical adaptation of the controlled experiment, a research procedure that offers the best approximation to causal inference yet devised. RCTs have been convincing in comparing psychopharmacological agents with placebos or each other. However, as we discuss later in this chapter, the application of RCTs to psychotherapy is beset with methodological and epistemological problems that render it more equivalent in value to other (also problematic) types of evidence (see also Haaga & Stiles, 2000).

In addition, conducting RCTs for psychotherapy is enormously time consuming and costly. Even clinical scientists who believe RCTs represent the gold standard of evidence must somehow deal with complex clinical presentations while waiting for such high-quality research evidence to be amassed. Clinicians must somehow decide what is the best evidence available when making the complex decisions with which they are faced. Therefore, as evidence slowly accumulates about the effectiveness of various approaches it is imperative that clinicians who often operate under the most challenging circumstances know which sources of evidence are most credible.

EVIDENCE-BASED PRACTICE

Evidence-based practice (EBP)—a broader category than ESTs—may be understood as using the best evidence available in making clinical treatment decisions (Sackett, Rosenberg, Gray, Haynes, & Richardson, 1996). EBP can be distinguished from ESTs in at least two major ways. First, the evidence-based approach is more broadly defined, considering a wide range of evidence that includes but is not limited to RCTs (see Figure 1.1). Basing one's clinical approach on ESTs is highly limiting, not least because very few RCT studies

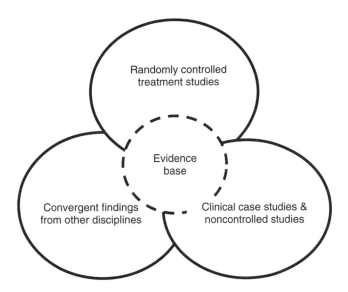

Figure 1.1. Three converging domains of evidence-based practice.

on personality disorders are available. Second, EBP recognizes that evidence about psychotherapeutic treatments is not applied mechanically by technicians but is integrated and applied by practitioners using their professional judgment to assess when evidence is relevant and to decide how it should be used in practice.

The APA (2005) report contains the following statement: "Evidence-based practice in psychology is the integration of the best available research with clinical expertise in the context of patient characteristics, culture, and preferences" (para. 1). Also, according to Spring (2007):

> Psychologists can have three primary kinds of relationship to research evidence. First, as researchers, they can design, conduct, analyze, and report research, thereby contributing directly to creating evidence. Second, as systematic reviewers, they can locate, appraise, and quantitatively synthesize research for evidence users. Third, as research consumers, they can access research evidence, appraise its quality and relevance for their context, and integrate research into their practical decision-making. Each of these three ways of relating to research assumes some common base of research knowledge, and each also entails some specialized skills. (p. 620)

We hope readers of this volume will critically examine various lines of evidence when making treatment planning decisions and developing a collaborative plan with their patients. Evidence that can enhance effectiveness has been published in disparate sources and integrated only occasionally in special review articles (e.g., Leichsenring & Leibing, 2003; Perry, Banon, & Ianni, 1999), special editions of journals, and of course books such as this one.

The first author of this chapter was once asked to hypnotize a patient to help him with a problematic habit. I knew of no scientific basis for the effectiveness of hypnosis for this problem. After about three requests, at the end of what seemed like a very productive session, the patient announced he was not coming back because his request for hypnosis had been ignored. This reminded me of what a supervisor early in my career used to say: "The operation was a success, but the patient died." The best approach may not always be best for the therapeutic alliance, and without a patient there is no hope of engaging in the change process.

THREE PILLARS OF EVIDENCE-BASED PRACTICE

The three essential elements of EBP are (a) the best evidence guiding a clinical decision (the *best evidence domain*); (b) the clinical expertise of the health-care professional to diagnose and treat the patient's problems (the *clinical expertise domain*); and (c) the unique preferences, concerns, and expectations that the patient brings to the health-care setting (the *client domain*). These three elements are often referred to as the *three pillars of EBP* (Bauer, 2007, p. 686). Appropriate types of evidence and their sources are not always obvious in complex clinical phenomena. It is a challenge to distinguish which evidence to use for conceptualizing and treating personality dysfunction. The domain of the best evidence to guide clinical decision making includes several components:

- Data about the *etiological factors* and *pathogenesis* that lead to certain personality configurations and treatment implications. Understanding the pathogenesis and etiological factors is critical for prevention, early intervention, and treatment. Patients have the right to know what the best evidence suggests about the clinical syndromes and personality system they manifest.
- *Theoretical modeling* used as a pattern recognition tool to guide the clinician in organizing the data sets into a coherent picture. A *theoretical system* is a framework for constructs that are useful for clinical practice. For example, research showing that individuals who have suffered from neglect and trauma early in life are more likely to have a smaller hippocampus and an overactive amygdala may be useful in understanding and strategizing affect-regulating strategies for patients with emotional dysregulation.

Understanding the neurobiology and dynamic processes is critical to working with any system as complex as humans. Lambert (2005) reported that better outcomes were achieved when treatment was theory driven than when it was not.

- *Epidemiological findings* that inform practitioners about incidence and pattern of particular types of personality dysfunction.

The clinical expertise domain comprises the following components the:

- familiarity with various diagnostic systems to identify and categorize the various manifestations of personality dysfunction;
- training in various models of EBP and the ability to use methods and techniques that are effective;
- familiarity with relational and alliance processes essential for working with patients who manifest personality dysfunction;
- understanding of and expertise in various modalities of treatment, such as individual psychotherapy, couples psychotherapy, family psychotherapy, group psychotherapy, ecosystem interventions, and psychobiological treatment (e.g., medication, neurofeedback, biofeedback) in that treating personality dysfunction, especially the more severe manifestations, often requires multimodal and sequential treatment planning;
- familiarity with concurrent and sequential treatment approaches incorporating various modalities, formats, and settings to obtain optimal results; and
- experience with a range of cases, gained through practice, observation, or reading reports of others' cases.

Interrelated areas in the client domain include the following:

- patient characteristics and expectations;
- level of adaptive capacities and resources, such as family and social networks;
- cultural considerations and ethnic variations;
- patient expectancies and motivational factors; and
- patient resources and the logistics of attending treatment.

As we can see from the preceding summary of the three pillars and subdomain systems, a tremendous amount of information must be distilled and synthesized to truly practice EBP. Such practice requires methods for synthesizing and reporting these types of data and training practitioners in the needed skill sets. The contributors to this volume attempt to bring these data sets together by distilling the best evidence on which to base clinical practice in the treatment of personality disorders and related syndromes.

HIERARCHY OF EVIDENCE IN EVIDENCE-BASED PRACTICE

In the traditional hierarchy of evidence (e.g., Gray, 1997), clinical case material and uncontrolled case studies are at the bottom, and RCTs are at the top. This hierarchy is being questioned, however, even in medicine (e.g., Rawlins, 2008). In psychotherapy research, streams of evidentiary support from research located lower on the hierarchy should not be easily dismissed.

In a RCT, randomization ensures that all initial differences are spread randomly between groups, which then receive different treatments so that, on average, differences in outcomes can be attributed to the treatment each group received.

Experimental logic requires that everyone within a particular group receive the same treatment. Krause and Lutz (2009) argued that clients in a psychotherapy treatment condition do not receive the same treatment because of casual entanglements. Treatment, therapist, client, and context variables depend on each other, confounding the manipulation. Even worse, psychotherapeutic treatment (the supposed independent variable) also depends on the dependent variables. Therapists use the tools at their disposal to overcome treatment problems as they emerge; this appropriate responsiveness works to defeat differential treatment effects (Stiles, 2009; Stiles, Honos-Webb, & Surko, 1998). For example, various therapists might implement a particular treatment differently, and each therapist behaves differently with different sorts of clients yet yields similar outcomes (e.g., Hardy et al., 1998). As a result, even the best studies do not always shed light on which components of psychotherapy are critical to the change process.

On the other end of the traditional hierarchy are *case studies*, which are receiving significant new attention in psychotherapy research (e.g., Elliott, 2002; Fishman, 1999; McLeod, 2003). Case studies have well-known problems, including selective sampling, low power, and investigator biases. Nevertheless, they offer a method for disciplined observation and can inform practitioners about possible phenomena and contingencies at a level of depth and detail far beyond what can be accomplished in hypothesis-testing studies. A case study can yield a large number of theory-relevant observations on *different* aspects of a theory, which may be considered analogous to degrees of freedom on the *same* theoretical aspect (a hypothesis deduced from the theory) in statistical hypothesis testing (Campbell, 1979). Each theory-relevant observation serves as positive or negative evidence and may point to specific modifications or extensions that would improve the theory. Thus, although case studies cannot yield high confidence in isolated conclusions, they may be as powerful as hypothesis-testing studies for building and gaining confidence in a psychological conceptualization or theory (Stiles, 2007, in press).

Such considerations by no means dictate that RCTs should be abandoned and replaced with case studies. Our point instead is that because psychotherapy is complex, responsive, difficult to control for practical and ethical reasons, and not plausibly accessible to double-blind designs, traditional approaches to medical research cannot be implemented properly, and the traditional hierarchy of evidence may be flattened. Many sorts of evidence are worth considering critically, but one must recognize that all of them have problems. We suspect such considerations were implicitly or explicitly responsible for the relatively greater inclusiveness of the APA (2005) EBP report compared with evaluations of evidence types in many other areas of clinical research.

EVIDENCE-BASE AND THEORETICAL MODELS FROM OTHER DISCIPLINES

Findings from the field of neuroscience are addressing many previously unsubstantiated psychological constructs, such as unconscious learning and emotional processing (Hassin, Uleman, & Bargh, 2005). Tools of cognitive neuroscience, such as psychophysiological measures, brain imaging (e.g., positron emission tomography, functional magnetic resonance imaging), and others, are being used to create an increasing evidence base that supports many important observations made by clinicians (Lane & Nadel, 2000). Animal models of emotion and psychopathology have significant implications for clinical practice and provide very compelling lines of convergent evidence (Panksepp, 1998). For example, Harlow's (1971) primate studies on attachment demonstrated the veracity of attachment theory for the shaping of personality.

EVIDENCE USED BY THIS BOOK'S AUTHORS

One way to assess what evidence is useful is to consider what authors discuss when they write about clinical issues. We read drafts of many of this book's chapters before we wrote this introductory chapter. We were struck by how little of what the authors wrote was based on evidence from RCTs. Should this observation be considered a criticism or an implicit statement of how experts value sources of evidence about personality disorders and their treatment?

Chapter 2, which focuses on the assessment of personality disorders, makes extensive use of research on the structure, reliability, and validity of particular instruments instead of inferential studies of effectiveness. The question asked and the problems encountered in assessment research are different from those in treatment research. There are, nevertheless, fundamental questions; for example, do the distinctions made in assessing personality disorders justify conceptualizing them as discrete phenomena? Do the personality disorders comprise unique, natural types of dysfunction, or are they arbitrarily imposed distinctions within multidimensional continua?

In several chapters of this book there is a curious disjunction, well illustrated in Chapter 4, between the clinical suggestions and the questions addressed by the research. Whereas most of the research concerns the outcomes of whole treatments—short-term dynamic therapy, dialectical behavior therapy, milieu therapy, and so forth—the treatment suggestions concerns processes within sessions. For example, the authors' most detailed clinical suggestions were based on Davanloo's (1980), Magnavita's (1997), and McCullough Vaillant's (1997) distinctions among defensive restructuring, affective restructuring, and cognitive restructuring, which emerged from clinical experience, microanalysis of audiovisual tapes, and psychodynamic theory as opposed to formal research. The chapter's section on techniques and methods of treatment uses a case study approach.

Somewhat similarly, the authors of Chapter 6 base their analysis of treating personality disorders not on explicit findings but on a theory of alliance rupture and repair called *brief relational therapy* (BRT). They offer a series of clinical vignettes with brief transcribed examples used not only to illustrate but also to convince. The richness of an actual (transcribed) encounter offers more than a single datum, insofar as the whole dialogue—not just an isolated data point—is consistent with the theory. BRT presumably was built from the team's clinical experience and thus represents, in condensed form, the team's empirical observations of many previous cases (cf. Stiles, 2007). Late in the chapter, the authors review some outcome studies showing that BRT is effective, but this is almost incidental to the thrust of the chapter.

Chapter 8, which discusses integrated treatment, draws broadly on systems conceptualizations to emphasize the value of a varied repertoire of conceptual and technical tools. The author makes little reference to specific findings of inferential research, although, as in many sections of the chapter, he does present exemplar passages to demonstrate key points.

IS THE TREATMENT OR THE CLINICIAN EVIDENCE BASED?

Another debate is whether a task as complex as the treatment of psychological disorders and personality dysfunction is based on the application of *treatments* that are empirically supported or whether it is the *clinician* who is evidence based (Krause, Lutz, & Saunders, 2007). "The fact is that all psychotherapeutic treatment is undoubtedly deeply affected by the natures of therapist and patient and their evolving and often unavoidably and repeatedly perturbed relationship as therapist and patient" (Krause et al., 2007, p. 349). It is clear that therapist and patient factors interact with treatment methods in a very complex way. Accordingly, perhaps, as Krause et al. (2007) wrote, it is more important that the clinician, instead of a particular treatment approach, be empirically certified. It does seem clear from a review of the literature that therapist factors are critical to successful outcomes when treating patients with personality disorders. These factors include the following characteristics:

- open-minded, flexible, and creative in one's approach (necessitated by the complexity of personality disorder treatments and psychopathology);
- comfortable with long-term, emotionally intense relationships;
- tolerance of own negative feelings regarding the patient and treatment process;
- patience; and
- training and experience with a specific Axis II disorder (Fernandez-Alvarez, Clarkin, del Carmen Salgueiro, & Critchfield, 2006, p. 215).

THE CHALLENGE OF KEEPING CURRENT WITH THE RAPIDLY EXPANDING EVIDENCE BASE AND ACCESS TO INFORMATION

Clinicians need to have the most current evidence base at their fingertips to be able to provide the most informed treatment. However, this is a daunting task because of the vast quantity of literature published and the considerable lag time between publication of empirical findings and their uptake by the practice community. It is estimated that if physicians were to read all the articles concerning practice they would have to spend 600 hours reading every month just to stay current (Alper et al., 2004). With the explosion in journals and research in the behavioral sciences, it is likely that mental health clinicians would also be faced with an enormous challenge to their time and resources just to stay current:

> Psychologists and other health care professionals need efficient methods not only for finding answers to clinically relevant questions, but also for staying up-to-date with the scientific literature. It is clear that it is no longer possible to stay informed by reading a few journals every month; skills that ensure lifelong learning have become essential for all health care professionals. (Walker & London, 2007, p. 634)

EBP has been adopted as a theme for medicine and psychology (APA, 2005) as well as for other professions whose members have been publishing articles and books that disseminate relevant information (Walker & London, 2007). There has been a growing demand for databases "of secondary, synthesized literature [that] has evolved to meet practitioners' needs" (Spring, 2007, p. 618). One such database is the Cochrane Collaboration's online database of Systematic Reviews of Health Care Practices (http://cochcrane.org/). Readers may also refer to Norcross, Hogan, and Koocher's (2008) *Clinician's Guide to Evidence-Based Practices*, in which they review many of the essential elements of EBP as well as the databases available and how to access them.

EVIDENCE-BASED PRACTICE AND THERAPIST RESPONSIVENESS

Responsiveness refers to behavior being influenced by emerging contexts (i.e., by new events), in particular those that include interpersonal cues (Stiles et al., 1998). This can be illustrated by imagining mothers and babies interacting: Each attends to the other and responds meaningfully. Responsiveness occurs on time scales from months to milliseconds in all human interaction, and in particular in psychotherapy. Therapists' skills and goals involve responsiveness; for example, treatment assignment, treatment planning, active listening, timing, staying on topic, turn taking, attunement, and adjusting interventions already in progress illustrate therapeutic responsiveness on different time scales.

Because therapy interaction is responsive, psychological interventions cannot be specified in the same way as pharmacological interventions. Manuals and other written descriptions of treatment recognize this implicitly. A quote from Chapter 4 of this volume is characteristic: "The point for clinicians to keep in mind is to apply various techniques flexibly according to the patient's capacities, the state of the therapeutic alliance, and the stage of treatment" (p. 100). This is a clear description of responsiveness. It undoes the myth of treatment specification, reducing the recommendations to the status of ideas to be considered.

Personality dysfunction encompasses a particularly complex and heterogeneous group of disorders, and no single approach can be expected to benefit every patient. Various streams of evidence can inform practice, but synthesizing this information and making it relevant for practitioners is a challenge. Kazdin (2008) put it this way:

> The challenge of clinical decision making can be conveyed by the effort
> to "tailor treatment to meet the needs of individual patients." This state-

ment is one we make and accept routinely in our clinical work, but researchers have yet to help us do that. A clinician might use an eclectic therapy and draw on multiple resources (including EBTs) to develop a treatment package suited to the individual. There are no formal or clearly replicable procedures for how to do this, in terms of selecting one or more treatments or components of treatment among all available therapies and deciding in what proportion and sequence they ought to be delivered to patients. As clinicians, we have an idea of how to do this, but it is not yet well established that different clinicians would select the same or a similar individualized treatment plan (i.e., reliability) when presented with the same case. (p. 149)

EBP offers a way through this complex maze. If we consider evidence as something to be used responsively by professional practitioners, instead of as instructions to be followed by technicians, then all sorts of research can be understood as potentially valuable. *Research,* as we use the term, is quality control on ideas though observation—checking whether the ideas match the world. EBP respects the complexity and variety of the individuals and contexts that clinicians encounter and the need to adapt treatments to these variations; it also respects clinicians' potential ability to use information flexibly and responsibly. Any observations that are accurate and relevant to the nature and treatment of personality disorders can prove valuable, as can conceptualizations that organize and synthesize the observations. Clinical practice is evidence based to the extent that it systematically makes use of these reality checks—drawing on others' observations of the world instead of on prejudice and preconception. The chapters in this book offer substance for EBP, summarizing the observations of those who have studied and dealt with personality disorders. The encompassing potential of EBP is summarized in the concept of a unified psychotherapy, described in Chapter 10.

WHAT WE KNOW, WHAT THE EVIDENCE SUGGESTS, AND WHAT REMAINS TO BE KNOWN

There is some good news: Personality disorders are treatable with contemporary forms of psychotherapy. Often those that cannot be effectively treated can now be managed so as to reduce the individual's harm to self and others. There are now a number of approaches that have been validated using RCTs, which are considered the gold standard of scientific support. Many of these studies are presented in this volume, but researchers are publishing new findings regularly, so it would behoove the reader to become an evidence-based practitioner.

REFERENCES

Alper, B. S., Hand, J. A., Elliott, S. G., Kinkade, S., Hauan, M. J., & Onion, D. K. (2004). How much effort is needed to keep up with the literature relevant for primary care? *JAMA, 92*, 429–437.

American Psychological Association. (2005). *Policy statement on evidence-based practice in psychology*. Retrieved from http://www2.apa.org/practice/ebpstatement.pdf

Bauer, R. M. (2007). Evidence-based practice in psychology: Implications for research and research training. *Journal of Clinical Psychology, 63*, 685–694.

Campbell, D. T. (1979). "Degrees of freedom" and the case study. In T. D. Cook & C. S. Reichardt (Eds.), *Qualitative and quantitative methods in evaluation research* (pp. 49–67). Beverly Hills, CA: Sage.

Chambless, D. L., Baker, M. J., Baucom, D. H., Beutler, L. E., Calhoun, K. S., Crits-Christoph, P., . . . Woody, S. R. (1998). Update on empirically validated therapies II. *The Clinical Psychologist, 51*, 3–16.

Davanloo, H. (Ed.). (1980). *Short-term dynamic psychotherapy*. New York, NY: Jason Aronson.

Elliott, R. (2002). Hermeneutic single case efficacy design. *Psychotherapy Research, 12*, 1–20.

Fernandez-Alvarez, H., Clarkin, J. F., del Carmen Salgueiro, M., & Critchfield, K. L. (2006). Participant factors in treating personality disorders. In L. G. Castonguay & L. E. Beutler (Eds.), *Principles of therapeutic change that work* (pp. 203–218). New York, NY: Oxford University Press.

Fishman, D. B. (1999). *The case for a pragmatic psychology*. New York, NY: New York University Press.

Haaga, D. A. F., & Stiles, W. B. (2000). Randomized clinical trials in psychotherapy research: Methodology, design, and evaluation. In C. R. Snyder & R. E. Ingram (Eds.), *Handbook of psychological change: Psychotherapy processes and practices for the 21st century* (pp. 14–39). New York, NY: Wiley

Hardy, G. E., Stiles, W. B., Barkham, M., & Startup, M. (1998). Therapist responsiveness to client interpersonal styles during time-limited treatments for depression. *Journal of Consulting and Clinical Psychology, 66*, 304–312.

Harlow, H. F. (1971). *Learning to love*. San Francisco, CA: Albion.

Hassin, R. R., Uleman, J. S., & Bargh, J. A. (2005). *The new unconscious*. New York, NY: Oxford University Press.

Kazdin, A. E. (2008). Evidence-based treatment and practice. *American Psychologist, 63*, 146–159.

Klerman, G. L. (1990). The psychiatric patient's right to effective treatment: Implications of *Osheroff v. Chestnut Lodge. American Journal of Psychiatry, 147*, 409–418.

Krause, M. S., & Lutz, W. (2009). Process transforms inputs to determine outcomes: Therapists are responsible for managing process. *Clinical Psychology: Science and Practice, 16*, 73–81.

Krause, M. S., Lutz, W., & Saunders, S. M. (2007). Empirically certified treatments or therapists: The issue of separability. *Psychotherapy: Theory, Research, Practice, Training, 44,* 347–353.

Lambert, M. J. (2005). Early response in psychotherapy: Further evidence for the importance of common factors rather than "placebo effects." *Journal of Clinical Psychology, 61,* 855–869.

Lane, R. D., & Nadel, L. (2000). *Cognitive neuroscience of emotion.* New York, NY: Oxford University Press.

Leichsenring, F., & Leibing, E. (2003). The effectiveness of psychodynamic therapy and cognitive behavior therapy in the treatment of personality disorders: A meta-analysis. *American Journal of Psychiatry, 160,* 1223–1232.

Magnavita, J. J. (1997). *Restructuring personality disorders.* New York, NY: Guilford Press.

Magnavita, J. J. (Ed.). (2005). *Handbook of personality disorders: Theory and practice.* Hoboken, NJ: Wiley.

McCullough Vaillant, L. (1997). *Changing character: Short-term anxiety regulating psychotherapy for restructuring of defenses, affects, and attachments.* New York, NY: Basic Books.

McLeod, J. (2003). *Doing counselling research* (2nd ed.). London, England: Sage.

Norcross, J. C., Hogan, T. P., & Koocher, G. P. (2008). *Clinician's guide to evidence-based practices: Mental health and the addictions.* New York, NY: Oxford University Press.

Muir Gray, J. A. (1997). *Evidence-based health care.* New York, NY: Churchill Livingston.

Oldham, J. M. (2007). Psychodynamic psychotherapy for personality disorders. *American Journal of Psychiatry, 163,* 1465–1467.

Panksepp, J. (1998). *Affective neuroscience: The foundations of human and animal emotions.* New York, NY: Oxford University Press.

Perry, J., Banon, E., & Ianni, F. (1999). Effectiveness of psychotherapy for personality disorders. *American Journal of Psychiatry, 156,* 1312–1321.

Rawlins, M. D. (2008). *De testimonio: On the evidence for decisions about the use of therapeutic interventions.* London, England: Royal College of Physicians.

Sackett, D. L., Rosenberg, W. M. C., Gray, J. A. M., Haynes, R. B., & Richardson, W. S. (1996). Evidence based medicine: What it is and what it isn't. *British Medical Journal, 3123,* 71–72.

Smith, K. R. (2009). Psychotherapy as applied science or moral praxia: The limitations of empirically supported treatment. *Journal of Theoretical and Philosophical Psychology, 29,* 34–46.

Spring, B. (2007). Evidence-based practice in clinical psychology: What it is, why it matters; what you need to know. *Journal of Clinical Psychology, 63,* 611–631.

Stewart, R. E., & Chamless, D. L. (2007). Does psychotherapy research inform treatment decisions in private practice? *Journal of Clinical Psychology, 63,* 267–281.

Stiles, W. B. (2007). Theory-building case studies of counselling and psychotherapy. *Counselling and Psychotherapy Research, 7,* 122–127.

Stiles, W. B. (2009). Responsiveness as an obstacle for psychotherapy outcome research: It's worse than you think. *Clinical Psychology: Science and Practice, 16,* 86–91.

Stiles, W. B. (in press). Logical operations in theory-building case studies. *Pragmatic Case Studies in Psychotherapy.* Retrieved from http://pcsp.libraries.rutgers.edu/index.php/pcsp/article/viewFile/973/2384

Stiles, W. B., Honos-Webb, L., & Surko, M. (1998). Responsiveness in psychotherapy. *Clinical Psychology: Science and Practice, 5,* 439–458.

Walker, B. B., & London, S. (2007). Novel tools and resources for evidence-based practice in psychology. *Journal of Clinical Psychology, 63,* 633–642.

2

EVIDENCE-BASED ASSESSMENT AND INSTRUMENTATION FOR PERSONALITY DISORDERS

STEPHEN STRACK

This chapter focuses on empirically validated methods for assessing personality dysfunction. The lion's share of research in this area has focused on the personality disorders (PDs) found on Axis II of the *Diagnostic and Statistical Manual of Mental Disorders* (4th edition, text revision; *DSM–IV–TR*; American Psychiatric Association, 2000), with a growing literature in the past decade on the dimensional assessment of maladaptive personality traits and a reconceptualization of PDs within a psychodynamic framework (e.g., Bornstein, 2006; PDM Task Force, 2006; Shedler, 2002). Space considerations prevent exhaustive coverage of the literature on PD assessment, but readers may find recent reviews in a number of sources (e.g., Clark, 2007; Clark & Harrison, 2001; O'Donohue, Fowler, & Lilienfeld, 2007; Widiger & Coker, 2002; Widiger, Costa, & Samuel, 2006; Widiger & Samuel, 2005). Here I provide specific recommendations on well-tested methods for assessing personality disturbance in clinical practice that have emerged from the three areas of research just mentioned. I also discuss the assumptions and theoretical constructs that underlie these three ways of conceptualizing personality pathology, address measurement problems that should be considered by anyone

Preparation of this chapter was supported by the U.S. Department of Veterans Affairs.

who assesses PDs, and highlight relational issues that may affect outcomes when testing therapy clients.

Methods available to clinicians for the assessment of maladaptive personality traits are unstructured, semistructured, and fully structured clinical interviews; self-report inventories; and performance-based tests. *Unstructured interviews* are the most common form of assessment in clinical practice, consisting of a series of questions selected by the interviewer for the purpose of eliciting from the client the information needed to make a clinical decision. The content, wording, and sequencing of unstructured interview questions are usually idiosyncratic to the interviewer and will be unspecified before and after the interview. Unstructured interviews are, by nature, unstandardized, and because of this they are not favored by clinical researchers. Although I comment on unstructured interviews in this chapter, they are not recommended for evidence-based practice because of their unreliability (Widiger & Coker, 2002).

Semistructured interviews (e.g., the International Personality Disorder Examination [IPDE]; Loranger, 1999; see Exhibit 2.1) provide a standard set of questions that are asked in a specified sequence, along with explicit rules for scoring responses. However, they also encourage follow-up queries that

EXHIBIT 2.1
Recommended Instruments for Assessing Personality Pathology as defined in the *Diagnostic and Statistical Manual of Mental Disorders* (4th ed., text revision; *DSM–IV–TR;* American Psychiatric Association, 2000)

Diagnostic Interviews for *DSM–IV–TR* Personality Disorders

International Personality Disorder Examination (Loranger, 1999). Description: Measures all *DSM–IV–TR* personality disorders (PDs) as well as *ICD–10* (World Health Organization, 1992) PDs. Includes a self-report screening form that takes the client 15 min to complete. The screener is given to identify patients who are likely to have PDs and who should then be evaluated with the semistructured diagnostic interview, which takes 90 to 120 min to complete. The interview is organized around topic areas rather than diagnostic category, with open-ended inquiries provided at the beginning of each section to enable smooth transition. Results allow the examiner to assign a definite, probable, or negative diagnosis for each PD. **Cost:** introductory kit with manual, 25 screening questionnaires, 15 interview booklets, and 50 answer sheets, $206.00 (2009 price). **Available from:** Psychological Assessment Resources, Inc., 16204 N. Florida Avenue, Lutz, FL 33549. Toll-free order line, 800-331-8378. Web site, http://www.parinc.com

Personality Disorders Interview—IV (Widiger, Manguine, Corbitt, Ellis, & Thomas, 1995). Description: Measures all *DSM–IV–TR* PDs. This semistructured interview takes approximately 120 min to complete and is offered in two formats, in which diagnostic criteria and corresponding questions are arranged by PD or by thematic content areas. A score summary and profile booklet allow users to summarize interview responses by diagnostic criteria and to plot an overall dimensional profile of the client, which can assist users in rank ordering multiple diagnoses by order

EXHIBIT 2.1
Recommended Instruments for Assessing Personality Pathology
as defined in the *Diagnostic and Statistical Manual of Mental
Disorders* (4th ed., text revision; *DSM–IV–TR;* American
Psychiatric Association, 2000) *(Continued)*

of importance. **Cost:** introductory kit with manual, two each of interview booklets arranged by diagnostic category and thematic content area, 10 score summaries, and 10 profile booklets, $156.00 (2008 price). **Available from:** Psychological Assessment Resources, Inc., 16204 N. Florida Avenue, Lutz, FL 33549. Toll-free order line, 800-331-8378. Web site, http://www.parinc.com

Structured Clinical Interview for *DSM–IV* Axis II Personality Disorders (First & Gibbon, 2004). Description: Measures all *DSM–IV–TR* PDs. Includes a self-report questionnaire (15 min to complete) that can be used as a screening tool to identify clients who are likely to have PDs and to shorten the interview by identifying the diagnostic categories to target. The interview, which takes approximately 60 min to complete, begins with a brief overview that characterizes the client's typical behavior and relationships and elicits information about his or her capacity for self-reflection. Questions cover each diagnostic criterion and were written to reflect the client's inner experience. Probes are encouraged to obtain specific examples from clients about their thoughts, feelings, and behaviors. A summary score sheet is completed at the end of the interview, which provides a dimensional score for each PD. **Cost:** starter kit with manual and five each of the self-report questionnaires, interview booklets, and summary score sheets, $106.00 (2009 price). Computer software for the self-report questionnaire and interview, with unlimited uses, $510.00 (2009 price). **Available from:** paper products only, American Psychiatric Publishing, Inc., 1000 Wilson Blvd., Suite 1825, Arlington, VA 22209-3901. Toll-free order line, 800-368-5777. Web site, http://www.appi.org. Paper products and software, Multi-Health Systems, Inc., P.O. Box 950, North Tonawanda, NY 14120-0950. Toll-free order line, 800-456-3003. Web site: http://www.mhs.com

Structured Interview for *DSM–IV* Personality Disorders (Pfohl, Blum, & Zimmerman, 1997). Description: Measures all *DSM–IV–TR* PDs. This semistructured interview uses positive and neutral questions to examine behavior and traits from the client's perspective. Organized by topic rather than diagnostic criteria, the interview is designed to be conversational in tone and takes approximately 90 min to complete. Topics include emotions, interests and activities, perception of others, relationships, self-image, stress, social conformity, and work. A score sheet is used to tally indicators for each PD and provides a quick summary of likely diagnoses. **Cost:** set of five interviews that includes an introduction to the instrument, instructions, space for scoring, and score sheet, $59.00 (2009 price). **Available from:** American Psychiatric Publishing, Inc., 1000 Wilson Blvd., Suite 1825, Arlington, VA 22209-3901. Toll-free order line, 800-368-5777. Web site, http://www.appi.org

Self-Report Measures of *DSM–IV–TR* Personality Disorders

Millon Clinical Multiaxial Inventory—III (Millon, 2009). Description: Measures all *DSM–IV–TR* PDs. Respondents answer "true" or "false" to each of 175 statements. For use with clients 18 years of age and older who read at the eighth-grade level. Takes approximately 30 min to complete. Contains a validity scale, 3 response style scales, 14 PD scales, and 10 clinical syndrome scales. Raw scores are transformed into base rate scores using norms from 998 male and female psychiatric patients. Scale elevations are plotted as continuous scores, but cutoffs above a base rate of 75

(continues)

EXHIBIT 2.1
Recommended Instruments for Assessing Personality Pathology
as defined in the *Diagnostic and Statistical Manual of Mental
Disorders* (4th ed., text revision; *DSM–IV–TR;* American
Psychiatric Association, 2000)   *(Continued)*

are indicative of psychiatric diagnosis. Can be administered in paper-and-pencil format, by computer, and with an audio CD. May be hand scored or computer scored; computer-generated profile and narrative reports are available. **Cost:** starter kit with manual, three answer sheets, one test booklet, and three mail-in interpretive reports, $158.50 (2009 price). **Available from:** Pearson Assessments, Inc., P.O. Box 1416, Minneapolis, MN 55440. Toll-free order line, 800-627-7271. Web site: http://www.pearsonassessments.com

Personality Diagnostic Questionnaire—4 (PDQ–4; Hyler, 1994). Description: Measures all *DSM–IV–TR* PDs. This 99-item true–false questionnaire takes 20 to 30 min to complete and is appropriate for use with clients 18 years of age and older. Can be administered in paper-and-pencil form or by computer using the Internet. Scores for each PD can be graphically displayed with indicators of whether the elevations are clinically significant, marginally significant, and not significant. **Cost:** paper-and-pencil test kit with instructions, scoring sheet, and a screening interview is provided on a CD with unlimited uses for $18.00 (2009 price). Internet-based computerized administration and scoring, $29.99–$59.99 per month (2009 price). **Available from:** paper-and-pencil test, http://www.pdq4.com; Internet version, http://www.pdqtest.com

Schedule of Normal and Abnormal Personality—2 (SNAP–2; Clark, Simms, Wu, & Casillas, 2008). Description: Assesses all *DSM–IV–TR* PDs. This newly published update to the SNAP (Clark, 1993) is a 390-item true–false questionnaire designed for use with clients 18 years of age and older and takes approximately 90 min to complete. The SNAP–2 retains the same item content for substantive scales as its predecessor but includes a new validity scale (Back Deviance), improved norms (community-based nonpatient adults), and better coordination of scales with *DSM–IV–TR* PDs. The SNAP was developed using a factor analytic approach, the goal of which was to identify all dimensional traits underlying personality pathology. The SNAP–2 contains 7 validity indices, 15 trait and temperament measures, and 10 *DSM–IV–TR* PD scales. A limitation is that the measure is available only in paper-and-pencil form and must be hand scored. A graphic profile of test results makes it easy to identify how high or low a client's scores are vis-à-vis the norm sample. **Cost:** manual, $20.00; 10 test booklets, $15.00; 100 answer sheets, $20.00; scoring keys, $60.00; 25 profile sheets, $10.00 (2009 prices). **Available from:** University of Minnesota Press Test Division, 111 Third Avenue South, Suite 290, Minneapolis, MN 55401-2520. Telephone, 612-627-4821. Web site, http://www.upress.umn.edu/tests

Self-Report Measures of Personality Dysfunction

Dimensional Assessment of Personality Pathology (Livesley & Jackson, 2008). Description: This 290-item questionnaire is answered on a 5-point Likert scale (1 = *very unlike me,* 5 = *very like me*). It is appropriate for clients 18 years of age and older and takes approximately 90 min to complete. The test can be administered in paper-and-pencil form or via the Internet. May be hand scored or computer scored (via the Internet). Dimensional plots of scores are provided to indicate how high or low a client is vis-à-vis the trait being assessed. This instrument was developed using a factor analytic approach, the goal of which was to identify all dimension traits underlying personality pathology. Eighteen factor-derived scales may be

EXHIBIT 2.1
Recommended Instruments for Assessing Personality Pathology
as defined in the *Diagnostic and Statistical Manual of Mental
Disorders* (4th ed., text revision; *DSM–IV–TR;* American
Psychiatric Association, 2000)   *(Continued)*

scored that cover the traits underlying the *DSM–IV–TR* PDs. Four higher order scales may also be calculated that are highly correlated with four of the Big Five dimensions of Neuroticism, Extraversion, Agreeableness, and Conscientiousness. **Cost:** start-up kit with manual, three answer sheets, one test booklet, and three mail-in interpretive reports, $125.00 (2009 price). **Available from:** Sigma Assessment Systems, Inc., P.O. Box 610984, Port Huron, MI 48061-0984. Toll-free order line, 800-627-7271. Web site, http://www.sigmaassessmentsystems.com

Revised NEO Personality Inventory (Costa & McCrae, 1992). Description: This 240-item questionnaire is answered on a 5-point Likert scale and can be used with clients 18 years of age and older. It provides measures of five broad normal personality dimensions (Neuroticism, Extraversion, Openness, Agreeableness, and Conscientiousness) as well as six facets of each dimension. The dimensions and facet scales have been reliably linked to *DSM–IV–TR* PDs. An observer rating form is available that allows the therapist or a significant other to provide assessment of the client. The extensive norm base includes a cross-section of nonpatient adults. Can be given as a paper-and-pencil measure or via personal computer. May be hand scored or computer scored. Dimensional plots of scores make it easy to assess whether a respondent is high or low on a particular trait vis-à-vis the norm sample. **Cost:** comprehensive kit with manual, 25 answer sheets, 10 test booklet, 50 profile forms, and 25 summary feedback sheets, $260.00 (2009 price). **Available from:** Psychological Assessment Resources, Inc., 16204 N. Florida Avenue, Lutz, FL 33549. Toll-free order line, 800-331-8378. Web site, http://www.parinc.com

Minnesota Multiphasic Personality Inventory—2 (Butcher et al., 2001). Description: Clients answer "true" or "false" to 567 statements that were written at a sixth-grade reading level. Takes approximately 90 to 120 min to complete. Appropriate for clients 18 years of age and older (a separate version for adolescents is available). Provides over 100 validity and clinical measures. *T* scores indicate the client's degree of deviation from the norm sample made up of over 2,000 nonpatient adults from across the United States and Canada. Can be administered in paper-and-pencil form, by computer, and with an audio CD. May be hand scored or computer scored; computer-generated profiles and narrative reports are available. **Cost:** starter kit with Adult Clinical Systems—Revised user's guide, three answer sheets, one test booklet, and three mail-in interpretive reports, $132.00 (2009 price). **Available from:** Pearson Assessments, Inc., P.O. Box 1416, Minneapolis, MN 55440. Toll-free order line, 800-627-7271. Web site, http://www.pearsonassessments.com

Personality Assessment Inventory (Morey, 1991). Description: This questionnaire contains 344 statements answered on a 4-point Likert scale ranging from 1 = totally false to 4 = very true. Appropriate for persons 18 years of age and older; statements were written at the fourth-grade reading level. The instrument may be scored for 22 nonoverlapping scales, including 4 validity indices, 11 clinical measures, 5 treatment-related scales, and 2 interpersonal variables. Can be administered in a paper-and-pencil form, by computer, and with an audio CD. May be hand scored or computer-scored; computer-generated profiles and narrative reports are available. **Cost:** comprehensive kit with manual, 2 test booklets, 25 answer sheets,

(continues)

EXHIBIT 2.1
Recommended Instruments for Assessing Personality Pathology
as defined in the *Diagnostic and Statistical Manual of Mental
Disorders* (4th ed., text revision; *DSM–IV–TR;* American
Psychiatric Association, 2000)   *(Continued)*

25 profile forms, and 25 critical items forms, $295.00 (2009 price). **Available from:** Psychological Assessment Resources, Inc., 16204 N. Florida Avenue, Lutz, FL 33549. Toll-free order line, 800-331-8378. Web site, http://www.parinc.com

Temperament and Character Inventory (Cloninger, Przybeck, Svrakic, & Wetzel, 1994). Description: This 240-item true–false questionnaire comes in an adult form for clients 15 years of age and older and a child–adolescent form for persons 7 to 14 years of age. Both forms take approximately 45 to 60 min to complete. The instrument measures seven dimensions of personality, including four temperament variables (novelty seeking, harm avoidance, reward dependence, persistence) and three character traits (self-directedness, cooperativeness, and self-transcendence). Scales for three to five subcomponents of each dimension are also measured (there are a total of 25 dimensional facet scales). Extensive norms are available for adults, adolescents, and children. The test can be administered in a paper-and-pencil form, via personal computer, or on the Internet. Scale scores may be plotted on a profile, and an interpretive report is also available. **Cost:** starter set with manual, test protocol, and scoring keys, $85.00; computer program with unlimited uses, $400.00 (2009 prices). **Available from:** C. Robert Cloninger, MD, Center for Well-Being, Department of Psychiatry, Washington University Medical School, 660 S. Euclid—Campus Box 8134, St. Louis, MO 63110. Web site, http://psychobiology.wustl.edu

Performance-Based Measures of Personality Dysfunction

Rorschach—Exner Comprehensive System (Exner, 2003). Description: The Comprehensive System is a method of administering and scoring the Rorschach (1921/1942) test, which consists of 10 colored plates containing designs created from folded ink blots. The Rorschach test may be administered to adults, adolescents, and children as young as 5 years of age. Exner's administration method takes approximately 60to 90 min to complete, with coding and scoring taking an additional 60 to 120 min, depending on the length and complexity of the test protocol. Norms are available for 600 nonpatient adults. Results are summarized in a Structural Summary that contains over 50 scores and indices. There are no scores or indices for *DSM–IV–TR* PDs, but several variables have been reliably linked to personality pathology that is associated with *DSM–IV–TR* PD diagnoses. **Cost:** Rorschach test plates, $100.00; 100 Structural Summary Blanks, $30.00; Rorschach Interpretation Assistance Program, Version 5, for computer scoring, $675.00 (2009 prices). **Available from:** Paper products only, Rorschach Workshops, P.O. 9010, Asheville, NC 28805. Telephone, 828-298-7200 Web site, http://www.rorschachworkshops.com. Paper products and computer software, Psychological Assessment Resources, Inc., 16204 N. Florida Avenue, Lutz, FL 33549. Toll-free order line, 800-331-8378. Web site, http://www.parinc.com

Note. The measures listed in this exhibit assess a wide variety of PDs and traits, have good empirical support, and are readily available for purchase in forms that most clinicians will find useful. Excluded were measures that assess only one or two PDs and traits, have limited or equivocal empirical support, and/or are not practical for clinical use.

can be worded in a manner that is idiosyncratic to the interviewer, may allow the exclusion of certain questions when the interviewer judges them to be unnecessary for rendering a confident assessment, and typically require the scoring of some diagnostic criteria on the basis of the interviewer's observational impressions of the respondent. Semistructured interviews usually include a mix of items with standard scoring options (e.g., present vs. absent) and open-ended questions, the responses to which can be idiosyncratic to the respondent and complex in content.

Fully structured interviews (e.g., the Diagnostic Interview Schedule; Leaf, Myers, & McEvoy, 1991) provide a systematic assessment by standardizing the questions used by an interviewer, the sequence of the questions, and the scoring of responses (Rogers, 2001). Structured interviews provide little to no allowance for deviation from the specified procedures (e.g., few or no follow-up queries are allowed). Fully structured interview questions are generally phrased in a manner such that the scoring of the response will be unambiguous (e.g., questions that can be answered by "yes" or "no"). Many fully structured interviews are so straightforward that they can be administered and scored by laypersons.

Self-report inventories (e.g., the Millon Clinical Multiaxial Inventory—III [MCMI–III]; Millon, 2009; see Exhibit 2.1) consist of written statements, adjectives, or questions, to which a person responds in terms of a specified set of options (e.g., true or false, or agree vs. disagree along a 5-point scale). Most such inventories are administered in private settings that minimize distractions and maximize confidentiality, although they can as easily be given in public and group settings (e.g., clinic waiting rooms and testing rooms that accommodate multiple clients). They can usually be administered by secretaries or clerks, because the instructions are designed to be self-explanatory.

Performance-based tests (e.g., the Rorschach; Exner, 2003; see Exhibit 2.1) present clients with a standard set of stimuli that can vary in structure and complexity. Respondents are asked to consider the stimuli and give responses that may be specific (e.g., answers to intelligence test questions) or open ended. Probes by the administrator are regulated by the specific test, but they may be exact or general, and either simple or complex, with some tests, such as the Rorschach (Exner, 2003), allowing for extended queries to ensure accurate coding of the client's responses. Many performance-based tests are administered during face-to-face meetings with the client, but some, such as sentence completion tests, can be administered as self-report forms.

THEORETICAL UNDERPINNINGS AND ASSUMPTIONS

The three major systems of conceptualizing personality dysfunction addressed in this chapter share a number of theoretical assumptions, but they also demonstrate critical differences in the way problems are defined and therefore measured. In this section I present the key conceptual elements that differentiate each approach.

DSM–IV–TR

PDs were first placed on a separate axis from other mental disorders in *DSM–III* (American Psychiatric Association, 1980). The assumption that guided this decision is that personality is a pervasive and ingrained feature of psychiatric patients, whereas most mental disorders are fleeting, with courses that typically wax and wane on the basis of underlying disease factors and psychosocial stressors.

The group of 10 PDs diagnosed on Axis II of *DSM–IV–TR* (paranoid, schizoid, schizotypal, antisocial, borderline, histrionic, narcissistic, avoidant, dependent, and obsessive–compulsive; American Psychiatric Association, 2000) is not based on a theoretically derived taxonomy. The diagnoses are the product of a consensus of opinion among the scientists and practitioners who made up the PDs work group authorized by the American Psychiatric Association to develop Axis II. Reports from those who participated in the work group indicated that their decisions about which PDs to include were informed by current summaries of personality theory and empirical research (Livesley, 1995). Extensive literature searches were conducted, and both published and unpublished data were scrutinized (in some cases, they were reanalyzed). Although field trials were advocated, only one was actually carried out (for antisocial PD), and it proved to be controversial. Although Axis II of *DSM–IV–TR* was not based on a coherent taxonomy, its authors attempted to cover the most common forms of personality pathology evident in psychiatric settings, and a provision was made to allow clinicians to diagnose other forms of PD using the Not Otherwise Specified category. It is interesting to note that this category is often more frequently used by clinicians than any other PD diagnosis (Livesley, 2001a).

The basic assumptions underlying *DSM–IV–TR* are that PDs are categorically distinct from normal range personality styles, can be assessed by a limited set of diagnostic criteria, and can be descriptively grouped into three clusters. There are 80 criteria for the 10 officially recognized PDs, and *DSM–IV–TR* provides specific rules for distinguishing between the presence and absence of each PD. For example, at least four of the seven listed features must be present to diagnose schizoid PD (American Psychiatric Association, 2000). Most of the criteria address overt behaviors (e.g., for schizoid PD: almost always chooses solitary over social pursuits), but some require inference on the part of the clinician (e.g., for paranoid PD: suspects—without sufficient basis—that others are exploiting, harming, or deceiving him or her). Cluster A personalities are those that appear odd or eccentric to others (paranoid, schizoid, schizotypal); and individuals with Cluster B disorders often appear dramatic, emotional, or erratic (antisocial, borderline, histrionic, narcissistic); whereas those with Cluster C personalities often appear anxious or fearful (avoidant, dependent, obsessive–compulsive).

Dimensional Assessment of Personality Traits

Current models of personality and psychopathology view normality and abnormality as end points on a continuum, with no sharp dividing line differentiating the two domains (e.g., Clark, Simms, Wu, & Casillas, 2008; Costa & Widiger, 2002; Livesley, 2001b; Livesley & Jackson, 2008; Millon, 1996). The assumption in these models is that the same traits underlie normal and abnormal personality. Abnormality is presumed to be caused by too much or too little of a given trait or set of traits, which leads to ineffective coping and responding. For example, a high level of neuroticism (which includes high sensitivity to unpleasant, negative emotions) may, by itself, place an individual at risk of mood disorders, but more pervasive problems may obtain if the same person has low levels of agreeableness and openness to experience (which, at moderate levels, might help the person cope with his or her emotional sensitivity). Persons without PDs are presumed to have moderate or high levels of adaptive traits and low levels of maladaptive traits and to be able to respond flexibly and adaptively to a wide range of stressors. Each personality model specifies which traits are involved in differentiating normal and abnormal personality, and the levels of specific traits, or profile of multiple traits, that are associated with dysfunctional behavior.

Psychodynamic Assessment

The system of conceptualizing pathological personality from a psychodynamic perspective represents an integration of more classical psychoanalytic classifications of character structure with Kernberg's (1970) integration of modern object relations theory with ego psychology regarding levels of personality organization (Bornstein, 2005, 2006; Lerner & Lerner, 2007; Trimboli & Farr, 2000). This diagnostic system involves assessing clients along two relatively independent dimensions. The first dimension consists of a descriptive characterological diagnosis organized in terms of distinct character structures. Character, from a psychoanalytic perspective, involves habitual modes of behavior and refers to constant, stereotyped modes of response the ego makes in mediating the demands of internal and external reality. Character traits are descriptive attributes representing a compounded synthesis that expresses a combination of psychic factors, including drives, defenses, identifications, superego aspects, modes of relating, attitudes, values, and moods.

Character structure refers to a cluster of traits that typically go together to form a particular personality style. Representative character structures include the hysterical, obsessive–compulsive, depressive, masochistic, infantile, narcissistic, and paranoid personalities (Lerner & Lerner, 2007).

The second dimension involves an evaluation of the underlying level of personality organization (Bornstein, 2005, 2006; Lerner & Lerner, 2007; Trimboli & Farr, 2000). Arguing that a descriptive characterological diagnosis is necessary but not sufficient, Kernberg (1970) devised a system for classifying levels of personality organization based on an assessment of psychological structures. The specific structures that are appraised include level of instinctual development, manifestations of ego weaknesses, level of defensive organization, level of internalized object relations, level of superego development, and attainment of ego identity. Each structure is placed on a continuum ranging from higher level (neurotic organization), through intermediate level (borderline organization), to lower level (psychotic organization). In this way, the diagnostic schema includes categorical (character structure) and dimensional (levels of personality structure based on several clinically relevant dimensions) components that are clinically important and assessable (Lerner & Lerner, 2007).

ESSENTIAL THEORETICAL CONSTRUCTS

The conceptual distinctions just reviewed can be further differentiated into constructs that provide the variable domains to be measured and the criteria by which personality pathology—and personality health—are to be judged. Presented here are the most important elements used to operationalize the three approaches into distinct measurement systems.

DSM–IV–TR

The general diagnostic criteria include the determination of whether there is an enduring pattern of inner experience and behavior that deviates markedly from the expectations of the individual's culture and whether this enduring pattern is manifested in two or more of the following four ways: (a) cognitively, (b) affectively, (c) interpersonally, and/or (d) through impulse dyscontrol (American Psychiatric Association, 2000). Clinicians must also determine whether the enduring pattern is inflexible and pervasive across a broad range of personal and social situations; whether the enduring pattern leads to clinically significant distress or impairment in social, occupational, or other important areas of functioning; whether the enduring pattern is indeed stable, of long duration, and can be traced back at least to adolescence or early adulthood; whether the enduring pattern is not better accounted for as a manifestation or consequence of another mental disorder; and, finally, whether the enduring pattern is due to the direct physiological effects of a substance or a medical condition, such as head trauma. If all of these criteria are met, then a PD diagnosis can be provided (Widiger et al., 2006; Widiger & Samuel, 2005).

Dimensional Assessment of Personality Traits

There are several competing dimensional models of personality that use varying numbers of factors to explain individual differences (e.g., Clark et al., 2008; Costa & Widiger, 2002; Livesley, 2001b; Livesley & Jackson, 2008; Millon, 1996). Most of these describe traits hierarchically such that lower order traits represent specific personal characteristics and higher order traits are more broad and subsume the lower order traits. An example of this is the *five-factor personality model* (FFM; e.g., Costa & Widiger, 2002), which posits five broad dimensions of personality (Neuroticism, Extraversion, Agreeableness, Conscientiousness, and Openness) that are measured by 30 lower order traits or facets. Dimensional models do not specify when traits become inflexible and maladaptive, and there is no consensus on how many, and which, traits are needed to cover the domain of normal and abnormal functioning.

Dimensional models of personality are concerned with multiple traits that underlie the specific personality types or categories. However, traits are typically not "all or none" (present or absent within a person); they are often viewed as being broad or narrow in their effects on behavior, and they are believed to be hierarchical in nature, with broader traits subsuming more narrow traits (e.g., Markon, Krueger, & Watson, 2005). Because of this, most personality measurement systems assess not the presence or absence of traits within an individual but the *level* of various traits on separate continua. As well, some measures assess aggregate personality types (or styles), whereas others measure broad or narrow traits. For example, MCMI–III scales measure individual personality styles that are linked to the PDs diagnosed on Axis II of *DSM–IV–TR* (Strack, 2008; Strack & Millon, 2007). This is the broadest (or highest) level of measurement, because each personality style is believed to be the expression of (and result of) many traits in interaction with each other. The NEO Personality Inventory–Revised (NEO-PI-R; Costa & McCrae, 1992) measures five broad trait dimensions and several subtrait dimensions that are nested under each of the five broader traits. Even at the broadest level of measurement, the NEO-PI-R does not offer a personality portrait of an individual until the profile configuration of traits and subtraits is examined as a whole.

Psychodynamic Assessment

Three psychodynamic constructs are key to understanding the nature of personality pathology: (a) ego strength, (b) defense style, and (c) object relations (Bornstein, 2005, 2006; Trimboli & Farr, 2000). Early experiences help determine the developing child's ego strength, that is, the degree to which the ego carries out reality-testing functions and deals effectively with impulses. Adequate parenting and minimal disruptions and traumas enable a child to devote considerable psychic energy to developing good reality-testing skills and acquiring effective self-control strategies. Inadequate parenting and/or significant disruption in the child–caregiver relationship divert psychic energy from these adaptation-enhancing ego functions, because at least some of the child's psychological resources must be used to cope with various stressful and hurtful experiences. Studies indicate that ego strength in adolescents and adults varies to some degree as a function of situational factors (e.g., mood, anxiety level), but they also suggest that two key elements of ego strength—reality testing and impulse control—are relatively consistent over time, with enduring, traitlike qualities.

As children move through adolescence and into adulthood, they develop a stable *defense style*, that is, a characteristic way of managing anxiety and coping with external threat (Bornstein, 2005, 2006; Cramer, 2000). Positive early experiences are associated with a flexible, adaptive defense style wherein mature defenses (e.g., sublimation, intellectualization) predominate (Vaillant, 1994). Negative early experiences lead to a less effective, and less mature, defense style characterized by coping strategies that entail greater distortion of internal and external events (e.g., repression, projection). Psychodynamic researchers have conceptualized defense style differently, but evidence from different research programs confirms that well-validated measures of defense style predict adjustment and functioning in a broad array of psychological domains (Cramer, 2000; Ihilevich & Gleser, 1986; Perry, 1991).

Early in life, a child internalizes mental representations of the self and significant others (Bornstein, 2005, 2006). These object representations—sometimes called *introjects*—evolve over time, but they also have enduring qualities that are relatively resistant to change (Westen, 1991). Studies conducted by Blatt (1991) and others (e.g., Bornstein & O'Neill, 1992) have confirmed that qualitative and structural aspects of an individual's object representations help determine interpersonal functioning and psychological adjustment throughout life: A person who has internalized introjects that are conceptually sophisticated and affectively positive is unlikely to develop psychopathology, whereas a person who has internalized introjects that are conceptually primitive and affectively negative is at increased risk of pathology.

Psychoanalytic theory classifies psychological disorders into three levels of severity, with each level characterized by differences in ego strength, ego defenses, and introjects (Bornstein, 2005, 2006; Trimboli & Farr, 2000). The least severe level of psychopathology in the psychoanalytic model (i.e., *neurosis*) is characterized by high levels of ego strength, mature defenses, and relatively benign introjects. The middle level of psychopathology (i.e., *personality disorder* or *character disorder*) is defined by less adequate ego strength, immature defenses, and introjects that are structurally flawed and/or malevolent. The most severe form of psychopathology in the psychoanalytic model (i.e., *psychosis*) is characterized by low levels of ego strength, immature (or even nonexistent) defenses, and primitive, malevolent introjects.

MEASUREMENT CONSIDERATIONS

Although the definitions of personality dysfunction differ for the three conceptual systems addressed in this chapter, a number of measurement problems are common to all of them. The most important among these are differentiating normal from abnormal personality functioning, differentiating personality pathology from other forms of psychiatric disorder, gender bias, and consideration of culture and ethnicity.

Differentiating Normal From Abnormal Personality Functioning

Personality pathology should be diagnosed only if a client demonstrates clinically significant levels of personal distress and/or clinically significant impairments in social or occupational functioning that can be directly attributed to rigid, inflexible, and maladaptive personality attributes. Assessment methods that focus on *DSM–IV–TR* diagnostic criteria, in particular the semistructured and fully structured interviews, offer measurement thresholds that are sufficiently high that diagnosable individuals will be highly likely to demonstrate these additional features. Because of its categorical nature, and the limited number of diagnostic indicators for each PD, the *DSM–IV–TR* system is more likely to produce false negative diagnoses than false positive diagnoses. Self-report inventories and performance-based tests cannot be used, by themselves, to diagnose *DSM–IV–TR* PDs because they do not assess all of the diagnostic criteria (e.g., that problems are evident before age 18).

Dimensional and psychodynamic models of personality do not offer evidence-based rules for determining when a client will have personality pathology. However, in essence all provide definitions of what constitutes PD and offer theoretical and/or normative indicators as guidelines for clinicians.

Furthermore, a variety of assessment measures offer normative data against which a respondent can be compared to determine degree of deviance. All of the self-report measures listed in Exhibit 2.1, except the Personality Diagnostic Questionnaire—4 (PDQ-4; Hyler, 1994), provide standardized test scores based on norms. The Millon Clinical Multiaxial Inventory—III (MCMI–III; Millon, 2009) uses psychiatric patients as the comparison group and offers cutoff scores that are useful in identifying clients who are likely to meet DSM–IV–TR PD criteria. Many psychodynamic personality pathology indicators, such as low ego strength and defense style, can be measured using norm-based instruments such as the Minnesota Multiphasic Personality Inventory—2 (MMPI–2; Butcher et al., 2001) and the Rorschach (Exner, 2003).

Differentiating Personality Disorders From Other Psychiatric Disorders

The DSM system since 1980 (American Psychiatric Association, 2000) has placed PDs on a separate axis from other psychiatric disorders to acknowledge them as pervasive and ingrained forms of pathology that are relatively stable. In spite of this conceptual distinction, clinicians often find it difficult to differentiate personality features from other psychiatric disorders. There are a number of reasons for this. Of significance is that there are many overlapping criteria for PDs and symptom disorders (e.g., depressive PD, dysthymic disorder, major depressive disorder). As well, many individuals with PD present for help only when they exhibit serious psychiatric symptoms. When interviewing a depressed psychiatric patient it may be difficult or impossible to get an accurate reading of the symptoms that arise from PD and those that stem from other causes. Except among researchers who diagnose PD according to physiological markers that remain relatively unchanged throughout adulthood, a persistent problem is how to differentiate personality from psychiatric disorders and vice versa. This is because trait expression on a superficial (phenotypic) level can vary greatly across persons and because most of the current methods for diagnosing PDs rely on observation, interview, and self-report.

Although there are no simple solutions to this problem, clinicians would do well to assume that a client's presentation, as well as responses to questions and performance-based tests, will be affected by significant emotional and cognitive symptoms. Whenever feasible, clinicians should use multiple assessment measures that separately assess psychiatric symptoms and personality problems. Assessment reports should routinely note the presence of psychiatric symptoms whenever personality diagnosis is also considered. Research has shown that semistructured and fully structured interviews for PDs are less susceptible to symptom-based distortions than unstructured interviews, self-report inventories, and performance-based tests, but they are not immune to these effects (Widiger & Coker, 2002).

Gender Bias

The potential for gender bias in the diagnosis of personality pathology has been hotly debated over the past 25 years (Garb, 1997; Widiger & Coker, 2002). Many of the DSM–IV–TR PDs have a differential sex prevalence rate, and some appear to involve maladaptive variants of gender-related personality traits. Gender bias concerns have been raised with respect to the conceptualization of PDs, the wording of diagnostic criteria, the application of diagnostic criteria by clinicians, thresholds for diagnosis, clinical presentation, research sampling, the self-awareness and openness of respondents, and the items included within self-report inventories (e.g., Bornstein, 1996; Clark, 2007; Widiger & Samuel, 2005). Most, if not all, of these concerns apply to other domains of psychopathology (as well as to the assessment of personality in general). Research has shown that the failure of clinicians to assess diagnostic criterion sets in a thorough or systematic manner has contributed to excessive diagnoses of histrionic PD in women (Garb, 1997). Studies have not yet been conducted to determine whether semistructured interviews are prone to gender bias, although gender biases that are inherent within the diagnostic criterion sets would be evident in the findings obtained through semistructured interviews (e.g., Bornstein, 1996; Sprock, Crosby, & Nielsen, 2001).

Studies have suggested that some self-report inventories are providing gender-biased assessments (Widiger, 1998). Some self-report inventories include gender-related items that are keyed in the direction of adaptive rather than maladaptive functioning. When these items are related to the sex or gender of respondents, as many are in the case of the histrionic, dependent, narcissistic, and obsessive–compulsive PD scales of the MCMI–III and MMPI-2 (Colligan, Morey, & Offord, 1994), they may contribute to gender-biased assessments.

Consideration of Culture and Ethnicity

In DSM–IV–TR, PD diagnosis can be made only when the individual's pattern of inner experience and behavior deviate markedly from his or her culture. One might expect considerable variation in the diagnosis and assessment of PDs across different cultural and ethnic groups (Alarcón, 1996). As one example, DSM–IV–TR's narcissistic PD is not included within the World Health Organization's (1992) international classification of mental disorders. However, there has been relatively little research on the impact of culture and ethnicity on the diagnosis or assessment of PDs (Alarcón, 1996).

Items on self-report inventories are generally written from the perspective of the dominant ethnic cultural group and thus may not have the same meaning or implications when applied to members of ethnic minority groups (Okazaki,

Kallivayalil, & Sue, 2002). Hindering the effort of psychologists to identify the cultural contexts in which assessment techniques should be interpreted differently, or the adjustments in test interpretation that should be made across different ethnic groups, is the absence of research on the mechanisms for cultural or ethnic group differences (Widiger & Coker, 2002; Widiger et al., 2006). Much of the existing research has been confined to the reporting of group differences, without an assessment of the purported mechanism by which the differences could be explained or understood (Okazaki et al., 2002). For example, studies have reported significantly higher scores obtained by African Americans (compared with Caucasian Americans) on the MCMI–III's narcissistic, antisocial, and paranoid PD scales (Craig, 1999), but as yet no published research has attempted to explain or account for these group differences. One possible social–cultural explanation for the different elevations is the presence of racial discrimination and prejudice (Whaley, 1997).

Membership in a minority ethnic group that has historically been mistreated and exploited by the dominant culture, and still experiences prejudicial and discriminatory behaviors, would understandably contribute to feelings of mistrust, skepticism, and suspicion that would not be shared by members of the majority ethnic group. African Americans who have experienced a history of racial discrimination might respond differently than Caucasian Americans to such paranoid PD items as "I am sure I get a raw deal from life" or "The people I work with are not sympathetic with my problems" (Colligan et al., 1994; Millon, 2009). Similar hypotheses might be generated for the interpretation of PD test items by members of other ethnic or cultural groups.

RELATIONAL CONSIDERATIONS IN PERSONALITY DISORDER ASSESSMENT

Research has consistently demonstrated a strong link between the therapist–client therapeutic alliance and the outcome of psychotherapy interventions (Horvath, 2001; Martin, Garske, & Davis, 2000; Zuroff & Blatt, 2006). A healthy alliance between therapist and client in the first three sessions appears to be especially predictive of positive treatment outcomes, and it is usually in the first few sessions that most assessment is completed (Hilsenroth & Cromer, 2007). When psychological assessment is integrated into the therapeutic process clients report increased satisfaction, and this is especially true when the assessment process is implemented as a collaborative dialogue between the therapist and client. The aim of therapeutic assessment is to integrate data from clinical interviews, self-report instruments, and performance-based measures, using a client-centered dialogue to arrive at a mutually agreed-on understanding of the client's problems and goals for treatment (Finn & Tonsager,

1997; Fischer, 1994). Although many elements are important for making this process successful, four critical factors are (a) obtaining the client's cooperation in the assessment from the outset; (b) staying attuned to the client's response as the assessment process unfolds; (c) providing feedback that matches the client's level of personal awareness, education, and sophistication; and (d) integrating the assessment findings with treatment in such a way that the client can see that they inform one other (Hilsenroth & Cromer, 2007).

Positive psychotherapy outcomes are not associated with the use of particular assessment measures, and whether interviews and tests are administered by the therapist or an associate does not appear to be critical (Hilsenroth & Cromer, 2007). For clinicians, the most important relational factors in assessment are reported to be time, flexibility, and accuracy. Interviews and performance-based measures such as the Rorschach take the most time to administer (often 2–4hr) and require face-to-face contact with the client. Self-report measures may require less time of both the client and the therapist. Some self-report instruments take 45 minutes or less to complete (e.g., the MCMI–III), and once the instructions are explained most clients can finish the measures without further assistance.

Accuracy in assessment is a function of clinician skill, the methods used, and the diagnostic criterion selected by the clinician. One of the principal arguments for using unstructured clinical interviews and performance-based tests to assess PDs is that they may be less susceptible to the distortions in perception, insight, and presentation that are evident in persons with PDs (e.g., Bornstein, 1999; Westen, 1997); for example, the self-descriptions of persons exhibiting grandiose narcissism, antisocial motives, and paranoid distrust should not always be taken at face value. Semistructured and fully structured interviews, as well as self-report inventories, have sometimes been characterized as simplistic inquiries into the presence of each *DSM–IV–TR* PD criterion (Shedler, 2002; Westen, 1997). There are indeed items within most of the inventories and interviews that have at least the appearance of naively trusting a person's insight or forthrightness.

Unstructured interviews offer clinicians a great amount of freedom in directing their questioning and probes according to their knowledge base and intuition about the client. However, for good reliability and validity unstructured interviews require expert clinical skills and a complete grasp of the diagnostic features being assessed. It is not surprising that research has consistently showed that assessments based on unstructured clinical interviews do not consider all of the necessary or important diagnostic criteria (e.g., Blashfield & Herkov, 1996; Garb, 2005). Studies have also indicated that PD assessments in the absence of structured clinical interviews are often unreliable (Garb, 2005). Clinicians tend to diagnose PDs hierarchically, failing to assess additional symptoms once they reach a conclusion that a particular PD is present (e.g., Herkov & Blashfield, 1995). The identified PD may even be based on idiosyncratic interests (Livesley, 2001a).

When it comes to diagnostic accuracy, semistructured and fully structured interviews have several advantages over unstructured interviews (Rogers, 2001, 2003). Semistructured interviews ensure and document that a systematic and comprehensive assessment of each PD diagnostic criterion has been made. This documentation can be particularly helpful in situations in which the credibility or validity of the assessment might be questioned, such as forensic or disability evaluations. Semistructured interviews also increase the likelihood of reliable and replicable assessments (Rogers, 2001, 2003), and they provide specific, carefully selected questions for the assessment of each diagnostic criterion, the application of which increases the likelihood that assessments will be consistent across interviewers.

Self-report measures are the most structured of all the assessment techniques because the instructions and items are standardized; however, they offer respondents a measure of privacy not afforded in other assessment methods. Persons who find it difficult to respond openly in an interview situation may have no trouble answering a set of written questions or statements that ask about sensitive matters. However, a client's account of his or her functioning and symptoms may be skewed consciously or unconsciously, resulting in inaccurate or unreliable assessment (Widiger & Coker, 2002; Widiger et al., 2006).

Self-report inventories are also useful in alerting clinicians to maladaptive personality functioning that might otherwise be missed because of false expectations or assumptions, such as failing to notice antisocial personality traits in female clients (Garb, 2005). A further advantage of a well-validated self-report inventory is the presence of normative data to facilitate interpretation. A substantial amount of normative data have been obtained and reported for some of the self-report inventories (e.g., Colligan et al., 1994; Costa & McCrae, 1992; Millon, 2009).

However, self-report questionnaires are susceptible to biased responding and faking (Ganellen, 2007). Additional problems may accrue in trying to get an accurate assessment from individuals who may not understand what they are supposed to do or are uncooperative, confused, tired, distressed, or under the influence of psychotropic medication.

TECHNIQUES AND METHODS OF ASSESSMENT

The increased interest in PDs that followed publication of *DSM–III* (American Psychiatric Association, 1980) resulted in the development of several new measures for assessing PDs as well as dimensions of pathological personality traits. There are now dozens of diagnostic interviews available to clinicians, and dozens of self-report measures, although there are fewer performance-based instruments, because these have had a history of reliability and validity problems (Clark & Harrison, 2001; Widiger & Coker, 2002; Widiger et al., 2006). A list of instruments that have a proven record of empirical support, cover a broad range of DSM–IV–TR PDs and/or pathological traits, and are readily available for purchase and use by practitioners are described in Exhibit 2.1. Some well-known instruments are not included in Exhibit 2.1 because they were not updated to cover DSM–IV–TR PDs, have limited empirical support as measures of DSM–IV–TR PDs or the traits that underlie most forms of personality pathology, address a single PD, and/or are not currently packaged and readily available in forms likely to be used by practicing clinicians (e.g., the Coolidge Axis II Inventory [Coolidge, 2006], Defense Mechanisms Inventory [Gleser & Ihilevich, 1969], Diagnostic Inventory for Personality Disorders [Zanarini, Frankenburg, Chauncey, & Gunderson, 1987], Hare Psychopathy Checklist—Revised [Hare, 1991], Inventory of Interpersonal Problems [Horowitz, Rosenburg, Baer, Ureño, & Villaseñor, 1988], Shedler–Westen Assessment Procedure [Shedler & Westen, 2004], and Thematic Apperception Test [Murray, 1943]).

Diagnostic Interviews for DSM–IV–TR Personality Disorders

Each of the diagnostic interviews listed in Exhibit 2.1 cover all of the DSM–IV–TR PDs, including the provisional disorders (depressive, negativistic). The IPDE, Structured Clinical Interview for DSM–IV Axis II Personality Disorders (SCID–II; First & Gibbon, 2004), and Structured Interview for DSM–IV Personality Disorders (SIDP–IV; Pfohl, Blum, & Zimmerman, 1997) have been more frequently used, and have more empirical support, than the Personality Disorders Interview—IV (PDI–IV; Widiger, Manguine, Corbitt, Ellis, & Thomas, 1995). The IPDE and PDI–IV take longer to complete (90–120 min) than the SCID–II and SIDP–IV (60–90 min). Both the IPDE and the SCID–II come with a self-report screening tool that can be used to identify clients who are likely to exhibit personality problems as well as their likely PD diagnoses, thus saving time with the interview. All of the interviews would be classified as semistructured, although the level of structure is perhaps greatest in the SCID–II. The IPDE and SIDP–IV are organized around topic areas (e.g., relationships, work), which may afford better rapport with clients than the SCID–II, which is organized around PD diagnosis. The PDI–IV offers the option of having the interview organized by PD or thematic content areas. The PDI–IV has the most complete administration manual among the four interviews, and the manuals for the SCID–II and SIPD–IV provide limited information. Clinicians should be aware that unlike most self-report instruments, none of the interviews has normative data. The strength of the interviews is that they compel users to cover all relevant *DSM–IV–TR* diagnostic criteria, thereby increasing reliability of diagnosis over unstructured interviews (Rogers, 2003).

Self-Report Measures of *DSM–IV–TR* Personality Disorders

All three of the recommended self-report measures in this group cover the 10 formally diagnosed *DSM–IV–TR* PDs. Only the MCMI–III has measures for the two provisionally diagnosed disorders (depressive, negativistic). The PDQ–4 takes less time to complete than the other instruments (20–30 min vs. 30–90 min) but assesses only PDs. The MCMI–III includes 10 scales that measure *DSM–IV–TR* Axis I disorders, and the SNAP–2 includes measures of 15 additional trait and temperament features. Each of the instruments includes validity and response style measures, which are important for assessing a client's approach to the test. The norm group for the MCMI–III is adult psychiatric patients, so it is not possible to assess whether a client is truly "normal"; instead, the test's strength is in identifying clients who are likely to meet *DSM–IV–TR* diagnostic criteria. The SNAP–2 norm group comprises community-dwelling nonpatient adults, so scale scores indicate how much a client deviates from a normal average score. The PDQ–4 does not have normative data; instead, the test measures each *DSM–IV–TR* diagnostic criterion, and so a PD scale score offers the number and proportion of diagnostic criteria endorsed by the client. Both the MCMI–III and PDQ–4 can be administered via computer; only the MCMI–III offers a narrative interpretation of results that covers *DSM–IV–TR* Axis I and II disorders.

Self-Report Measures of Personality Dysfunction

With the exception of the NEO-PI-R, all of the instruments listed for this group in Exhibit 2.1 were designed to assess both normal and pathological personality traits. The NEO-PI-R is included because its scores have been empirically linked to *DSM–IV–TR* PDs, although clinicians will need to use an additional instrument to understand the nature of the problems identified by the NEO-PI-R. In terms of time commitment, the NEO-PI-R and Temperament and Character Inventory (TCI; Cloninger, Przybeck, Svrakic, & Wetzel, 1994) take 45 to 60 min to complete, the Dimensional Assessment of Personality Pathology (DAPP; Livesley & Jackson, 2008) and Personality Assessment Inventory (PAI; Morey, 1991) take 60 to 90 min, and the MMPI–2 takes 90 to 120 min. All of the instruments include measures of validity and response style and were standardized on the basis of normal adult samples instead of psychiatric patients. However, the DAPP, PAI, MMPI–2, and TCI offer extensive comparative data from many different samples, including psychiatric samples, and separate norms are available with the PAI and MMPI–2 for various applications (e.g., employment selection, forensic assessment). Each of the measures can be administered and scored by computer. The PAI and MMPI–2 offer a wide array of reporting options, whereas the DAPP, NEO-PI-R, and TCI offer a couple of choices.

Performance-Based Measures of Personality Dysfunction

As mentioned earlier, several well-known instruments are not included Exhibit 2.1 for a number of reasons. Only the Rorschach (1921/1942) inkblot test, as administered and scored using Exner's (2003) Comprehensive System, is included in this section because it is the only method that has substantial empirical evidence of reliability and validity in measuring *DSM–IV–TR* PD categories and traits (e.g., Blais & Bistis, 2004; Huprich, 2006). This test must be administered face to face with the client by a skilled examiner, and considerable time resources are required to yield valid, interpretable findings (often 2–4 hr). Norms for the Comprehensive System are 600 normal adults, as opposed to psychiatric patients. Although expensive, the available computerized scoring program can save time, and it provides an interpretive report of the Structural Summary that can be useful for quickly identifying clients with potential PDs and other forms of psychiatric pathology.

CONVERGENT AND DISCRIMINANT VALIDITY

Except for the Rorschach (1921/1942; Exner, 2003), the instruments summarized in Exhibit 2.1 have been widely used in mainstream PD research and are likely to demonstrate good convergent validity, because they were constructed to measure all *DSM–IV–TR* PDs and/or the dimensional traits that underlie these disorders. The interview and self-report instruments do, in fact, appear to be readily integrated within a common hierarchical structure (Markon et al., 2005; Widiger & Samuel, 2005).

With regard to convergent validity, only three studies have made comparisons among the semistructured interviews. In only two of these did the researchers administer the interview schedules to the same clients, and all three studies were confined to two semistructured interviews (Widiger & Coker, 2002). Comparisons across the interviews are therefore precluded, but one particularly rigorous study that used the IPDE and SCID–II among psychiatric inpatients yielded a median convergence coefficient (kappa) of .53 (Skodol, Oldham, Rosnick, Kellman, & Hyler, 1991).

Several studies have been published on the convergent validity of PD semistructured interviews with self-report inventories as well as the convergent validity among self-report inventories. Widiger and Coker (2002) tabulated the findings from 41 of these studies. They noted that convergent validity increased as the structure of the assessment increased. The weakest convergent validity was obtained with unstructured clinical interviews (Mdn κ = .15) and the highest with self-report inventories (Mdn κ = .57). The convergence of semi-structured interviews with self-report inventories fell in between (Mdn κ = .37).

One implication of Widiger and Coker's (2002) analysis is that self-report inventories might provide a more valid assessment of PDs than semi-structured interviews, yet semistructured interviews are often used as the criterion with which the validity of self-report inventories are tested. Rarely are self-report inventories used as criterion measures for the validity of a semi-structured interview, although there are exceptions.

Only a few studies have provided discriminant validity data on inter-view and self-report measures of PD (Widiger & Coker, 2002). This may reflect, in part, an awareness that the diagnostic constructs assessed by these measures do not themselves have compelling discriminant validity. For exam-ple, Skodol et al.'s (1991) report was confined to the convergent validity of the IPDE and SCID–II and did not discuss nor provide any data on discrim-inant validity. Because the DSM–IV–TR PDs overlap extensively (Livesley, 2001a), a valid assessment of an individual PD should perhaps obtain weak discriminant validity with respect to its near neighbor diagnostic constructs. For example, perhaps a valid assessment of borderline PD should not result in the absence of overlap with the dependent, histrionic, and narcissistic PDs. The scales of some PD self-report inventories (e.g., the MCMI–III and MMPI–2) overlap substantially in order to compel the obtainment of a par-ticular degree and direction of co-occurrence that would be consistent with theoretical expectations.

Morey et al. (2002) administered the NEO PI-R to 86 clients diagnosed with schizotypal PD, 175 with borderline PD, 157 with avoidant PD, and 153 with obsessive–compulsive PD in the multisite Collaborative Longitudinal Personality Disorders Study. A discriminant function analysis indicated that the four PDs were differentiated significantly in terms of the 30 facets of the FFM, but it was also apparent from a visual inspection of the FFM profiles that each PD displayed a similar configuration of FFM traits (Morey et al., 2002).

SUMMARY OF EVIDENCE-BASED PRINCIPLES AND STRATEGIES

PDs are difficult to assess accurately, because DSM–IV–TR diagnostic criteria offer a small set of behavioral and inferential indicators that are expected to encompass a client's characteristic way of thinking, feeling, and behaving in major life areas. Perhaps because of this, only antisocial PD has been found to be reliably diagnosed in clinical practice (Widiger & Coker, 2002). Additional problems manifest because clients often present with symptom disorders that are difficult to differentiate from PDs and because many people with PDs are poor reporters of their own behavior and experience. Considerable time must be invested by the clinician if he or she is to assess the client for all of the diagnostic criteria. As a result, clinicians often cut corners, which results in more frequent diagnostic errors.

Although unstructured interviews appear to be clinicians' favorite method for assessing all forms of pathology, including PDs, much of the empirical literature shows that these lack consistent reliability and validity (Widiger & Coker, 2002; Widiger & Samuel, 2005). The three main problems appears to be that clinicians (a) fail to consider all diagnostic criteria, (b) overlook client factors that may diverge from the clinician's preconceived ideas about diagnosis, and (c) prematurely end their interview when they have identified a single PD that appears to account for the client's presenting problems.

Semistructured and fully structured interviews reduce the kinds of errors found in unstructured interviews by forcing clinicians to cover all diagnostic criteria, and they have a track record of empirical reliability and validity (Widiger & Coker, 2002; Widiger & Samuel, 2005). Although some clinicians will find semistructured and fully structured interviews confining and time consuming compared with unstructured interviews, the methods listed in Exhibit 2.1 offer some flexibility in terms of how the interview can be conducted, and two come with a self-report screening tool to help identify clients who are likely to have PDs, which can be a significant time-saver.

Self-report measures are, in essence, self-administered interviews. They are relatively quick and ease to give, and they can involve very little clinician time because they can be administered by nonclinicians (e.g., administrative staff). They have a significant advantage over interview methods in that they offer normative data, which allows clinicians an objective measuring stick for determining how normal or deviant a client is on the various constructs being assessed. Disadvantages include bias in self-report (e.g., faking) and the need to interview the client to determine whether he or she will meet diagnostic criteria for a PD.

Except for the Rorschach, performance-based measures have not established an extensive research base as measures of PD; however, the recent resurgence of interest in psychodynamic formulations of PDs makes it appear likely that this gap will be filled in the near future. Among the measures listed in Exhibit 2.1, the Rorschach is the one that best straddles the boundary between idiographic and nomothetic assessment. As with diagnostic interviews, the Rorschach in an individualized assessment measure and, like self-report questionnaires, the Exner (2003) scoring system incorporates norms to offer an objective measure of the client's function vis-à-vis normal adults.

Drawbacks with the Rorschach include the large amount of time needed to administer and score the test and its limited coverage of some *DSM–IV–TR* Axis II diagnostic features (Ganellen, 2007; Huprich, 2006).

There clearly is no gold standard for assessing PDs; however, Widiger and Samuel (2005) argued for an evidence-based practice model that involves first administering a self-report measure of PD to identify clients who are likely to meet *DSM–IV–TR* criteria for PD and then administering portions of a semi-structured interview that address the PD features identified by the self-report measure. Their rationale is that self-report inventories are good at identifying clients with likely PDs while also minimizing false negatives. This means that most self-report measures are known to magnify a client's problems rather than minimize them, and so there is decreased risk in falsely identifying a client as not having a PD when one might actually exist. Self-report questionnaires will typically identify a small set of likely PD diagnoses (usually one or two), which should then be evaluated with a semistructured interview.

This strategy is not perfect, but it capitalizes on the strengths of self-report and interview measures of PD. For psychodynamic clinicians who do not use *DSM–IV–TR* as their diagnostic criterion, the strategy can be modified so that ego strength, defense mechanisms, and object representations are first assessed using self-report questionnaires and/or performance-based measures and then an interview is given to further assess and verify the problems noted by the other instruments.

CONCLUSION

The purpose of this chapter has been to provide evidence-based recommendations for assessing personality pathology in clinical practice. Since 1980, most of the research on the assessment of PDs has focused on the *DSM* model, now represented by the 10 PDs diagnosed on Axis II of *DSM–IV–TR*. During the past decade, there has been a growing literature on the dimensional assessment of maladaptive personality traits and a reconceptualization of PDs within a psychodynamic framework. I offered a limited set of measures culled from this literature that cover *DSM–IV–TR* PDs, dimensional models of personality pathology, and the central variables of interest to psychodynamic clinicians (ego strength, defense style, and object representations). The measures include four semistructured interviews and three self-report measures of *DSM–IV–TR* PDs, five self-report measures of dimensional traits, and one performance-based measure of personality pathology. As a context for assessing PDs in clinical practice, I presented the central assumptions and theoretical constructs of *DSM–IV–TR*, dimensional trait, and psychodynamic approaches; addressed measurement problems common to them; and discussed the relational issues that one should consider when conducting psychological assessments. I concluded with an evidence-based recommendation by Widiger and Samuel (2005) to first screen clients for PD using a norm-based self-report instrument (e.g., the MCMI–III) and then administer a semistructured interview to verify the presence of PDs in clients identified by the self-report measures as probable candidates.

REFERENCES

Alarcón, R. D. (1996). Personality disorders and culture in *DSM–IV*: A critique. *Journal of Personality Disorders, 10,* 260–270.

American Psychiatric Association. (1980). *Diagnostic and statistical manual of mental disorders* (3rd ed.). Washington, DC: Author.

American Psychiatric Association. (2000). *Diagnostic and statistical manual of mental disorders* (4th ed., text revision). Washington, DC: Author.

Blais, M. A., & Bistis, K. (2004). Projective assessment of borderline psychopathology. In M. J. Hilsenroth, D. L. Segal, & M. Hersen (Eds.), *Comprehensive handbook of psychological assessment: Vol. 2. Personality assessment* (pp. 485–499). Hoboken, NJ: Wiley.

Blashfield, R. K., & Herkov, M. J. (1996). Investigating clinician adherence to diagnosis by criteria: A replication of Morey and Ochoa (1989). *Journal of Personality Disorders, 10,* 219–228.

Blatt, S. J. (1991). A cognitive morphology of psychopathology. *Journal of Nervous and Mental Disease, 179,* 449–458.

Bornstein, R. F. (1996). Sex differences in dependent personality disorder prevalence rates. *Clinical Psychology: Science and Practice, 3,* 1–12.

Bornstein, R. F. (1999). Criterion validity of objective and projective dependency tests: A meta-analytic assessment of behavioral prediction. *Psychological Assessment, 11,* 48–57.

Bornstein, R. F. (2005). Psychodynamic theory and personality disorders. In S. Strack (Ed.), *Handbook of personology and psychopathology* (pp. 164–180). Hoboken, NJ: Wiley.

Bornstein, R. F. (2006). A Freudian construct lost and reclaimed: The psychodynamics of personality pathology. *Psychoanalytic Psychology, 23,* 339–353.

Bornstein, R. F., & O'Neill, R. M. (1992). Parental perceptions and psychopathology. *Journal of Nervous and Mental Disease, 180,* 475–483.

Butcher, J. N., Graham, J. R., Ben-Porath, Y. S., Tellegen, A., Dahlstrom, W. G., & Kaemmer, B. (2001). *The Minnesota Multiphasic Personality Inventory—2: Manual for administration and scoring* (rev. ed.). Minneapolis: University of Minnesota Press.

Clark, L. A. (1993). *Schedule for nonadaptive and adaptive personality (SNAP)*. Minneapolis, MN: University of Minnesota Press.

Clark, L. A. (2007). Assessment and diagnosis of personality disorder: Perennial issues and an emerging reconceptualization. *Annual Review of Psychology, 58*, 227–257.

Clark, L. A., & Harrison, J. A. (2001). Assessment instruments. In W. J. Livesley (Ed.), *Handbook of personality disorders* (pp. 277–306). New York, NY: Guilford Press.

Clark, L. A., Simms, L. J., Wu, K. D., & Casillas, A. (2008). *Schedule for Nonadaptive and Adaptive Personality—2nd Edition.* Minneapolis: University of Minnesota Press.

Cloninger, C. R., Przybeck, T. R., Svrakic, D. M., & Wetzel, R. D. (1994). *The Temperament and Character Inventory (TCI): A guide to its development and use.* St. Louis, MO: Center for Psychobiology of Personality.

Colligan, R. C., Morey, L. C., & Offord, K. P. (1994). MMPI/MMPI–2 personality disorder scales: Contemporary norms for adults and adolescents. *Journal of Clinical Psychology, 50*, 168–200.

Coolidge, F. L. (2006). *Coolidge Axis II inventory manual.* Colorado Springs, CO: Author.

Costa, P. T., Jr., & McCrae, R. R. (1992). *Revised NEO Personality Inventory (NEO-PI-R) and NEO Five-Factor Inventory (NEO-FFI) professional manual.* Odessa, FL: Psychological Assessment Resources.

Costa, P. T., & Widiger, T. A. (Eds.). (2002). *Personality disorders and the five-factor model of personality* (2nd ed.). Washington, DC: American Psychological Association.

Craig, R. J. (1999). Overview and current status of the Millon Clinical Multiaxial Inventory. *Journal of Personality Assessment, 72*, 390–406.

Cramer, P. (2000). Defense mechanisms in psychology today: Further processes for adaptation. *American Psychologist, 55*, 637–646.

Exner, J. E. (2003). *The Rorschach: A comprehensive system: Vol. 1. Basic foundations* (4th ed.). Hoboken, NJ: Wiley.

Finn, S. E., & Tonsager, M. E. (1997). Information-gathering and therapeutic models of assessment: Complementary paradigms. *Psychological Assessment, 9*, 374–385.

First, M. B., & Gibbon, M. (2004). The Structured Clinical Interview for DSM–IV Axis I Disorders (SCID–I) and the Structured Clinical Interview for DSM–IV Axis II Disorders (SCID–II). In M. J. Hilsenroth, D. L. Segal, & M. Hersen (Eds.), *Comprehensive handbook of psychological assessment: Vol. 2. Personality assessment* (pp. 134–143). Hoboken, NJ: Wiley.

Fischer, C. (1994). *Individualized psychological assessment.* Hillsdale, NJ: Erlbaum.

Ganellen, R. J. (2007). Assessing normal and abnormal personality functioning: Strengths and weaknesses of self-report, observer, and performance-based methods. *Journal of Personality Assessment, 89*, 30–40.

Garb, H. N. (1997). Race bias, social class bias, and gender bias in clinical judgment. *Clinical Psychology: Science and Practice, 4*, 99–120.

Garb, H. (2005). Clinical judgment and decision making. *Annual Review of Clinical Psychology, 1*, 67–89.

Gleser, G. C., & Ihilevich, D. (1969). An objective instrument for measuring defense mechanisms. *Journal of Consulting and Clinical Psychology, 31*, 51–60.

Hare, R. D. (1991). *The Hare Psychopathology Checklist—Revised.* Toronto, Canada: Multi-Health Systems.

Herkov, M. J., & Blashfield, R. K. (1995). Clinicians diagnoses of personality disorder: Evidence of a hierarchical structure. *Journal of Personality Assessment, 65*, 313–321.

Hilsenroth, M. J., & Cromer, T. D. (2007). Clinical interventions related to alliance during the initial interview and psychological assessment. *Psychotherapy: Theory, Research, Practice, Training, 44*, 205–218.

Horowitz, L. M., Rosenberg, S. E., Baer, B. A., Ureño, G. & Villaseñor, V. S. (1988). Inventory of Interpersonal Problems: Psychometric properties and clinical applications. *Journal of Consulting and Clinical Psychology, 56*, 885–892.

Horvath, A. (2001). The alliance. *Psychotherapy, 38*, 365–372.

Huprich, S. K. (Ed.). (2006). *Rorschach assessment of the personality disorders.* Mahwah, NJ: Erlbaum.

Hyler, S. E. (1994). *Personality Diagnostic Questionnaire—4.* New York: New York State Psychiatric Institute.

Ihilevich, D., & Gleser, G. C. (1986). *Defense mechanisms.* Owosso, MI: DMI Associates.

Kernberg, O. (1970). A psychoanalytic classification of character pathology. *Journal of the American Psychoanalytic Association, 18*, 800–822.

Leaf, P. J., Myers, J. K., & McEvoy, L. T. (1991). Procedures used in the Epidemiologic Catchment Area Study. In L. N. Robins & D. A. Regier (Eds.), *Psychiatric disorders in America: The Epidemiologic Catchment Area Study* (pp. 11–32). New York, NY: Free Press.

Lerner, P. M., & Lerner, H. D. (2007). A psychoanalytic clinician looks at diagnostic labels and diagnostic classification systems. *Journal of Personality Assessment, 89*, 70–81.

Livesley, W. J. (Ed.). (1995). *The DSM–IV personality disorders.* New York, NY: Guilford Press.

Livesley, W. J. (2001a). Conceptual and taxonomic issues. In W. J. Livesley (Ed.), *Handbook of personality disorders* (pp. 3–38). New York, NY: Guilford Press.

Livesley, W. J. (Ed.). (2001b). *Handbook of personality disorders.* New York, NY: Guilford Press.

Livesley, W. J., & Jackson, D. (2008). *Manual for the Dimensional Assessment of Personality Pathology—Basic Questionnaire.* Port Huron, MI: Sigma Press.

Loranger, A. W. (1999). *International Personality Disorder Examination*. Odessa, FL: Psychological Assessment Resources.

Markon, K. E., Krueger, R. F., & Watson, D. (2005). Delineating the structure of normal and abnormal personality: An integrative hierarchical appraisal. *Journal of Personality and Social Psychology, 88,* 139–157.

Martin, D. J., Garske, J. P., & Davis, M. K. (2000). Relation of the therapeutic alliance with outcome and other variables: A meta-analytic review. *Journal of Consulting and Clinical Psychology, 68,* 438–450.

Millon, T. (1996). *Disorders of personality* (2nd ed.). New York, NY: Wiley.

Millon, T. (2009). *Millon Clinical Multiaxial Inventory—III manual* (4th ed.). Minneapolis, MN: National Computer Systems.

Morey, L. C. (1991). *The Personality Assessment Inventory professional manual*. Odessa, FL: Psychological Assessment Resources.

Morey, L. C., Gunderson, J. G., Quigley, B. D., Shea, M. T., Skodol, A. E., McGlashan, T. H., . . . Zanarini, M. C. (2002). The representation of borderline, avoidant, obsessive–compulsive, and schizotypal personality disorders by the five-factor model. *Journal of Personality Disorders, 16,* 215–234.

Murray, H. A. (1943). *Thematic Apperception Test manual*. Cambridge, MA: Harvard University Press.

O'Donohue, W., Fowler, K. A., & Lilienfield, S. O. (Eds.). (2007). *Personality disorders: Toward the DSM–V*. Thousand Oaks, CA: Sage.

Okazaki, S., Kallivayalil, D., & Sue, S. (2002). Clinical personality assessment with Asian Americans. In J. T. Butcher (Ed.), *Clinical personality assessment: Practical approaches* (2nd ed., pp. 135–153). New York, NY: Oxford University Press.

PDM Task Force. (2006). *Psychodynamic diagnostic manual*. Silver Spring, MD: Alliance of Psychodynamic Organizations.

Perry, J. C. (1991). *Defense Mechanisms Rating Scale*. Boston, MA: Cambridge Hospital.

Pfohl, B., Blum, N., & Zimmerman, M. (1997). *Structured Interview for DSM–IV Personality*. Washington, DC: American Psychiatric Press.

Rogers, R. (2001). *Diagnostic and structured interviewing: A handbook for psychologists*. New York, NY: Guilford Press.

Rogers, R. (2003). Standardizing *DSM–IV* diagnoses: The clinical applications of structured interviews. *Journal of Personality Assessment, 81,* 220–225.

Rorschach, H. (1942). *Psychodiagnostic* (H. H. Verlag, Trans.). Bern, Switzerland: Bircher. (Original work published 1921)

Shedler, J. (2002). A new language for psychoanalytic diagnosis. *Journal of the American Psychoanalytic Association, 50,* 429–456.

Shedler, J., & Westen, D. (2004). Dimensions of personality pathology: An alternative to the five-factor model. *American Journal of Psychiatry, 161,* 1743–1754.

Skodol, A. E., Oldham, J. M., Rosnick, L., Kellman, H. D., & Hyler, S. E. (1991). Diagnosis of *DSM–III–R* personality disorders: A comparison of two structured interviews. *International Journal of Methods in Psychiatric Research, 1*, 13–26.

Sprock, J., Crosby, J. P., & Nielsen, B. A. (2001). Effects of sex and sex roles on the perceived maladaptiveness of DSM–IV personality disorder symptoms. *Journal of Personality Disorders, 15*, 41–59.

Strack, S. (Ed.). (2008). *Essentials of Millon inventories assessment* (3rd ed.). Hoboken, NJ: Wiley.

Strack, S., & Millon, T. (2007). Contributions to the dimensional assessment of personality disorders using Millon's model and the Millon Clinical Multiaxial Inventory (MCMI–III). *Journal of Personality Assessment, 89*, 56–69.

Trimboli, F., & Farr, K. (2000). A psychodynamic guide for essential treatment planning. *Psychoanalytic Psychology, 17*, 336–359.

Vaillant, G. E. (1994). Ego mechanisms of defense and personality pathology. *Journal of Abnormal Psychology, 103*, 44–50.

Westen, D. (1991). Social cognition and object relations. *Psychological Bulletin, 109*, 429–455.

Westen, D. (1997). Divergences between clinical and research methods for assessing personality disorders: Implications for research and the evolution of Axis II. *American Journal of Psychiatry, 154*, 895–903.

Whaley, A. L. (1997). Ethnicity/race, paranoia, and psychiatric diagnoses: Clinician bias versus sociocultural differences. *Journal of Psychopathology and Behavioral Assessment, 19*, 1–20.

Widiger, T. A. (1998). Sex biases in the diagnosis of personality disorders. *Journal of Personality Disorders, 12*, 95–118.

Widiger, T. A., & Coker, L. A. (2002). Assessing personality disorders. In J. N. Butcher (Ed.), *Clinical personality assessment: Practical approaches* (2nd ed., pp. 407–434). New York, NY: Oxford University Press.

Widiger, T. A., Costa, P. T., & Samuel, D. B. (2006). Assessment of maladaptive personality traits. In S. Strack (Ed.), *Differentiating normal and abnormal personality* (2nd ed., pp. 311–335. New York, NY: Springer.

Widiger, T. A., Manguine, S., Corbitt, E. M., Ellis, C. G., & Thomas, G. V. (1995). *Personality Disorder Interview—IV: A semistructured interview for the assessment of personality disorders*. Odessa, FL: Psychological Assessment Resources.

Widiger, T. A., & Samuel, D. B. (2005). Evidence-based assessment of personality disorders. *Psychological Assessment, 17*, 278–287.

World Health Organization. (1992). *The ICD–10 classification of mental and behavioral disorders: Clinical descriptions and diagnostic guidelines*. Geneva, Switzerland: Author.

Zuroff, D. C., & Blatt, S. J. (2006). The therapeutic relationship in the brief treatment of depression: Contributions to clinical improvement and advanced adaptive capacities. *Journal of Consulting and Clinical Psychology, 74*, 130–140.

RESOURCES FOR CLINICIANS

Beutler, L. E., & Groth-Marnat, G. (Eds.). (2003). *Integrative assessment of adult personality*. New York, NY: Guilford Press.

Costa, P. T., & Widiger, T. A. (Eds.). (2002). *Personality disorders and the five-factor model of personality* (2nd ed.). Washington, DC: American Psychological Association.

Huprich, S. K. (Ed.). (2006). *Rorschach assessment of the personality disorders*. Mahwah, NJ: Erlbaum.

O'Donohue, W., Fowler, K. A., & Lilienfield, S. O. (Eds.) (2007). *Personality disorders: Toward the* DSM–V. Thousand Oaks, CA: Sage.

Rush, A. J., Jr., First, M. B., & Blacker, D. (2008). *Handbook of psychiatric measures* (2nd ed.). Washington, DC: American Psychiatric Publishing.

3

DIALECTICAL BEHAVIOR THERAPY

CLIVE J. ROBINS, M. ZACHARY ROSENTHAL,
AND PRUDENCE F. CUPER

Dialectical behavior therapy (DBT) grew out of Marsha Linehan's attempts in the 1970s and 1980s to apply the standard behavior therapy of that time, which had already demonstrated efficacy with a range of disorders, to chronically suicidal individuals (Linehan, 1987). The assumption was that suicidal behaviors are usually attempts to escape a life perceived to be not worth living, and therefore these individuals need to develop skills not only to better tolerate emotional distress but also to create a life that they view as worth living. Helping clients learn these skills would involve direct skills training through instruction, modeling, rehearsal, and coaching as well as the use of principles of reinforcement and exposure. However, clients who have made multiple suicide attempts tend to be sensitive to criticism and prone to emotion dysregulation, and a strong focus only on change strategies can lead them to feel that their level of distress is not understood, or even that they are being blamed for their problems. They may respond with anger at the therapist or withdrawal from treatment. On the other hand, letting go of an emphasis on change can lead the client to feel that the therapist is not taking his or her pain seriously, which in turn may generate hopelessness or anger. This observation led Linehan to develop a treatment that attempts to balance and integrate acceptance and change through a dialectical process.

Because most of the chronically suicidal individuals treated with this approach met criteria for borderline personality disorder (BPD), the treatment manuals were developed for that disorder (Linehan, 1993a, 1993b).

The most fundamental dialectic addressed by DBT is that of acceptance and change. The difficulties Linehan encountered with a more purely change-oriented treatment led to attempts to balance the therapist's focus on helping the client change with communicating acceptance of the client as he or she is. The difficulties BPD clients commonly have in tolerating distress, and in accepting themselves and others, led to attempts to help them develop acceptance-oriented skills as well as change-oriented skills. In addition to change-oriented treatment strategies that draw primarily on standard cognitive behavior therapy and from basic principles from psychological science, DBT includes strategies for the therapist to communicate his or her acceptance of the client that draw primarily on client-centered and emotion-focused therapies. Finally, DBT includes treatment strategies to help the client develop greater acceptance of the self, of others, and of life in general that draw primarily on Zen principles and mindfulness practice (Robins, 2002).

THEORETICAL FOUNDATION

In this section, we describe DBT's conceptual model for understanding the development and maintenance of BPD, principles of change derived from basic psychological science that are the foundation of DBT treatment strategies, a conceptual framework for understanding the nature of the difficulties experienced and expressed by the individual with DBT, and the structural elements of DBT.

Biosocial Theory

The development and maintenance of BPD behaviors are viewed in DBT as resulting from a transaction of a *biological component*, dysfunction of the emotion regulation system, with a *social–environmental component*, an invalidating environment (Linehan, 1993a). BPD may involve a dysfunction of parts of the central nervous system involved in regulating emotions. There is evidence for genetic influences on emotion dysregulation and on BPD, and early life trauma can have enduring structural effects on the developing limbic system, which is central to emotion regulation (Sapolsky, 1996). In an invalidating environment, the individual's communications about his or her private experiences are frequently met with responses that suggest they are invalid or inappropriate or that oversimplify the ease of problem solving. As a consequence, the individual may come to self-invalidate and not learn how to accurately label, communicate about, or regulate his or her emotions. Communication of negative emotions may be ignored or punished, but extreme communications are taken more seriously so that the individual is reinforced for either inhibiting emotional expression or responding to distress with extreme behaviors.

Over time, as the individual's behavior becomes more extreme, in attempts to regulate emotion or to communicate, he or she is increasingly likely to experience invalidation from the environment (often including the mental health system), and in response the sensitive individual is likely to feel even more emotionally vulnerable and react more intensely, thereby generating further invalidation. Thus, in this transactional model the individual and those in his or her interpersonal environment continuously influence one another. The individual comes to experience frequent and pervasive emotion dysregulation and has poor emotion regulation skills, often relying on ultimately maladaptive coping behaviors.

Principles of Change

DBT assumes that the BPD clients' difficulties are a result of both inherent biological tendencies and their individual learning histories that have led to skills deficits and to deficits in motivation to use whatever skills they do have. Skillful use of the therapeutic relationship, which we discuss later in this chapter, is one avenue through which motivational problems are addressed.

DBT assumes that many maladaptive behaviors have been learned by the three primary ways in which organisms learn: (a) respondent (classical) conditioning, (b) operant (instrumental) conditioning, and (c) modeling. The same methods can also be used to help the client develop more adaptive behaviors.

In *respondent conditioning*, two or more stimuli co-occur closely in time, thereby becoming associated, so that the natural response to one becomes a learned response to the other; this was famously illustrated by the salivation of Pavlov's dogs in response to a tone previously paired with food. Involuntary responses, such as emotional reactions, both negative and positive, are often learned through classical conditioning. For example, if a person is raped in a dark alley, being near a dark alley may elicit fear. After many instances of drug use, the sight of drug paraphernalia may come to elicit drug cravings. In treatment, maladaptive emotional reactions may be reduced by removing relevant stimuli or by developing new associations with them.

In *operant conditioning*, when positively valued consequences follow a behavior they may lead to a subsequent increase in that behavior, and negatively valued consequences lead to a decrease, processes referred to as *reinforcement* and *punishment*, respectively. When previously reinforced behavior no longer is reinforced, the behavior will decrease, a process called *extinction*.

When desired or adaptive behavior does not occur, and so cannot be reinforced, reinforcement of successively closer approximations of the behavior can lead to the desired behavior, a process referred to as *shaping*. DBT, like many other behavioral therapies, pays considerable attention to behavior–consequence contingencies.

Modeling refers to the process by which humans and other organisms learn both emotional responses and overt behaviors by observing the responses of others and the consequences of those responses. Maladaptive behaviors may have been learned through modeling by parents, siblings, other clients, and other individuals in the client's environment. In the context of a strong therapeutic alliance, therapists can serve as effective models of more skillful behavior.

Domains of Operation

DBT organizes the nine *Diagnostic and Statistical Manual of Mental Disorders* (4th ed., text revision; *DSM–IV–TR*; American Psychiatric Association, 2000) criteria for BPD into five broad areas of dysregulation, described in the following sections, because this clarifies what skills the client needs to learn and practice. Dysregulation in any one area can have effects on each of the others, but in DBT emotion dysregulation is viewed as the most central problem. All components of DBT are used to address these five domains. After describing each of these domains, we identify and highlight the role of the four sets of skills that are taught to clients.

Emotion Dysregulation

In addition to high reactivity and instability of mood, the baseline mood in a person with BPD often is one of chronic dysphoria. Although *DSM–IV* specifies intense, inappropriate expressions of anger as a separate criterion, many BPD clients are at least as likely to be underexpressive of anger, and they typically have as much difficulty regulating sadness, anxiety, guilt, and shame as they do regulating anger. In DBT, clients are taught and practice specific emotion regulation strategies.

Relationship Dysregulation

Unstable, intense relationships may result from the interpersonal impact of clients' intense emotions and accompanying behaviors, such as anger outbursts or self-injury, or from their own difficulty in being assertive about relationship problems. Frantic efforts to avoid abandonment may reflect this relationship history and/or rejection, neglect, or abandonment in childhood.

DBT targets interpersonal problems, in part, through training and practice of interpersonal skills.

Self-Dysregulation

The experience of intense, frequently changing emotions and behaviors makes it difficult to predict one's own behavior, which probably is an important component of developing a coherent sense of self. In addition, BPD clients' repeated experience of invalidation usually leads to self-invalidation of their own preferences, goals, perceptions, and so on, which therefore do not become well developed or stable. Mindfulness skills taught in DBT can help clients to observe their own experiences and behavior without judgment and are one means through which DBT helps clients develop a clearer sense of self.

Behavior Dysregulation

DSM–IV criteria include suicidal and other self-injurious behaviors specifically, and other impulsive and potentially harmful behaviors, such as substance abuse or binge eating, generally. These behaviors may serve a variety of functions, including interpersonal communication, but their most common function seems to be to escape or decrease aversive emotions. In DBT, skills are taught that can help clients to better tolerate strong distress without resorting to maladaptive escape behaviors.

Cognitive Dysregulation

Some BPD clients experience transient paranoia, dissociation, or hallucinations when under stress. These biased or distorted perceptions and beliefs may reflect the influence of strong emotions on cognitive processes. Mindfulness skills can help clients attend carefully to external reality in the present moment and thereby counteract paranoid ideas and dissociation.

Process of Therapy

Stages of treatment and treatment targets

One of the challenges in working with clients with BPD is the sheer number of problems with which they often present and the fact that the problem viewed as most urgent by the client and/or therapist often changes from session to session. A loss of focus and continuity can easily result. This is addressed in DBT, in part, by establishing a clear list of therapy targets and arranging these in a hierarchical order of priority that depends on their severity and impact on long-term functioning rather than on a short-term sense of urgency. Treatment of DBT is generally grouped into four stages, according to the client's level of dysfunction.

Clients who have severe behavioral dyscontrol, such as repeated self-injury, hospitalization, or a severe eating disorder or substance abuse, are considered to have the highest level of severity and to require *Stage 1* treatment, in which the primary focus is simply on getting those behaviors under control. Within Stage 1, the highest priority is given to life-threatening behaviors, including not only suicide attempts but also any deliberate self-injury, regardless of intent or severity, as well as major changes in suicidal ideation and behaviors related to harming others. When one of these has occurred since the last therapy session, understanding the incident and problem solving for similar circumstances in the future become the primary session foci. The second highest priority is therapy-interfering behavior, because insufficient attention to this can lead to the therapist losing motivation to work with the client or the client prematurely dropping out of treatment. The third priority is severe quality-of-life–interfering behaviors, such as serious substance abuse, major depression, or other mental health or social problems.

Stage 2 focuses on some of the sources of the client's misery, which he or she is likely to still experience even after behaviors are more under control. This might include exposure to trauma-related cues and other trauma-focused work and on helping the client to be more willing and able to tolerate experiencing a full range of emotions that he or she may have been avoiding and escaping from through self-injurious or other problematic behaviors. The most important thing is to not embark on this until there is evidence that the client is sufficiently equipped to handle the strong emotions such exposure may elicit without resorting to extreme behaviors.

If the client no longer has serious difficulties with severe behavioral dyscontrol or posttraumatic stress disorder–related phenomena, *Stage 3* treatment, in which the goal is to help the person solve the ordinary problems in living that bring most people to psychotherapy, such as relationship problems, self-esteem, and dysthymia, can proceed.

To complete the continuum from extreme mental illness to optimal mental health, Linehan (1999) added a Stage 4 to her treatment model. In this stage, the goal is to help the individual develop a greater capacity for joy and freedom.

DBT explicitly includes a pretreatment stage, in which therapist and client reach agreements about the most important treatment targets and the treatment structure, among other things. We discuss these agreements further in the section titled Alliance Factors Related to Process and Outcome.

Treatment Modes. Comprehensive treatment for clients with BPD needs to address four functions: (a) help the client develop new skills, (b) address motivational obstacles to skills use, (c) help the client generalize to daily life what he or she learns; and (d) keep therapists motivated and skilled. In standard outpatient DBT these four functions are addressed primarily through four modes of treatment: (a) group skills training, (b) individual psychotherapy, (c) telephone coaching, and (d) a therapist consultation team meeting, respectively.

Linehan (1993a) found that it was extremely difficult for the therapist to focus on long-term skills acquisition in individual therapy because of the need simultaneously to respond to current crises, dysregulated emotions, and recent instances of behavioral dyscontrol; thus, she separated these two treatment functions into different treatment modes. Skills are taught in four modules: (a) mindfulness, (b) distress tolerance, (c) emotion regulation, and (d) interpersonal effectiveness. During each skills group session, homework practice from the previous session is reviewed for each participant, followed by the teaching of new material and assignment of new homework practice.

In individual therapy, the therapist helps the client use whatever skills he or she has to more effectively navigate crises and reduce problem behaviors. This frequently occurs in the context of a behavioral analysis of a recent incident of problem behavior, which we discuss and illustrate in detail later in this chapter. Problems in motivation to use the skills that the client actually has need to be addressed in individual therapy; these can include environmental punishment of adaptive behaviors or reinforcement of maladaptive ones, hopelessness, fear, or other cognitive and emotional inhibiting factors.

Clients are instructed to call their individual therapist for skills coaching when they are in crisis or having difficulty controlling urges to self-injure, drink alcohol, leave work, or engage in other problem behaviors. Clients are expected to call before, rather than after, engaging in high-priority target behaviors, and specifically not to call within 24 hours of self-injury (to avoid reinforcing the behavior). If the client does call in that circumstance, the therapist only assesses and responds to possible medical risk. Other than the 24-hour rule, therapists determine their own limits regarding out-of-session contacts.

Most experts in treatment of clients with BPD agree that, because of the difficulty in treating these clients, including the stress often experienced by therapists, obtaining regular consultation is essential. A consultation team that meets regularly is therefore a required component of DBT. The purpose is to keep therapists motivated and to provide guidance in conducting the treatment. Team members agree to accept a dialectical philosophy in which useful truths are seen as emerging from the transactions between opposing ideas. The team members use with each other the same DBT strategies used with clients, including balancing validation and problem solving, and help each therapist find an optimal balance of acceptance and change strategies.

RELATIONAL CONSIDERATIONS

There currently is little empirical evidence regarding which client characteristics, therapist characteristics, and therapeutic alliance characteristics influence the process or outcomes of DBT. However, this treatment model assigns high priority to monitoring and attempting to resolve any problems in these relational domains that interfere with clinical progress. We describe here the therapist behaviors and attitudes and therapeutic relationship qualities that are encouraged or required in DBT.

Alliance Factors Related to Process and Outcome

Three elements of a therapist–client relationship constitute the therapeutic alliance: (a) the collaborative nature of the relationship, (b) the affective bond between therapist and client, and (c) the dyad's ability to agree on treatment goals and tasks (Martin, Garske, & Davis, 2000). The therapeutic alliance is often viewed as one of the common factors that underlies client improvement regardless of the practitioner's theoretical orientation or the type of intervention used. A recent meta-analysis of 79 studies yielded a moderate correlation ($r = .22$) between quality of alliance and treatment outcomes, with no evidence that this relation differs by type of treatment (Martin et al., 2000).

Given that interpersonal difficulties are a hallmark of many personality disorders, forging a strong therapeutic alliance with clients with Axis II disorders is both important and challenging (J. S. Beck, 1995; Bender, 2005). We discussed earlier the emphasis in DBT on targeting treatment-interfering behaviors in order to develop a collaborative relationship. Similarly, developers of other cognitive–behavioral approaches to treatment of personality disorders, such as cognitive therapy (A. T. Beck, Freeman, & Associates, 2004), emphasize the importance of understanding the causes of noncollaborative behavior and approaching those causes in an objective and nonjudgmental manner. They suggest numerous potential causes of noncollaborative behavior from the client, many arising from skills deficits of the client or therapist, interfering beliefs on the part of the client or therapist, or contingencies or environmental variables that impede compliance. Therapists are advised to adopt a stance of "friendly advisor" instead of "expert helper," to examine their own emotions that arise in session, and to expect more noncollaboration than in clients with only an Axis I disorder.

In DBT, alliance issues are targeted, in part, by orientation sessions and strategies designed to elicit commitment to therapy. During pretreatment orientation, the therapist educates the client about DBT, and the client makes an informed decision about whether to proceed. Both client and therapist make specific agreements regarding treatment goals, targets, and structure, and they discuss at the outset the possibility of difficulties in the relationship and how they might best be handled. The client agrees to remain in treatment for one year; attend all scheduled sessions; work on reducing suicidal, self-injurious, and therapy-interfering behaviors; attend skills group; and pay all fees. The therapist agrees to make all efforts to practice competent psychotherapy, obey ethical and professional codes, attend scheduled sessions, provide phone coaching and back-up therapists as needed, respect the integrity of the client, adhere to confidentiality guidelines, and obtain consultation as needed. The therapist provides an explicit definition of *dropping out* of therapy: A client may miss up to three sessions, but upon missing the fourth he or she will be considered to have dropped out and may not return until the end of the treatment year. This policy, designed to prevent clients from drifting out of therapy, may be responsible for superior attendance rates of DBT in some trials (e.g., Linehan, Armstrong, Suarez, Allmon, & Heard, 1991).

Both cognitive therapy and DBT emphasize respect for the client and the need for therapists to examine their own contributions to the relationship, by means such as eliciting verbal and/or written feedback from clients, observing in-session therapist behaviors and emotions, and participating in a consultation team or obtaining supervision. Working with clients who have more severe dysfunction will inevitably lead to the making of some mistakes; the mistakes themselves are less important than how the therapist recovers from them and works to mend the relationship. A study of cognitive therapy for clients with depression plus avoidant personality disorder (AVPD) or obsessive–compulsive personality disorder (OCPD) recently provided support for this principle; in it, the presence of alliance rupture–repair episodes, as well as strength of early alliance, predicted reductions in personality disorder symptoms, reductions in depression symptoms, and better therapy attendance (Strauss et al., 2006).

Client Characteristics Related to Process and Outcome

In an early review of 166 studies, Luborsky, Chandler, Auerbach, Cohen, and Bachrach (1971) examined a wide range of client characteristics and their associations with treatment success. Factors predicting success included general personality functioning, less severe diagnoses, high motivation and expectation of change, high initial anxiety, higher intelligence, and greater social achievements. In short, higher functioning clients fared better. However, Luborsky et al. excluded from their review all studies of behavior therapy. Sloane, Staples, Cristol, Yorkston, and Whipple (1976) looked at the relationship between client characteristics and outcomes in two treatment conditions: (a) psychotherapy (psychoanalytically oriented) and (b) behavior therapy. As in Luborsky et al.'s meta-analysis, the authors found that variables associated with higher general functioning predicted success in psychotherapy. High scores on the Mania and Hysteria scales of the Minnesota Multiphasic Personality Inventory, which Sloane et al. described as reflecting acting-out behaviors, predicted poorer outcomes. In contrast, fewer factors predicted success in behavior therapy and, in fact, the clients who did exceptionally well in behavior therapy were those who scored highest on the "acting-out" scales. This study suggests that clients with severe personality symptoms, in particular the impulsive and dramatic behaviors of Cluster B disorders, may be best served by behavior therapies.

Sloane et al.'s (1976) results are consistent with those from studies of newer behavior therapies, such as DBT. In a controlled trial of DBT conducted in the Netherlands, investigators found that DBT was more effective than treatment as usual for clients who had the most severe symptoms (i.e., those who reported more frequent episodes of self-mutilation) at intake (Verheul et al., 2003). As in the first DBT outcome study conducted by Linehan et al. (1991), Verheul et al. (2003) found that although DBT provided superior results for reducing parasuicidal acts, it showed no advantage over treatment as usual in treating depression, hopelessness, or the BPD symptoms of emptiness and boredom (van den Bosch, Verheul, Schippers, & van den Brink, 2002). Because the presence of Axis II symptoms predicts poorer outcomes for treatment of Axis I disorders (Reich & Vasile, 1993), DBT may be an optimal intervention for early treatment of severe personality symptoms, which need to be controlled before interventions for an Axis I disorder can be useful.

Client characteristics certainly are one factor that predict treatment outcomes, but therapists' beliefs or assumptions about such characteristics may be equally important. DBT recommends a number of assumptions about clients that are believed to facilitate therapy, the adoption of which requires a dialectical stance, because some of them might appear at first glance to be in opposition to one another. These seven assumptions, described in detail by Linehan (1993a) are as follows: that (a) clients are doing the best they can; (b) clients want to improve; (c) clients need to do better, be more motivated, and try harder in their lives; (d) clients have to solve their own problems, regardless of who caused them; (e) the lives of suicidal BPD clients are currently unbearable; (f) failures in therapy are not failures of the client; and (g) clients need to learn behaviors across many contexts, and in particular they need to practice new behaviors in times of stress.

Therapist Characteristics Related to Process and Outcome

Successful therapists generally have more experience and a higher level of skill, and they display warmth, genuineness, and empathy (Luborsky et al., 1971). In cognitive and behavioral therapies, such as DBT, *skill* can be operationalized as adherence to the treatment manual and guidelines. In one controlled trial of DBT in the treatment of BPD and co-occurring substance use disorder (Linehan et al., 1999), clients whose DBT therapists were judged by expert raters to be treatment adherent had better outcomes than those whose therapists were less adherent.

Therapists range in their natural levels of warmth, genuineness, and empathy, but cognitive and behavioral approaches provide strategies that can enhance these assets within the therapeutic relationship. For example, DBT therapists use a variety of validation strategies with the aim of helping the client see that they are actively listening; can take the client's perspective; and understand why a particular maladaptive behavior made sense for the client, given his or her developmental history and the current context in which the behavior occurred. Validation strategies work so well that, in a study of clients with BPD and comorbid substance use disorders, a treatment condition that included only DBT's validation strategies (and a 12-step program) had zero dropouts, a retention rate that was significantly higher than in the DBT group, which had already fared well in terms of retention compared with most studies of substance abuse treatment (Linehan et al., 2002). Within DBT, such strategies are balanced with change procedures and irreverent communication style strategies. Irreverent strategies, such as calling the client's bluff and "going where angels fear to tread" can help the client to see the therapist as genuine, someone who is going to call it as he or she sees it and who is able to tolerate the higher levels of distress that might result from such conversations.

Overall, DBT is well suited for therapists who can model a nonjudgmental attitude and those who are comfortable with ambiguity. The dialectical stance and strategies require the acceptance of apparent paradoxes such as the one mentioned earlier in this section, the concurrent beliefs that a client is doing the best that she can and that he or she needs to try harder and be more motivated to change. Therapists need to flex between the two poles on several dimensions: change and acceptance, centeredness and flexibility, and nurturance and benevolent demandingness. This flexibility, along with the concurrent use of reciprocal and irreverent strategies, helps create an atmosphere that is both challenging and accepting, one that optimally keeps the client slightly off balance, making it difficult for him or her to fall back into rigid or overlearned patterns of behavior, cognition, and emotion.

TECHNIQUES AND METHODS OF TREATMENT

A variety of strategies, which we detail in this section, are used to help clients to do four things: (a) be more motivated to change maladaptive behaviors (which in DBT refers not only to overt behaviors but also to thoughts and emotional responses); (b) accept the current state of their own behaviors, other people, and their environments without judgment; (c) learn new skill-ful behaviors, strengthen them, and generalize their use outside the therapy setting; and (d) adopt a more flexible, dialectical stance toward life.

Description of Methods Used

There are four primary sets of DBT strategies used to support therapists and strengthen their skills, each of which includes both acceptance-oriented and change-oriented strategies. *Core strategies* include validation (acceptance) and problem solving (change). *Dialectical strategies* present or highlight extreme positions that tend to elicit their antithesis. *Communication style strategies* include a reciprocal style (acceptance) and an irreverent one (change). *Case management strategies* include intervening in the environment for the client (acceptance), being a consultant to the client (change), and obtaining consultation from the team (balancing acceptance and change).

Compendium of Techniques That Are Consistent With the Dialectical Behavior Therapy Approach

Commitment Strategies

In discussing alliance factors in DBT, we have described a number of agreements that clients and therapists are expected to make before therapy proceeds (and that may need to be revisited at times). To facilitate those agreements, as well as to increase motivation to try new behaviors during treatment, Linehan (1993a) suggested several commitment strategies that have been found effective in research in social psychology, marketing, and motivational interviewing:

- evaluating the pros and cons of changing and of not changing;
- *foot-in-the-door* techniques, in which eliciting agreement to a small request increases the probability of subsequent agreement to a larger one;
- *door-in-the-face* techniques, in which refusal of a large request increases the probability of subsequent agreement to a smaller one;
- *devil's advocate,* in which the therapist tries to strengthen a weak commitment by noting the difficulty of, or obstacles to, change;
- connecting the present commitment to previous commitments the client has made; and
- highlighting the client's freedom to choose whether to commit, while acknowledging the consequences of the choice (e.g., the

client may continue to get hospitalized; the therapist can choose not to treat the client).

Validation Strategies

Validation means to communicate to the client that his or her response is valid, that is, that it makes sense or is reasonable. Although some instances of a behavior would almost universally be considered either valid or invalid, in many situations a behavior can be valid in some ways but not in others. For example, self-injury may be invalid in that it usually has some negative consequences and interferes with the client's longer term goals, but it may also be valid insofar as it reduces emotional pain in the short term. Whether or not to validate a behavior therefore is often a strategic choice on the part of the therapist. The therapist would be more likely to acknowledge or highlight the valid aspects of ultimately maladaptive behaviors when the therapeutic alliance is weak or when the client is currently emotionally dysregulated or self-judgmental. Validation may be accomplished through a variety of techniques:

- unbiased listening and observing, which communicates to the client that he or she is important;
- accurate reflection, which communicates to the client that he or she has been understood;
- articulating emotions, thoughts, and behavior patterns that the client has not yet put into words, which, when accurate, may help the client to feel deeply understood;
- validation in terms of past learning history or biological dysfunction, which communicates to the client that, even if a behavior currently is maladaptive, its occurrence nonetheless makes sense;
- validation in terms of the present context or normative functioning, which lets the client know that that is how most people would respond in that situation; and
- Radical genuineness on the part of the therapist, who does not treat the client as overly fragile, which validates the client's capability.

Problem-Solving Strategies

The principal approach to helping the client change a problem behavior pattern is, first, to repeatedly examine particular instances of it, that is, to attempt to understand the variables that maintain the behavior by examining its antecedents and its consequences. A helpful behavioral analysis will point to one or more solutions, that is, changes that would lead to more desired outcomes. To facilitate those changes, the therapist uses standard cognitive behavior therapy procedures, which can be usefully classified into four groups: (a) skills training, if the client does not know how to behave more skillfully; (b) contingency management, if the client's maladaptive behavior is being reinforced, or adaptive behavior is being punished or not reinforced; (c) exposure, if conditioned emotional reactions to particular stimuli interfere with adaptive behavior; and (d) cognitive modification, if the client's beliefs, attitudes, and thoughts interfere with adaptive behavior.

Example of a Clinical Process Highlighting Technique

In the following dialogue, the therapist is conducting a chain analysis on problem behavior and, while doing so, is weaving in validation, irreverence, and skill rehearsal and is modeling nonjudgmental and dialectical thinking.

Therapist (T): So, let's talk a bit about what happened earlier in the week when you cut yourself with a razor. (*Chain analysis begins*)

Client (C): OK.

T: It was yesterday, right?

C: Yeah, it was yesterday.

T: OK, so let's do what we do now and take a closer look at what happened just before, during, and after you harmed yourself.

C: Fine.

T: What was it that prompted you to eventually cut yourself? What started the chain?

C: [*Pauses, head begins to look down, eyes averted*] Well, you know how my mom just makes me so mad sometimes? She can just downright piss me off, you know? And I don't know why she does it. It's like she just can't help herself but say mean things sometimes.

T: I know. She hasn't exactly been the warmest and kindest person in your life. From everything you have ever told me it sounds like she has said and done a lot of things that have really hurt you, deeply, over the years. And we know that when the two of you have an argument, the outcome is not exactly good for you. So it sounds like maybe something happened with her yesterday that may have eventually led to you harming yourself. But I may be jumping to conclusions here, because you haven't told me anything specific yet. So tell me, what exactly was it that happened that led to you harming yourself? (*Validation*)

C: It was my mom. She called and left a message. And I was sleeping. And she kept going on and on over the answering machine. And that thing is loud! You know how when you're just trying to sleep and that's the only thing you really want in the world, and someone or something wont let you?

T: Oh yeah, I know that feeling well. (*Validation*)

C: That's what happened. So I'm sitting there and she's carrying on about how she knows I am in bed, and I need to wake up and take her call, and she's going to keep talking until I get up and pick up the phone . . . It was driving me insane, and I just kept getting more and more angry.

T: Yeah, I imagine. That sounds like it could be a really aggravating situation for anyone. So there you are, listening, getting more and more angry, and when did you start to think about hurting yourself? (*Validation*)

C: [*Looking down, shaking her head back and forth restlessly now*] I don't know. I just got up out of the bed, picked up the phone, and told her to stop calling me.

T: You told her?

C: No, I screamed it in her ear so she would know where I was coming from.

T: Did she seem to know where you were coming from when you screamed at her? (*Irreverence*)

C: I don't think so, because she kept on calling me names and telling me I was lazy.

T: So screaming didn't exactly work to get her to know where you were coming from? (*Irreverence*)

C: No, I guess not. But she's not just gonna get away with callin' me and bein' nasty!

T: I totally agree that this is a problem. But I want to be sure that we both agree that the solution to her calling you and interrupting your sleep is not you screaming at her. (*Irreverence*)

C: I know you're right. But what am I supposed to do? Just sit there and take it?

T: That's one option. But [it's] a hard thing to do. If someone is talking that way to me, I have a hard time simply sitting and taking it too. Sitting and taking it is kind of an extreme thing to do, just like screaming back is kind of an extreme thing to do. (*Validation*)

C: So you're saying I shouldn't do either?

T: I'm saying there may be more solutions than those two extremes. Coming up with solutions that are neither of those extremes is the really important thing. And my guess is that you are able to come up with some good ideas, if you stop and think. (*Modeling dialectical thinking*)

C: [*Pauses*] No. I can't think of anything . . . [*Looks away, appears ashamed*]

T: I notice you are starting to look away from me as you talk more and more about this. Can you try to look up at me? It's really hard when you feel this way to look me in the eyes, isn't it? (*Validation*)

C: Yeah.

T: What are you feeling right now? Which emotion or emotions are you experiencing, right now?

C: I don't know . . . [*Pauses for a long time*] ashamed I guess . . .

T: OK, that would make sense given that you keep looking away and we are talking about something that you and I both know you would like to do less of (*Validation*). So, try as best you can to look up towards me as keep going. This is the same skill to use when you are upset and want to avoid others, but need to avoid avoiding. You know I am going to support you through thick and thin here. (*Skill rehearsal*)

C: OK. [*Looks up*]

T: Great. Let's continue. We were trying to think of a solution to the problem of being angry, having urges to scream, but neither screaming nor being too passive. Try and think, for this situation with your mom, what is a skillful thing you can do? (*Modeling dialectical thinking*)

C: I don't know.

T: OK, we need to get you to be able to be open to finding new solutions to this problem. Let's take a minute or two and do a brief mindfulness practice, just as we have many times before. OK?

C: Fine.

T: OK, I will ring my mindfulness bell several times to start, and to finish the practice. During the practice, I would like you to focus on your breath, noticing when your mind wanders away from observing your breath, and gently returning your focus back to your breath, without judgment. Remember, it is not important whether you lose your focus. It is only important that you practice coming back to your breath after you lose your focus. (*Skill rehearsal*)

C: OK. [*Bell rings, followed by several minutes of mindfulness practice*]

T: [*Bell rings to end practice*] OK. Now, on a scale of 0 to 10, with 10 being the highest, how much are you able to stay focused right now on your breath, in this moment?

C: Pretty well. Like a 7.

T: Great work. You are so much more skillful when you can bring your attention to the present moment. Now, let's think about solving this problem of being angry, without screaming.

C: I don't know. I realize that I should not yell, but I just want to when she gets like that. The only thing I can think of is if I got up and turned off the answering machine, and then went back to bed.

T: Terrific idea. But you would still be mad, right?

C: Yes, definitely.

T: So what else could you do, in addition to turning off the answering machine, to calm down and avoid screaming at her?

C: I don't know. I can't just ignore her. I guess I could wait until later to talk with her about it, after I cool down a bit.

T: Yes. Good idea. So let's suppose you did those things with her yesterday. Do you think you would have ended up harming yourself?

C: Probably not.

T: OK, so let's keep those two good solutions on the table, and let's go back to a chain analysis of yesterday. (*Modeling dialectical thinking*) You screamed at her, and then what happened? Did you have urges to hurt yourself?

C: No. I hung up on her and then my stepdad called for her, like five minutes later. And he just kept on with the same attitude. So I'm pissed, right? And I finally told him, look, you know what happens when she pisses me off? And he says yes. And I said, so don't keep it up or I'll probably end up doing something to hurt myself.

T: Did you have urges to harm yourself at that point?

C: Not until I said that. But we hung up, and then I started to get to thinking about it, and it seemed like a pretty good idea.

T: There's nothing about self-harm that makes it a good idea. (*Irreverence*) It's just another thought in an unending stream of thoughts, neither good nor bad, that you have across your life . . . But we can come back to this in a minute. First, let me make sure I understand you. Once you got off the phone and started to think about hurting yourself did your anger go up or down?

C: It was really weird. It was like I realized I could just cut myself and then I started thinking about it more and more, and then I started to feel less and less angry. It was kind of messed up how that happened, you know?

T: I'm not sure that it was weird or messed up. It was your experience, and it is really great that you are able to remember it so well. (*Modeling nonjudgmentalism*) This will help us know what you can do differently next time. But tell me more. When did you actually cut yourself?

C: Like five minutes later. I went into the kitchen, grabbed the knife, and slit my wrist. Not too hard. It's not like I wanted to die. I definitely didn't want to go to the hospital or nothin'.

T: So you were aware at the time of your intent to hurt yourself, but not to die or go to the hospital?

C: Yeah. I was thinkin' about it. And then I just went ahead and cut. And you know, it really didn't hurt that much (shows her wrist to the therapist, and it is a superficial cut).

T: And did your anger go down after you cut?

C: Yeah, a little. But I wasn't really that angry any more. I just needed to do it once I started thinkin' about it.

T: Did you do anything right after you cut? Did you tell anyone about it?

C: No, I didn't tell anyone. Just you. I'm wearing long sleeves to make sure no one sees. It's really embarrassing, you know? It just seems like it is the only thing I can do when I get like that. But after I do it, there is no way I want anyone to find out. The whole thing is kind of pathetic [*starts to cry*].

T: OK. Notice you are feeling a strong negative emotion right now. And when you feel strong negative emotions in here you often start to be self-judgmental. (*Validation*) Would you be willing to say what you just again, but this time without any self-judgment? (*Modeling nonjudgmentalism*)

C: OK. I don't want anyone to know when I cut because I am embarrassed by it, and I wish I would stop doing it.

T: Very skillfully said. Nice. So you don't want to keep cutting yourself, but once you start getting the urge when you are angry, you're telling me that it's as if nothing can stop you.

C: Right.

T: If it's literally true that nothing can stop you, then I'm afraid there will be literally nothing we can do to make things better. But let me ask you, do you think it is literally true that nothing can stop you for cutting once the urge starts when you are angry?

C: [*pauses*] I guess I could go do something else.

T: I think we both know from everything we have ever talked about over the past six months that there are times when you have urges to hurt yourself and you use skills to keep from doing so. Even when you are angry. What I am suggesting is that you are not, as your emotion[al] mind may tell you, a robot that has no ability to choose not to cut yourself. You have proven over and over again that you can choose not to cut yourself.

C: That's true, I guess.

T: So coming back to the solutions you came up with yourself a few minutes ago, what would have happened if you did not answer the phone, and talked to your mom later, after you had slept more and calmed down?

C: Oh, I would not have cut myself.

T: Is this a solution, or are we missing something here? (*Modeling dialectical thinking*)

C: I think if I keep the answering machine volume down or off when I sleep I won't get mad when she calls, because I won't even know until I wake up that she called.

T: And if you get mad once you check the machine after you wake up?

C: Then I'll . . . I guess I have to make a commitment not to confront my mom when I am angry at her.

T: OK, that seems like a good idea. So how about this week when you get mad at her, which just might happen, you make a commitment to wait until your anger comes down to a 4 out of 10 before you talk to her about why you are angry?

C: OK. I'll have to use those other skills we talked about last time to tolerate my anger until it comes down. I'll try doing the pros and cons thing, and I'll try to stay busy with my Sudoku, or even go on the web.

T: Great.

Treatment of Comorbid Conditions

Individuals with BPD commonly present for treatment with a wide range of problems. Diagnostically, co-occurring Axis I and/or II disorders are more the rule, and not the exception, among individuals with BPD presenting for treatment. Among problems on Axis I, BPD is associated with posttraumatic stress disorder, major depressive disorder, social anxiety disorder, eating disorders, and substance use disorders (American Psychiatric Association, 2000). The presence of BPD is associated with poorer treatment outcomes for major depression and several other Axis I disorders (Robins, Fenwick, Donnelly, & Lacy, 2008). On Axis II, BPD is commonly associated not only with other Cluster B personality disorders (e.g., histrionic personality disorder) but also with Cluster A (e.g., paranoid personality disorder) and Cluster C (e.g., AVPD) disorders. Perhaps of most concern, however, is that these individuals are at high risk of self-injurious or suicidal behavior (Black, Blum, Pfohl, & Hale, 2004).

In addition to the complicated diagnostic presentation, it is not uncommon among treatment-seeking individuals with BPD for there to be multiple persisting life crises that are deemed as highly important, in any given week, by either the therapist or the client. For example, clients with BPD may present with high negative affect due to an interpersonal situation, after using cocaine and heroin that week, contemplating self-harm earlier in the day, and restricting food intake. In addition to the myriad treatment targets identified by the client as problematic, in this same hypothetical therapy session the client may be 20 minutes late, not have completed therapy homework from the previous week, and be talking about how mad he or she is at the front desk staff in the clinic. In such a session, there simply is no way to address all of these problems adequately within the usual outpatient time frame of 50 to 60 minutes.

As we discussed earlier, DBT provides a principle-based framework for organizing treatment targets. Using a hierarchy, the therapist would elect to target problems associated with the client physically harming him- or herself or others. Self-harm, violence toward others, and changes in suicidal ideation, for example, are treatment targets at the top of the hierarchy. If none of these targets is relevant in any given session, the therapist will target *therapy-interfering behavior*. This class of behavior includes anything that the therapist believes interferes with the client's therapeutic progress. Not completing therapy homework, coming to sessions late, missing sessions, and arriving at sessions intoxicated are examples of therapy-interfering behavior. The last category of treatment targets includes *quality of life–interfering behavior*. These are often the problems that clients prefer to talk about and include such things as difficulties in relationships or at work, problems with sleep, mood and anxiety, eating, and anger. Using this treatment hierarchy, the DBT therapist is able to make quick decisions about which problems to try to address when there are many to choose from and a short amount of time. As such, the hierarchy provides principles to inform decision making, keeping the therapist from feeling easily overwhelmed with uncertainty about in which direction to proceed.

Many co-occurring disorders can be targeted in the first year, or Stage 1, of DBT. For example, major depressive disorder is targeted through behavioral activation, cognitive restructuring, emotion regulation skill training, and mindfulness-based interventions (Robins et al., 2008). Social anxiety disorder can be targeted by using exposure-based interventions to increase the client's willingness to tolerate anxiety associated with feared social situations, until such anxiety extinguishes. Substance use disorders are conceptualized as quality-of-life problem behaviors and treated using many of the same DBT strategies (Rosenthal, Lynch, & Linehan, 2005).

Although many problems can be addressed in the first stage of DBT, some co-occurring disorders are not immediately addressed. When DBT clients have learned the skills in all skill modules, have demonstrated a capability to use these skills to prevent extreme behavioral dyscontrol (e.g., self-injury), and are no longer displaying major therapy-interfering behaviors, the second stage of DBT may begin. In Stage 2, the primary goal is to increase the client's ability to experience emotions without using dysfunctional means of coping to escape from or otherwise regulate emotional arousal. In this stage of treatment, clients with co-occurring posttraumatic stress disorder will commonly begin exposure therapy targeting their hyperarousal, intrusive re-experiencing, and avoidance symptoms (Foa & Rothbaum, 1998).

SUMMARY OF EVIDENCE-BASED PRINCIPLES AND STRATEGIES

Some guidelines may be relevant for treatment of all personality disorders. For example, when considering specific behaviors to target, two complementary forms of change will likely be needed: (a) the adoption and practice of adaptive behaviors and (b) the reduction of maladaptive behaviors (Critchfield & Benjamin, 2006). Furthermore, although clinicians may see similarities in the behavioral patterns exhibited by various clients (e.g., the behaviors that comprise *DSM* diagnoses), and adopt a particular treatment model, a key element to treating individuals with personality pathology is tailoring the treatment to the individual client (Piper & Joyce, 2001).

Because DBT was developed for BPD and there are no writings or data regarding its utility with disorders in Clusters A or C, we include in this section a discussion of what is known about the treatment of Cluster A and C disorders with other cognitive–behavioral approaches.

Cluster A Disorders

Specific Treatment Considerations

No studies to date have examined the efficacy of any psychotherapy interventions for Cluster A personality disorders in a randomized trial. Nevertheless, several authors of cognitive and behaviorally oriented treatment guides suggest therapeutic techniques for treating specific behaviors that commonly appear in the Cluster A disorders (A. T. Beck et al. 2004; Cuper, Merwin, & Lynch, 2007; Farmer & Nelson-Gray, 2005). Within the emotional domain, for example, clinicians may address general reactivity, anger, and anxiety, using techniques such as skills training, graded exposure, and exposure and response prevention. Maladaptive cognitive patterns in paranoid personality disorder might include suspiciousness, paranoia, negative self-views, and low perceived self-efficacy; vigilance to signs of bad intentions in others; and the misinterpretation of benign acts as deceptive. In schizotypal personality disorder (STPD) and schizoid personality disorder, suspiciousness or paranoia may also be present, as well as obsessiveness, maladaptive thoughts about close relationships and independence, and thoughts of the self as abnormal. When perceptual anomalies occur in STPD, A. T. Beck and colleagues (2004) suggested psychoeducation about the prevalence of hallucinatory experiences, and Farmer and Nelson-Gray (2005) indicated that techniques used for clients with schizophrenia may be applicable.

In general, individuals with Cluster A disorders tend to exhibit experiential avoidance and interpersonal detachment, which clinicians may influence with skills training and exposure exercises. More specifically, clinicians can watch for and address such in-session behaviors as avoiding eye contact, hiding affect, or reluctance to discuss personal information. Outside of the therapy office, clients may avoid situations that elicit positive emotions, interactions with other people, and confiding in other people, and they may neglect to engage in small prosocial behaviors, such as saying "thank you" or making small talk. To work on these behaviors, clinicians may give homework assignments that clients are to track with activity logs, such as those used in behavioral activation (Martell, Addison, & Jacobson, 2001). Clinicians should be aware, though, that clients may not yet possess the interpersonal skills necessary to carry out these activities. After assessing abilities, client and therapist can spend time in session conducting role plays and watching videos of others interacting. For clients with paranoid personality disorder who exhibit behaviors associated with entitlement or grandiosity (e.g., overreaction to small slights or an unwillingness to compromise), validation and acceptance early in therapy can be followed by motivational interviewing and then training in communication skills such as perspective taking, listening and reflection, appropriate assertiveness, and anger management.

Attachment, Relational, and Familial Factors

Discussions of a client's history may enhance self-awareness; however, within most cognitive and behavioral approaches conversations about the past will be limited to information that is relevant to the client's current problems. For example, A. T. Beck et al. (2004) suggested that bullying or peer rejection may be found in the histories of clients with STPD and schizoid personality disorder; both lead to views of self as bad, abnormal, or a "misfit," which in turn can lead to lack of engagement.

Focusing on the client–therapist relationship may shed some light on interpersonal functioning. Critchfield and Benjamin (2006) described the therapy relationship as a "crucible" in which new behaviors can be tried out. As such, the relationship should be warm and genuine, with the therapist using self-disclosure as appropriate and showing comfort with the expression of affect. In Cluster A disorders in particular, enhancing the relationship should be an emphasis of treatment. A. T. Beck and colleagues (2004) suggested using relationship-building techniques. For example, early in therapy the clinician may focus on less sensitive topics, or discuss the client's difficulties indirectly, by using phrases such as "Some people have difficulty with X." Beck et al. also suggested giving the client ample control over session content and frequency, and they advised clinicians to respect the client's goals for treatment, even if they are less ambitious than the therapist's goals. Clients with Cluster A disorders may feel suspicious about therapy and/or the therapist. Beck et al. suggested checking in with the client to see how much trust he or she feels toward the therapist, and, if trust is low, asking the client whether he or she would be willing and able to suspend disbelief early in treatment. Also, as with all clients, the therapist should assess for any ambivalence the client feels about giving up some of the symptomatic behaviors.

Extant Evidence Base for Clinical Intervention

As mentioned earlier, the treatment strategies described here are general treatment strategies used across disorders to treat specific symptoms. Evidence of their efficacy with individuals diagnosed with Cluster A disorders would be a welcome addition to the personality disorders literature.

Cluster B Disorders

There has been relatively little research on the use of cognitive–behavioral treatments for narcissistic, histrionic, and antisocial personality disorders. In regard to the treatment of BPD using DBT, we have already discussed some specific treatment considerations and attachment and relational factors. In this section, we summarize the evidence base for DBT.

DBT has now been empirically evaluated in at least 10 randomized clinical trials (RCTs). Overall, the clinical outcome data support the efficacy of DBT as a treatment for women with BPD, warranting its designation as *empirically supported* by Division 12 (Clinical Psychology) of the American Psychological Association. Four RCTs have found DBT to have superior efficacy when compared with treatment as usual for women with BPD and suicidal or other self-injurious behavior (Koons et al., 2001; Linehan et al., 1991, 2006; Verheul et al., 2003), in particular in reducing the frequency and medical severity of suicide attempts, self-injurious behavior, frequency and total days' duration of psychiatric hospitalizations, and client anger, as well as in increasing treatment compliance and social adjustment (Linehan, Tutek, Heard, & Armstrong, 1994). These changes appear to endure over at least a one-year follow-up period (Linehan, Armstrong, & Heard, 1993; van den Bosch et al., 2002). The results of Linehan et al.'s (2006) study are particularly compelling, because the comparison group was treatment by clinicians nominated by their peers as experts in the treatment of BPD.

Standard DBT also has been adapted for several other populations and treatment settings. RCTs have supported the efficacy of adaptations of DBT for women with BPD in a community mental health clinic (Turner, 2000), women with BPD and substance abuse or dependence (Linehan et al., 1999, 2002), women with binge eating disorder (Telch, Agras, & Linehan, 2001) and bulimia (Safer, Telch, & Agras, 2001), and depressed elderly individuals (Lynch, Morse, Mendelson, & Robins, 2003). Controlled but nonrandomized studies also suggest that adaptations of DBT may have efficacy for BPD clients in longer term inpatient settings (Barley et al., 1993; Bohus et al., 2004) and for suicidal adolescents (Rathus & Miller, 2002; for a review of treatment outcome studies of DBT, see Robins & Chapman, 2004).

Cluster C Disorders

Specific Treatment Considerations

In treating clients with the Cluster C disorders—AVPD, dependent personality disorder (DPD), and OCPD—clinicians can expect to devote a good portion of treatment to problems related to anxiety. Cognitive treatment targets that have been suggested (A. T. Beck et al., 2004; Cuper et al., 2007; Farmer & Nelson-Gray, 2005) include obsessiveness, paranoia, maladaptive thoughts about rejection and inferiority (including thoughts that the therapist is rejecting), inaccurate self-evaluation, beliefs about abandonment, dysfunctional beliefs about making mistakes, and chronic worry. Interpersonal targets may include reducing dependency and increasing autonomy in clients diagnosed with AVPD and DPD and working on detachment and valuing the beliefs and opinions of others in clients with OCPD. Behavioral goals for clients with AVPD could be increased social interactions, increased expressions of intimacy and vulnerability, and not distracting oneself from or avoiding distressing emotions. In DPD, potential behavioral targets include not asking for assistance when making decisions, increasing the amount of time spent alone, voicing opinions, and assuming responsibility for tasks (e.g., setting the therapy agenda) instead of asking for help. With clients diagnosed with OCPD, overt behaviors to decrease include checking details of tasks, spending excessive time on tasks, hoarding, working excessively, not delegating tasks to others, and procrastination.

Attachment, Relational, and Familial Factors

A. T. Beck and colleagues (2004) offered conceptualizations of the relational and familial factors that may shape Cluster C personality disorder behaviors. They suggested that individuals with AVPD may have spent time with a significant other who was critical or rejecting, which could lead to assumptions that take the form of negative beliefs about the self ("I'm inadequate") and others ("They'll reject me"). As adults, these clients then expect rejection and feel unable to cope with rejection, they may believe a façade is necessary for approval, and they may misevaluate others' reactions or discount positive data. Beck et al. suggested that the key relational assumptions for individuals with DPD are "I'm inherently inadequate" and "I'm unable to cope." These assumptions can lead individuals to rely on others instead of learn skills for independent living and to resist asserting themselves within relationships for fear of losing the all-important relationship.

A. T. Beck et al. (2004) also warned clinicians that, despite the fact that clients diagnosed with Cluster C disorders may appear attentive and eager to please, the therapy relationship may be challenging. Clients diagnosed with DPD can be slow to change, and clients diagnosed with OCPD often desire complete control over themselves and their environments and exhibit dichotomous thinking about right and wrong. Beck et al. suggested that the therapy relationship can be strained when these clients feel discomfort with emotion and downplay interpersonal relationships.

Extant Evidence Base for Clinical Intervention

A small number of controlled and noncontrolled trials have shown group cognitive–behavioral treatments to be effective in alleviating some symptoms of AVPD. Alden (1989) examined the efficacy of three types of group treatment: (a) graduated exposure, (b) graduated exposure plus skills training, and (c) graduated exposure + skills training with an interpersonal focus. All three groups showed significantly more improvement than a wait list control group and maintained the gains at three months posttreatment. Overall, there were no differences in the effectiveness of the three groups, leading Alden to conclude that the graduated exposure and common group elements were probably the most effective strategies. Indeed, when interviewed, clients stated that the factors most helpful to them were meeting and talking with others who had similar difficulties, analyzing specific social activities and behaviors, and setting behavioral targets and getting the encouragement to follow through in meeting them.

Rennenberg, Goldstein, Phillips, and Chambless (1990) conducted a noncontrolled study of an intensive behavioral group treatment for AVPD. Treatment targeted fear of criticism, fear of rejection, and negative self-image, using techniques that included continuous monitoring of distress, progressive relaxation and imaginal exposure to feared situations (desensitization), paradoxical intention exercises (in which clients exaggerated feared symptoms while reading aloud before the group), positive self-statements, coaching in communication skills, and role playing anxiety-producing situations with other clients. There were no dropouts, and clients improved or recovered from pre- to posttreatment and maintained their gains at follow-up.

Finally, in an open trial of cognitive therapy for AVPD or OCPD, Strauss et al. (2006) found that only two of 30 subjects (7%) still met criteria for their respective personality disorder posttreatment.

REFERENCES

Alden, L. (1989). Short-term structured treatment for avoidant personality disorder. *Journal of Consulting and Clinical Psychology, 57,* 756–764.

American Psychiatric Association. (1994). *Diagnostic and statistical manual of mental disorders* (4th ed.). Washington, DC: Author.

American Psychiatric Association. (2000). *Diagnostic and statistical manual of mental disorders* (4th ed., text revision). Washington, DC: Author.

Barley, W. D., Buie, S. E., Peterson, E. W., Hollingsworth, A. S., Griva, M., Hickerson, S. C., . . . Bailey, B. J. (1993). The development of an inpatient cognitive–behavioral treatment program for borderline personality disorder. *Journal of Personality Disorders, 7,* 232–240.

Beck, A. T., Freeman, A., & Associates. (2004). *Cognitive therapy of personality disorders* (2nd ed.). New York, NY: Guilford Press.

Beck, J. S. (1995). *Cognitive therapy: Basics and beyond.* New York, NY: Guilford Press.

Bender, D. (2005). The therapeutic alliance in the treatment of personality disorders. *Journal of Psychiatric Practice, 11,* 73–87.

Black, D. W., Blum, N., Pfohl, B., & Hale, N. (2004). Suicidal behavior in borderline personality disorder: Prevalence, risk factors, prediction, and prevention. *Journal of Personality Disorders, 18,* 226–239.

Bohus, M., Haaf, B., Simms, T., Limberger, M. F., Schmal, C., & Unckel, C. (2004). Effectiveness of inpatient dialectical behavioral therapy for borderline personality disorder: A controlled trial. *Behaviour Research and Therapy, 42,* 487–499.

Critchfield, K. L., & Benjamin, L. S. (2006). Principles for psychosocial treatment of personality disorder: Summary of the APA Division 12 Task Force/NASPR review. *Journal of Clinical Psychology, 62,* 661–674.

Cuper, P. F., Merwyn, R. M., & Lynch, T. R. (2007). Personality disorders. In P. Sturmey (Ed.), *Functional analysis in clinical treatment* (pp. 403–427). San Diego, CA: Academic Press.

Farmer, R. F., & Nelson-Gray, R. O. (2005). *Personality-guided behavior therapy.* Washington, DC: American Psychological Association.

Foa, E. B., & Rothbaum, B. O. (1998). *Treating the trauma of rape: Cognitive–behavioral therapy for PTSD.* New York, NY: Guilford Press.

Koons, C. R., Robins, C. J., Tweed, J. L., Lynch, T. R., Gonzales, A. M., Morse, J. Q., . . . Bastian, L. A. (2001). Efficacy of dialectical behavior therapy in women veterans with borderline personality disorder. *Behavior Therapy, 32,* 371–390.

Linehan, M. M. (1987). Dialectical behavioral therapy: A cognitive behavioral approach to parasuicide. *Journal of Personality Disorders, 1,* 328–333.

Linehan, M. M. (1993a). *Cognitive–behavioral treatment of borderline personality disorder.* New York, NY: Guilford Press.

Linehan, M. M. (1993b). *Skills training manual for treating borderline personality disorder.* New York, NY: Guilford Press.

Linehan, M. M. (1999). Development, evaluation, and dissemination of effective psychosocial treatments: Levels of disorder, stages of care, and stages of treatment research. In M. G. Glantz & C. R. Hartel (Eds.), *Drug abuse: Origins and interventions.* Washington, DC: American Psychological Association.

Linehan, M. M., Armstrong, H. E., & Heard, H. L. (1993). Naturalistic follow-up of a behavioral treatment for chronically suicidal borderline patients. *Archives of General Psychiatry, 50,* 971–974.

Linehan, M. M., Armstrong, H. E., Suarez, A., Allmon, D., & Heard, H. L. (1991). Cognitive–behavioral treatment of chronically parasuicidal borderline patients. *Archives of General Psychiatry, 48,* 1060–1064.

Linehan, M. M., Comtois, K. A., Murray, A. M., Brown, M. Z., Gallop, R. J., Heard, H. L., . . . Lindenboim, N. (2006). Two-year randomized controlled trial and follow-up of dialectical behavior therapy versus therapy by experts for suicidal behaviors and borderline personality disorder. *Archives of General Psychiatry, 63,* 757–766.

Linehan, M. M., Dimeff, L. A., Reynolds, S. K., Comtois, K. A., Shaw Welch, S., Heagerty, P., & Kivlahan, D. R. (2002). Dialectical behavior therapy versus comprehensive validation plus 12-step for the treatment of opioid dependent women meeting criteria for borderline personality disorder. *Drug and Alcohol Dependence, 67,* 13–26.

Linehan, M. M., Schmidt, H., Dimeff, L. A., Craft, J. C., Kanter, J., & Comtois, K. A. (1999). Dialectical behavior therapy for patients with borderline personality disorder and drug-dependence. *American Journal on Addiction, 8,* 279–292.

Linehan, M. M., Tutek, D., Heard, H. L., & Armstrong, H. E. (1994). Interpersonal outcome of cognitive–behavioral treatment for chronically suicidal borderline patients. *American Journal of Psychiatry, 51,* 1771–1776.

Luborsky, L., Chandler, M., Auerbach, A. H., Cohen, J., & Bachrach, H. M. (1971) Factors influencing the outcome of psychotherapy: A review of quantitative research. *Psychological Bulletin, 75,* 145–185.

Lynch, T. R., Morse, J. Q., Mendelson, T., & Robins, C. J. (2003). Dialectical behavior therapy for depressed older adults: A randomized pilot study. *American Journal of Geriatric Psychiatry, 11,* 33–45.

Martell, C. R., Addis, M. E., & Jacobson, N. S. (2001). *Depression in context: Strategies for guided action*. New York, NY: W. W. Norton.

Martin, D. J., Garske, J. P., & Davis, M. K. (2000). Relation of the therapeutic alliance with outcome and other variables: A meta-analytic review. *Journal of Consulting and Clinical Psychology, 68,* 438–450.

Piper, W. E., & Joyce, A. S. (2001). Psychosocial treatment outcomes. In W. J. Livesley (Ed.), *Handbook of personality disorders* (pp. 323–343). New York, NY: Guilford Press.

Rathus, J. H., & Miller, A. L. (2002). Dialectical behavior therapy adapted for suicidal adolescents. *Suicide and Life Threatening Behavior, 32,* 146–157.

Reich, J. H., & Vasile, R. G. (1993). Effect of personality disorders on the treatment outcome of Axis I conditions—An update. *Journal of Nervous and Mental Disease, 181,* 475–484.

Rennenberg, B., Goldstein, A. J., Phillips, D., & Chambless, D. L. (1990). Intensive behavioral group treatment of avoidant personality disorder. *Behavior Therapy, 21,* 363–377.

Robins, C. J. (2002). Zen principles and mindfulness practice in dialectical behavior therapy. *Cognitive and Behavioral Practice, 9,* 50–57.

Robins, C. J., & Chapman, A. L. (2004). Dialectical behavior therapy: Current status, recent developments, and future directions. *Journal of Personality Disorders, 18,* 73–89.

Robins, C. J., Fenwick, C. V., Donnelly, J. E., & Lacy, J. (2008). Borderline personality disorder. In M. A. Whisman (Ed.), *Adapting cognitive therapy for depression: Managing complexity and comorbidity* (pp. 280–305). New York, NY: Guilford Press.

Rosenthal, M. Z., Lynch, T. R., & Linehan, M. L. (2005). Dialectical behavior therapy for individuals with borderline personality disorder and substance use disorders. In R. J. Frances, S. I. Miller, & A. H. Mack (Eds.), *Clinical textbook of addictive disorders* (3rd ed., pp. 615–636). New York, NY: Guilford Press.

Safer, D. L., Telch, C. F., & Agras, W. S. (2001). Dialectical behavior therapy for bulimia nervosa. *American Journal of Psychiatry, 158,* 632–634.

Sapolsky, R. M. (1996, August 9). Why stress is bad for your brain. *Science, 273,* 749–750.

Sloane, R. B., Staples, F. R., Cristol, A. H., Yorkston, N. J., & Whipple, K. (1976). Patient characteristics and outcome in psychotherapy and behavior therapy. *Journal of Consulting and Clinical Psychology, 44,* 330–339.

Strauss, J. L., Hayes, A. M., Johnson, S. L., Newman, C. F., Brown, G. K., Barber, J. P., . . . Beck, A. T. (2006). Early alliance, alliance ruptures, and symptom change in a nonrandomized trial of cognitive therapy for avoidant and obsessive–compulsive personality disorders. *Journal of Consulting and Clinical Psychology, 74,* 337–345.

Telch, C. F., Agras, W. S., & Linehan, M. M. (2001). Dialectical behavior therapy for binge eating disorder. *Journal of Consulting and Clinical Psychology, 69,* 1061–1065.

Turner, R. M. (2000). Naturalistic evaluation of dialectical behavior therapy–oriented treatment for borderline personality disorder. *Cognitive and Behavioral Practice, 7,* 413–419.

van den Bosch, L. M. C., Verheul, R., Schippers, G. M., & van den Brink, W. (2002). Dialectical behavior therapy for borderline patients with and without substance use problems: Implementation and long term effects. *Addictive Behaviors, 27,* 911–923.

Verheul, R., van den Bosch, L. M. C., Koeter, M. W. J., de Ridder, M. A. J., Stijnen, T., & van den Brink, W. (2003). Dialectical behavior therapy for women with borderline personality disorder. *British Journal of Psychiatry, 182,* 135–140.

4

EVIDENCE-BASED PSYCHODYNAMIC THERAPY WITH PERSONALITY DISORDERS

STANLEY B. MESSER AND ALLAN A. ABBASS

Mental health clinicians have come to recognize that symptoms or complaints are frequently embedded in personality functioning and that treatment, to be optimal, needs to take into account the client's personality. In a clinical situation it is not only normal (i.e., unimpaired) personality functioning that must be considered but, typically, personality disorder (PD). As Wilhelm Reich (1949) stated over 60 years ago, "If one recognized the fact that the basis of a symptom neurosis is always a neurotic character, then it is clear that we shall have to deal with character-neurotic resistances in every analysis" (p. 42). One way in which the close connection of clinical syndromes and personality disorders has been empirically demonstrated is the high incidence of individuals with dual diagnoses based on the *Diagnostic and Statistical Manual of Mental Disorders* (e.g., 4th ed., *DSM–IV*; American Psychiatric Association, 1994), namely, an Axis I clinical syndrome, such as anxiety or depression, and an Axis II PD, such as obsessive–compulsive PD or borderline PD (BPD; see e.g., McGinn & Sanderson, 1995, regarding panic disorder and PD, and Shea et al., 1990, regarding depression and PD; for a special journal issue on treating comorbid PDs, see Dimaggio & Norcross, 2008).

THEORETICAL UNDERPINNINGS AND ASSUMPTIONS

Essential Theoretical Constructs

Psychoanalysis first categorized personality styles according to the vicissitudes of the psychosexual stages of development, that is, oral, anal, or phallic. Thus, a person who was especially orderly, miserly, and obstinate was said to be (or have) an anal character, based on the eroticism of the anal stage (Abraham, 1923/1942; Freud, 1908/1959). W. Reich (1949) brought the notion of character front and center in psychoanalysis. He considered character to be made up of particular drive–defense constellations that were based on childhood conflicts. Regarding treatment, he said, character resistance expressed itself

> not in the content of the material, but in the formal aspects of the general behavior, the manner of talking, of the gait, facial expression and typical attitudes such as smiling, deriding, haughtiness, over-correctness, the manner of the politeness or of the aggression, etc. (p. 47)

He also considered a lack of insight into one's condition as a prime characteristic that distinguishes the bearer of character traits or dysfunction from a person with neurotic symptoms. Even today, we often consider symptoms to be *ego dystonic* and character traits or disorders to be *ego syntonic*; that is, symptoms trouble the individual, whereas character is rationalized and usually troubles others more so than oneself. Of course, this is a rough characterization: A person who sabotages himself over and over, for example, may well regard this pattern as ego dystonic, especially after this fact has been pointed out to him. In addition to one's style of coping with and defending against inner conflict as a major factor in the formation of character, psychoanalytic theorizing posits that character stems from the child's identification with significant others, in particular the parents.

An important way in which these defining concepts of dysfunctional drive–defense constellations and maladaptive interpersonal patterns have been harnessed in the psychodynamic treatment of PD is by means of the *triangles of conflict* (Ezriel, 1952) and insight or person (Menninger, 1958; see Figure 4.1). Regarding the triangle of conflict, a person experiences a forbidden or otherwise unpleasant impulse or feeling (I/F; e.g., guilt), which triggers a defense (D; e.g., intellectualization). If the defense is not successful, the person experiences anxiety (A). Another way in which the triad of I/F, D, and A helps to conceptualize psychopathology is that the impulse produces a subliminal signal of anxiety, which is then defended against in an adaptive or maladaptive way. In either scenario, the person is said to be in conflict over

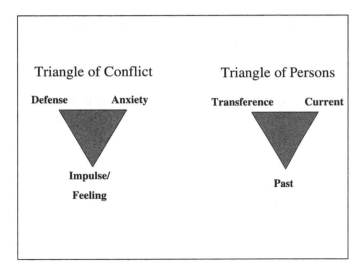

Figure 4.1. Triangles of conflict and persons.

the recognition and expression of a strong and unacceptable feeling (or drive or impulse), which is largely unconscious.

The second triangle—that of insight or person—refers to the major interpersonal venues in which the conflict or maladaptive pattern has been, or is being, enacted or played out. *Past* (P; see Figure 4.1) refers to the interpersonal patterns that formed early on, usually in childhood. *Current* (C) refers to the way in which the patient interacts with others in the present, especially in maladaptive interpersonal cycles, and *transference* (T) refers to the interactions with the therapist. See the Techniques and Methods of Treatment section for a discussion of how the psychotherapist uses these two triangles therapeutically.

To these elements, McCullough Vaillant (1997) added the concept of *self,* pictured within the triangle as observer and observed. It points the psychotherapist toward exploring the self-concept, especially self-esteem, the self as seen by others, and one's perspective on others.

Mechanisms of Change

Insight

Clarification and interpretation of the conflict among I/F, D, and A, and connecting the interpersonal corners of the triangle (P, C, and T) are said to provide the insight that helps to bring about character change. If the therapist illuminates these intrapsychic patterns and demonstrates how they operate interpersonally, awareness is enhanced, and new learning can occur.

The Therapeutic Relationship

The patient's experience of a new and better relationship with the therapist compared with those he or she has had in the present or past is also said to bring about change. This constitutes what is often referred to as a *corrective emotional experience*.

According to McCullough Vaillant (1997), "By changing the long-standing and repetitive 'transferring' of the patient's maladaptive patterns onto current relationships, we are changing character" (p. 11). Within the two broad mechanisms of change—namely, insight and a new and improved relationship with the therapist compared with the client's typical dysfunctional relationships—are three specific mechanisms of change that are hypothesized to restructure the personality: (a) defensive restructuring, (b) affective restructuring, and (c) cognitive restructuring (Magnavita, 1997; McCullough Vaillant, 2007).

Defensive Restructuring

Within the *defensive restructuring* modality the therapist attempts to break through the client's character defenses to expose underlying feelings and repressed experiences. In their review of the empirical psychotherapy process literature, Blagys and Hilsenroth (2000) found that this is one of the ways in which short-term psychodynamic–interpersonal psychotherapy differs from cognitive–behavioral treatment. In defensive restructuring, the therapist helps turn the patient against the defense, thereby making it ego dystonic. The therapist works on the Current (C) and Transference (T) corners of the triangle of insight, and the defense (D) corner of the triangle of conflict. Challenging defenses often elicits anger or disguised anger toward the therapist, which, when interpreted, may open channels to past (P) memories and feelings. The therapist carefully monitors the process so that the client does not become overwhelmed or flee treatment. The therapist should monitor not only individual defenses but also the constellation of defenses that coalesce into a character style or disorder, such as obsessive-compulsive, narcissistic, or histrionic. For a very useful categorization of the defenses at varying levels of maturity, see Magnavita (1997).

Affective Restructuring

In the *affective restructuring* mode the therapist bypasses the defenses and tries to arouse affect directly, using experiential techniques (e.g., Greenberg & Pascual-Leone, 2006), with the object of improving anxiety tolerance.

Thus, the main emphasis is on the I/F corner of the triangle of conflict and the C corner of the triangle of insight. As links to the past (P) emerge, the therapist connects C to T and P. To increase emotional arousal, the therapist may point to a client's nonverbal gestures, such as a clenched fist or incongruous smile, or ask the client to recount an emotional event in detail. In support of the importance of accessing client affect, a recent meta-analysis of 10 samples of short-term psychodynamic therapy found that "therapist facilitation of patient affective experience/expression is associated with patient improvement" (Diener, Hilsenroth, & Weinberger, 2007, p. 936).

Cognitive Restructuring

In *cognitive restructuring* the therapist elicits the client's thoughts, characteristic beliefs, and schemas, using more direct advice giving, support, and information sharing than in the other modalities to bring about change. It revolves around the T and C corners of the triangle of person and the D and A corners of the triangle of conflict. The therapist helps the client problem solve, enhance coping skills, and differentiate feelings. If the client confuses a feeling or thought with a presumed necessity to take action, for example, the therapist clarifies this for him or her. Research has shown that more structured variants of psychodynamic therapy (basically, those that include elements such as contract setting and cognitive restructuring) with a mixture of PDs result in lower dropout rates than those that are more exclusively expressive or interpretive (Verheul & Herbrink, 2007). However, active forms of brief psychodynamic therapy have also been found to be effective, especially with mild and moderately severe forms of PD (see Table 4.1, discussed later in this chapter, for the effect sizes of outcome measures from such treatment).

Domains of Operation Within the Total Ecological System

The major format in treating PD within a psychodynamic framework is one-on-one psychotherapy, with exploration and interpretation of intrapsychic conflict and interpersonal dysfunction being paramount. However, dyadic and triangular familial configurations are taken account of through an understanding of oedipal relationships and rivalries that stem from the interaction of biological drives (sex and aggression) and typical family constellations in childhood. Regarding sociocultural and systemic factors, group therapy and group process also have been used in the treatment of PDs. For example, individuals with PDs and those with affective disorders were treated within a day hospital milieu, which included, among other interventions, a daily group therapy meeting of 50 patients and staff that addressed emotional concerns of the entire treatment milieu as well as smaller therapy groups conducted according

TABLE 4.1
Treatment Descriptors and Effect Sizes (ESs) of Brief Psychodynamic Psychotherapy Randomized Clinical Trials of Individuals With Personality Disorders (PDs)

Study	STPP intervention	N	PD diagnosis (cluster/type)	Mean total sessions	Mean length follow-up (months)	SCL-90, BSI, or GSI ES	IIP ES	GAF ES
Abbass, Sheldon, et al. (2008)	ISTDP (Davanloo, 2000)	27	A, B, and C	28	24	1.78	1.39	2.26
Hardy et al. (1995)	Psychodynamic–interpersonal (Hobson, 1985)	13	C	12	12	1.21	1.13	—
Hellerstein et al. (1998)	STDP (Davanloo, 1980)	25	A, B, and C	29	6	0.27	0.31	—
Munroe-Blum et al. (1999)	Dynamic psychotherapy (Kernberg, 1975)	26	Borderline	40	24	0.92	—	—
Svartberg et al. (2004)	STDP (McCullough Vaillant, 1997)	25	C	40	24	0.95	1.04	—
Vinnars et al. (2005)	SE psychotherapy (Luborsky, 1984)	61	A, B, and C	26	24	0.63	—	0.68
Winston et al. (1994)	STDP (Davanloo, 1980)	15	A, B, and C	40	18	0.58	—	—
Mean (SD)				30.7 (10)	18.9 (7.3)	0.91 (0.5)	0.97 (0.5)	1.47 (1.1)

Note. Effect size was computed by dividing the pre versus post score difference by the pooled standard deviation. Data from the longest follow-ups were used to calculate the mean treatment effects. Effects sizes of 0.2 are small, those of 0.5 are medium, and those 0.8 and higher are large. An eighth study, Emmelkamp et al. (2006), did not use any of the common measures listed. STPP = short-term psychodynamic psychotherapy; SCL-90 = Symptom Checklist–90; BSI = Brief Symptom Inventory; GSI = Global Symptom Index; IIP = Inventory of Interpersonal Problems; GAF = Global Assessment of Functioning; ISTDP = intensive short-term dynamic psychotherapy; STDP = short-term dynamic psychotherapy; SE = supportive–expressive. Dashes indicate that no data are available.

to psychodynamic principles. Compared with a delayed-treatment control, individuals who received the group interventions had significantly more positive results posttreatment and at an 8-month follow-up (Piper, Rosie, Azim, & Joyce, 1993).

RELATIONAL CONSIDERATIONS

Alliance Factors Related to Process and Outcome

Freud (1913/1958) presaged the current emphasis on the therapeutic alliance when he stated the importance of the psychoanalytic patient attaching him- or herself to the psychotherapist for the progress of therapy. What we have learned from a scientific perspective since then is that the correlation between the therapeutic alliance and therapy outcome is modest but consistent, ranging from .22 to .29; the client's rating is more predictive than that of the therapist or researcher; and the measurement of alliance taken early in therapy is as good as, or better than, one taken later (Horvath, 2005; Martin, Garske, & Davis, 2000). Although these are findings from across many patient groups, they are likely to apply to persons with PDs even more so than to others, given the difficulties such individuals have with interpersonal relationships. Thus, it behooves the therapist to pay careful attention to the therapeutic alliance from the very beginning of therapy and watch for ruptures in that alliance in response to clinical interventions (Messer & Wolitzky, in press; Safran & Muran, 2000; see also Chapter 6, this volume).

Bender (2005) reviewed the literature on the role of the therapeutic alliance in the treatment of PDs, pointing out that because of the significant impairment in interpersonal relationships people with PDs often have, special problems arise in the formation of the alliance with this diagnostic group. However, the quality of those interpersonal relationships affects the alliance more than the particular diagnosis (Hersoug, Monsen, Havik, & Høglend, 2002), and it is the quality of the clients' object relationships (i.e., schemas of self–other relationships) that predicts outcome (Piper et al., 1991). Bender pointed out that in practical terms different aspects of a patient's personality pathology may be in focus, and it is to them that the psychotherapist must be attuned to maintain the alliance.

Patient Characteristics Related to Process and Outcome

There is a large and growing literature on the effect of patient characteristics on psychotherapy outcome (Clarkin & Levy, 2004). Here, we focus on those studies that pertain specifically to PD and how it moderates psychodynamic treatment outcome. The most frequent finding is that the presence of PD reduces the treatment effect on symptoms of Axis I disorders (J. H. Reich & Vasile, 1993) and lengthens the treatment time needed for change (Messer & Warren, 1995). For example, PD clients were randomly assigned either to Luborsky's (1984) manualized, time-limited, supportive–expressive psychotherapy or a nonmanualized, open-ended, community-delivered, psychodynamic treatment (Vinnars et al., 2007). Across the entire sample, clients with a greater number of positive PD criteria showed less symptomatic change.

The presence of PD also increases the need for psychotherapy instead of medication alone. In a randomized clinical trial, Kool, Dekker, Duijsens, de Jonghe, and Puite (2003) studied the effects of pharmacotherapy with or without short psychodynamic supportive psychotherapy in persons with major depression. They found that the combined therapy was more effective than pharmacotherapy for the depressed persons with PD, whereas pharmacotherapy alone was equivalent to the combined condition for those without PD. Similarly, in a naturalistic study of clients in long-term psychodynamic therapy, Bond and Perry (2006) found that PD pathology and being on medication at intake moderated the effects of therapy; specifically, the presence of PD was associated with a smaller reduction in depression and general functioning, whereas medication use predicted a smaller effect on depression only.

A recent study of clients who had a diagnosis of comorbid panic disorder and PD compared panic-focused psychodynamic psychotherapy (PFPP) with applied relaxation training (Milrod, Leon, Barber, Markowitz, & Graf, 2007), with findings unlike the modal ones just described. Presence of Axis II diagnoses, most of which were Cluster C (with conflicts over self-assertion and autonomy) moderated treatment outcome; that is, the effect of PFPP was enhanced in clients with Axis II comorbidity. The authors explained this in terms of the PFPP's exploration of the kind of issues that plague people with Cluster C personalities. By articulating the fantasies that underlay the clients' inhibitions about being more autonomous, the PFPP empowered them to become more active and assertive, something that was overlooked in applied relaxation training.

Psychotherapist Characteristics Related to Process and Outcome

Beutler et al. (2004) conducted a comprehensive review of psychotherapist variables predictive of psychotherapy outcome. Their findings can be summarized in three observations: (a) Psychotherapist sex, age, and race, taken by themselves rather than studied in conjunction with how they correspond to patient characteristics, are poor predictors of outcome; (b) classes of psychotherapist interventions, without taking patient factors into account, are also poor predictors of outcome; and (c) psychotherapist training skill, experience, and style are weak contributors to outcome, but there is considerable variability among studies. The authors concluded that patient moderating variables are repeatedly shown to affect outcome and that there is a "need to integrate patient, therapist, procedural and relationship factors" in future research (p. 292).

A study of psychotherapist countertransference reactions to different kinds of personality pathology illustrates the value of examining therapist factors in conjunction with patient characteristics (Betan, Heim, Conklin, & Westen, 2005). It is particularly relevant to this chapter because it concerns personality disorder Clusters A, B, and C and because the largest contingent of clinicians in the study were psychodynamically oriented. A countertransference questionnaire was created and its items subjected to factor analysis, yielding eight factors that were independent of therapist theoretical orientation. The eight factors were associated in predictable ways with Axis II pathology. The countertransference reaction with Cluster A PDs (odd/eccentric) was feeling criticized or mistreated; with Cluster B PDs (dramatic/erratic) it was feeling overwhelmed/disorganized, helpless/inadequate, sexualized, disengaged, criticized/mistreated and lack of positive countertransference; and with Cluster C PDs (anxious) it was feeling parental/protective. The authors also looked within the clusters at the specific PDs, (e.g., BPD and narcissistic PD) to refine the association further.

Racial and Cultural Factors

Just as for clinicians with other theoretical orientations, it is important for psychodynamic clinicians to be aware of and take seriously cultural, racial, ethnic, religious, class, and gender differences among their clients and in particular to know what is normative for different subgroups. Otherwise, there is the danger of pathologizing what is merely a usual cultural phenomenon (Messer & Wolitzky, 2007). It has been posited, for example, that there are predominant personality styles among different nationalities such that one should not be too quick to diagnose histrionic PD in someone of Latino background or obsessive–compulsive PD in a person from northern Europe.

At the same time, psychoanalytic approaches stress that people are all more or less alike under the skin in that we have to deal with universals such as injury, loss, raising or relating to children, life transitions, death, and so forth, even if the way in which we do so may differ markedly from culture to culture and even from person to person. Psychoanalysis, until recently, was relatively neglectful of multicultural features of practice, but this is being corrected. For a well-informed, clinically relevant volume on how social class, culture, and race have been brought into the psychoanalytic object relations domain, we recommend Altman's (1995) book *The Analyst in the Inner City: Race, Class and Culture Through a Psychoanalytic Lens*.

TECHNIQUES AND METHODS OF TREATMENT

There is no single psychodynamic method for working with all types of PDs, although most rely on psychodynamic concepts about treatment as outlined in the beginning of this chapter (e.g., working with the triangles of conflict and insight; the unconscious, the self, transference, and resistance; defense, affect, and cognitive restructuring). In this section, we draw most from the literature on the more active, expressive, and interpretive forms of brief dynamic therapy, in particular Davanloo's (2000) intensive short-term dynamic psychotherapy (ISTDP). Perhaps among the best researched of the brief psychodynamic models, Davanloo's method is focused on challenges to defenses, mobilization of underlying emotions, and working through these emotions. This method is now supported by 17 studies (six randomized controlled trials, two controlled trials, and nine case series) that have examined individuals with somatic problems, PDs, anxiety disorders, treatment-resistant depression, and mixed problems. (For a recent summary of these studies, see Abbass, Lovas, & Purdy, 2008.) After describing the main features of psychodynamic therapy, we present a case vignette to illustrate ISTDP.

The process of psychodynamic psychotherapy with PD patients often includes the 12 features described in the following sections.

1. Establishment of Shared Objectives

All methods of psychodynamic psychotherapy aim to develop a collaborative process whereby the client and psychotherapist agree on the treatment focus and objectives. This process of developing rapport, or a therapeutic alliance, enables assessment and therapy to take place. Barriers against such an engagement often need to be explored, and this in itself is an important part of the therapy.

2. Therapeutic Focus

Formulating and making interventions around a focus is a key therapy ingredient across the more active, short-term dynamic therapies and is correlated with good outcomes (Messer, 2001). Psychodynamic therapies, in general, focus on making manifest, and helping the client experience, unconscious emotions and conflicts surrounding difficult or traumatic events from the past.

This includes working with specific defenses the client brings into the treatment relationship as a product of transference feelings. An initial focus also may be on reducing anxiety in a client who is extremely anxious or even frightened about therapy.

3. Inquiry Into the Problem Areas

It is essential to have an overall picture of the client's background and the problems to be addressed. The therapist explores the client's symptoms and characterological problems by taking a personal, family, psychiatric, and medical history.

4. Dynamic Exploration and Assessment

Specific areas that are noted and explored are the client's capacity to tolerate unconscious anxiety and how this anxiety manifests itself physically. The defensive patterns and the client's awareness of them, the degree to which such defenses are syntonic or dystonic, and the client's willingness to examine his or her difficulties, are noted and explored as well. This allows assessment of psychological mindedness and quality of object relations, both of which are predictors of treatment outcome (Ogrodniczuk, Piper, Joyce, & McCallum, 1999), as well as the ability to establish shared objectives (see feature 1, Establishment of Shared Objectives).

5. Mobilization of Unconscious Emotions, Anxiety, and Defenses

The psychotherapist's efforts to examine the client's problems and to form a therapeutic bond inevitably activate feelings about past attachments. In the case of clients with PD, these relationship efforts were often fraught with abuse, neglect, or trauma, leading to complex feelings of disappointed love, grief, rage, guilt about rage, and a craving for attachment. As the psychotherapist engages the client, these complex feelings are activated, resulting in unconscious anxiety and defenses, which constitute PD behaviors. This is both a potential barrier to engagement and an opportunity for the psychotherapist to assess the client, help him or her to see what is happening, and make changes. Winston et al. (1991) found that Davanloo's (2000) ISTDP used more challenge to defenses and elicited more affect than brief adaptive psychotherapy, a more cognitively oriented psychodynamic treatment. ISTDP was superior to brief adaptive psychotherapy in reducing depression and improving social/interpersonal adjustment in clients with PDs, whereas it was less effective at reducing anxiety in clients with PDs. Similarly, Winston et al. found that clients with good outcomes had a greater ratio of affective to defensive responses over the course of treatment (Taurke et al., 1990) and that transference interventions followed by affect correlated with better outcomes than when the same interventions were followed by defensive responses. A meta-analysis conducted by Diener et al. (2007) further supports the notion that emotional focus is an important contributor to good outcomes in brief dynamic psychotherapy.

6. Handling Resistance

The central focus of dynamic psychotherapy with highly defended PD clients is on examining and removing the various destructive major defenses, including repression of affect. Interventions include exploration of the nature of the defense, the impact of the defense, and the client's willingness to give it up. Such interventions render a defense more ego dystonic; that is, the client is turned against the defense. As resistance is overcome, collaborative tasks of therapy can proceed.

Defenses may be most fruitfully challenged when they are being manifested within the therapeutic relationship and have been significantly clarified so that the client recognizes that the challenge is leveled against the defenses and not against the person him- or herself. Thus, the defensive barriers against closeness and intimacy, against self-care, and against the experience of emotions are challenged by the therapist and client as a team. Clarification and challenge exist on a continuum (see Exhibit 4.1).

In support of this approach, Abbass, Joffres, and Ogrodniczuk (2008, 2009) found, in a case series that comprised over 90% PD clients undergoing brief dynamic trial therapy (i.e., an extended ISTDP interview), that therapists had higher rates of emotion mobilization efforts, clarification of defense, challenge to defense, and linking past to present in an affective way compared with therapists who conducted standard psychiatric intake assessments. In addition, greater symptomatic improvement was noted in the ISTDP intervention versus the comparison group.

EXHIBIT 4.1
Continuum of Clarification to Challenge of Resistance and Defense

Clarification ———————————————————→ Challenge		
Exploration of destructive effects; e.g., "Do you notice you become detached when you talk about anger?"	Pointing out to stop defensive behaviors; e.g., "What is the effect if you do that here?", "Where will we get if this continues?"	Confronting the client-specific behaviors; e.g., "*Again* you put up a wall with me."

7. Maintenance of the Therapeutic Alliance and Repair of Ruptures

Maintenance of the therapeutic alliance is crucial with PD clients who have suffered from broken bonds and subsequently have themselves ruptured bonds, hurting others. Thus, psychotherapists working with these clients must have a central intention of building and maintaining the therapeutic alliance and make efforts to prevent ruptures and repair them when they occur. Examples of efforts to maintain the alliance and avoid serious rupture are having clear, shared tasks and obtaining the client's moment-to-moment consent to examine difficult emotional areas. Psychotherapist self-awareness, including acknowledgment of one's own contribution to ruptures, is a crucial feature of the work with these clients (e.g., Safran & Muran, 2000; see Chapter 6, this volume).

8. Building Anxiety Tolerance and Self-Reflective Capacity

It is the task of therapy not to strip away all defenses but instead to improve self-regulation and emotion regulation while reducing destructive defenses. Depending on the physical manifestations of anxiety (e.g., voluntary muscle tension, such as neck pain, or involuntary muscle tension, such as gastrointestinal tract discomfort), the therapy process may help either regulate or reduce anxiety and/or to mobilize it toward consciousness along with the underlying feelings. According to the nature of the defenses and the degree to which they are syntonic or dystonic, the process may aim either to reduce them or augment healthier defenses or other capacities, such as self-reflection.

Because relinquishing defenses can mobilize overwhelming anxiety in some cases, psychodynamic models have various mechanisms of helping the client regulate anxiety. One such method, referred to as the *graded format* of ISTDP (Davanloo, 1989), allows the psychotherapist and client to improve anxiety tolerance through stepwise increases in, and examination of, complex feelings. When the anxiety becomes too high, the therapist helps the client reduce it by intellectually reviewing the links among phenomena, exploring the physical concomitants of the anxiety, and shifting from one area of focus to another. In this way, the client's ability to *mentalize*—that is, to be cognizant of the mental states of self and other (Fonagy & Bateman, 2006b) or to isolate affect—is increased, replacing repression, dissociation, or somatization. Similar processes used in transference-focused psychotherapy are described later in this chapter.

Such efforts may have a very positive effect on the therapeutic alliance because clients get to experience a helping relationship instead of being left alone with their distress, as was so often the case in their early lives. This work builds anxiety tolerance and allows eventual emotional experiencing to take place in a safe and comfortable fashion.

9. Working With Mobilized Unconscious Feelings

Once unconscious emotions, anxiety, and defenses are mobilized, various methods work to help the client identify, experience, and integrate the underlying affect. For example, Davanloo's (2000) method highlights the use of the therapeutic relationship, or the *transference*, to activate unconscious mixed feelings and subsequent character defenses. When these defenses crystallize in the transference, they can then be examined and overcome. The underlying complex transference feelings inevitably include positive feelings, anger, guilt, and sadness, which are all linked to feelings about broken attachments in the past. When these complex feelings are experienced, viscerally and cognitively, it brings about what Davanloo referred to as the "unlocking of the unconscious."

After this unlocking of the unconscious, the client's anxiety and defenses are reduced, the therapeutic alliance increases, and the client is able to recognize the feelings in the past that led to the original defensiveness. This process is applicable across a range of clients with character neuroses. According to Davanloo (2000), enabling the client to experience these transference feelings is crucial to preventing the buildup of unconscious transference feelings and the development of a *transference neurosis*, which is a risk factor for prolonged or interminable therapy and treatment failure with PD clients. Through these types of therapeutic efforts, clients experience grief about suffering caused by their long-standing destructive behavior. Hope and positive feelings for themselves and others result, leading to corrective actions in key relationships.

10. Recapitulation and Integration

Efforts to link the relationship patterns between the triangle of person and the triangle of conflict (see the Essential Theoretical Constructs section) is a common process across the many forms of dynamic psychotherapy. Along with this effort, the psychotherapist helps the client differentiate among the visceral experience of emotions, anxiety about the feelings, and defenses against anxiety. This is best done at the time of, or soon after, the experience of unconscious feelings. On its own, linking elements of the triangle can also mobilize unconscious feelings further. Many models highlight the need for a review with the client of the two triangles after some unconscious feelings have been experienced. Davanloo (2000) and Malan (1976), among others, have found, through case-based research, that this linking of elements of the triangles needs to take place to bring about character change and symptomatic relief in resistant clients.

Research (e.g., Ogrodniczuk et al., 1999) has shown that patients with a low quality of object relations (e.g., those with BPD) benefit more from interpretation than those with a high quality of object relations (e.g., clients with obsessive–compulsive PD). Thus, the relative use and timing of these interventions must be tailored to the client.

11. Dynamic Exploration of the Unconscious

The above-mentioned processes weaken the defenses the client has been using to ward off old, pathogenic emotions. Unconscious emotions from past traumatic experiences and losses will be more or less accessible depending on the client's degree of resistance and the degree to which the therapeutic alliance is mobilized. When this mobilization is happening on a high level, linkages to past trauma will start to take place. These activities have been described and demonstrated in some detail over the past 30 years by Davanloo (2000), who called this the *activation of the unconscious therapeutic alliance* (Davanloo, 1987). It is in this state of openness that the unconscious emotions about trauma will be mobilized, often with accompanying visual imagery, and experienced (e.g., see the Clinical Case Vignette section). Each such experience is generally followed by further recapitulation and analysis, which builds self-reflective capacity, mindfulness, and anxiety tolerance as described in feature 8, Building Anxiety Tolerance and Self-Reflective Capacity.

12. Working Through and Consolidation

After repeated experiences of access to unconscious emotions, a phase of *working through* takes place in which other related emotions are mobilized and experienced. In collaboration with the psychotherapist, clients put these findings together, broadening their own awareness of their narrative of life and putting the past into context. In this phase, residual strong emotions are brought to the surface and experienced, each time broadening the richness and color of the client's narrative. Grieving of other losses, as well as the upcoming loss of the therapeutic relationship, then take place.

Termination

Depending on the complexity of the client's problems and the length of the treatment, a termination phase may occur, with the client's expression of grief in relationship to the lost therapeutic attachment coupled by mobilization of past losses and grief. This provides another opportunity to experience here-and-now emotional processing.

CLINICAL CASE VIGNETTE

The patient is a married, 45-year-old, highly educated businessman with a long history of destructive behaviors and dysfunctional relationship patterns, such as emotional detachment, a sarcastic defensive pattern, avoidance of conflict, and an explosive temper. At work, these included panic attacks while in meetings, underperformance, suspicions that he is being schemed against, and destruction of property. On several occasions, with no one looking, he dumped coffee on the floor, and he once urinated on the floor in the coffee room. He could not clearly explain what motivated these behaviors. He also has had major depressive episodes and generalized anxiety with headaches and irritable bowel syndrome. Diagnostically speaking, he met *DSM–IV* criteria for paranoid PD, BPD, and avoidant PD; dysthymic disorder, and generalized anxiety disorder. He had failed to respond to two antidepressants at adequate dosages. (N.B.: The numbers in parentheses in the following paragraphs refer to the number of the technique or principle described in the preceding sections.)

In the first meeting, when focusing on his feelings about recent events, the client experienced a sensation of dark liquid going over his head and became mentally confused at or during a rise in anxiety, confirming the diagnosis of fragile character structure. A graded format of ISTDP was used to build his emotion and anxiety tolerance. Through the first five sessions of therapy, he experienced grief over failed relationship efforts as well as grief, rage, and guilt related to childhood physical and emotional abuse (No. 5). These emotions were seen as directly driving his current anxiety and behavior problems. In the fifth session, for example, he experienced rage and guilt related to his mother taking him, when he was 5 years old, to watch while she drowned kittens in a bucket (No. 5). Through experiencing these feelings and becoming aware of the links between past and present feelings, anxiety, and defenses, his anxiety significantly subsided (No. 10). By the sixth session, he arrived with a positive feeling toward the psychotherapist and treatment process:

> It just seems that when I am dealing with people, that I can distance myself from other people's emotions. . . . This is something I have never, mentally been able to do. I never had a technique to just disassociate myself from other people's anger. It seems that this is starting to happen without me even really thinking about techniques or anything like that. (*Describing self-reflective capacity and awareness of projection*)

The client went on to describe an incident when his wife was very angry and distraught. Instead of becoming anxious or hostile, he helped calm her down. He was amazed afterward that he could see that the distress was hers, separate himself from it, and be helpful. This brought a positive feeling toward the psychotherapist regarding treatment thus far.

Client (C):   It feels good, it feels like I don't have a weight on my shoulders. [Big sigh—marker of a rise in unconscious feelings]

Therapist (T):   So your priimary thing is a positive feeling. (Focus on feelings, No. 5)

C: It is a positive feeling, whereas every time I met with you before it started with some sort of aggression or anger. I had said things last time that I hadn't thought about in a long time about the two instances that mother drowned the kittens in front me. The amazing thing is it was almost just talking about it, and even saying things like wanting to kill my mother and I never would have ever thought that or said that to anybody, but for some reason it was almost like exorcising demons by just saying it.

T: To get it out of you. (No. 10)

C: I said it and now it's like you are almost at peace with yourself, which is a good feeling. I suppose there are other demons to talk about but it seems like this is definitely on a road to feeling good about myself. So that's where it stands right now! [Laughs boisterously]

This highlights a change mechanism considered central in psychodynamic psychotherapy of PD, namely, experiencing hitherto-unconscious pathogenic emotions, including grief, rage, and guilt about rage.

T: So when you think about that, we talked about that, at some point when you get to look at what we have done, and look at it in terms of victories for yourself, that you get to the place where you feel stronger and these things are not a problem or less of a problem, that you and I have done that working together and it gives you a good feeling in the end. (Nos. 8, 10, 12, 13)

This recap underscores the therapeutic task and the results of working together (No. 10). This is done repeatedly, especially after a rise in, or experience of, unconscious emotions. This typically brings a rise in the next series of unconscious emotions.

C: I feel positive about it. [*Another big sigh*]

T: How else do you feel inside at this point when you talk about these things, because I see some tension there. (*No. 5*)

C: [*Sighs*] I feel good about it, but I am getting tense. [*Sighs again*]

T: How do you feel beneath this tension? (*No. 5*)

C: There's some anger coming up. OK? But I want to stay with that good feeling.

T: You have some anger coming? (*No. 5*)

C: Yes, I do, really. It is just coming up. [*Points to abdomen and upward movement to chest*]

T: How do you experience this anger physically? (*No. 5*)

C: Well apart from that positive feeling with you that I truly do have. Have you ever felt evil?

T: That rage? (*No. 5*)

C: Yes, that rage is coming again.

T: How do you experience it with me here? (*No. 5*)

There is then a sequence of 15 minutes of focus on the somatic experience of the rage in the transference where the feeling is gradually activated and internally experienced. The anxiety about this feeling drops sequentially as the feeling is experienced.

C: There is this heat. . . . Just thinking of you right now, I want to grab you by the collar. [*Makes grabbing motion; the anxiety has now stopped entirely*]

T: How physically would that go if you totally lost control of it? (*No. 5*)

C: I'd grab you and push you back over and over. [*Makes shaking motion*]

One minute passes with this focus.

T: Then what happens? (*No. 5*)

C: As soon as the anger goes, I'm thinking of sympathy, that I wouldn't do that. Those tears are coming back.

T: A painful feeling. (*No. 10*)

C: [*Weeping*] That guilt, that I've hurt you, I've hurt a friend.

T: So that rage comes, and a guilt comes as if you damaged me. (*No. 10*)

C: But I didn't even do it! But the guilt anyway.

T: Which brings a question . . . (*of where this is coming from.*) (*No. 11*)

C: Yeah. [*Looks around room*] it is like . . . a river . . . My father comes right to mind when you said that, like a picture. (*Unconscious therapeutic alliance*)

T: Your father . . . and rivers? (*No. 11*)

C: Yeah. First I saw my father, then I saw this river with dark water, with bits of foam on it. I don't know what that means. . . . You know, there was something. I remember I was 4 years old, my father and I were on a ferry going over the river and I remember he held me over the edge like he was going to dump me over. But you know that is just something fathers do to their kids. (*The rationalization that kept feelings buried*)

T: So how do you feel when you recall this? (*No. 5, No. 11*)

C: That rage is coming back. I just want to grab him and hold him over the edge of the ferry . . . and so how do you like it? . . . As soon as I feel that, the guilt comes back, like how could I do that, but another part of me wants to dump him over.

T: Very mixed feelings. How would you feel if you dumped him off the ferry? (*No. 5, No. 11*)

C: [*In tears, can't speak*] . . . Bad.

A few minutes later:

C: I always thought doing things like that was normal, like my mother drowning kittens.

T: So if we look at it, what happened when you felt positive with me earlier? First the positive feelings, then this rage that came up and guilt as if you damaged me. But we see the next thing is your father and the ferry incident came up. Was it this rage toward your father that made so much anxiety when you felt close to me? (*Linking two triangles, No. 10*)

C: It must have been, because that's what happened.

T: Like you were afraid of what you would do if you felt close to me . . . (*Analysis and linking of the two triangles [No. 10] of T-C-P and I/F-A-D*)

C: . . . Or afraid of what you would do and how I'd react, but I didn't even realize it. God, this must have been happening all the time! (*Client does his own linking and analysis, No. 10*)

T: Do you think that you have been transferring all these feelings and anxieties? (*No. 10*)

C: Yeah, there is no doubt, that picture just came into my head after the anger with you. I feel a huge relief but how many times I've done that. I didn't see it. [*In tears*]

Once this material was reviewed further, it was apparent to both therapist and client that his "dark liquid" panics were a product of the guilt-laden urge to drown the father in the dark water. He was physically experiencing the drowning of his father each time. No doubt the fact that his mother drowned kittens increased his anxiety about this event and his feelings about it. The guilt about the rage had driven him to do provocative things at home (e.g., throwing rocks at windows) such that it elicited memories of being beaten repeatedly by his father. This was all paralleled at work with now-explainable defensiveness and destruction of property.

This client noted marked improvement both at home with family and at work. He stopped his antidepressant medication, without event. At termination, after 18 one-hour sessions of therapy, his score on the Brief Symptom Inventory (Global Symptom Index; Derogatis & Melisaratos, 1983) had gone from 2.47 to 0.12, and his Inventory of Interpersonal Problems (Horowitz, Rosenberg, Baer, Ureno, & Villaseñor, 1988) global mean rating had dropped from 2.11 to 0.19. Both of these represent decreases from the high pathological range to the normal range. He became more of a visible leader in his corporation, sustained his gains in a 6-year follow-up, and has not required further treatment sessions.

TREATMENT OF COMORBID CONDITIONS

In general, psychodynamic psychotherapy approaches do not focus only on specific conditions comorbid with PDs, such as anxiety, minor behavioral problems, a depressive tendency or intermittent substance abuse. Such behavioral difficulties and anxiety-linked phenomena are viewed as linked to complex unconscious emotions that are part and parcel of the PD (see the quote from W. Reich, 1949, in the opening paragraph of this chapter). However, when patients with comorbid Axis I and II diagnoses have been treated psychodynamically, the treatment has proven effective for depression (Hilsenroth,

Defife, Blake, & Cromer, 2007; Kool et al., 2003) and panic disorder (Milrod et al., 2007).

SPECTRUM OF CLIENTS WITH PERSONALITY DISORDERS WHO ARE SUITABLE FOR PSYCHODYNAMIC THERAPIES

Psychodynamic theorists have defined categories or spectra of clients who are suitable for dynamic therapies, which are detected through specialized evaluation methods. These psychodynamic categories are arguably far more important than DSM categories in helping design and guide psychodynamic treatment (PDM Task Force, 2006). For example, Davanloo (1995) named two spectra of PD patients: (a) those with psychoneurotic disorders and (b) those with fragile character structure, which are diagnosable by means of a trial therapy interview (Abbass, Joffres, & Ogrodniczuk, 2008). Clinical case research and anecdotal evidence suggest that where the client lies on these two continua predicts the length of treatment and relative effectiveness of short-term dynamic therapy efforts. The general finding has been that the more resistant the client, the longer and less effective is the treatment, especially in the hands of an early career psychotherapist. Fragile patients require longer treatment overall than nonfragile PD patients (i.e., those with character neuroses; Abbass, 2002; Abbass, Sheldon, Gyra, & Kalpin, 2008). Moreover, the treatment may be tailored according to where the client lies on these continua (Davanloo, 1995).

The first spectrum extends from low-resistant clients, who may be suffering from grief about a loss in their past without repressed rage and guilt, to extremely highly resistant clients, who have had repeated, massive trauma regarding attachments and have a punitive superego and a large amount of unconscious guilt about their rage.

Individuals with fragile character structure range from mild, in which there is transient cognitive and perceptual disruption, to severe, in which there is prolonged cognitive disruption and tendencies toward projective defenses and psychotic phenomena. These clients experience the phenomenon of *drifting,* or dissociation within the interview at a rise in unconscious anxiety (Danvaloo, 1995). Such clients must build their capacity to tolerate anxiety, as described in transference-focused psychotherapy (Clarkin, Levy, Lenzenweger, & Kernberg, 2007) and in ISTDP, among other psychotherapy models.

SUMMARY OF EVIDENCE-BASED PRINCIPLES AND STRATEGIES

There have been two very recent reviews of the empirical literature on psychological treatment of PDs from which we have culled the clinically useful principles and strategies applicable to psychodynamic approaches

(Crits-Christoph & Barber, 2007; Verheul & Herbrink, 2007). Note that most of the psychodynamically oriented empirical studies on PD include a mixture of clients from Clusters A, B, and C; however, there are a number of studies pertaining to the brief dynamic treatment of Cluster C clients whose results we summarize after discussing the more general results. Finally, we give special attention to BPD, which falls in Cluster B.

Intervention Strategies Applying to Personality Disorders in General

Two meta-analyses (Leichsenring & Leibing, 2003; Perry, Banon, & Ianni, 1999) have demonstrated that psychodynamically oriented individual psychotherapy (as well as cognitive behavior therapy) reduces symptoms and personality pathology and improves social functioning among a mixture of clients diagnosed with PDs from Clusters A, B, and C as well as PD not otherwise specified (NOS). However, the forms of psychodynamic therapy that include elements such as encouragement, validation, and advice result in lower dropout rates than therapy styles that are more exclusively expressive (emphasizing clarification, confrontation, and interpretation); specifically, depending on the capacities of the client (e.g., frustration and anxiety tolerance, impulse control and the capacity for reality testing), more emphasis should be placed on such elements at least in the first phase of treatment, and the switch to more interpretive and expressive elements should be made only when these capacities have improved. In the first phase of treatment the psychotherapist should focus on motivating PD clients who are resistant and have limited reflective capacities (Verheul & Herbrink, 2007). At the same time, with clients with Cluster C PDs, and with some Cluster B clients as well, there is often more opportunity to conduct an actively exploratory, emotion-eliciting therapy from the outset than with clients who have Cluster A or some Cluster B PDs, which may be why the studies that combine Clusters A, B, and C emphasize the importance of more empathic, cognitive, and structured elements compared with those that focus solely on Cluster C PDs.

Manualized treatments of PDs, regardless of the theoretical orientation followed, frequently draw eclectically from more than one approach. For example, Verheul and Herbrink (2007) pointed out that these therapies may include cognitive behavior therapy elements, such as cognitive restructuring, and psychodynamic elements, such as interpretation of defense mechanisms and of transference. The point for clinicians to keep in mind is to apply various techniques flexibly according to the client's capacities, the state of the therapeutic alliance, and the stage of treatment. However, it is important that they not avoid helping even Cluster B clients face their anxieties.

Brief Psychodynamic Therapy With Clients With PD

A variety of psychodynamically based short-term therapies (fewer than 40 sessions) conducted with mostly Cluster B, Cluster C, and NOS PDs have been studied in eight randomized clinical trials, yielding robust positive effects that have persisted at follow-ups averaging 18.9 months ($SD = 7.3$; see the effect sizes of seven of these studies in Table 4.1). These include three studies that rely on Davanloo's (2000) approach, as described earlier in this chapter. Davanloo's earlier method (before 1980) was found to be similar in overall outcome to two other forms of more supportive dynamic models and superior to a wait-list control group (Hellerstein et al., 1998; Winston et al., 1994). More recently, his technique has evolved to include methods to build anxiety tolerance in fragile and somatizing clients, enabling treatment of a far broader PD sample (Abbass, 2002). A study using the current ISTDP model (Davanloo, 2000) found greater effects with a shorter treatment course than did Hellerstein et al. (1998) and Winston et al. (1994) even while including 12 out of 27 PD patients with BPD (Abbass, Sheldon, Gyra, & Kalpin 2008).

A study of Cluster C PDs based on McCullough Vaillant's (1997) model of brief dynamic therapy found positive change for clients treated in this modality and in cognitive therapy. The dynamic therapy also brought a significant decrease in symptoms, which was not the case for cognitive therapy (Svartberg, Stiles, & Seltzer, 2004). In terms of strategies, this psychodynamic therapy uses defense, affect, cognitive, and self–other restructuring as described in the Mechanisms of Change section.

In a different study, another form of time-limited, manualized therapy, known as *supportive–expressive therapy* (Luborsky, 1984), which is based on standard psychodynamic principles, was compared with community-delivered, nonmanualized psychodynamic therapy conducted with clients who had Cluster C PDs; both yielded comparable, positive results (Vinnars, Barber, Norén, Gallop, & Weinryb, 2005). Finally, brief relational therapy (BRT) was compared with brief dynamic therapy based on standard psychodynamic principles and with cognitive behavior therapy in clients with Cluster C PDs and PDs NOS (Muran, Safran, Samstag, & Winston, 2005). The results indicated that the three treatments were equally effective, although there were fewer dropouts in BRT. The strategies used in BRT are to track alliance ruptures and to communicate about what is happening for client and psychotherapist, thereby cultivating awareness of self in relation to the other.

These data, gathered from a group of reasonably good quality studies from several different research centers, offer empirical support for short-term dynamic therapies for a range of PDs. They do not, however, indicate the superiority of psychodynamic therapy over other therapies.

Intervention Strategies Applying to Borderline Personality Disorder

We turn now to principles and strategies for treating BPD clients, who are well known to be particularly difficult to treat and who are heavy users of both general medical and psychiatric services (Bender et al., 2001; Zanarini, Frankenburg, Hennen, & Silk, 2003). Fortunately, the past few years have seen a substantial increase in psychodynamically based, empirically supported interventions to treat this disorder, which we now describe.

Transference-Focused Psychotherapy

Clarkin et al. (2007) compared TFP, dialectical behavior therapy (DBT), and supportive therapy (ST) in a randomized clinical trial with a sample of seriously disturbed clients with BPD (Clarkin et al., 2007). TFP is based on object relational psychoanalytic principles as conceptualized by Clarkin, Yeomans, and Kernberg (1999); DBT is an empirically supported, cognitive–behavioral treatment for BPD developed by Marsha Linehan (1993); and ST is a psychodynamically oriented but nontransference based therapy for BPD developed by Rockland (1992) that emphasizes the psychotherapist's engagement with BPD clients to help them deal with their daily difficulties in a constructive way.

Clarkin et al.'s (2007) study was very sophisticated, combining elements of both efficacy (internal validity) and effectiveness (external validity). Adherence and competence were monitored; allegiance effects were controlled; and progress and outcome were measured on a wide variety of measures, which went well beyond symptomatic improvement. Furthermore, the therapies were of 50-session duration, which is considerably longer than most psychotherapy studies and were geared conceptually to the specific population at hand.

The three treatment groups showed significant positive changes in depression, anxiety, global functioning, and social adjustment after 1 year of treatment. Both TFP and DBT were significantly associated with improvement in suicidality. Only TFP and ST were associated with improvement in anger and in facets of impulsivity, and only TFP was significantly predictive of change in irritability and verbal and direct assault (Clarkin et al., 2007, p. 922). Overall, of the 12 outcome variables evaluated, TFP showed improvement in 10, DBT in six, and ST in five.

The mechanisms of change contributing to good outcomes with TFP were described by Levy, Clarkin, et al. (2006) as follows. The creation of a safe relationship enables clients to experience affect without being overwhelmed by it and to reflect on what is happening in the therapeutic relationship. Clients are helped to become aware of the extent to which their perceptions are based more on internalized representations than on what is really occurring and then they are taught to understand, modify, and integrate these representations via techniques of clarification, confrontation, and transference interpretation. The psychotherapist, while staying focused on what is being enacted in therapy, continues to monitor what is happening in the client's life. The psychotherapist tries to repair splits in clients' object relations and splits between cognitions and affects by helping them to become more self-reflective:

> The therapist's timely, clear and tactful interpretations of the dominant, affect-laden themes and patient enactments in the here and now of the transference are hypothesized to shed light on the reasons that representations remain split off and thus facilitate integrating polarized representations of self and others. (Levy, Clarkin, et al., 2006, p. 487)

In another article based on the same clients as in Levy, Clarkin, et al. (2006), Levy, Meehan, et al. (2006) provided empirical support for the value of some of the elements that improved after treatment with TFP but not after treatment with DBT or ST. These included changes in self-reflection and what they called *attachment representations* in BPD. In brief, "Patients treated with TFP evidenced increases in [reflective function], attachment coherence, and rates of being classified as secure with respect to attachment as compared with the other treatment conditions" (Levy, Meehan, et al., 2006, p. 1035). (TFP did not, however, lead to a resolution of loss or trauma.) Studies are now underway to test whether these changes endure.

Mentalization-Based Treatment

Bateman and Tyrer (2004) compared mentalization-based treatment, administered within the context of a psychodynamically oriented partial hospitalization program, with standard psychiatric care for BPD clients. Interventions in the individual and group psychoanalytic therapies were aimed at increasing patients' reflective or mentalizing capacity. "Mentalisation entails making sense of the actions of oneself and others on the basis of intentional mental states such as desires, feelings and beliefs" (Bateman & Tyrer, 2004, p. 381; see also Fonagy & Bateman, 2006a, for a fuller description of the mechanisms of change in mentalization-based treatment of BPD). It involves the recognition of what is in one's mind and the minds of others, or recognizing that others have feelings and conceptions that are different from one's own—capacities that are diminished in BPD clients. Treatment was provided for up to 18 months. Compared with the control group, individuals in the partial hospitalization program showed a significant decrease on a number of outcome measures, such as frequency of suicide attempts, inpatient admissions, and use of psychotropic medication, as well as a variety of self-report measures of symptoms, interpersonal functioning, and social adjustment (Bateman &

Fonagy, 1999). The control group participants showed limited change or some deterioration over the same time period. When participants were followed up after 18 months, those in the psychodynamically oriented partial hospitalization program continued to show better functioning compared with the participants in standard care and continued improvement on social and interpersonal variables (Bateman & Fonagy, 2001).

Although the effective components of treatment are hard to tease out in this study (Bateman & Fonagy, 1999), Bateman and Fonagy (2000, p. 141) contended that there are seven common features across the successful approaches, including DBT: They (a) are well structured; (b) enhance compliance; (c) have a clear focus, be it a problem behavior or interpersonal pattern; (d) are highly coherent theoretically to both psychotherapist and client; (e) are relatively long term; (f) encourage a powerful attachment between client and therapist, enabling an active therapeutic stance; and (g) are integrated with other services available to the client. It should be noted in this connection that many clients, when offered open-ended, unstructured psychodynamic therapy, drop out within a few months (Gunderson et al., 1989; Skodal, Buckley, & Charles, 1983).

Bateman (2004) also teased out the commonality between mentalization-based treatment and TFP, which is instructive for practicing clinicians. Both focus on affect, emphasize awareness of countertransference, consider mental representations of relationships, and draw parallels between relationship patterns (cf. the earlier discussion of the triangle of insight). They de-emphasize deep unconscious concerns and stick closer to the surface.

A Psychodynamic–Interpersonal Model

A psychodynamic–interpersonal therapy that blends self and object relations concepts was applied to BPD clients for 1 year. The clients showed improvements at 1 and 5 years following treatment (Stevenson, Meares, & D'Angelo, 2005), and there were considerable cost savings due largely to reduced hospital admissions (Hall, Caleo, Stevenson, & Meares, 2001). This model of treatment seems to share some strategies and principles with treatments previously described.

Inpatient and Psychodynamic Outpatient Therapy Combined

Finally, we report briefly on a research program that compared the effectiveness of two psychodynamically oriented treatment models for PD; 70% of the participants had BPD (Chiesa & Fonagy, 2000). One model was a long-term residential treatment that used a therapeutic community approach, which included formal psychodynamic therapy (individual and group), whereas the other was a briefer inpatient treatment of the same kind but was followed by twice-weekly, small-group psychodynamic psychotherapy along with some other outreach services. The latter, known as a *step-down program*, was found to be more effective than the former, especially for the BPD clients. At a 3-year follow-up, improvements were significantly greater in the step-down program in terms of social adjustment, global assessment of mental health, attempted suicide, self-mutilation, and hospital readmission. It appears that small group psychodynamic therapy, provided alongside ancillary community support services, is important to the stabilization of severe PD following hospitalization.

CONCLUSION

Psychodynamically based therapies for treating PDs have fared well in recent years, both in terms of the number of studies conducted and their outcomes. That the studies tend to support the effectiveness of psychodynamic therapies with PDs, including therapies that are 1 year or less in duration and those conducted in very different locales; and even when compared with other established therapies, such as DBT, suggests that the psychodynamic approach to therapy is quite robust. Although all the therapies we have discussed in this chapter rely on psychoanalytic concepts, they are not unimodal in execution but vary in their way of using psychodynamic ideas and techniques. In particular, they differ in how they treat the healthier clients with PD (i.e., those in Cluster C) and those who are more fragile (i.e., those whose PDs are in Clusters B and C), with the latter seeming to require more structure and attention to emotional regulation and modulation. In addition, even within Cluster B there are a variety of psychodynamic approaches to treatment, all of which have at least some empirical backing in treating BPD, including TFP, mentalization-based treatment, and ISTDP. Despite the promising results, we are still some way from knowing how to effect change in many clients with PD who seek our help or even understanding exactly which mechanisms are at play. We need more process and outcome research to place psychodynamic therapy on a firmer empirical footing and to extend its reach to the more dysfunctional PDs.

REFERENCES

Abbass, A. A. (2002). Office-based research in intensive short-term dynamic psychotherapy (ISTDP): Data from the first 6 years of practice. *Ad Hoc Bulletin of Short-Term Dynamic Psychotherapy, 6*, 5–13.

Abbass, A. A. , Joffres, M. R., & Ogrodniczuk, J. S. (2008). A naturalistic study of intensive short-term dynamic psychotherapy trial therapy. *Brief Treatment and Crisis Intervention, 8*, 164–170.

Abbass, A. A., Joffres, M. R., & Ogrodniczuk, J. S. (2009). Intensive short-term dynamic psychotherapy trial therapy: Qualitative description and comparison to standard intake assessments. *Ad Hoc Bulletin of Short-Term Dynamic Psychotherapy, 13*, 6–14.

Abbass, A. A., Lovas, D., & Purdy, A. (2008). Direct diagnosis and management of emotional factors in chronic headache patients. *Cephalalgia, 28*, 1305–1314.

Abbass, A., Sheldon, A., Gyra, J., & Kalpin, A. (2008). Intensive short-term dynamic psychotherapy for *DSM–IV* personality disorders: A randomized controlled trial. *Journal of Nervous and Mental Disease, 196*, 211–216.

Abraham, K. (1942). Contributions to the theory of anal character. In *Selected papers of Karl Abraham* (pp. 370–392). London: Hogarth Press. (Original work published 1923)

Altman, N. (1995). *The analyst in the inner city: Race, class, and culture through a psychoanalytic lens* (Vol. 3). Hillsdale, NJ: Analytic Press.

American Psychiatric Association. (1994). *Diagnostic and statistical manual of mental disorders* (4th ed.). Washington, DC: Author.

Bateman, A. W. (2004). Psychodynamic psychotherapy for personality disorders. *Psychiatric Times, 21*(8). Retrieved from http://www.psychiatrictimes.com/personality-disorders/article/10168/47031.

Bateman, A., & Fonagy, P. (1999). Effectiveness of partial hospitalization in the treatment of borderline personality disorder: A randomized controlled trial. *American Journal of Psychiatry, 156*, 1563–1569.

Bateman, A. W., & Fonagy, P. (2000). Effectiveness of psychotherapeutic treatment of personality disorder. *British Journal of Psychiatry, 177*, 138–143.

Bateman, A. W., & Fonagy, P. (2001). Treatment of borderline personality disorder with psychoanalytically oriented partial hospitalization: An 18-month follow-up. *American Journal of Psychiatry, 158*, 36–42.

Bateman, A. W., & Tyrer, P. (2004). Psychological treatment for personality disorders. *Advances in Psychiatric Treatment, 10*, 378–388.

Bender, D. S. (2005). The therapeutic alliance in the treatment of personality disorders. *Journal of Psychiatric Practice, 11*, 73–87.

Bender, D. S., Dolan, R. T., Skodol, A. E., Sanislow, C. A., Dyck, I. R., McGlashan, T. H., . . . Gunderson, J. G. (2001). Treatment utilization by patients with personality disorders. *American Journal of Psychiatry, 158*, 295–302.

Betan, E., Heim, A. K., Conklin, C. Z., & Westen, D. (2005). Countertransference phenomena and personality pathology in clinical practice: An empirical investigation. *American Journal of Psychiatry, 162*, 890–898.

Beutler, L. E., Malik, M., Alimohamed, S., Harwood, T. M., Talebi, H., Noble, S., & Wong, E. (2004). Therapist variables. In M. J. Lambert (Ed.), *Bergin and Garfield's handbook of psychotherapy and behavior change* (5th ed., pp. 227–306). New York, NY: Wiley.

Blagys, M. D., & Hilsenroth, M. J. (2000). Distinctive features of short-term psychodynamic–interpersonal psychotherapy: A review of the comparative psychotherapy process literature. *Clinical Psychology: Science and Practice, 7*, 167–188.

Bond, M., & Perry, J. C. (2006). Psychotropic medication use, personality disorder and improvement in long-term dynamic psychotherapy. *Journal of Nervous and Mental Disease, 194*, 21–26.

Chiesa, M., & Fonagy, P. (2000). Cassel personality disorder study methodology and treatment effects. *British Journal of Psychiatry, 176*, 485–491.

Clarkin, J. F., & Levy, K. N. (2004). The influence of client variables on psychotherapy. In M. J. Lambert (Ed.), *Bergin and Garfield's handbook of psychotherapy and behavior change* (5th ed., pp. 194–226). New York, NY: Wiley.

Clarkin, J. F., Levy, K. N., Lenzenweger, M. F., & Kernberg, O. F. (2007). Evaluating three treatments for borderline personality disorder: A multiwave study. *American Journal of Psychiatry, 164*, 922–928.

Clarkin, J. F., Yeomans, F., & Kernberg, O. F. (1999). *Psychotherapy of borderline personality*. New York, NY: John Wiley & Sons.

Crits-Christoph, P., & Barber, J. P. (2007). Psychological treatments for personality disorders. In P. A. Nathan & J. M. Gorman (Eds.), *A guide to treatments that work* (3rd ed., pp. 641–658). New York, NY: Oxford University Press.

Danvaloo, H. (1980). *Short-term dynamic psychotherapy*. New York, NY: Jason Aronson.

Davanloo, H. (1987). Unconscious therapeutic alliance. In P. Buirski (Ed.), *Frontiers of dynamic psychotherapy* (pp. 64–88). New York: Brunner/Mazel.

Davanloo, H. (1989). The technique of unlocking the unconscious in patients suffering from functional disorder: Part I. Restructuring ego's defenses. *International Journal of Short-Term Psychotherapy, 4*, 93–116.

Davanloo, H. (1995). Intensive short-term dynamic psychotherapy: Spectrum of psychoneurotic disorders. *International Journal of Short-Term Psychotherapy, 10*, 121–155.

Davanloo, H. (2000). *Intensive short-term dynamic psychotherapy: Selected papers of Habib Davanloo*. Chichester, England: Wiley.

Derogatis, L. R., & Melisaratos, N. (1983). The Brief Symptom Inventory: An introductory report. *Psychological Medicine, 13*, 595–605.

Diener, M. J., Hilsenroth, M. J., & Weinberger, J. (2007). Therapist affect focus and patient outcome in psychodynamic psychotherapy: A meta-analysis. *American Journal of Psychiatry, 164*, 936–941.

Dimaggio, G., & Norcross, J. C. (2008). (Eds.). Treating comorbid personality disorders [Special issue]. *Journal of Clinical Psychology, 64*(2).

Emmelkamp, P. M., Benner, A., Kuipers, A., Feiertag, G. A., Koster, H. C., & van Apeldoorn, F. J. (2006). Comparison of brief dynamic and cognitive–behavioural therapies in avoidant personality disorder. *British Journal of Psychiatry, 189*, 60–64.

Ezriel, H. (1952). Notes on psychoanalytic group therapy: Interpretation and research. *Psychiatry, 15,* 119–126.

Fonagy, P., & Bateman, A. W. (2006a). Mechanisms of change in mentalization-based treatment of BPD. *Journal of Clinical Psychology, 62,* 411–430.

Fonagy, P., & Bateman, A. W. (2006b). Progress in the treatment of borderline personality disorder. *British Journal of Psychiatry, 188,* 1–3.

Freud, S. (1958). On the beginning of treatment: Further recommendations on the technique of psychoanalysis. In J. Strachey (Ed. and Trans.), *Standard edition of the complete psychological works of Sigmund Freud* (Vol. 12, pp. 122–144). London, England: Hogarth Press. (Original work published 1913)

Freud, S. (1959). Character and anal eroticism. In J. Strachey (Ed. and Trans.), *The standard edition of the complete psychological works of Sigmund Freud* (Vol. 14, pp. 145–156). London, England: Hogarth Press. (Original work published 1908)

Greenberg, L. S., & Pascual-Leone, A. (2006). Emotion in psychotherapy: A practice-friendly research review. *Journal of Clinical Psychology, 62,* 611–630.

Gunderson, J. G., Frank, A. F., Ronningstam, E. F., Wachter, S., Lynch, V. J., & Wolf, P. J. (1989). Early discontinuance of borderline patients from psychotherapy. *Journal of Nervous and Mental Disease, 177,* 38–42.

Hall, J., Caleo, S., Stevenson, J., & Meares, R. (2001). An economic analysis of psychotherapy for borderline personality disorder patients. *Journal of Mental Health Policy and Economics, 4,* 3–8.

Hardy, G. E., Barkham, M., Shapiro, D. A., Stiles, W. B., Rees, A., & Reynolds, S. (1995). Impact of Cluster C personality disorders on outcomes of contrasting brief psychotherapies for depression. *Journal of Consulting and Clinical Psychology, 63,* 997–1004.

Hellerstein, D. J., Rosenthal, R. N., Pinsker, H., Samstag, L. W., Muran, J. C., & Winston, A. (1998). A randomized prospective study comparing supportive and dynamic therapies. *Journal of Psychotherapy Practice and Research, 7,* 261–271.

Hersoug, A. G., Monsen, J. T., Havik, O. E., & Høglend, P. (2002). Quality of early working alliance in psychotherapy: Diagnoses, relationship and intrapsychic variables as predictors. *Psychotherapy and Psychosomatics, 71,* 18–27.

Hilsenroth, M. J., Defife, J. A., Blake, M. M., & Cromer, T. D. (2007). The effects of borderline pathology on short-term psychodynamic psychotherapy for depression. *Psychotherapy Research, 17,* 175–188.

Hobson, R. F. (1985). *Forms of feeling: The heart of psychotherapy.* London, England: Tavistock.

Horowitz, L. M., Rosenberg, S. E., Baer, B. A., Ureno, G., & Villaseñor, V. S. (1988). Inventory of Interpersonal Problems: Psychometric properties and clinical applications. *Journal of Consulting and Clinical Psychology, 56,* 885–892.

Horvath, A. O. (2005). The therapeutic relationship: Research and theory [Introduction to the special issue]. *Psychotherapy Research, 15,* 3–7.

Kernberg, O. F. (1975). *Borderline conditions and pathological narcissism*. New York, NY: Jason Aronson.

Kool, S., Dekker, J., Duijsens, I. J., de Jonghe, F., & Puite, B. (2003). Efficacy of combined therapy and pharmacotherapy for depressed patients with or without personality disorders. *Harvard Review of Psychiatry, 11*, 133–141.

Leichsenring, F., & Leibing, E. (2003). The effectiveness of psychodynamic therapy and cognitive behavior therapy in the treatment of personality disorders: A meta-analysis. *American Journal of Psychiatry, 160*, 1–10.

Levy, K. N., Clarkin, J. F., Yeomans, F. E., Scott, L. N., Wasserman, R. H., & Kernberg, O. F. (2006). The mechanisms of change in the treatment of borderline personality disorder with transference focused psychotherapy. *Journal of Clinical Psychology, 62*, 481–501.

Levy, K. N., Meehan, K. B., Kelly, K. M., Reynoso, J. S., Weber, M., Clarkin, J. F., & Kernberg, O. F. (2006). Change in attachment patterns and reflective function in a randomized control trial of transference-focused psychotherapy for borderline personality disorder. *Journal of Consulting and Clinical Psychology, 74*, 1027–1040.

Linehan, M. M. (1993). *Cognitive–behavioral treatment of borderline personality disorder*. New York, NY: Guilford Press.

Luborsky, L. (1984). *Principles of psychoanalytic psychotherapy: A manual for supportive–expressive treatment*. New York, NY: Basic Books.

Magnavita, J. J. (1997). *Restructuring personality disorders*. New York, NY: Guilford Press.

Malan, D. H. (1976). *The frontier of brief psychotherapy*. New York, NY: Plenum Press.

Martin, D. J., Garske, J. P., & Davis, K. M. (2000). Relation of the therapeutic alliance with outcome and other variables: A meta analytic review. *Journal of Consulting and Clinical Psychology, 68*, 438–450.

McCullough Vaillant, L. (1997). *Changing character*. New York, NY: Basic Books.

McGinn, L. K., & Sanderson, W. C. (1995). The nature of panic disorder. *In Session: Psychotherapy in Practice, 1*, 7–19.

Menninger, K. (1958). *Theory of psychoanalytic technique*. New York, NY: Basic Books.

Messer, S. B. (2001). What makes brief psychodynamic therapy time efficient? *Clinical Psychology: Science and Practice, 8*, 5–22.

Messer, S. B., & Warren, C. S. (1995). *Models of brief psychodynamic therapy: A comparative approach*. New York, NY: Guilford Press.

Messer, S. B., & Wolitzky, D. L. (2007). The psychoanalytic approach to case formulation. In T. Eells (Ed.), *Handbook of psychotherapy case formulation* (2nd ed., pp. 67–104). New York, NY: Guilford Press.

Messer, S. B., & Wolitzky, D. L. (in press). The therapeutic alliance: A psychodynamic perspective on theory, practice and research. In J. C. Muran & J. P. Barber (Eds.), *The therapeutic alliance: An evidence-based approach to practice and training*. New York, NY: Guilford Press.

Milrod, B. L., Leon, A. C., Barber, J. P., Markowitz, J. C., & Graf, E. (2007). Do comorbid personality disorders moderate panic-focused psychotherapy? An exploratory examination of the American Psychiatric Association practice guideline. *Journal of Clinical Psychiatry, 68,* 885–891.

Munroe-Blum, H., & Marziali, E. (1995). A controlled trial of short-term group treatment for borderline personality disorder. *Journal of Personality Disorders, 9,* 190–198.

Muran, J. C., Safran, J. D., Samstag, L. W., & Winston, A. (2005). Evaluating an alliance-focused treatment for personality disorders. *Psychotherapy, 42,* 532–545.

Ogrodniczuk, J. S., Piper, W. E., Joyce, A. S., & McCallum, M. (1999). Transference interpretations in short-term dynamic psychotherapy. *Journal of Nervous and Mental Disease, 187,* 571–578.

PDM Task Force. (2006). *Psychodynamic diagnostic manual.* Silver Spring, MD: Alliance of Psychoanalytic Organizations.

Perry, J., Banon, E., & Ianni, F. (1999). Effectiveness of psychotherapy for personality disorders. *American Journal of Psychiatry, 156,* 1312–1321.

Piper, W. E., Azim, H .F. A., Joyce, A. S., McCallum, M., Nixon, G. W. H., & Segal, P. S. (1991). Quality of object relations versus interpersonal functioning as predictors of therapeutic alliance and psychotherapy outcome. *Journal of Nervous and Mental Disease, 179,* 432–438.

Piper, W. E., Rosie, J. S., Azim, H. F. A, & Joyce, A. S. (1993). A randomized trial of psychiatric day treatment for patients with affective and personality disorders. *Hospital and Community Psychiatry, 44,* 757–763.

Reich, J. H., & Vasile, R. G. (1993). Effect of personality disorders on the treatment outcome of Axis I conditions—An update. *Journal of Nervous and Mental Disease, 181,* 475–484.

Reich, W. (1949). *Character analysis* (T. P. Wolfe, Trans.). New York, NY: Orgone Institute Press.

Rockland, L. H. (1992). *Supportive therapy for borderline patients: A psychodynamic approach.* New York, NY Guilford Press.

Safran, J. D., & Muran, C. (2000). *Negotiating the therapeutic alliance: A relational treatment guide.* New York, NY: Guilford Press.

Shea, M. T., Pilkonis, P. A., Beckham, E., Collins, J. F., Elkin, I., Sotsky, S. M., Docherty, J. P. (1990). Personality disorders and treatment outcome in the NIMH Treatment of Depression Collaborative Research Program. *American Journal of Psychiatry, 147,* 711–718.

Skodal, A., Buckley, P., & Charles, E. (1983). Is there a characteristic pattern to the treatment history of clinical outpatients with borderline personality disorder? *Journal of Nervous and Mental Disease, 171,* 405–410.

Stevenson, J., Meares, R., & D'Angelo, R. (2005). Five-year outcome of outpatient psychotherapy with borderline patients. *Psychological Medicine, 35,* 79–87.

Svartberg, M., Stiles, T. C., & Seltzer, M. H. (2004). Randomized, controlled trial of the effectiveness of short-term dynamic psychotherapy and cognitive therapy for Cluster C personality disorders. *American Journal of Psychology*, *161*, 810–817.

Taurke, E., Flegenheimer, W., McCullough, L., Winston, A., Pollack, J., & Trujillo, M. (1990). Change in patient affect/defence ratio from early to late sessions in brief psychotherapy. *Journal of Clinical Psychology*, *46*, 657–666.

Verheul, R., & Herbrink, M. (2007). The efficacy of various modalities of psychotherapy for personality disorders: A systematic review of the evidence and clinical recommendations. *International Review of Psychiatry*, *19*, 25–38.

Vinnars, B., Barber, J. P., Norén, K., Gallop, R., & Weinryb, R. M. (2005). Manualized supportive–expressive psychotherapy versus nonmanualized community-delivered psychodynamic therapy for patients with personality disorders: Bridging efficacy and effectiveness. *American Journal of Psychiatry*, *162*, 1933–1940.

Vinnars, B., Barber, J. P., Norén, K., Thormählen, B., Gallop, R., Lindgren, A., & Weinryb, R. M. (2007). Who can benefit from time-limited dynamic psychotherapy? A study of psychiatric outpatients with personality disorders. *Clinical Psychology and Psychotherapy*, *14*, 198–210.

Winston, A., Laikin, M., Pollack, J., Samstag, L. W., McCullough, L., & Muran, J. C. (1994). Short-term psychotherapy of personality disorders. *American Journal of Psychiatry*, *151*, 190–194.

Winston, A., McCullough, L., & Laikin, M. (1993). Clinical and research implications of patient–therapist interaction in brief psychotherapy. *American Journal of Psychotherapy*, *47*, 527–539.

Winston, A., Pollack, J., McCullough, J., Flegenheimer, W., Kestenbaum, R., & Trujillo, M. (1991). Brief psychotherapy of personality disorders. *Journal of Nervous and Mental Disease*, *179*, 188–193.

Zanarini, M. C., Frankenburg, F. R., Hennen, J., & Silk, K. R. (2003). The longitudinal course of borderline psychopathology: 6-year prospective follow-up of the phenomenology of borderline personality disorder. *American Journal of Psychiatry*, *160*, 274–283.

5

EVIDENCE-BASED INTERPERSONAL PSYCHOTHERAPY WITH PERSONALITY DISORDERS: THEORY, COMPONENTS, AND STRATEGIES

JACK C. ANCHIN AND AARON L. PINCUS

Compelling bodies of scientific evidence have converged to indicate that "interpersonal relationships are the foundation and theme of human life" (Reis, Collins, & Berscheid, 2000, p. 844). The centrality of processes between self and others to human evolutionary history; their ubiquity throughout the life cycle; and their powerful influence on development, motivation, and behavior are well documented (Reis et al., 2000; Ryff & Singer, 1998; Siegel, 1999). Highlighting their profound significance in the human experience, Berscheid and Reis (1998) concluded that "relationships are people's most frequent source of both happiness and distress" (p. 243).

Chronic dysfunction in self–other processes and its painful consequences are perhaps nowhere more prominent than in the case of personality disorder (PD; Livesley, 2001; Skodol et al., 2002), at the very heart of which indeed lie "problems with self or identity and chronic interpersonal dysfunction" (Clarkin, 2006, p. 2; cf. Livesley, 2001; Pincus, 2005a). In this chapter, we synthesize principal themes in the theory, research, and practice of interpersonal psychotherapy with PD clients, a paradigm that directly targets the multiple maladaptive self–other processes fundamental to this complex and challenging class of disorders. In highlighting both the covert and overt levels of these relational phenomena and their reciprocality, the interpersonal approach also

113

provides a framework for seamlessly integrating concepts and techniques associated with other treatment approaches to PDs (Anchin, 1982a, 1982b, 2002; Pincus & Cain, 2008). Overarchingly informing this chapter is the contemporary conception of evidence-based practice in psychology (American Psychological Association Presidential Task Force on Evidence-Based Practice, 2006). Grounded in the continuing effort to optimize syntheses between science and practice, this framework emphasizes the integration of research findings, clinical expertise, and patient factors in guiding clinical processes and practices.

THEORETICAL UNDERPINNINGS AND ASSUMPTIONS

In the following sections, we delineate essential theoretical constructs and intimately related assumptions that are foundational to interpersonal approaches to psychotherapy, followed by an encapsulation of core mechanisms that account for change in effective interpersonal treatment of PDs. Interpersonal psychotherapy is then placed in broader context by specifying principal domains of functioning targeted within the total ecological system, followed by an overview of the prototypic therapy process characterizing interpersonal treatment of PD clients.

Essential Theoretical Constructs

Contemporary interpersonal theory (e.g., Pincus, 2005a) is based on four broad assumptions. The first assumption is that the most important expressions of personality and psychopathology occur in phenomena involving more than one person (i.e., interpersonal situations). An *interpersonal situation* is defined as the experience of a pattern of relating self with other, associated with varying levels of anxiety (or security), in which learning takes place that significantly influences the development of self-concept and social behavior. The interpersonal situation is intimately tied to the genesis, development, maintenance, and mutability of personality and PD through the continuous patterning and repatterning of interpersonal experience in an effort to satisfy fundamental human motives (e.g., attachment and communion, autonomy and agency) in ways that increase security and self-esteem (positively reinforcing) and avoid anxiety (negatively reinforcing). Over time, this gives rise to social–cognitive–affective schemas of self and others and enduring patterns of adaptive or disturbed interpersonal relating (Critchfield & Benjamin, 2008).

The second assumption is that interpersonal situations occur both between proximal interactants and within the minds of those interactants via the capacity for perception, mental representation, memory, fantasy, expectancy, and emotion. This assumption allows interpersonal psychotherapy to incorporate important pantheoretical representational constructs such as cognitive–affective interpersonal (self–other) schemas, internalized object relations, and internal working models (Pincus & Cain, 2008). At the core of these different conceptions of covert interpersonally related structure and processes is the view that earlier experiences in family and peer relationships (Benjamin, 2003), in dynamic interaction with biological temperament (Livesley, 2001), have ingrained into the patient's biocognitive unconscious (see Hooker, 2008) internal representations of self and others and their interactions. These representational structures, elaborated over the life span by one's interpersonal experiences and metacognitive processes (e.g., self-reflection), act as templates that reflexively guide and organize one's network of perceptions, thoughts, feelings, and motivations in significant relationships (Anchin, 2002)—processes that in real time function as a system and therefore in thoroughly interrelated fashion (Anchin, 2003, 2008c; Anchin & Magnavita, 2006; Magnavita, 2005). Thus, although contemporary interpersonal theory suggests that the most important personality and psychopathological phenomena are relational in nature, these phenomena and their operative dynamics are not limited to contemporaneous, observable interpersonal behavior.

The third assumption is that *agency* and *communion*, core domains of human existence, provide an integrative metastructure for conceptualizing interpersonal situations and their internal representations (e.g., Wiggins, 2003). *Agency* refers to the condition of being a differentiated individual, and it is manifested in strivings for power and mastery that can protect and enhance one's differentiation. *Communion* refers to the condition of being part of a larger social entity, and it is manifested in strivings for intimacy, union, and solidarity with the larger entity. These metaconcepts form a superordinate structure, referred to as the *interpersonal circle* (IPC; Leary, 1957) or *interpersonal circumplex* (Wiggins, 1996), which can be used to derive descriptive and explanatory concepts of personality, mental health, and psychopathology at different levels of specificity (see Figure 5.1). At the broadest and most interdisciplinary level, agency and communion encompass the fundamental interpersonal motives, strivings, and values of human relations (Horowitz, 2004). Thus, when seeking to understand essential motivations in interpersonal situations, one may consider both the agentic and communal nature of the individual's personal strivings or current concerns (e.g., to be in control, to be close to others) and the specific behaviors enacted to achieve those goals. At a sharper level of resolution the IPC provides conceptual coordinates for describing and measuring interpersonal traits and behaviors (Locke, 2006). Agentic and communal traits imply enduring patterns of perceiving, thinking, feeling, and behaving that describe an individual's relational tendencies aggre-

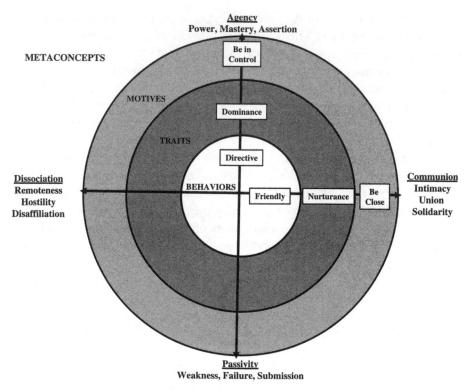

Figure 5.1. Agency and communion.

gated across interpersonal situations. At the greatest level of specificity, the IPC can classify the nature and intensity of distinct interpersonal acts. IPC categories are also valuable in capturing specific ways that an individual may treat and react to him- or herself, self-schema processes of vital import in interpersonal psychotherapy. Benjamin's (1996) *structural analysis of social behavior model*, an interpersonal circumplex constructed around the horizontal axis of *affiliation* (similar to the IPC communion dimension) and the vertical axis of *interdependence* (overlapping with the IPC agency dimension), maps within circumplicial space not only reciprocal interpersonal behavior by the self in reaction to specified interpersonal behavior by others but also differential ways that an individual will interact with him- or herself (Westen & Heim, 2003) through *introjection*, that is, internalizing and turning inward on the self forms of behavior directed at the self by others.

The fourth and final assumption asserts that interpersonal behaviors create *reciprocal influences* on interactants and that these patterns of reciprocity can be defined in reference to the IPC. The most fundamental interpersonal pattern is referred to as *interpersonal complementarity* (Carson, 1969; Kiesler, 1983), and it can be defined by reciprocity on the vertical dimension (i.e., dominance pulls for submission; submission pulls for dominance) and correspondence for the horizontal dimension (friendliness pulls for friendliness; disaffiliation pulls for disaffiliation). Although complementarity is neither the only reciprocal interpersonal pattern that can be described by the IPC nor proposed as a universal law of interaction, empirical studies consistently find support for its probabilistic predictions (e.g., Locke & Sadler, 2007). However, complementarity should not be conceived of as simply a behavioral stimulus—response chain of events. Rather, mediating internal psychological processes (e.g., each interactant's self–other schemas, the motives and needs embedded in these schemas, and their effects on subjective experience) influence the likelihood of complementary patterns, and thus complementarity is most helpful if it is considered a common baseline for the field-regulatory pulls and invitations of interpersonal behavior associated with healthy socialization. Used this way, an individual's chronic deviations from complementary reciprocal patterns when interacting with others may be indicative of PD because it suggests impairments in three areas: (a) recognizing the consensual understanding of interpersonal situations (e.g., psychotherapy), (b) adaptively communicating one's own interpersonal needs and motives, and (c) comprehending the needs of others and the intent of their interpersonal behavior. In such cases, the individual pulls consistently and rigidly for responses that complement his or her own interpersonal behavior but has significant difficulty reciprocating with responses that are complementary to others' behavior. This reduces the likelihood that the agentic and communal motives of both persons will be satisfied in the interpersonal situation, creating disturbed interpersonal relations (Sullivan, 1953).

Mechanisms of Change

The primary mechanism of change in interpersonal psychotherapy with PD clients is new social learning through examination of the proximal reciprocal influences unfolding within the therapeutic relationship as well as by linking identified interpersonal patterns with current symptoms and functional impairments, including the nature of the client's relationships with extratherapy others and exploring the origins and functions of maladaptive interpersonal patterns in the client's developmental history. This promotes new interpersonal awareness and learning, resulting in improved relational capacity and symptom reduction. These social learning processes promote both intrapersonal and interpersonal change, with changes in each domain affecting the other in reciprocal, or bidirectional, fashion. In the intrapersonal domain, new social learning aims to modify motivational, cognitive, and affective content and processes relating the self and others. In the interpersonal domain, new social learning aims to modify the client's maladaptive patterns of interaction with others, which concomitantly modifies how others recip-rocally experience and interact with the client. Examining the reciprocal effects of changes in interpersonal behavior on self, others, and symptoms consolidates therapeutic gains by fostering and reinforcing constructive, adaptive changes in the person's relational functioning and its self-schema underpinnings. In summary, interpersonal psychotherapy promotes personality change by modi-fying the "relatively enduring pattern of recurrent interpersonal situations which characterize a human life" (Sullivan, 1953, pp. 110–111).

Domains of Operation Within the Total Ecological System

Interpersonal psychotherapy with PD clients primarily operates within the intrapsychic/biological and interpersonal/dyadic domains of functioning. The former emphasizes motivational, cognitive, and affective processes underlying relational functioning. These include schemata, expectancies, wishes, and fears that strongly influence—and, in the case of PD clients, distort—perception, subjective experience, and meaning-making regarding the self, others, and relationships. The latter emphasizes overt transactional processes between the self and others, their reciprocal influences, and the covert processes that mediate interpersonal transaction (Anchin, 1982a, 1987, 2002). Interpersonal psychotherapy links the intrapsychic/biological and interpersonal/dyadic domains by conceptualizing interpersonal situations as ongoing adaptive or maladaptive transaction cycles that include the overt behaviors and covert interpretations and experiences of both self and other (Benjamin, 2005). Note that although interpersonal psychotherapy is most often conducted in one-to-one sessions (Benjamin, 2003), the approach can be logically extended to the relational/triadic and sociocultural/familial domains constituting multiple dyads and relationships and has applications for group psychotherapy (Benjamin, 2000) and family therapy (Benjamin & Cushing, 2004).

Process of Therapy

Therapists generally attempt to work in the client's best interest and promote a positive therapeutic alliance. Using the IPC as a lens, therapists typically adopt a warm and moderately dominant interpersonal position com-mensurate with offering help and structuring treatment based on their expert-ise. Clients who are free of personality pathology tend to enter therapy seeking relief from their symptoms and may be highly distressed. Despite their distress, such clients typically begin treatment with the expectation that the therapist is a benign expert who is working in their best interest, and they are hopeful of receiving effective help. In other words, they grasp the normative understanding of the therapeutic relationship (i.e., interpersonal situation), accurately decode the interpersonal behavior of the therapist, and can engage in the role relationships prescribed by the particular treatment approach. Simply put, these clients can adopt a complementary interpersonal position of friendly submissiveness (e.g., trusting) in relation to the therapist's friendly dominance (i.e., understanding, leading). Such *positive complementarity* promotes formation of the therapeutic alliance rather quickly (e.g., Schauenburg, Kuda, Sammet, & Strack, 2000; Tasca & McMullen, 1992).

However, the existence of positive complementarity is clearly not always the case. Despite psychotherapists' attempts to take a similar stance with PD clients, the beginning of therapy is often quite rocky because such clients tend to view their therapists with suspicion, fear, contempt, and so on. Their ability to view and experience therapist behavior and psychotherapy in normative ways is impaired, as are their own patterns of interpersonal behavior and communication. Treatment often begins with the therapist and client experiencing either mutually disaffiliative *negative complementarity* (e.g., Strupp, 1998) or noncomplementary reciprocal patterns that require further negotiation of the therapeutic relationship and an extended period of alliance formation. In fact, a central aspect of psychotherapy for PD clients involves working through their relational impediments to both alliance formation and making use of therapy. Treatment generally proceeds through a sequence of pathological interpersonal enactments; establishing collaboration; recognizing maladaptive interpersonal patterns and their reciprocal impacts on the self, others, and symptoms; understanding the origins and functions of these maladaptive patters; learning new adaptive patterns within the context of the therapeutic relationship; and generalizing new social learning beyond the psychotherapy context (Anchin & Kiesler, 1982; Pincus & Cain, 2008).

RELATIONAL CONSIDERATIONS

The process and outcome of interpersonal psychotherapy with PDs is strongly influenced by an exceedingly complex network of interacting variables—alliance factors, patient and therapist characteristics, and racial and cultural factors—intrinsic to the relational nature of treatment. It is essential when working with PD clients that the growing evidence bases pertaining to these relationship factors inform the therapist's clinical formulations, hypotheses, and practices.

Alliance Factors Related to Process and Outcome

Among the most robust results in the therapy research literature is the positive relationship between the therapeutic alliance and treatment outcome

(Castonguay & Beutler, 2006). However, given that disturbed interpersonal relating is a hallmark of PDs (Critchfield & Benjamin, 2006), "therapists must be experts in fostering relationships with individuals who have difficulty doing this" (Clarkin & Levy, 2004, p. 211). Yet, therapists can develop expertise in building alliances with PD clients only through ongoing and at times painful experience. Interpersonal theory and research (Kiesler, 1982, 1996) emphasize that negative impact messages are a key source of this challenge, and hence effectively managing these impacts is an important focus of developing one's clinical expertise.

Impact messages are the therapist's internal engagements and reactions evoked by the client's interpersonal behavior and that parallel in thematic content those experienced by others. These impacts are experienced as direct feelings (e.g., complimented, angry), action tendencies (e.g., "I'd like to tell her to start taking responsibility for her own actions"); perceived evoking messages/cognitive attributions (e.g., "I feel like she's trying to bait me"), and fantasies (e.g., picturing oneself and the client sparring in a boxing ring; Anchin, 2002; Kiesler, 1988). These covert engagements pull for complementary responses, which, when enacted, satisfy the client's skewed communal and agentic motives, confirm supervenient cognitive–affective self–other schemas, and reinforce the client's interpersonal style. The difficulty and protractedness of building a solid alliance with a PD client is bound up with the latter "interact[ing] with the therapist in the same dysfunctional way that characterizes his or her interactions with significant others (i.e., transference)" (Levenson, 2004, p. 257) and the therapist's reciprocal negative impact messages. Thus, a critical alliance-building skill with PD clients is not one of avoiding the experience of negatively engagement but instead handling these aversive impacts constructively. Acting out negative feelings toward the client has been shown to be associated with a weaker therapeutic alliance, whereas greater ability to manage negative feelings is predictive of a stronger alliance (Gelso & Hayes, 2002). Moreover, in the Vanderbilt I and II studies of time-limited dynamic psychotherapy (Strupp & Binder, 1984), a brief interpersonal approach to treating chronic and pervasive interpersonal dysfunction, Binder and Strupp (1991) found that "experienced therapists often engage in countertherapeutic [e.g., negative and hostile] interpersonal processes with difficult patients" (p. 191), which was integral to their conclusion that "the absence of poor process does not ensure good outcomes, but the presence of certain types of poor process is almost always linked to bad outcomes" (p. 191). It is thus essential that from the outset therapists be attuned to their inner reactions, label their emotional themes, and manage these reactions in ways that foster the therapeutic alliance.

Once established, ongoing monitoring and maintenance of the alliance is a must. Particularly vital is detecting *alliance ruptures* (Safran, Muran,

Samstag, & Stevens, 2002) and engaging the client in the collaborative repair of these ruptures. This potent intervention, which has been empirically associated with positive outcome (Safran et al., 2002), carries particular therapeutic import with PDs, given that a client's intrasession maladaptive enactments are among the very processes that can spawn breakdowns (i.e., ruptures) in the alliance.

Patient Characteristics Related to Process and Outcome

Although the quality of the therapeutic alliance is a critical contributor to psychotherapy outcome, Norcross and Lambert (2005) concluded that "without question, the largest determinant of . . . outcome [accounting for 25% to 30% of the variance] is the patient" (p. 209). The array of client variables influencing outcome is indeed enormous (Clarkin & Levy, 2004), but reviews of the empirical literature point to nondiagnostic client characteristics that may exert particular influence on alliance formation, therapy process, and outcome with PD clients (Benjamin & Karpiak, 2002, Critchfield & Benjamin, 2006, Fernandez-Alvarez, Clarkin, Salgueiro, & Critchfield, 2006). Examples include the client's willingness and ability to engage with treatment; expectations (e.g., about success and the therapist's role) and preferences (e.g., regarding what the client desires from treatment); severity, chronicity, and comorbidity of functional impairment; level of resistance/reactance; quality of object relations (i.e., quality of past and present relationships with significant others and the internalization of these relationships), including the extent to which the client has a history of positive attachments; and degree of trauma resolution. An interpersonal perspective emphasizes that client characteristics influence therapy process and outcome through interactions with therapist factors (Clarkin & Levy, 2004).

Therapist Characteristics Related to Process and Outcome

The quality of therapist responsiveness to client variables is integral to the latters' impact on therapy process and outcome. *Responsiveness* refers to "behavior being affected by emerging context" and in "psychotherapeutic interaction . . . responsive[ness occurs] on time scales that range from months to milliseconds" (Stiles & Wolfe, 2006, p. 158). Especially vital for the therapist is *appropriate responsiveness*, that is, taking into account "the client's characteristics, needs, resources, and ongoing behavior, as well as aspects of the setting and context" (Newman, Stiles, Janeck, & Woody, 2006, p. 187) and in response "doing what is required to produce some positive, beneficial, or desired effect, as judged from the perspective of the treatment approach and the participants' purposes in the encounter" (Stiles & Wolfe, 2006, p. 158).

The therapist's appropriate responsiveness may be enhanced by the following characteristics inferred to be predictive of therapy outcome with PDs:

> (1) open-minded, flexible, and creative in approach (necessitated by the complexity of PD treatments and psychopathology); (2) comfortable with long-term, emotionally intense relationships; (3) tolerance of own negative feelings regarding the patient and the treatment process; (4) patience; and (5) training and experience with a specific Axis II disorder. (Fernandez-Alvarez et al., 2006, p. 215)

Manifesting these attributes may also help create an interpersonal climate that fosters adaptive client responsiveness to several "therapist relational stance principles" linked to positive outcome with PDs (Critchfield & Benjamin, 2006, p. 261): relatively high activity level (but not necessarily directive), structuring treatment and setting limits on unacceptable behavior, expressing empathy, showing positive regard for the client, and congruence in expression of feelings (including strategic self-disclosure) and transmission of knowledge. Sensitively tailoring a given relational stance in ways responsive to a client's distinct PD and the focus of the work is essential.

Racial and Cultural Factors and Considerations

The investigation of psychotherapy with racially, ethnically, and culturally diverse clients (e.g., African Americans, American Indians, Asian Americans, and Latino/a Americans; Zane, Hall, Sue, Young, & Nunez, 2004) remains among the most underaddressed areas within therapy research (Sue & Zane, 2005). However, Zane et al. (2004) concluded from their review that "We now know that ethnic and cultural group variations are related to certain processes and outcomes in psychotherapy" (p. 796). Thus, it is clinically advisable that therapists treating PD clients who are members of an ethnic minority group proactively cultivate *cultural competence*, encompassing "the cultural knowledge and skills of a particular culture to deliver effective interventions to members of that culture" (Sue, 1998, p. 441). However, to our knowledge no empirical studies have yet examined cultural factors in interpersonal treatment of PD clients who are members of ethnic minority groups.

TECHNIQUE AND METHODS OF TREATMENT

The most enduring and overarching theme of interpersonal technique and methods with PD clients is the therapist's modus operandi as a participant observer (Anchin, 1982b; Kiesler, 1996; Pincus & Cain, 2008; Sullivan, 1954). Underpinning this stance is the recognition that the therapist, no less than the patient, is an external, real person (Frank, 2002). Thus, despite certain unique features, the client–therapist relationship is itself a very real one indeed (Anchin, 2002). The client will therefore inevitably enact with the therapist the same maladaptive patterns of interaction that characterize his or her troubled relationships with others. Bradley, Heim, and Westen (2005) found that, independent of therapists' theoretical orientation, clients diagnosed with different PDs enacted in relation to therapists predictable, differential interpersonal patterns, providing valuable information about clients' personality pathology, attachment patterns, and interpersonal functioning. Interpersonal theory conceptualizes these maladaptive patterns as self-perpetuating, and thus the client unwittingly brings about and maintains the problems in living associated with his or her distress and symptomatology. This self-perpetuating process, which has been labeled a *maladaptive transaction cycle* (Kiesler, 1996), *vicious circle* (Millon & Davis, 1996), *self-confirmation process* (Andrews, 1991), *self-fulfilling prophecy* (Carson, 1982), and *cyclical maladaptive pattern* (Strupp & Binder, 1984), proceeds through "an unbroken causal loop" (Carson, 1982, p. 66) between the client's pathologic schemas about the self and others, rigid agentic and communal motives, inflexible and extreme interpersonal behavior, and others' pathology-maintaining complementary responses. Darley and Fazio (1980), Jussim (1986), and Rosenthal and Rubin (1978) have reported empirical evidence verifying the operation of interpersonal self-perpetuating cycles, and the powerful role of self-verification processes in interpersonal situations in maintaining psychological coherence and minimizing anxiety was supported by Swann, Rentfrow, and Guinn's (2003) research.

Against this backdrop, the interpersonal psychotherapist's prime directive when treating clients with PDs is "interrupting and altering this self-perpetuating cycle" (Carson, 1982, p. 66). In implementing this principle the therapist oscillates between fully participating in and experiencing the evolving intrasession relationship and observing these processes and developing hypotheses about their meanings and implications for understanding the client's chronic interpersonal difficulties. The therapist uses these data and hypotheses to facilitate clinical judgments regarding ways of relationally and interventionally participating in the ongoing interaction to optimize its mutative effects on disturbed self–other processes. These decisions are partially guided by the principle of complementarity and its variants, applied initially to alliance building but also informing the therapist's participatory processes throughout treatment.

Forging the Therapeutic Alliance

Forging a therapeutic alliance with a given PD client is facilitated by keeping front and center the essentiality of creating an interpersonal climate of safety and security—which is vital for cultivating the client's trust, attachment, and collaboration. The client must not feel "stripped" (Cashdan, 1982, p. 221) of his or her familiar way of navigating the social world, which would only heighten feelings of vulnerability and anxiety, thereby impeding development of a trusting bond. However, the negative impact messages therapists commonly experience early in the treatment of PDs can be obstacles to forming a positive alliance. These impacts fall in the cold, hostile side of the IPC (Smith, Barrett, Benjamin, & Barber, 2006; Wagner, Riley, Schmidt, McCormick, & Butler, 1999), for example, feeling frustrated, irritated, angry, critical, rejecting, defeated, controlled, or shut out. Yet "The therapist cannot *not* be hooked or sucked in by the client, because the client is more adept, more expert in his distinctive, rigid, and extreme game of interpersonal encounter" (Kiesler, 1982, p. 281). The therapist's challenge is managing these negative reactions in ways that promote development of a working alliance, as opposed to acting them out and risking embroilment in countertherapeutically disaffiliative (e.g., hostile) transactional cycles.

Constructive handling of negative impact messages is aided by a flexible, idiographic alliance-building strategy that strikes an effective therapeutic balance between Livesley's (2001) generic alliance-building modes of responding (e.g., careful listening, empathy, acceptance, a nonjudgmental attitude), all anchored within the friendly side of the IPC (cf. Ackerman & Hilsenroth, 2003; Benjamin, 2003), and Tracey and Ray's (1984) caveat that it is "important for the counselor to follow (*to some extent* [emphasis added]) the client's definition of the relationship" (p. 14). This approach, in recognizing "the possible need for different relational strategies to achieve positive alliances with different Axis II patients" (Critchfield & Benjamin, 2006, p. 269), draws on the principle of complementarity for implementation. Thus, to the extent that in early sessions negative impact messages are salient therapist reactions, selective overt responding with hostile-side complementarity allows a client with prominent hostile-side stylistics (whether hostile–dominant or hostile–submissive) to occupy his or her familiar way of being, thereby reducing threat and feelings of vulnerability and enhancing safety and security.

However, given empirical findings that therapist hostility has toxic effects on outcome (Hatcher & Barends, 2006), negative complementarity in the service of alliance building must be enacted with particular sensitivity. We recommend that when the therapist judges that responding to the client's hostile-side behaviors with negative complementarity may facilitate establishing an alliance, this be limited to varying degrees of *cordial distance*. Cordiality maintains the overarchingly benign therapeutic climate essential to cultivating the alliance while incorporating complementary communication that conveys respect for and acceptance of the client's early need to self-protectively distance the other. This therapist stance ensures that the client is not confronted with uncomfortable, threatening levels of therapist closeness and friendliness. As the client's trust grows and, with it, more appropriate responsiveness to the therapist, the alliance can be nurtured through therapist matching with increased friendly-side behavior, cultivating and strengthening the safe, secure relational base necessary for collaboratively working on emotionally sensitive domains of the client's interpersonal pathology.

Disengagement and Noncomplementary Responding

Getting hooked by the client's interpersonal pathology in the course of attempting to forge an alliance provides opportunities to experience the negative impacts others experience and thus learn how the client entangles others into becoming accomplices (Wachtel, 1982) in his or her self-perpetuating cycles. Thus, "it is not an error for the therapist to become engaged . . . However, [it] is an error to stay engaged" (D. Young & Beier, 1982, p. 268); ongoing complementary enmeshment enables the client's dysfunctionality and steadily hinders the capacity to therapeutically intervene. Therefore, it is vital that the therapist disengage, or "unhook," from these complementary reactions (Kiesler, 1996), freeing him- or herself to enact mutative, noncomplementary responses that replace the complementarity the patient reflexively expects, which is pivotal to providing "*new experiences* and *new understandings*" (Levenson, 2004, p. 258).

Foundational to disengagement is becoming aware of and labeling the recurring internal engagements and reactions induced by the client, advanced by asking oneself "phenomenological questions" (D. Young & Beier, 1982, p. 267) that address the four types of impact messages (i.e., direct feelings, action tendencies, perceived evoking messages/cognitive attributions, and fantasies; see Exhibit 5.1).

Given the emotional force of most PD clients, the cognitive–linguistic symbolization necessary for internally addressing these questions valuably

EXHIBIT 5.1
Phenomenological Questions That Address
the Four Classes of Impact Messages

1. Direct feelings: "What feelings does the client make me experience?"
2. Action tendencies: "What do I want to do/say or not do/not say to this client?
3. Perceived evoking messages/cognitive attributions: "What is the client trying to do or not do to me?", "What is the client trying to get me to do or not do?", "What is the client saying to him- or herself and/or feeling about me?
4. Fantasies: "What fantasies, images, or metaphors come to mind that capture my reaction to this client?

Note. Adapted from *Contemporary Interpersonal Theory and Research: Personality, Psychopathology, and Psychotherapy* (pp. 116–118), by D. J. Kiesler, 1996, New York, NY: Wiley. Copyright 1996 by Wiley. Adapted with permission.

"provides an organized experience of a coherent self as an 'agent' experiencing . . . nameable feeling[s], rather than being a passive victim of the feeling[s]" (Greenberg & Paivio, 1997, p. 101). The resultant loosening from the grip of these inner reactions enables sharpened observations of dyadic processes, especially how the client is verbally and nonverbally evoking these impacts and the extent to which the therapist is overtly responding in complementary ways. This configuration of experiential and observational data, in conjunction with descriptions of extrasession relationships, accelerates the therapist's initial conceptualization of the client's central relational difficulties, interpersonally anchoring the PD technique principle advising "early formulation and identification of patterns of cognition, affect, and behavior linked to problem maintenance" (Critchfield & Benjamin, 2006, p. 263).

Another key therapist-disengagement step is discontinuing enactment of overt complementary responses, thereby effectively managing countertransference, an element of the relationship empirically associated with positive outcomes (Steering Committee, 2002). The criticality of knowing one's felt-engagements is underscored by evidence that managing countertransference is facilitated by both awareness of and having a theoretical framework for understanding feelings toward the client (Gelso & Hayes, 2002).

Shifting to noncomplementary responding provides the client with a new experience by terminating reinforcement of his or her rigid evoking style, disconfirming interpersonal expectancies, and opening space for more adaptive communication and interaction. Bernier and Dozier (2002) documented a positive association between therapist–client noncomplementarity and positive outcomes but noted that the temporal context of noncomplementarity is a key: Most successful cases are characterized by predominantly complementary therapist–client exchanges early in treatment; more frequent noncomplementarity during treatment's middle, "working" stage; and reversion to mostly complementary interactions in the last stage. Adding nuance, "harmonious and gentle switches between complementary and noncomplementary exchanges over the course of treatment may maximize therapeutic gains, presumably by providing . . . a safe and confirming environment along with appropriate challenges likely to induce change and growth" (Bernier & Dozier, 2002, p. 36).

Forms of therapist noncomplementarity optimally suited to different PDs have yet to be empirically validated. However, empathically understanding that aversive interactional behavior is an expression of emotional pain facilitates disengagement from negative complementarity and clinical judgments about therapeutic noncomplementary responses in light of here-and-now contextual factors (e.g., quality of the alliance, current content). These include asocial responses (e.g., silence, delay responses, reflection of content and feeling; D. Young & Beier, 1982), appropriate techniques that interrupt personality pathology by therapeutically pressing the client to attend to aspects of internal experience and to communicate in ways that salubriously diverge from subjective experience and communication modes (Kiesler, 1996), and therapist enactment of specific noncomplementary styles of interaction (e.g., antithesis [Benjamin, 1996], acomplementarity, and anticomplementarity [Kiesler, 1996]) intended to elicit client enactment of specific healthier modes of interpersonal behavior.

Therapeutic Metacommunication

A central form of therapist disengagement and intervention in the interpersonal treatment of PDs is "*therapeutic metacommunication* or *metacommunicative feedback*[,which] refers to any instance in which the therapist provides to the patient verbal feedback that targets the central, recurrent, and thematic relationship issues occurring between them in their therapy sessions" (Kiesler, 1996, p. 284). This often entails expression and discussion of negatively toned feelings stemming from the client's maladaptive transaction cycle but also includes sharing and processing positive feelings between client and therapist (Hill et al., 2008; Kaspar, Hill, & Kivlighan, 2008). Hill (2004) referred to this process of conjointly analyzing the therapeutic relationship as a vehicle for the client's social learning as *immediacy* and it also is highly akin to relational psychoanalytic transference–countertransference analysis (Anchin, 2002).

Research has demonstrated that therapist–client metacommunicative processes help clients express immediate feelings toward the therapist (Hill et al., 2008); improve the therapeutic alliance (Foreman & Marmar, 1985); provide a corrective relational experience (Kaspar et al., 2008); and resolve alliance ruptures, misunderstanding in the therapy dyad, and client anger toward the therapist (see Hill et al., 2008). However, depending on the client, metacommunication can also engender some negative in-session effects (e.g., the client feeling somewhat awkward, pressured, and uneasy) that may be associated with mixed treatment outcomes (Kaspar et al., 2008). Moreover, high levels of interpretation addressing the therapy relationship lead to poor outcome, especially with clients with low-quality object relations (Crits-Christoph & Gibbons, 2002). Clinical judgment is thus essential with regard to deploying interventions that focus directly on the therapy relationship: "Immediacy can be a powerful and helpful intervention if used at the right time with the right client for therapeutic reasons in a way that fits the client's needs" (Hill et al., 2008, p. 314).

Maladaptive Overt Processes in Relation to the Therapist

As delineated by Kiesler (1996), a chief metacommunicative procedure for bringing to light the client's maladaptive transaction cycle is the therapist's skillful disclosure of the recurrent negative impacts he or she experiences when interacting with the client and, to the extent that these overtly emerge, associated complementary behaviors the therapist finds him- or herself enacting. It is crucial that the therapist also pinpoint the client's verbal and nonverbal behavior that evoked those reactions, thereby enabling the client to learn what he or she overtly says and does to elicit these self-defeating consequences. This feedback's assimilability can also be enhanced by underscoring both positive and negative dimensions of the client's maladaptive relational style. A prototypic technique for therapist impact disclosure is illustrated in the following:

> [*Therapist:*] I realize it's important to you to be cautious and rational in what you do or say to others, and I agree that it's important in many situations (*recognizing the patient's positive intent*). Yet in our sessions, you seem to send messages you don't intend as a result of this caution (*a negative consequence of this style*). For example, you often show long, silent pauses with me after I've said something to you, and frequently a quick smile flashes on and off (*overt pinpointing*). Several times when you did that I felt you were really disagreeing with what I was saying, or were thinking that my comment was a little stupid (*impact disclosure*). But I found out later that wasn't the case, that actually you were feeling a little stupid about yourself. (Kiesler, 1996, p. 293; italicized commentary added)

Empirical evidence demonstrates that effective feedback also requires *follow-through*, that is, dialogical exploration and processing of the client's reactions (Clairborn, Goodyear, & Horner, 2002). This also often serves a crucial function as a context that spawns more extensive metacommunicative discussion about the therapy relationship, including, as warranted, the therapist openly examining—and, if accurate, owning—his or her contributions to a client's enactment (Anchin, 2002). This emotionally demanding collaborative process is intended to progressively heighten awareness of and insight into the client's problematic transaction cycle, salutary changes in the therapy relationship, and healthy modifications in disordered self–other schema processes. Intervening with therapist impact disclosure also necessitates a caveat: Before metacommunicating with clients about their impact, therapists "must accurately determine that their reactions are due to the client's evoking style and not to their own issues" (Marcus & Buffington-Vollum, 2005, p. 265), which would place the metacommunicative work on inaccurate and hence countertherapeutic footing. Supervision and consultation—another technique principle associated with positive treatment outcome of PD clients (Critchfield & Benjamin, 2006)—can be an invaluable arena for attaining insight into sources of one's internal reactions.

Maladaptive Covert Processes in Relation to the Therapist

The interior of an intrasession enactment is a charged configuration of thoughts, feelings, and motivations in relation to the therapist. Thus, as Safran and Segal (1990) noted, enactments also serve as *interpersonal markers* (p. 82) that problematic self–other schema(s) have been activated, heightening their accessibility. Examining schemas in the context of immediate affective experience is also more powerful than discussing them abstractly (J. E. Young, 1999). This internal focus adheres to the principle advising *holistic understanding* of PDs (see Anchin & Magnavita, 2006), that is, use of strategies and methods that "facilitate knowledge and awareness of links between the problem and environment, cognition, affect, and behavior" (Critchfield & Benjamin, 2006, p. 264).

Cognitive, constructivist, humanistic–experiential, and solution-based therapies (e.g., Beck, Freeman, & Associates, 2004; Bertolino, Kiener, & Patterson, 2009; Greenberg, Watson, & Lietaer, 1998; Rosen & Kuehlwein, 1996; Safran & Segal, 1990; J. E. Young, Klesko, & Weishaar, 2003) provide a treasure trove of integrative treatment strategies and interventions for targeting an intrasession enactment's self–other schema underpinnings (Anchin, 2002). This work implements not only the PD technique principle that the therapist "challenge specific 'dysfunctional thoughts' and 'negative core beliefs'" (Critchfield & Benjamin, 2006, p. 262) but also integrates, as warranted, work on related pathologic affects and motivations. This said, it is important to be mindful of four levels of schema change that exist on a continuum: (a) *reconstruction* (the most ambitious level, entailing replacement of a maladaptive schema with a thoroughly new and healthier schema), (b) *modification* (changes in some, but not all, aspects of a schema), (c) *reinterpretation* (understanding and reframing a schema by giving it more constructive expression and/or identifying contexts in which it may serve the client well), and (d) camouflage (teaching social skills enabling the client to "cover over" a maladaptive schema in particular situations; Cottraux & Blackburn, 2001; Freeman, Pretzer, Fleming, & Simon, 2004). The therapist needs to be realistic about the degree of schema change that may be achievable, and we caution against premature conclusions.

In this illustrative prototype, the therapist blends metacommunication with cognitive, constructivist, solution-focused, and experiential technique to identify and gain insight into internal facets of the client's charged reaction to seeing him glance at his desk clock. Therapist questions and statements are preceded by brief explanations of the underlying therapeutic strategy.

> Therapist (T): (*Pinpointing overt, observable behavior, focusing inward, and pinpointing affect*) Bob, you just stopped talking about the argument you and your wife had this morning and

stared at me; then you looked away, shook your head, and gave this deep sigh. What are you feeling?

Client (C): To be honest, I'm pissed off!

T: (*Encouraging client to elaborate*) About?

C: You; what you just did. I'm telling you about something that was very upsetting and you're looking at your clock.

T: (*Not getting hooked by client's anger; instead validating his observation*) You're right; I did. (*Preparing the way for explaining link between meaning given to other's behavior and consequent feeling*) How are you interpreting that?

C: What interpretation?! It's obvious that you can't wait for me to leave.

T: (*Probing for automatic thoughts*) Is that what went through your head when you just saw me look at the clock?

C: Yeah, like, "He's not really interested; he doesn't really give a shit about me."

T: (*Empathy-based pinpointing of additional affects*) It sounds like you feel like I'm not taking you seriously—that you felt dismissed, rejected.

C: Absolutely! Hopefully, you can see why I'd feel that way!

T: (*Conveying acceptance of client's subjective affective state while continuing to set the ground for explaining relationship between interpretations and feelings*) Yes; I can—interpreting what I did as meaning that I don't care about you, it makes sense that you'd feel dismissed, rejected, angry. I understand. (*Beginning to engage client in the metacommunicative process of stepping back and collaboratively reflecting on the interaction in order to turn this intrasession incident to therapeutic advantage*) But can we step back and look at this? Because maybe we can both learn something from what just happened.

C: It just really hit me wrong. But, yeah, go ahead, I'm listening.

T: (*Brief psychoeducation regarding the link between thoughts and feelings*) Even when we're not aware of it, we interpret and give meaning to things people say and do to us; there's "what happened" and then the meaning we give to it, and those interpretations have a strong effect on our emotional reaction; different interpretations of the same situation can create very different feelings. (*A concrete illustration could be given here*)

C: I hear ya.

T: (*Fostering collaboration, encouraging the search for alternative interpretations*) So—go with me on this—could there be other ways to interpret my looking at my clock while you were talking?

C: I suppose; maybe you're hungry and you can't wait for the session to end so you can get something to eat.

T: (*Fostering experiential understanding of the cognitive–affective link*) And if it was that, how do you think that would make you feel?

C: Maybe a little less pissed, but you'd still be thinking about how hungry you are, like it's more important than me.

T: (*Encouraging the search for additional alternative interpretations*) OK; but are there other possible reasons why I looked at the clock, other possible interpretations?

C: Hmm . . . I suppose; maybe you just wanted to see what time it was so that you knew how much time we had left in the session to deal with what I was talking about.

T: (*Confirming the client's interpretation*) Exactly; that's exactly why I looked at my clock. (*Explaining the intent behind his actions*) I know that this was a very upsetting situation between you and your wife, and I wanted to be sure we'd have time to home in on what was happening there.

C: I suppose [*nods head*]; that makes sense.

T: (*Using immediacy to further enhance interpersonal–experiential change*) Understanding it that way, do you experience at this moment a change in how you feel?

C: I guess not really pissed off. I guess I appreciate that you understand this was an extremely upsetting situation [this morning] and that you wanted to make sure we had time to figure it out.

T: (*Reciprocating the expression of appreciation*) Good; I appreciate that you're willing to rethink this. (*Refuting client's misconstrual of therapist's behavior with honest self-disclosure of nurturing feelings*) And can you see, too, that in wanting

C: to make sure we had enough time, that I do care, that I'm genuinely interested in what's happening in your life—that I care about you, that you do matter?

C: Yes, I can see where you're also kind of saying that, too.

T: (*Further honest therapist self-disclosure to underscore his genuine interest*) Good—because the last thing I would want you to feel is dismissed or rejected by me.

C: [*Listening, nodding head*]

T: (*Identifying cognitive distortions—selective abstraction, magnification, and jumping to conclusions*) So if we go back to what just happened, it's like you tuned in on that one piece of behavior on my part, magnified it, and then jumped to a conclusion—and a negative one, at that! And given that conclusion, you got really angry with me.

C: Yeah, I guess it's true, I definitely do that . . . Somebody says or does something and I lose it; it's like a switch goes off.

T: (*Applying this analogy to the immediate context to advance client's social–cognitive learning*) Bob, if we use what just happened here between us, what do you think flipped that switch?

C: I guess at some level I think that people don't really care about me, that I'm insignificant, I don't matter . . . it's like this feeling is in the background; it nags at me!

T: (*Drawing from this intrasession process, planting a seed intended to facilitate client's generalizing this healthy revision in his core belief about others to extrasession interpersonal situations*) So it sounds like there's these two central beliefs—maybe core beliefs—that you have. One is that "I'm insignificant" and the other sounds like you believe "People don't care about me." (*With an eye on maintaining the alliance, promotes collaborative exploration*) Does that feel like it fits?

C: Yeah, definitely . . . I've always felt . . . "haunted" is the best word . . . by this terrifying feeling, deep down, that I'm completely insignificant, that I really mean nothing . . . nothing!—and that that's also what I mean to people who know me: nothing; that deep down they don't care about me.

T: (*Client is speaking the language of self and relational disorder; therapist homes in on its core-belief-about-others component,*

holding up his hands as if to say "Let's just wait a moment")
Let's just take that belief that "To people who know me,
I mean nothing, and they don't really care about me."
(*Exploring whether this belief is being tacitly applied to therapist*) Since I fit in that category—people who know you—
do you think at some level you maintain the belief that to
me you meaning nothing and that I don't care about you?

C: [*Thinks for a moment*] I must think that—after what just
happened . . .

T: (*Extending the analogy and having client step back*) And so,
in terms of what flips the switch, maybe this belief that
to people who know you, you mean nothing and that
they don't really care about you, is like the circuitry
attached to the switch. (*Pulling this together as a hypothesis
linking his negative core belief about others, distorted social–
cognitive interpretations, emotional reactions, and overt behavior*) When someone says or does something, like when I
looked at my clock, that in the slightest way could be
interpreted as meaning "They don't care about me,"
that's the meaning you automatically give it; that they—
and in this case I—don't really care about you. That sets
off those feelings of being dismissed, of being insignificant; those feelings hurt and—like when someone hits
their finger with a hammer—that pain sparks anger, and
it can suddenly show itself—like the way you reacted
when you saw me look at my clock.

C: Hmm. [*Sits back, reflects*] That feels pretty right—yeah, I
think that's what's going on.

T: (*Using constructivist technique within the immediate relational situation*) So if we could redo what happened
between you and me, and this time you completely knew
and believed "[therapist's name] really is interested in
and cares about what happens to me," then when I
looked at my clock, do you think the switch would have
been flipped?

C: No. I think I still would've seen you check it, but it
wouldn't have bothered me. I might have even thought
"He wants to make sure we have enough time."

T: (*Taking advantage of an opportunity to show the client how
his core belief gives rise to the content of his interpretation*) So
that's an example of your underlying belief—"I know
[therapist's name] cares about me"—affecting how you
interpret my behavior.

C: Yeah, I see that now.

T: (*Gathering evidence from previous therapeutic interactions to further change the client's other-schema as it relates to him*) Bob, since knowing and believing that I do care can make such a difference in how you interpret and react to me, I'd like to ask you to think back to previous sessions we've had: Can you see other evidence that demonstrates that I'm truly interested in how things go in your life?

C: When I think about it, you did give me more time a few weeks ago when I came late after that crazy situation at work.

T: (*Confirming and reinforcing this accurate relational interpretation*) Yes, I'm glad you can see the meaning in that; (*Encouraging the search for additional memories reflecting this positive relational theme*) anything else that you remember?

C: Hmm, I don't know . . . You usually do seem to listen closely to what I'm saying, and that you're glad when I tell about something that's gone well.

T: (*Confirming and reinforcing the accuracy of his interpretation*) Yes, that's true. (*Using this intrasession evidence to challenge client's core belief about others*) So even though you have this deep-down core belief that "I don't mean anything to other people and they don't care about me," can you see that it's not 100% accurate: that there's somebody [*Points to himself*] who does care?

C: Yeah, when I look at it—like you said, at the evidence—I can see that.

T: (*On the basis of this intrasession process, planting a seed intended to facilitate generalization in healthy revision in this core belief in relation to extrasession others, that is, generalization*) So here's something to also think about: I'd bet there are other people who also genuinely care about you, and that if you look more closely at the evidence from your experiences with them over time, you'll see that that's the case.

C: I will think about that. If I could really believe that, I think I'd be a lot less sensitive and less likely to fly off the handle.

T: (*Casting client's prediction as accurate, expressed in a way intended to convey that this healthy change is entirely feasible*) I think that's true . . . (*Having client concretize a more adaptive alternative*) What do you think would take its place?

C: Well, I think I wouldn't take things so personally, and I wouldn't get so hooked in by the some of the things other people do; I think I'd be able to roll with things more . . . And it would also be pretty different to believe—to feel—like I mean something to other people and they do care about me.

T: (*Again, casting client's predictions as accurate*) Again, I think that's all true. (*Promoting client's experience of the positivity of these relational changes and to heighten motivation*) So what do you think that would feel like?

C: That would be very cool. It would feel great.

T: [*Vigorously nods in agreement*]

A maladaptive schema activated in relation to the therapist can also serve as a springboard for working on the client's intimately connected self-issues. Focusing on the narrow and rigid self-schemas characteristic of PDs (Westen & Heim, 2003) often elicits emotional pain, necessitating therapist support and empathy. These segments also offer opportunities to access formative developmental experiences that have shaped the client's maladaptive self–other schemas as well as positive self-related information that has long been under-attended to and remains to be brought forth, processed, and integrated.

The following dialogue draws off the prior example to demonstrate work on the negative self-schema identified in the course of processing Bob's intrasession enactment:

T: (*Creating a transitional bridge between the negative core belief about others and about self*) It sounds like this negative core belief that you have about others—that you don't mean anything to them and they don't care about you—is very tied up with that strong belief that you have about yourself—that you mean nothing, that you're insignificant.

C: I think you're right . . . If I felt better about myself, I don't think it'd be an issue whether people care about me or not—or at least less of an issue.

T: (*Validating client's insight*) I think that's true. How do you see that? (*Open-ended question to promote further discussion*)

C: Because if I really felt worthwhile, I think I'd be, I don't know, more secure, stronger . . .

T: (*Validating the accuracy of this understanding*) Again, I think you're absolutely right. It would make a very meaningful difference. (*Advancing guided discovery into interpersonal–developmental understanding*) So where do you think this fundamental belief that you're insignificant is coming from?

C: I've had it all my life. Even when I've felt decent about myself, there's still this feeling of doubt, like a voice in my head saying, "Yeah, right—you know you're really a piece of shit; and no one gives a shit about you. Who are you kidding?"

T: (*Continuing guided discovery, focused on understanding this covert self-attacking process*) That voice sounds very, very nasty—what do you think that's about?

C: What's coming into my head are memories of when my father came home drunk after work, which, when I was a kid, seemed like just about every night; and he'd always go after somebody.

T: (*Inviting client's historical narrative about his family of origin*) In what way?

C: With words. He was vicious. He'd call my sister a whore, or tell my mother how miserable it was to be married to her; or if he went after me or one of my brothers, he'd criticize us or make fun of us. A lot of times he'd make fun of me because I wasn't much of an athlete, or something else that his venom would land on.

T: (*Eliciting detail, which is also intended to arouse affect*) Can you remember the kinds of things he'd say to you?

C: Yeah. I can remember him saying, in this drunk, slurring voice, "You little pipsqueak, you can't even hit a baseball . . . .you're pathetic!" Nasty things, critical things; he'd get really cruel.

T: (*Expanding the lens to learn about additional family system dynamics*) And what would your mother do when this was happening to you?

C: She'd just stand there, terrified to open her mouth. He got so loud, and forget about reasoning with him.

T: (*Making an empathy-based query*) So how protected did you feel?

C: I think sometimes she tried. But as soon as she'd say something—"He's a good boy, leave him alone"—he'd start on her. All I wanted to do was get to my room and hide. It was awful. [*Tears up*]

T: (*Experiential focusing*) What are you feeling right now?

C: Very sad. [*Reaches for a tissue and wipes away tears on his cheeks*] It was horrible . . . [*Cries more openly*]

T: (*Communicating empathic understanding*) It sounds like it was just awful, Bob; I have the sense that it was so frightening, and so painful, to grow up in that kind of environment.

C: You said it . . . I hated him, and the whole damn thing. [*Takes deep breath; crying lessens*] My mother, she was nice, but she was so busy trying to run the house I don't think she had time to really pay lots of attention to any one of us. For her it was a matter of just surviving daily life with my father and seven kids.

T: (*Crystallizing*) So your father, when he was drunk verbally and emotionally abused you; your mother, because of what she was going through, wasn't there, maybe couldn't be there, to give you what you needed emotionally. (*Focuses on self-schema implications*) How do you think growing up in that environment affected how you felt about yourself?

C: I felt ashamed. And even with a sister and five brothers, I think I felt alone, like the "real me" was invisible. I felt pretty lousy about myself—when I think back, like this worthless, lost, pathetic kid, like I meant nothing.

T: (*Validating negative self-schema effects*) It couldn't help but significantly affect how you felt about yourself.

C: It left some pretty deep scars . . . [*Eyes tear, looks down*]

T: (*Offering support, empathy, and validation*) I understand, Bob—it really hurts; it's very painful to think back to this, to remember what it was like and to see the damage it caused . . . (*Using client's metaphor as a context for injecting hope*) But sometimes scars can heal.

C: [*wearily*] Good luck . . . [*Continues to stare at the floor, but crying comes to an end*]

T: (*Expanding the metaphor, and not reinforcing client's pessimism with complementary negativism but instead enacting the noncomplementary response of optimism*) With the right ingredients, some scars really can heal.

C: It'll take a lot . . .

T: (*Offering a solution-focused response, that is, not drawing conclusions, encouraging openness to other possibilities, and maintaining optimism*) We'll see; but understanding can help; it can really make a difference.

C: But I think I do understand it; it doesn't take a rocket scientist. My father was a bastard and my mother wasn't there for me like other kids' moms. So I felt worthless and insignificant.

T: (*Challenging the accuracy of client's negative core self-belief by proposing that a distortion was at play*) Bob, I think you assumed you were worthless and insignificant.

C: Wouldn't you?

T: (*Validating accuracy of client's assertion*) Yes, I probably would. (*Using the concept of introjection to explain processes at play*) But let me share this observation that we can see only in later years: Kids don't have the mental sophistication to step back and realize things like "Well, my father's an abusive alcoholic, and my mother's terrified and preoccupied with surviving, so they're really the ones with the problems. I'm still a good kid!" And unless you had someone essentially saying that to you, you couldn't help but internalize into your self-image—and your self-feelings—the negative things your father said to you about you. And with what your mom was going through, she wasn't able to offset it. So you couldn't help but take it all in and think, and feel like "This is who I am; I don't matter."

C: So how do you get rid of that?!

T: (*Responding in complementary fashion to this request for change-related input by articulating a constructivistically based pathway to change*) Part of the process involves rethinking who you were and are. We can't change events that have happened to us, but we can change the meanings we've given them—including the meanings about ourselves. Even though you inevitably took in the ways you were—and weren't—treated in this dysfunctional family environment, it doesn't mean they were accurate statements about who you really were, and have continued to believe you are. A person can re-examine and alter negative, toxic beliefs they've come to hold about themselves so they're more accurate. (*Suggesting the positive relationship with self thereby instantiated*) Doing that is also a way to be compassionate with yourself—that can really help the healing process.

C: Easier said than done. What do I have to go on?

T: Great question! (*Client's question provides an opportunity to expand his lens regarding the past*) Think about this: (*Having the client begin to gather evidence to support constructive change in his negative self-schema*) When you look back at that kid that you were, and I mean really take a close look, are there things about him that you like?

C: I don't really think about that . . . but I guess he—I—was pretty tough. I kept going . . . I started working when I was 15 just to get out of the house. I worked at a deli, stocking the shelves, on weekends making sandwiches at lunchtime, sweeping the floor.

T: (*Drawing out positive self-meanings in this behavior*) So you were doing what you had to do to try to make things better for yourself.

C: Yeah, I guess I was. I never thought of it that way.

T: (*Affirming the client while also hypothesizing an additional positive self-meaning*) My hunch is that you also handled this responsibility well.

C: Yeah, that's true. My boss loved me; he'd say to me "I can really count on you."

T: That's terrific. (*In the immediacy of the moment, having client use this evidence to foster a more positive experience of self*) So if we take just this example, and you look back at yourself more mindful of the fact that that kid—who was you—was tough and at 15 went to work: Even just sitting here now, does it create any change at all in how you see yourself and feel about yourself?

C: [*Reflects*] Yeah, it does . . . Maybe I wasn't so pathetic. I guess that was pretty good, what I did.

T: (*Supporting and reinforcing this more positive self-appraisal*) Absolutely! (*Having client cull additional evidence to support self-schema change*) And what about how your boss regarded you? What do you think that says about you?

C: Well, he liked me. I guess to him I wasn't insignificant; he really did count on me.

T: (*Again, in the here-and-now moment, having the client experience a positive shift in self-image*) And right here, now, when you really see that, do you experience a change in your sense of self?

C: Yeah . . . my father made fun of me, but here was someone who valued me. [*Tears up slightly*]

T: Clearly! I'm glad you can see and experience that. (*If time allowed, the therapist could encourage the client to recall other adult figures [e.g., teachers] who explicitly or implicitly regarded him positively. But with time in the session winding down, the therapist shifts the reflective focus.*) So Bob, let's step back. We're almost down in time for today, but let me ask you: When you think just about what you've remembered about yourself today, and some of the things you realized about who and how you were, and how your first boss regarded you, does it in any way change your view of that boy—of you?

C: Yeah, he was a pretty neat kid. Sitting here right now, I like him; I'd like to put my arm around him and tell him what a great kid he is. (*With additional time, the therapist could also introduce an empty chair intervention, having the client directly speak with this boy—himself—about "what a great kid he is."*)

T: (*Promoting additional self-experiential change that may derive from this segment of work*) Is there anything else about yourself you're experiencing differently?

C: Yes, I feel like there was more to me than I realized. I don't feel that sense of insignificance right now. I have to admit I'm proud of myself for what I worked at overcoming, even while I was living through it.

T: (*Supporting and reinforcing the client's self-realizations and their implications, and in conveying that the change the client is experiencing is meaningful to him also communicates his valuing of the client—additional evidence to contribute to constructive self-schema change*) Justifiably! That's terrific—I'm really glad to hear this. I value you, and it's good to hear you value yourself. (*Bringing this segment of self-schema work full circle and underscoring the emergent positive self-meanings*) And, y'know, what we started with—that negative core belief you have about yourself, that you're worthless and insignificant—doesn't hold up when we start to understand more clearly how it got there and begin to look at real evidence that says some very positive things about you.

C: No, it doesn't seem to hold up. I know I have a lot more work to do on this, but right now I feel pretty good—and pretty good about myself.

T: (*Again supporting and expressing positive feelings about the here-and-now change client is experiencing, and in so doing again communicating valuing of the client*) That's great to hear.

Providing a Corrective Interpersonal Relationship

The very process of metacommunication and its central ingredients (e.g., honest self-disclosure, collaboration) provide the client with healthy, and hence reparative, relational experiences that differ from painful pathology-perpetuating experiences often encountered in extrasession relationships. In addition, akin to Alexander and French's (1946) concept of the *corrective emotional experience*, the therapist can provide the client with salutary relational experiences by proactively cultivating, on the basis of his or her growing understanding of the client's clinical issues and needs, a type of relationship and interpersonal process that is itself intended to have therapeutic effects (see Anchin, 2006).

Interpersonal Work on Extrasession Relationships

PD clients' relationships and interpersonal experiences outside of treatment serve as another major arena for intensive therapeutic work. As when targeting intrasession enactments, the overarching therapeutic strategy centers on fostering awareness, understanding, and making adaptive changes in dysfunctional overt and covert self–other processes that play salient roles in the client's problematic relational functioning; however, tactics of intervention are modified and tailored in ways suited to the extratherapeutic realm. In the course of extrasession work it is also valuable to identify positive interpersonal experiences and relationships, past and present, as well as strengths and healthy psychosocial capacities—potent resources that expedite therapeutic change.

The following prototypic dialogue illustrates technical and processural facets of extrasession relational work integrating interpersonal, experiential, cognitive, constructivist, and solution-focused methods.

C: I had a fight with Elise [her separated 33-year-old daughter] today; she infuriates me!

T: (*Pursuing descriptive reconstruction of the interactional exchange, including mentally "coding" in IPC terms the client's and daughter's reciprocal interpersonal behaviors in order to crystallize the relational process being played out*) What happened?

C: Just thinking about it gets me mad. We were on the phone, and she was telling me that Joey [Elise's 10-year-old son] still isn't doing his homework, and so his grades are going down, and so I asked her what she was doing about it.

T: (*This and the therapist's four ensuing questions reflect tracking the sequential exchange*) What did she say?

C: It was ridiculous! She said she doesn't know what to do about it at this point; she's thinking of seeing the school psychologist to see if she has any ideas about what might be wrong, that she doesn't know what else to try.

T: How did you respond to that?

C: I told her flat out "That's ridiculous!" and that she needed to get tougher with him; that if he was my kid, I'd make him sit there until he did his homework, and if he didn't, he could forget about supper that night. And if that didn't work, I'd tell him that every time he didn't do his homework, he'd lose another weekend to play with his friends.

T: What did she say?

C: "Mom, I'm not that way." So I asked her what she meant, and she said "I don't think punishing him is the answer" and that it's been hard enough for him since his father moved out two months ago, and that threatening him would only make matters worse.

T: So what did you say?

C: I exploded! I asked her why the hell she brought this up if she didn't want my advice! She never listens to me; that's why her life's a mess! She never respects what I have to say.

T: Did you say that to her?

C: No, but I sure thought it.

T: (*In some previous work, the therapist and client had identified "No one ever respects me" as one of her core beliefs; here, the therapist is gathering data regarding the link between this belief and her angry reaction*) Do you remember, when you had that thought—"She never respects what I have to say"—what you were feeling?

C: Really, really mad! She's never respected me, and this time I just blew!

T: Yeah, it sounds like it. (*Continued tracking of the exchange*) So when you asked her why she brought this up if she didn't want your advice, what did she say?

C: I don't remember exactly. I was too mad at that point—I think she said something like "Ma, I wasn't looking for your advice" and that she just wanted to tell me what's been going on with Joey and how worried she is about him.

T: So what happened next?

C: I said to her "Stop worrying and do something about it!"

T: (*According to the IPC, thus far Elise's behavior could be coded as primarily entailing closeness and intimacy by virtue of honestly disclosing her current difficulties, whereas the client's reciprocal responses have been primarily noncomplementary, involving mixtures of dominance, assertion, and hostility*) Did she say anything back?

C: She's so weak—it sounded like she was starting to cry, and she said "I just can't talk to you," and then had the nerve to say something like "You'd think I'd know that by now," and then she hung up on me! (*A reciprocal hostile reaction by Elise*)

T: (*Ascertaining client's internal experience in reaction to the call ending in this way*) What were you thinking and feeling when she did that?

C: I was shocked! I think that's the first time she's done that. All I know is, I was furious. She's never had respect for me, and this just proves it.

T: (*Refocusing client*) So this happened earlier today. (*Gauging client's current subjective experience regarding the call*) What are your thoughts and feelings about it right now?

C: I'm still really mad about it, and hurt. If she just listened to me she'd get herself, and Joey, on the right track. But [*sarcastically*] I'm just her mother; I don't know anything . . .

T: (*Engaging client in stepping back and reflecting on the interaction through a solution-focused lens, that is, establishing client's preferred outcome*) Mary, let me ask you something: Is this how you want things to go between you and Elise?

C: Of course not! I wish we could get along, but it seems like we always end up fighting. If she'd just listen to me . . .

T: (*Sharpening focus on a key, emotionally charged component of the interaction*) You seem very frustrated by the fact that she doesn't listen to you.

C: I am! I mean, why would she ask for my advice if she's not gonna follow it?

T: (*Focusing client's attention on a tacit faulty belief*) Well, you're making an assumption that she was asking for your advice.

C: It sure seemed that way to me.

T: (*Identifying and affirming her positive intentions*) I can understand how you'd see it that way; she's having a hard time with Joey, and as her mother, I think you very much want to help her.

C: Of course!

T: (*Contrasting the client's positive intentions with the actual negative outcomes and framing this in a way designed to motivate change*) But since this didn't turn out the way you wanted it to—you ended up, it sounds like, enraged, and she hung up on you—it might help if we figured out what happened so that next time you try to help her, things go better.

C: I don't know what else to do; I always try to help her, but we end up fighting.

T: (*Validating client's positive motivation and the characteristically negative outcome of her interactions with Elise*) Yeah, it seems that way. (*Reinserting a change-oriented frame*) So in an effort to improve things, (*Laying groundwork to reappraise the accuracy of her assumption*) let's go back to your assumption, that she was looking for your advice.

C: Yeah . . .

T: (*Drawing on the therapeutic bond*) Stay with me on this. (*Therapeutically confronting the client with Elise's statement in the service of promoting cognitive reappraisal*) Later in the call she said she just wanted to tell you about the trouble she's been having with Joey, that he hasn't been doing his homework and his grades are going down; she said she didn't want advice, she just wanted to tell you what's been going on.

C: I see what you're saying, but still . . .

T: (*Expressing belief in client's positive intentions in order to protect her self-esteem and enhance receptivity to his next statement*) Mary, that's not to say you didn't want to help her; I think you really did. But once you made that assumption, that she was looking for your advice, it colored your reactions from then on.

C: I don't see that; how?!

T: (*Explaining by linking salient processes: the client's inaccurate assumption, the resultant meaning given to the daughter's differing opinion, the role of her negative core belief in coloring this interpretation, and her ensuing emotional and overt reaction*) Well, you offered advice, assuming she wanted that. But then she didn't accept the advice you gave and you interpreted that to mean she wasn't respecting you, which hit a nerve. We've seen that because of what it was like in your family when you were growing up, you came out of that with this deep, core belief that no one respects you.

C: [*Nods in agreement*]

T: So that's something, very understandably, you're sensitive about. So once you made that assumption that she wanted your advice, it seemed like you experienced her disagreeing with you as disrespect; and that just hit that nerve, that painful belief that no one respects you—that hurt, and so you exploded. (*Having client try on this explanation to ascertain its felt-accuracy*) Does that make sense?

C: [*Thinks for a moment*] Yeah, it does. I know this respect thing is an issue. But she didn't have to react the way she did.

T: (*Not getting diverted by this effort to shift blame; instead, drawing on the working alliance as a context for requesting clarification*) I want to make sure we're on the same page here; what part of her reaction are you referring to?

C: Her sarcastically saying "I should know by now that I can't talk to you," and then hanging up on me!

T: (*Clarifying meaning*) Her saying and doing that; what does that mean to you?

C: Well, I hate to say it, but again, there's that disrespect!

T: (*Responding to client's again shifting focus back to daughter with a noncomplementary response via inserting a change-oriented frame and eliciting collaboration*) OK, but again, so that we can figure this out so that maybe things can go better next time, are you willing to consider this from a different angle?

C: [*somewhat defensively*] Yeah, I have an open mind . . .

T: (*There is the option here of a technical shift aimed at pinpointing and discussing the relational feelings embedded in the client's statement—perhaps an intrasession enactment of not feeling respected by the therapist—but at this juncture the therapist chooses to maintain the extrasession focus*) An open mind is a definite asset. (*Moving toward fostering client's awareness of the impact of her intense anger*) So Elise makes this statement and then hangs up. But think back to the call; how angry were you as it played out?

C: I was livid; like you said before, I think I felt enraged.

T: (*Validating client's observation*) It sounds that way. (*Engaging client in perspective taking*) What do you think the impact of that intense anger—that rage—might have been on Elise?

C: [*Looks away, appearing to be somewhat embarrassed*] I didn't think about that.

T: (*Fostering empathy for the felt-impact of another's rage*) Mary, when your mother used to get so angry with you like that, do remember how it felt?

C: I hated it; it hurt so much. And I hated her; I just wanted to get away—from that anger and from her.

T: (*Joining perspective taking and empathy*) Is it possible Elise was feeling the same kind of thing?

C: I guess.

T: [*Remains silent*]

C: I probably would've done the same thing to my mother.

T: (*Recognizing and reinforcing this honesty with self*) I appreciate that you can see that.

C: I feel like I really screwed up in the call . . .

T: (*Client directs blame at self; therapist seeks to protect her self-esteem by blocking her self-denigration and encouraging a constructive mindset linked to her helpful intentions*) I don't think it's a matter of finding fault, or assigning blame. I think it's a matter of us getting a healthy understanding of what was involved in how the call played out and what it means in terms of changes that can be made so that you're desire to be helpful to her is effective. (*Planting a seed as to potential positive outcomes of these changes*) I think you'll both feel better when that happens.

C: So what do I do differently?

T: (*In this context, providing a complementary response: The overarching goal is change, the client is receptive to new social learning, and hence explicit recommendations are offered*) In some ways it's very straightforward. The short answer is: If Elise is going through something difficult, unless she explicitly asks for your advice, don't offer it, and instead just listen. (*Constructivistically recreating the situation as another way to promote change*) In fact, let's say you went into the call earlier today with this mind-set: "Elise doesn't want me to try to fix it; she just needs someone to talk to who can listen in a way that'll be helpful." With that mind-set, how might you have responded when she started telling you about Joey and her feelings about the situation?

C: Well, like you said, just listen.

T: (*Having client take this a step further, that is, translating this into overt expressive behavior*) And since it's over the phone, and she can't see you, how might you convey to her that you're listening from a place of wanting to be helpful to her?

C: Hmmm . . . I suppose I could tell her that it's too bad she's having this problem with Joey, and I see why she's upset. But I think I'd still be thinking "I know what to do; just listen to me . . ."

T: (*Attempting to reduce the probability of acting on that thought by having client consider potential negative consequences*) OK, but if you act on that?

C: I think we already know what's probably gonna happen.

T: (*Validating client's prediction and suggesting metaphorically a way to control this*) Exactly; so it would be a matter of turning the volume down on that thought and staying with the "I'm gonna listen" mind-set. (*Exploring additional response options*) What else could you do to let her know that your listening is coming from a place of wanting to help?

C: I don't know . . . No one ever really listened to me, so I don't have much to go on.

T: (*Drawing on the immediacy of the therapeutic relationship*) Well, let's tap into our process. (*The next question is risky, but on the basis of the positive tenor of the evolving therapeutic relationship, the therapist judges this to be a safe risk.*) Do you experience me as listening from a place of wanting to be helpful?

C: Yeah—I wouldn't keep coming back if I didn't.

T: (*Making honest self-disclosure in response to client's meta-message*) I'm glad that our meetings help. (*Pinpointing helpful facets of therapist's listening*) And how can you tell my listening comes from a place of wanting to be helpful?

C: Sometimes you repeat back what I'm feeling; like you bring feelings out—that helps me somehow, and it makes me feel like you care and that you're trying to understand. . . .

T: (*Making honest self-disclosure*) I'm glad that comes through. (*Encouraging client to make efforts to attempt a similar process with her daughter, and laying groundwork for empathy training*) Maybe that's the kind of thing you could try to do with Elise once things settle down—try to focus on what she might be feeling. That's something you can practice, and we can also talk about ways of expressing to her that you understand her feelings; I think this could make a very positive difference in your relationship.

C: It's worth a shot! . . . But you said the things we've been talking about my trying was the short answer about what I could do differently. Is there also a long answer?

T: (*Thinking that the "short-versus-long answer" distinction can be improved, and modeling fallibility*) I think I need to correct myself here; it's not so much a long answer, but it has to do with working on some other aspects of the kind of thing that happens between you and Elise. (*Laying groundwork for additional directions of work on the core belief abut others activated during client's interactions with Elise, e.g., developing insight into etiologically significant formative experiences, appraising its accuracy through gathering and closely examining evidence, culling out and working on change in the activated negative core belief(s) about self*) I think it could help if we also had a better understanding of where this strong belief that no one respects you is coming from; also, is it accurate? And how much is it tied up with some of the feelings you have about yourself—not necessarily easy things to look at, but it could also be very helpful.

C: Well, like you said, I do want to be better at helping her—even though she drives me nuts! Maybe if I understood what's going on better . . .

It is crucial that the client's growing awareness and understanding of overt and covert components of his or her maladaptive transaction cycles, as well as of alternative, more adaptive processes translate into actual change in extrasession relational functioning and experiencing. An interpersonal therapist proactively promotes these modifications in part by encouraging the client to bring to bear in specific problematic situations relevant new learnings about his or her dysfunctional processes. This on-the-spot awareness can function as a conscious cue to resist enacting a particular maladaptive process (e.g., negatively interpreting a particular action by another, responding impulsively). In addition, "structured skill intervention strategies" (Sperry, 2003, p. 28; e.g., emotional regulation training, assertiveness training, empathy training) can facilitate acquisition of specific skills in areas of deficit. Integrally related, interpersonal therapists also promote extrasession change through between-session homework assignments in which the client actively attempts more adaptive overt and/or covert actions in problematic interpersonal situations. It is vital, too, that the therapist and client collaboratively process experiential and interpersonal (self–other) consequences associated with real-world experimentation with more adaptive processes. PD clients' characteristic ambivalence about expanding beyond their timeworn yet familiar ways of viewing and interacting with self and others necessitates that they see and experience for themselves, through repeated real-world evidence across different interpersonal situations, that change is warranted, possible, and beneficial.

Integrating Intrasession and Extrasession Psychotherapeutic Work

The complex and rigidified nature of PDs characteristically necessitates persistent, long-term intervention in different components of a client's interpersonal dysfunctionality; focusing on both its intrasession and extrasession expressions maximizes interventional opportunities. In addition, knowledge about the client's maladaptive patterns gained in one arena enhances sensitivity to these processes in the other arena; for example, identifying a consistent problematic pattern in the client's extratherapy relationships sensitizes the therapist to its in-session occurrence, facilitating disengagement and metacommunicative processes as this pattern emerges in the therapy relationship.

Furthermore, examining self–other understandings developed in relation to the therapist for their pertinence to extrasession relationships is vital to fostering generalization of insights and their change implications to the client's naturalistic environment. In a reciprocal manner, linking a maladaptive pattern in the client's extratherapy relationships to its enactment in session enables the client to examine this pattern in a safe environment and to develop vivid, in vivo understanding of its composition, meanings, and interpersonal impact (Levenson, 2004). Metacommunicating about intrasession and extrasession enactments and linking the two is integral to time-limited dynamic psychotherapy, which has been found to yield positive outcomes with a population of PD clients (Levenson, 2004).

Combining Treatment Modalities

Sperry (2003) distinguished between *integrative treatment* (blending different treatment orientations) and *combined treatment* (concurrently or sequentially combining different treatment modalities, i.e., individual, group, marital and family therapy, day treatment, inpatient hospitalization, or medication). Advantages of combining modalities with PDs "include additive and even synergistic effects, diluting unworkably intense transference relationships, and rapid symptom relief (Francis, Clarkin, & Perry, 1984)" (Sperry, 2003, p. 9). Client strengths can also more vividly emerge in additional treatment contexts. Decisions incorporating any of these modalities into treatment must be made on a case-by-case basis and supported by a rationale. Recommending that one or more modalities be added to treatment (and regarding medication, referral for a medication evaluation) is of no small significance and triggers within the client reactions—at times schema related—that need to be processed. To facilitate informed decisions and discussion about adding modalities, we refer readers to excellent discussions of the benefits and processes of PD-adapted group therapy (MacKenzie, 2001), couple and family therapy (MacFarlane, 2004), day treatment (Ogrodniczuk & Piper, 2004), residential/inpatient treatment (Belnap, Iscan, & Plakun, 2004), and pharmacotherapy (Grossman, 2004; see Chapter 10, this volume).

TREATMENT OF COMORBID CONDITIONS

Dolan-Sewell, Krueger, and Shea (2001) reported that nearly 75% of clients diagnosed with a PD also present with an Axis I (clinical syndrome) disorder and indeed that "the modal treatment-seeking personality-disordered patient meets criteria for at least one Axis I disorder" (p. 84).

Complicating matters further, "PDs . . . are well-known for *dense patterns* [emphasis added] of co-morbidity on *both* [emphasis added] axes" (Critchfield & Benjamin, 2006, p. 257), underscoring the heterogeneity of clinical pathology in these disorders. Furthermore, although different conceptual models have been put forth to explain the high rate of Axis I and II comorbidity, none have emerged as definitive.

Although bases for comorbidity are far from having been unraveled, research tends to show that the prognosis for clients with an Axis I syndrome who have also been diagnosed with a PD is distinctly worse than for Axis I clients without a PD (Benjamin, 2003; Castonguay & Beutler, 2006). The interpersonal approach's holistic view of the client, wherein systems are embedded within systems, interprets this finding as reflecting a spurious distinction between Axis I and Axis II (see Benjamin, 2003, pp. 3–4); the disturbances in cognition and affect that are central to clinical syndromes are entwined with PD clients' deeply entrenched maladaptive modes of navigating the social world (Benjamin, 1996, pp. 377–381). Growing bodies of research (Kiesler, 1996; Magnavita, 2005) have demonstrated the interpersonal nexus of Axis I symptoms, which cyclically operate as both effects of and maintaining factors in clients' interpersonal pathology.

Translated into treatment implications, an interpersonal therapist's decision is not one of whether to initially emphasize treatment of either the Axis I or the Axis II disorder; instead, the treatment processes is dialectical (Anchin, 2002; Anchin & Magnavita, 2006), entailing a both/and approach: From the outset, the therapist shuttles between intervening in Axis II symptom-maintaining interpersonal processes and intervening in Axis I symptomatology with specific targeted interventions. McCullough's (2005) cognitive–behavioral analysis system of psychotherapy, an empirically supported approach to chronic depression, is an exemplar of a treatment model conceptualizing Axis I symptomatology as inseparably tied to chronic and pervasive interpersonal dysfunction. The cognitive–behavioral analysis system of psychotherapy integrates cognitive, behavioral, and interpersonal methods to concurrently and interactively reduce the client's depression and foster change in maladaptive interpersonal behavior.

Comorbidity of Axis I and Axis II conditions can also be among the primary contexts for medication evaluation, given that "the Axis I condition may be not only causing more dysphoria, but also exacerbating Axis II symptomatology. As such, pharmacological treatment can be more parsimonious if an agent treats both the Axis I condition and core features of that client's Axis II pathology" (Grossman, 2004, p. 334). The fundamentally biopsychosocial nature of PDs (Anchin, 2008c; Magnavita, 2005; Sperry, 2003) is integral to this pharmacologic treatment perspective.

SUMMARY OF EVIDENCE-BASED PRINCIPLES AND STRATEGIES

A unique aspect of the interpersonal approach involves use of the IPC to generate coordinated descriptions of individual differences in interpersonal motives, traits, and behaviors, as well as reciprocal interpersonal patterns (e.g., complementarity), that are used to differentiate normal and abnormal personality functioning in a variety of ways (Benjamin, 1994; Pincus & Gurtman, 2006). Efforts to map PDs onto the IPC and infer testable hypotheses regarding overt and covert interpersonal experience and relational developmental experience have existed since the first formal empirical derivation of the model (Leary, 1957) and have continued to the present (e.g., Benjamin, 1996; Horowitz & Wilson, 2005). Empirical research demonstrating that several PDs are related to unique pervasive and inflexible interpersonal styles with associated reciprocal relational impacts that lead to social reinforcement of early learning through vicious circles (Millon & Davis, 1996) and self-fulfilling prophecies (Carson, 1982) are summarized in Figure 5.2. Consistent with Millon's (2005) blueprint for a clinical science, the interpersonal approach can coordinate empirical assessment of interpersonal dysfunction with empir-

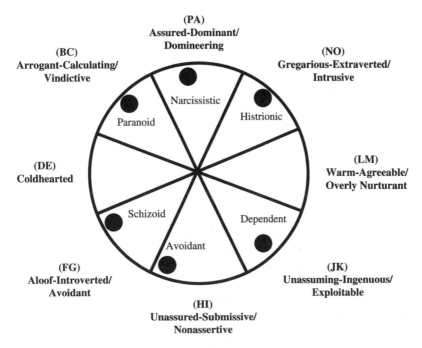

Figure 5.2. Empirically supported interpersonal styles associated with personality disorders.

ically supported clinical theory to provide a diagnostic nexus for personality and personality pathology (Pincus, 2005b).

Psychotic Level of Personality Organization: Cluster A Personality Disorders

Two Cluster A PDs have been consistently mapped onto the IPC. *Schizoid PD* is associated with an introverted–aloof interpersonal style reflecting low levels of both communion and agency. *Paranoid PD* is associated with a suspicious–vindictive interpersonal style reflecting low levels of communion and high levels of agency. Given that clients with these PDs lack communal motivation, alliance formation itself may actually be a significant long-term treatment goal and an important outcome of, rather than a preliminary step in, treatment. In both cases, asocial therapeutic responding and therapeutic metacommunication are highly challenging.

Specific Treatment Considerations

The interpersonal tendencies of individuals with schizoid PD include a lack of communal and agentic motives and behavior, sensitivity to intrusion, and expectations of being dominated and overwhelmed by others that distort the client's accurate decoding of most interpersonal situations (Benjamin, 1996; McWilliams, 2006). Such clients tend to ignore and wall themselves off from others. Consistent cold and aloof behavior and low levels of interpersonal responsiveness pull for others to either ignore these individuals or become frustrated when affiliative efforts are ineffective or rebuffed, reinforcing the person's expectancies. The clinical challenges are to form an alliance with a client who does not appear motivated to respond in a complementary way to the warmth of the therapist while simultaneously titrating the very strength or "volume" of the therapist's interpersonal presence to levels tolerable to the client.

The interpersonal tendencies of individuals with paranoid PD include a lack of communal motives in combination with strong agentic motives to block anticipated humiliation, exploitation, and attack from others that distort accurate decoding of most interpersonal situations (Benjamin, 1996; Horowitz, 2004). Expectations of malice from others lead these individuals to accuse, control, blame, attack, recoil, and wall themselves off from others. Consistent hostile dominant behavior combined with a quickly rising anger in response to perceived malice (Horowtiz & Wilson, 2005) pull for others to attack back or withdraw support, reinforcing the individual's expectancies. The clinical challenge is to form an alliance with a client who cannot trust that the therapist will work in his or her best interest and who uses active, hostile defensive tactics.

Adult attachment styles exhibit systematic relationships with interpersonal functioning assessed with the IPC model (Bartholomew & Horowitz, 1991). The low communion of paranoid and schizoid PDs is consistent with dismissive and disorganized attachment (Westen, Nakash, Thomas, & Bradley, 2006). Little is known about the family factors associated with schizoid PD, although cases treated by one of us have exhibited either unpredictable, intrusive parenting (e.g., spontaneous, illogical parental rage and physical attack), or significant schizoid family dynamics (e.g., a catatonic father). Benjamin (1996) suggested that individuals with paranoid PDs exhibit a history of sadistic, degrading, and controlling parenting leading to expectancies of harm and humiliation and simultaneous identification with the attacking parental style.

Borderline Level of Personality Organization: Cluster B Personality Disorders

Two Cluster B PDs have been consistently mapped onto the IPC. *Histrionic PD* is associated with an extraverted–intrusive interpersonal style reflecting high levels of both communion and agency. *Narcissistic PD* (at least as conceived by the *Diagnostic and Statistical Manual of Mental Disorders* [4th ed., text revision; American Psychiatric Association, 2000]; see Cain, Pincus, & Ansell, 2008) is associated with an arrogant–domineering interpersonal style reflecting average levels of communion and high levels of agency. Unlike individuals with schizoid PD and paranoid PD, who are disaffiliative, clients with histrionic PD and narcissistic PD are looking for something from others. Histrionic PD clients are looking for attention and connection, and narcissistic PD clients are looking for admiration. Finally, individuals with *borderline PD* (BPD) are interpersonally chaotic and affectively labile. Recent longitudinal research investigating interpersonal behavior and emotion in BPD confirms these characteristics. Russell, Moskowitz, Zuroff, Sookman, and Paris (2007) found that, over 20 days, BPD clients exhibited—relative to control participants—more variability in how dominant, hostile, and friendly they were; greater overall intensity and variability in their types of interpersonal behaviors; and more variability in affective states.

Specific Treatment Considerations

The interpersonal tendencies of clients with histrionic PD include strong communal and agentic motives and behavior, attention seeking, and sensitivity to signs of indifference from others that distort their accurate decoding of most interpersonal situations (Horowitz & Wilson, 2005). Such clients tend to approach others and to disclose and exhibit superficial but intensely experienced needs and emotions. Because of their sensitivity to indifference, they are also quick to become excessively disappointed or angry at others if needed attention is not provided. Consistent extraverted and intrusive behaviors may initially attract the attention of others and evoke affiliative reactions. However, histrionic PD clients' intense needs for attention, extreme and shifting moods, and low levels of interpersonal mutuality ultimately pull for others to become frustrated with their intrusiveness or indifferent to their affected style, reinforcing client expectancies. A person with histrionic PD is apt to form an alliance quickly, but this may be quite superficial. Therapists run the risk of becoming seduced by such presentations, absorbed in their client's dramatic expression and misconstruing it as evidence for a deepening alliance. However, if pressed for more intimacy, depth, and mutuality than is tolerable, such clients tend to terminate treatment and seek needed attention in a new therapeutic relationship.

The interpersonal tendencies of people with narcissistic PD reflect strong agentic motives to obtain admiration from others in support of an inflated self-image, as well as sensitivity to signs of disrespect that distorts their accurate decoding of most interpersonal situations (Cain et al., 2008). Such clients are apt to affirm their self-worth by exploiting other people and/or acting like someone who is special, important, and entitled (Horowitz & Wilson, 2005). When needed admiration is not received, these individuals are prone to blame and devalue others, and they become envious and enraged. Interpersonal behavior is consistently used in the service of self-enhancement. Although this can often lead to positive first impressions (e.g., Wagner et al., 1999), over time the inflexibility and derogation of others leads to interpersonal rejection (Paulhus, 1998), reinforcing client expectations. The clinical challenge is to form an alliance with a client who cannot allow the therapist to exhibit competence or expertise that threatens the client's inflated self-image.

Attachment, Relational, and Family Factors

The interpersonal style of people with histrionic PD is consistent with a preoccupied attachment style (Westen et al., 2006) that is compensated for by chronic attention seeking. Benjamin (1996) suggested that this arises from a history of being valued for appearance and entertainment value in the context of general neglect, requiring dramatic expressions of illness, distress, or incompetence to evoke care. Narcissistic PD is related to several insecure attachment variants (Dickinson & Pincus, 2003; Westen et al., 2006) and negative assessments of relational functioning by others (Clifton, Turkheimer, & Oltmanns, 2005). Two prominent developmental pathways to narcissism proposed in the literature are (a) the receipt of noncontingent love and praise, leading to expectations of admiration without requisite skills and accomplishments (Benjamin, 1996), and (b) defensive development of a grandiose self-image in response to hostile or rejecting developmental experiences (Kernberg, 1998).

Neurotic Level of Personality Organization: Cluster C Personality Disorders

Two Cluster C PDs have been consistently mapped onto the IPC. *Avoidant PD* is associated with a timid and nonassertive interpersonal style reflecting modestly low levels of communion and low levels of agency. *Dependent PD* is associated with a range of friendly–submissive behaviors (Pincus & Gurtman, 1995; Pincus & Wilson, 2001) enacted in the service of a needy and exploitable interpersonal style reflecting high communion and low agency. Individuals with these PDs see themselves as ineffective and weak, but low communion in avoidant PD leads them to be hypersensitive to rejection and to intensely fear others, whereas the high communion of dependent PD leads them to be hypersensitive to abandonment and to intensely need others for instrumental and emotional support.

Specific Treatment Considerations

The defective self-image and hypersensitivity to rejection of avoidant PD clients distorts their accurate decoding of most interpersonal situations, and their interpersonal style leads them to avoid discomfort by minimizing social contact, intimacy, and new relationships (Horowitz & Wilson, 2005). Such clients experience considerable anxiety if required to approach others and often maintain a passive and distant relational stance. Because of their low agency, they experience themselves as flawed and are quick to become self-critical. Clients with avoidant PD can form a positive therapeutic alliance once they are certain they will not be judged or rejected, but this may not generalize outside of therapy without more directive interventions (e.g., Alden, 1989). Alden and Capreol (1993) found that the client's level of communion interacted with treatment responsiveness. Clients with avoidant PD who have very low levels of communion benefited from graded exposure to social tasks but not from intimacy training, whereas clients with relatively higher levels of communion benefited from both interventions.

The incompetent self-image and fear of abandonment of clients with dependent PD distort their accurate decoding of most interpersonal situations, and their interpersonal style leads them to avoid feelings of helplessness by pleasing others and getting them to take charge (Horowitz & Wilson, 2005). However, the urgency with which they fear being alone can also lead to highly demanding behavior (e.g., frequent phone calls, suicidal threats). Although efforts to please and requests for guidance may first pull others to the aid of a person with dependent PD, his or her chronic lack of agentic motivation leads others to burn out, reinforcing client expectations. The clinical challenge is to form a true collaborative alliance with a client who is highly agreeable, wishes to please the therapist, and is most comfortable submitting to authority.

Attachment, Relational, and Family Factors

Research on attachment in avoidant and dependent PDs is inconsistent, suggesting a mix of fearful, dismissing, and preoccupied styles (Westen et al., 2006). This inconsistency may be related to the impact of variable levels of communion on the behavior and treatment response of these PDs (e.g., Alden & Capreol, 1993; Pincus & Wilson, 2001). Low levels of agency could be a complementary response to a shared developmental history of parental overcontrol. Also consistent with complementarity, their divergence in affiliation may reflect control within a blaming and hostile family environment for clients with avoidant PDs and for clients with dependent PD, control within an infantilizing family environment in which autonomy was prohibited (Benjamin, 1996; Thompson & Zuroff, 1998).

SUMMARY AND CONCLUSION

The treatment guidelines we have presented in this chapter integrate three components: (a) empirical evidence supporting interpersonal constructs and postulates about PDs and specific relational and technical interventions used in interpersonal psychotherapy; (b) research findings pertaining to participant, relationship, and technique factors found to be associated with effective PD treatment; and (c) multidimensional knowledge yielded by acquired clinical expertise. Synthesizing these bodies of scientific and clinical knowledge, and integrating them on a case-by-case basis with the ongoing data provided through traversing the participant-observer dialectic, yields a rich matrix of multifaceted evidence that supports an interpersonal approach to the psychotherapy of PDs that can be idiographically tailored to the given client at hand. This flexible approach to interpersonal treatment proceeds within the context of a coherent holistic framework that centers on reciprocally-connected dysfunctional covert and overt self–other processes definitive of the maladaptive self-perpetuating cycles fundamental to this complex and challenging class of disorders.

Helping to expand the evidence base of interpersonal psychotherapy with PDs is an ongoing process requiring *methodological pluralism* (Anchin,

2008b, 2008c). This is clearly apparent in recommendations of the American Psychological Association Presidential Task Force on Evidence-Based Practice (2006), which provided a highly articulated road map for directions of research on evidence-based practices; specifically, these entail clinical observation, qualitative research, systematic case studies, single-case experimental designs, public health and ethnographic research, process–outcome studies, studies of interventions delivered in naturalistic settings, randomized clinical designs and their equivalents, and meta-analyses. As indicated by the task force, "different research designs are better suited to address different types of questions (Greenberg & Newman, 1966)" (p. 274). Nor are these methods mutually exclusive (Anchin, 2008a). Adapting these research designs to the marked complexities of treating PDs poses major challenges for investigators, but successfully integrating clinical expertise with the growing knowledge yielded by these diverse methodologies will place the interpersonal psychotherapy of PDs on an ever more robust evidentiary base.

REFERENCES

Ackerman, S. J., & Hilsenroth, M. J. (2003). A review of therapist characteristics and techniques positively impacting the therapeutic alliance. *Clinical Psychology Review, 23*, 1–33.

Alden, L. E. (1989). Short-term structured treatment for avoidant personality disorder. *Journal of Consulting and Clinical Psychology, 57*, 756–764.

Alden, L. E., & Capreol, M. J. (1993). Avoidant personality disorder: Interpersonal problems as predictors of treatment response. *Behavior Therapy, 24*, 357–376.

Alexander, F., & French, T. M. (1946). *Psychoanalytic psychotherapy: Principles and applications*. New York, NY: Ronald Press.

American Psychiatric Association. (2000). *Diagnostic and statistical manual of mental disorders* (4th ed., text revision). Washington, DC: Author.

American Psychological Association Presidential Task Force on Evidence-Based Practice. (2006). Evidence-based practice in psychology. *American Psychologist, 61*, 271–285.

Anchin, J. C. (1982a). Interpersonal approaches to psychotherapy: Summary and conclusions. In J. C. Anchin & D. J. Kiesler (Eds.), *Handbook of interpersonal psychotherapy* (pp. 313–329). New York, NY: Pergamon Press.

Anchin, J. C. (1982b). Sequence, pattern, and style: Integration and treatment implications of some interpersonal concepts. In J. C. Anchin & D. J. Kiesler (Eds.), *Handbook of interpersonal psychotherapy* (pp. 95–131). New York, NY: Pergamon Press.

Anchin, J. C. (1987). Functional analysis and the social-interactional perspective: Toward an integration in the behavior change enterprise. *Journal of Integrative and Eclectic Psychotherapy, 6,* 398–389.

Anchin, J. C. (2002). Relational psychoanalytic enactments and psychotherapy integration: Dualities, dialectics, and directions: Comment on Frank (2002). *Journal of Psychotherapy Integration, 13,* 302–346.

Anchin, J. C. (2003). Cybernetic systems, existential phenomenology, and solution-focused narrative: Therapeutic transformation of negative affective states through integratively oriented brief psychotherapy. *Journal of Psychotherapy Integration, 13,* 334–442

Anchin, J. C. (2006). A hermeneutically informed approach to psychotherapy integration. In G. Stricker & J. R. Gold (Eds.), *A casebook of psychotherapy integration* (pp. 261–280). Washington, DC: American Psychological Association.

Anchin, J. C. (2008a). Comment: Integrating methodologies in the scientific study of interpersonal psychotherapy: A reaction to "Therapist Immediacy in Brief Psychotherapy: Case Study I and Case Study II." *Psychotherapy: Theory, Research, Practice, Training, 45,* 316–319.

Anchin, J. C. (2008b). Contextualizing discourse on a philosophy of science for psychotherapy integration. *Journal of Psychotherapy Integration, 18,* 1–24.

Anchin, J. C. (2008c). Pursuing a unifying paradigm for psychotherapy: Tasks, dialectical considerations, and biopsychosocial systems metatheory. *Journal of Psychotherapy Integration, 18,* 310–349.

Anchin, J. C., & Kiesler, D. J. (Eds.). (1982). *Handbook of interpersonal psychotherapy.* New York, NY: Pergamon Press.

Anchin, J. C., & Magnavita, J. J. (2006). The nature of unified clinical science: Implications for psychotherapeutic theory, practice, training, and research. *Psychotherapy Bulletin, 41*(2), 26–36.

Andrews, J. D. W. (1991). *The active self in psychotherapy.* Boston, MA: Allyn & Bacon.

Bartholomew, K., & Horowitz, L. M. (1991). Attachment styles among young adults: A test of a four-category model. *Journal of Personality and Social Psychology, 61,* 226–244.

Beck, A. T., Freeman, A., & Associates. (2004). *Cognitive therapy of personality disorders* (2nd ed.). New York, NY: Guilford Press.

Belnap, B., Iscan, C., & Plakun, E. M. (2004). Residential treatment of personality disorders: The containing function. In J. J. Magnavita (Ed.), *Handbook of personality disorders: Theory and practice* (pp. 379–397). New York, NY: Wiley.

Benjamin, L. S. (1994). SASB: A bridge between personality theory and clinical psychology. *Psychological Inquiry, 5,* 273–316.

Benjamin, L. S. (1996). *Interpersonal diagnosis and treatment of personality disorders* (2nd ed.). New York, NY: Guilford Press.

Benjamin, L. S. (2000). Use of structural analysis of social behavior for interpersonal diagnosis and treatment in group therapy. In A. P. Beck & C. M. Lewis (Eds.), *The process of group psychotherapy: Systems for analyzing change* (pp. 381–412). Washington, DC: American Psychological Association.

Benjamin, L. S. (2003). *Interpersonal reconstructive therapy: Promoting change in non-responders*. New York, NY: Guilford Press.

Benjamin, L. S. (2005). Addressing interpersonal and intrapsychic components of personality during psychotherapy. In S. Strack (Ed.), *Handbook of personology and psychopathology* (pp. 417–441). Hoboken, NJ: Wiley.

Benjamin, L. S., & Cushing, G. (2004). An interpersonal family-oriented approach to personality disorder. In M. M. MacFarlane (Ed.), *Family treatment of personality disorders: Advances in clinical practice* (pp. 41–69). Binghamton, NY: Haworth Clinical Practice Press.

Benjamin, L. S., & Karpiak, (2002). Personality disorders. In J. C. Norcross (Ed.), *Psychotherapy relationships that work: Therapist contributions and responsiveness to patients* (pp. 423–440). New York, NY: Oxford University Press.

Bernier, B., & Dozier, M. (2002). The client–counselor match and the corrective emotional experience: Evidence from interpersonal and attachment research. *Psychotherapy: Theory, Research, Practice, Training, 39,* 32–43.

Berscheid, E., & Reis, H. T. (1998). Attraction and close relationships. In D. T. Gilbert, , S. T. Fiske, & G. Lindzey (Eds.), *The handbook of social psychology* (4th ed., Vol. 2, pp. 193–281). New York, NY: McGraw-Hill.

Bertolino, B., Kiener, M., & Patterson, R. (2009). *The therapist's notebook on strengths and solution-based therapies*. New York, NY: Routledge.

Binder, J., & Strupp, H. H. (1991). The Vanderbilt approach to time-limited dynamic psychotherapy. In P. Crits-Christoph & J. Barber (Eds.), *Handbook of short-term dynamic psychotherapy* (pp. 137–165). New York, NY: Basic Books.

Bradley, R., Heim, A. K., & Westen, D. (2005). Transference patterns in the psychotherapy of personality disorders: Empirical investigation. *British Journal of Psychiatry, 186,* 342–349.

Cain, N. M., Pincus, A. L., & Ansell, E. B. (2008). Narcissism at the crossroads: Phenotypic description of pathological narcissism across clinical theory, social/personality psychology, and psychiatric diagnosis. *Clinical Psychology Review, 28,* 638–656.

Carson, R. C. (1969). *Interaction concepts of personality*. Chicago, IL: Aldine.

Carson, R. C. (1982). Self-fulfilling prophecy, maladaptive behavior, and psychotherapy. In J. C. Anchin & D. J. Kiesler (Eds.), *Handbook of interpersonal psychotherapy* (pp. 64–77). New York, NY: Pergamon Press.

Cashdan, S. (1982). Interactional psychotherapy: Using the relationship. In J. C. Anchin & D. J. Kiesler (Eds.), *Handbook of interpersonal psychotherapy* (pp. 215–226). New York, NY: Pergamon Press.

Castonguay, L. G., & Beutler, L. E. (2006). Common and unique principles of therapeutic change: What do we know and what do we need to know? In L. G. Castonguay

& L. E. Beutler (Eds.), *Principles of therapeutic change that work* (pp. 353–369). New York, NY: Oxford University Press.

Clairborn, C. D., Goodyear, R. K., & Horner, P. A. (2002). Feedback. In J. C. Norcross (Ed.), *Psychotherapy relationships that work: Therapist contributions and responsiveness to patients* (pp. 217–233). New York, NY: Oxford University Press.

Clarkin, J. F. (2006). Conceptualization and treatment of personality disorders. *Psychotherapy Research, 16,* 1–11.

Clarkin, J. F., & Levy, K. N. (2004). The influence of client variables on psychotherapy. In M. J. Lambert (Ed.), *Bergin and Garfield's handbook of psychotherapy and behavior change* (5th ed., pp. 194–226). New York, NY: Wiley.

Clifton, A., Turkheimer, E., & Oltmanns, T. (2005). Self and peer perspectives on pathological personality traits and interpersonal problems. *Psychological Assessment, 17,* 123–131.

Cottraux, J., & Blackburn, I.-M. (2001). Cognitive therapy. In W. J. Livesley (Ed.), *Handbook of personality disorders: Theory, research, and treatment* (pp. 377–399). New York, NY: Guilford Press.

Critchfield, K. L., & Benjamin, L. S. (2006). Integration of therapeutic factors in treating personality disorders. In L. G. Castonguay & L. E. Beutler (Eds.), *Principles of therapeutic change that work* (pp. 253–271). New York, NY: Oxford University Press.

Critchfield, K. L., & Benjamin, L. S. (2008). Internalized representations of early interpersonal experience and adult relationships: A test of copy process theory in clinical and non-clinical settings. *Psychiatry, 71,* 71–92.

Crits-Christoph, C., & Gibbons, M. B. C. (2002). Relational interpretations. In J. C. Norcross (Ed.), *Psychotherapy relationships that work: Therapist contributions and responsiveness to patients* (pp. 285–300). New York, NY: Oxford University Press.

Darley, J. M., & Fazio, R. H. (1980). Expectancy confirmation processes arising in the social interaction sequence. *American Psychologist, 35,* 867–881.

Dickinson, K. A., & Pincus, A. L. (2003). Interpersonal analysis of grandiose and vulnerable narcissism. *Journal of Personality Disorders, 17,* 188–207.

Dolan-Sewell, R.T., Krueger, R.F., & Shea, M.T. (2001). Co-occurrence with syndrome disorders. In W.J. Livesley (Ed.), *Handbook of personality disorders: Theory, research, and treatment* (pp. 84–104). New York, NY: Guilford Press.

Fernandez-Alvarez, H., Clarkin, J. F., Salgueiro, M. D. C., & Critchfield, K. L. (2006). Participant factors in treating personality disorders. In L. G. Castonguay, & L. E. Beutler (Eds.), *Principles of therapeutic change that work* (pp. 203–218). New York, NY: Oxford University Press.

Foreman, S. A., & Marmar, C. R. (1985). Therapist actions that address initially poor alliances in psychotherapy. *American Journal of Psychiatry, 142,* 922–926.

Frank, K. A. (2002). The "ins and outs" of enactment: A relational bridge for psychotherapy integration. *Journal of Psychotherapy Integration, 12,* 267–286.

Freeman, A., Pretzer, J., Fleming, B., & Simon, K. M. (2004). *Clinical applications of cognitive therapy* (2nd ed.). New York, NY: Kluwer Academic/Plenum Press.

Gelso, C. J., & Hayes, J. A. (2002). The management of countertransference. In J. C. Norcross (Ed.), *Psychotherapy relationships that work: Therapist contributions and responsiveness to patients* (pp. 267–283). New York, NY: Oxford University Press.

Goldfried, M. R., & Davila, J. (2005). The role of relationship and technique in therapeutic change. *Psychotherapy: Theory, Research, Practice, Training, 42,* 421–430.

Greenberg, L. S., & Paivio, S. C. (1997). *Working with emotions in psychotherapy.* New York, NY: Guilford Press.

Greenberg, L. S., Watson, J. C., & Lietaer, G. (Eds.). (1998). *Handbook of experiential psychotherapy.* New York, NY: Guilford Press.

Grossman, R. (2004). Pharmacotherapy of personality disorders. In J. J. Magnavita (Ed.), *Handbook of personality disorders: Theory and practice* (pp. 331–355). New York, NY: Wiley.

Hatcher, R. L., & Barends, A.W. (2006). How a return to theory could help alliance research. *Psychotherapy: Theory, Research, Practice, Training, 43,* 292–299.

Hill, C.E. (2004). *Helping skills: Facilitating, exploration, insight, and action* (2nd ed.). Washington, DC: American Psychological Association.

Hill, C. E., Sim, W., Spangler, P., Stahl, J., Sullivan, C., & Teyber, E. (2008). Therapist immediacy in brief psychotherapy: Case study II. *Psychotherapy: Theory, Research, Practice, Training, 45,* 298–315.

Hooker, C. A. (2008). Interaction and bio-cognitive order. *Synthese, 166,* 513–546. Retrieved from http://www.springerlink.com/content/2p1115hq36696v20/ doi: 10.1007/s11229-008-9374-y

Horowitz, L. M. (2004). *Interpersonal foundations of psychopathology.* Washington, DC: American Psychological Association.

Horowitz, L. M., & Wilson, K. R. (2005). Interpersonal motives and personality disorders. In S. Strack (Ed.), *Handbook of personology and psychopathology* (pp. 495–510). Hoboken, NJ: Wiley.

Jussim, M. (1986). Self-fulfilling prophecies: A theoretical and integrative review. *Psychological Review, 93,* 429–445.

Kaspar, L. B., Hill, C. E., & Kivlighan Jr., D. M. (2008). Therapist immediacy in brief psychotherapy: Case study I. *Psychotherapy: Theory, Research, Practice, Training, 45,* 281–297.

Kernberg, O. F. (1998). Pathological narcissism and narcissistic personality disorder: Theoretical background and diagnostic classification. In E. Ronningstam (Ed.), *Disorders of narcissism: Diagnostic, clinical, and empirical implications* (pp. 29–51). Washington, DC: American Psychiatric Press.

Kiesler, D. J. (1982). Confronting the client–therapist relationship in psychotherapy. In J. C. Anchin & D. J. Kiesler (Eds.), *Handbook of interpersonal psychotherapy* (pp. 274–295). New York, NY: Pergamon Press.

Kiesler, D. J. (1983). The 1982 interpersonal circle: A taxonomy for complementarity in human transactions. *Psychological Review, 90,* 185–214.

Kiesler, D. J. (1988). *Therapeutic metacommunication: Therapist impact disclosure as feedback in psychotherapy*. Palo Alto, CA: Consulting Psychologists Press.

Kiesler, D. J. (1996). *Contemporary interpersonal theory and research: Personality, psychopathology, and psychotherapy*. New York, NY: Wiley.

Leary, T. (1957). *Interpersonal diagnosis of personality*. New York, NY: Ronald Press.

Levenson, H. (2004). Time-limited dynamic psychotherapy. In J. J. Magnavita (Ed.), *Handbook of personality disorders: Theory and practice* (pp. 254–279). New York, NY: Wiley.

Livesley, W. J. (2001). A framework for an integrated approach to treatment. In W. J. Livesley (Ed.), *Handbook of personality disorders: Theory, research, and treatment* (pp. 570–600). New York, NY: Guilford Press.

Locke, K. D. (2006). Interpersonal circumplex measures. In S. Strack (Ed.), *Differentiating normal and abnormal personality* (2nd ed., pp. 383–400). New York, NY: Springer.

Locke, K. D., & Sadler, P. (2007). Self-efficacy, values, and complementarity in dyadic interactions: Integrating interpersonal and social-cognitive theory. *Personality and Social Psychology Bulletin, 33,* 94–109.

MacFarlane, M. M. (Ed.). (2004). *Family treatment of personality disorders*. Binghamton, NY: Haworth Press.

MacKenzie, K. R. (2001). Group psychotherapy. In W. J. Livesley (Ed.), *Handbook of personality disorders: Theory, research, and treatment* (pp. 497–526). New York, NY: Guilford Press.

Magnavita, J. J. (2005). *Personality-guided relational psychotherapy: A unified approach*. Washington, DC: American Psychological Association.

Marcus, D. K., & Buffington-Vollum, J. K. (2005). Countertransference: A social relations perspective. *Journal of Psychotherapy Integration, 15,* 254–283.

McCullough, J. P., Jr. (2005). Cognitive Behavioral Analysis System of Psychotherapy (CBASP) for chronic depression. In J. C. Norcross & M. R. Goldfried (Eds.), *Handbook of psychotherapy integration* (2nd ed., pp. 281–298). New York, NY: Oxford University Press.

McWilliams, N. (2006). Some thoughts about schizoid dynamics. *Psychoanalytic Review, 93,* 1–24.

Millon, T. (2005). Reflections on the future of personology and psychopathology. In S. Strack (Ed.), *Handbook of personology and psychopathology* (pp. 527–546). Hoboken, NJ: Wiley.

Millon, T., & Davis, R. D. (1996). *Disorders of personality: DSM–IV and beyond* (2nd ed.). New York, NY: Wiley.

Newman, M. G., Stiles, W. B, Janeck, A., & Woody, S. R. (2006). Integration of therapeutic factors in anxiety disorders. In L. G. Castonguay & L. E. Beutler (Eds.), *Principles of therapeutic change that work* (pp. 187–200). New York, NY: Oxford University Press.

Norcross, J. C., & Lambert, M. (2005). What should be validated? The therapy relationship. In J. C. Norcross, L. E. Beutler, & R. F. Levant (Eds.), *Evidence-based practices in mental health: Debate and dialogue on the fundamental questions* (pp. 209–218). Washington, DC: American Psychological Association.

Ogrodniczuk, J. S., & Piper, W. E. (2004). Day treatment of personality disorders. In J. J. Magnavita (Ed.), *Handbook of personality disorders: Theory and practice* (pp. 356–378). New York, NY: Wiley.

Paulhus, D. L. (1998). Interpersonal and intrapsychic adaptiveness of trait self-enhancement: A mixed blessing? *Journal of Personality and Social Psychology, 74,* 1197–1208.

Pincus, A. L. (2005a). A contemporary integrative interpersonal theory of personality disorders. In J. Clarkin & M. Lenzenweger (Eds.), *Major theories of personality disorder* (2nd ed., pp. 282–331). New York, NY: Guilford Press.

Pincus, A. L. (2005b). The interpersonal nexus of personality disorders. In S. Strack (Ed.), *Handbook of personology and psychopathology* (pp. 120–139). New York, NY: Wiley.

Pincus, A. L., & Cain, N. M. (2008). Interpersonal psychotherapy. In D. C. S. Richard & S. K. Huprich (Eds.), *Clinical psychology: Assessment, treatment, and research* (pp. 213–245). New York, NY: Academic Press.

Pincus, A. L., & Gurtman, M. B. (1995). The three faces of interpersonal dependency: Structural analyses of self-report dependency measures. *Journal of Personality and Social Psychology, 69,* 744–758.

Pincus, A. L., & Gurtman, M. B. (2006). Interpersonal theory and the interpersonal circumplex: Evolving perspectives on normal and abnormal personality. In S. Strack (Ed.), *Differentiating normal and abnormal personality* (2nd ed., pp. 83–111). New York, NY: Springer.

Pincus, A. L., & Wilson, K. R. (2001). Interpersonal variability in dependent personality. *Journal of Personality, 69,* 223–251.

Reis, H. T., Collins, W. A., & Berscheid, E. (2000). The relationship context of human behavior and development. *Psychological Bulletin, 126,* 844–872.

Rosen, H., & Kuehlwein, K.T. (Eds.). (1996). *Constructing realities: Meaning-making perspectives for psychotherapists.* San Francisco: Jossey-Bass.

Rosenthal, R., & Rubin, D. (1978). Interpersonal expectancy effects: The first 345 studies. *Behavioral and Brain Sciences, 3,* 377–415.

Russell, J. J., Moskowitz, D. S., Zuroff, D. C., Sookman, D., & Paris, J. (2007). Stability and variability of affective experience and interpersonal behavior in borderline personality disorder. *Journal of Abnormal Psychology, 116,* 578–588.

Ryff, C. D., & Singer, B. (1998). The contours of positive human health. *Psychological Inquiry, 9,* 1–28.

Safran, J. D., Muran, J. C., Samstag, L. W., & Stevens, C. (2002). Repairing alliance ruptures. In J. C. Norcross (Ed.), *Psychotherapy relationships that work: Therapist* contributions and responsiveness to patients (pp. 235–254). New York, NY: Oxford University Press.

Safran, J. D., & Segal, Z. V. (1990). *Interpersonal process in cognitive therapy*. New York, NY: Basic Books.

Schauenburg, H., Kuda, M., Sammet, I., & Strack, M. (2000). The influence of interpersonal problems and symptom severity on the duration and outcome of short-term psychodynamic psychotherapy. *Psychotherapy Research, 10,* 133–146.

Siegel, D. J. (1999). *The developing mind: How relationships and the brain interact to shape who we are*. New York, NY: Guilford Press.

Skodol, A., Gunderson, J., McGlashan, T., Dyck, I., Stout, R., Bender, D., . . . Oldham, J. M. (2002). Functional impairment in patients with schizotypal, borderline, avoidant or obsessive-compulsive personality disorder. *American Journal of Psychiatry, 159,* 276–282.

Smith, T. L., Barrett, M. S., Benjamin, L. S., & Barber, J. P. (2006). Relationship factors in treating personality disorders. In L. G. Castonguay & L. E. Beutler (Eds.), *Principles of therapeutic change that work* (pp. 219–238). New York, NY: Oxford University Press.

Sperry, L. (2003). *Handbook of diagnosis and treatment of* DSM–IV–TR *personality disorders* (2nd ed.). New York, NY: Brunner-Routledge.

Steering Committee. (2002). Empirically supported therapy relationships: Conclusions and recommendations of the Division 29 Task Force. In J. C. Norcross (Ed.), *Psychotherapy relationships that work: Therapist contributions and responsiveness to patients* (pp. 441–443). New York, NY: Oxford University Press.

Stiles, W. B., & Wolfe, B. E. (2006). Relationship factors in treating anxiety disorders. In L.G. Castonguay & L. E. Beutler (Eds.), *Principles of therapeutic change that work* (pp. 155–165). New York, NY: Oxford University Press.

Strupp, H. H. (1998). Negative process: Its impact on research, training, and practice. In R. F. Bornstein & J. M. Masling (Eds.), *Empirical studies of psychoanalytic theories: Vol. 8. Empirical studies of the therapeutic hour* (pp. 1–26). Washington, DC: American Psychological Association.

Strupp, H. H., & Binder, J. L. (1984). *Psychotherapy in a new key: A guide to time-limited dynamic psychotherapy*. New York, NY: Basic Books.

Sue, N. (1998). In search of cultural competence in psychotherapy and counseling. *American Psychologist, 53,* 440–448.

Sue, N., & Zane, N. (2005). How well do both evidence-based practices and treatments as usual satisfactorily address the various dimensions of diversity? Ethnic minority populations have been neglected by evidence-based practices. In J. C. Norcross, L. E. Beutler, & R. F. Levant (Eds.), *Evidence-based practices in mental health: Debate and dialogue on the fundamental questions* (pp. 329–337). Washington, DC: American Psychological Association.

Sullivan, H. S. (1953). *The interpersonal theory of psychiatry*. New York, NY: W. W. Norton.

Sullivan, H. S. (1954). *The psychiatric interview*. New York, NY: W. W. Norton.

Swann, W. B., Jr., Rentfrow, P. J., & Guinn, J. S. (2003). Self-verification: The search for coherence. In M. R. Leary & J. P. Tangney (Eds.), *Handbook of self and identity* (pp. 367–383). New York, NY: Guilford Press.

Tasca, G. A., & McMullen, L. M. (1992). Interpersonal complementarity and antitheses within a stage model of psychotherapy. *Psychotherapy: Theory, Research, Practice, Training, 29*, 515–523.

Thompson, R., & Zuroff, D. C. (1998). Dependent and self-critical mothers' responses to adolescent autonomy and competence. *Personality and Individual Differences, 24*, 311–324.

Tracey, T. J., & Ray, P. B. (1984). Stages of successful time-limited counseling: An interactional examination. *Journal of Counseling Psychology, 31*, 13–27.

Wachtel, P. L. (1982). Interpersonal therapy and active intervention. In J. C. Anchin & D. J. Kiesler (Eds.), *Handbook of interpersonal psychotherapy* (pp. 46–63). New York, NY: Pergamon Press.

Wagner, C. C., Riley, W. T., Schmidt, J. A., McCormick, M. G., & Butler, S. F. (1999). Personality disorder styles and reciprocal interpersonal impacts during outpatient intake interviews. *Psychotherapy Research, 9*, 216–231.

Westen, D., & Heim, A. K. (2003). Disturbances of self and identity in personality disorders. In M. R. Leary & J. P. Tangney (Eds.), *Handbook of self and identity* (pp. 643–664). New York, NY: Guilford Press.

Westen, D., Nakash, O., Thomas, C., & Bradley, R. (2006). Clinical assessment of attachment patterns and personality disorder in adolescents and adults. *Journal of Consulting and Clinical Psychology, 74*, 1065–1085.

Wiggins, J. S. (1996). An informal history of the interpersonal circumplex tradition. *Journal of Personality Assessment, 66*, 217–233.

Wiggins, J. S. (2003). *Paradigms of personality assessment*. New York, NY: Guilford Press.

Young, D., & Beier, E. (1982). Being asocial in social places: Giving the client a new experience. In J. C. Anchin & D. J. Kiesler (Eds.), *Handbook of interpersonal psychotherapy* (pp. 262–273). New York, NY: Pergamon Press.

Young, J. E. (1999). *Cognitive therapy for personality disorders: A schema-focused approach* (3rd ed.). Sarasota, FL: Professional Resource Press.

Young, J. E., Klesko, J. S., & Weishaar, M. E. (2003). *Schema therapy: A practitioner's guide*. New York, NY: Guilford Press.

Zane, N., Hall, G. C. N., Sue, S., Young, K., & Nunez, J. (2004). Research on psychotherapy with culturally diverse populations. In M. J. Lambert (Ed.), *Bergin and Garfield's handbook of psychotherapy and behavior change* (5th ed., pp. 767–804). New York, NY: Wiley.

6

A RELATIONAL APPROACH TO THE TREATMENT OF PERSONALITY DYSFUNCTION

J. CHRISTOPHER MURAN, CATHERINE EUBANKS-CARTER, AND JEREMY D. SAFRAN

Our relational approach to psychotherapy focuses on negotiating ruptures—disagreements and deteriorations—in the therapeutic alliance (Safran & Muran, 2000). This model has been informed by our research on identifying ruptures in the alliance and developing models of their resolution (e.g., Safran & Muran, 1996). We have defined *ruptures* as dysfluencies in relatedness, as markers of vicious cycles or enactments involving the unwitting participation of both client and therapist, and as ubiquitous phenomena that represent windows into the relational world of the client (as well as that of the therapist). We have defined *rupture resolutions*—efforts to address and repair alliance ruptures—as critical change events in the psychotherapy process. Our specific aim in these efforts has been to develop metatherapeutic strategies for negotiating the therapeutic alliance, that is, strategies that at once are informed by, as well as inform, many therapeutic traditions.

In the process of pursuing this metatherapeutic initiative, Safran and Muran (2000) developed a short-term psychotherapy treatment model identified as *brief relational therapy* (BRT). The development of this model has taken place primarily in the Brief Psychotherapy Research Program at Beth Israel Medical Center in New York City, where it has been evaluated on a sample of individuals with personality disorders (PDs). In addition to being informed by results from our rupture resolution research (Safran & Moran, 1996), the BRT model is also based to a great extent on principles and techniques associated with relational psychoanalysis and, to a lesser extent, on principles and techniques associated with cognitive (see Safran & Segal, 1990) and humanistic–experiential psychotherapies (see Greenberg, Watson, & Lietaer, 1998).

The BRT model is founded on a two-person psychology and a social constructivist epistemology (see Safran & Muran, 2000). It involves an ongoing collaborative exploration of both clients' and therapists' immediate experiences in the therapeutic relationship. What distinguishes the BRT model from other short-term dynamic models is that it eschews the establishment of a case formulation during the first phase of treatment, replacing a *content* focus with a *process* focus. The emphasis in BRT is on developing a generalizable skill of mindfulness rather than on gaining insight into and mastering a particular core theme. It makes extensive use of therapeutic *metacommunication*, or communication about the communication process (defined further later in this chapter), as a form of mindfulness in action.

THEORETICAL UNDERPINNINGS AND ASSUMPTIONS

Essential Theoretical Constructs

We have found a conceptualization of the therapeutic alliance along the lines that Bordin (1979) suggested to be useful in our work (see, e.g., Safran & Muran, 2000). Bordin defined the alliance as comprising three interdependent factors: the agreement between client and therapist on the (a) *tasks* and (b) *goals* of treatment as well as (c) the *affective bond* between client and therapist. This definition highlights the interdependence of relational and technical factors: It suggests that the meaning of technical factors can be understood only in the relational context in which they are applied. It also highlights the importance of negotiation between client and therapist on the tasks and goals of therapy, which is consistent with an increasingly influential way of conceptualizing the psychotherapy process as one involving the negotiation between the client's desires or needs and those of the therapist (see Mitchell & Aron, 1999).

Clients and therapists are always embedded in a *relational matrix* (Mitchell, 1988) that is shaped, moment to moment, by their implicit needs and desires. Ruptures in the therapeutic alliance mark when there is a tension between the client's and therapist's respective desires (see Safran & Muran, 2000). Ruptures indicate vicious cycles or enactments that can be unduly driven by one participant's dysfunctional *relational schemas*. Relational schemas shape a person's perceptions of the world, leading to cognitive processes and interpersonal behaviors that in turn shape the environment in a way that confirms the representational content of the schemas. To the extent that relational schemas are limited in scope of internalized interpersonal experiences, they will restrict the range of interpersonal behaviors, which pull for similar responses from a range of different people, resulting in redundant patterns of interaction. Thus, they limit the possibility of new interpersonal experiences and form the basis of personality dysfunction. Ruptures also invariably involve the unwitting participation of the other member of the dyad. Ruptures are inevitable events and are viewed not as obstacles to overcome but as opportunities for therapeutic change. They can be understood as windows into the relational worlds of both the client and therapist and thus as opportunities for expanded awareness and new relational experiences.

Ruptures can be organized into two main subtypes: (a) *withdrawal ruptures* and (b) *confrontation ruptures* (Harper, 1989a, 1989b). In withdrawal ruptures, clients withdraw from the therapist (e.g., through long silences) or from their own experience (e.g., by denying their emotions or by being overly deferential to the therapist's wishes). In confrontation ruptures, clients move against the therapist, either by expressing anger or dissatisfaction (e.g., complaining about the therapist or the treatment) or by trying to control the therapist (e.g., telling the therapist what to do). These markers can be understood as reflecting different ways of coping with the dialectical tension between the need for self-definition versus the need for relatedness: Withdrawal ruptures mark the pursuit of relatedness at the expense of the need for self-definition; confrontation ruptures mark the expression of self-definition at the expense of relatedness.

Mechanisms of Change

Change is essentially understood as involving the two parallel processes of (a) increasing immediate awareness of self and other and (b) providing a new interpersonal experience. Increasing immediate awareness begins with attending more closely to the details of experience at a molecular level. The client starts to develop a sense of the choices he or she is making on a moment-by-moment basis. With greater awareness of how he or she constructs his or her experience, the client develops an increased sense of responsibility and agency. This change process does not simply suggest a correction of a distorted interpersonal schema; instead, increasing the client's immediate awareness of the processes that mediate a dysfunctional interpersonal pattern leads to an elaboration and clarification of the client's self: in other words, expanded awareness of who one is in a particular interpersonal transaction. The clarification of the client's self invariably involves greater clarification of the therapist's self as well.

Following our relational understanding of the role of increased immediate awareness in the change process, we have identified a specific mechanism of change: *decentering*, which consists of inviting the client to observe his or her contribution to a rupture or enactment in the relational matrix of the therapeutic relationship. We find the notion of mindfulness to be particularly useful in this regard. A primary task for therapists is to direct clients' attention to various aspects of their inner and outer worlds as they are occurring. This attention promotes the type of awareness discussed earlier that de-automates habitual patterns and helps clients experience themselves as agents in the process of constructing reality rather than as passive victims of circumstances. We also believe that the principle of metacommunication captures the spirit of this type of collaborative exploration and the essence of what we mean by *decentering*. Metacommunication involves an attempt to disembed from the interpersonal claim that is being enacted by taking the current interaction as the focus of communication. It is an attempt to bring awareness to bear on the relational matrix as it unfolds.

It is also important to recognize that the psychotherapeutic process is not only discovery oriented but also constructive (Mitchell, 1993). Operating in parallel with the process of increasing immediate awareness, the constructive process of psychotherapy helps to bring about change by providing the client with a new interpersonal experience. In this regard, we have identified another specific mechanism of change: the *disconfirmation* of the client's maladaptive relational schema through the new interpersonal experience in the therapeutic interaction. By disembedding from a relational matrix, the therapist can provide opportunities for new learning. In practice, metacommunication about the therapeutic relationship plays a central role in facilitating the process of experiential disconfirmation in addition to that of decentering.

Domains of Operation Within the Total Ecological System

By increasing awareness of self and other and providing a new interpersonal experience, the relational approach operates in both the intrapsychic–biological and interpersonal–dyadic domains. Through this parallel focus, BRT seeks to achieve change in both dimensions. In the context of a new kind of relational experience with the therapist, the client becomes more aware and accepting of his or her intrapsychic experience as well as his or her characteristic ways of engaging in interpersonal–dyadic interactions. By expanding his or her awareness, the client becomes better able to recognize, challenge, and change self-defeating ways of thinking, feeling, and relating. This process of self-expansion also occurs for the therapist.

Process of Therapy

BRT consists of 30 weekly, 45-minute sessions. At the beginning of treatment, the therapist explains the rationale of the approach and tries to establish reasonable expectations for a short-term treatment. The therapist explains that the goal is not to "cure" the client but rather to cultivate a new skill of awareness and to examine what happens in the therapeutic relationship because that can shed light on the client's core relational themes. The therapist may provide the client with reading material or lead the client in a mindfulness task to demonstrate the concept of nonjudgmental awareness.

Over the course of treatment, the therapist and the client collaborate to determine the focus of each session. The therapist expresses curiosity about the client's inner experience and draws the client's attention to moments when the client seems to be avoiding or defending against certain emotional states. The therapist moves back and forth between *content* and *process*, that is, between what the client says and how he or she says it. The therapist remains alert to the client's experience and to his or her own experience. Through this close attention the therapist seeks to identify ruptures in the alliance when they occur and to address them in a nondefensive manner, as we describe in greater detail later in this chapter.

The end of treatment is the ultimate rupture. As the 30-session mark nears, the therapist must be especially sensitive to any indication of the client's feelings regarding separation and loss. The therapist also maintains awareness of his or her own reaction to the upcoming termination. In particular, the therapist seeks to recognize his or her limitations as a clinician and to accept what he or she was and was not able to accomplish during the treatment.

RELATIONAL CONSIDERATIONS

Despite the intrinsically relational nature of our approach, in this section we consider a number of specific factors that have important relational implications.

Alliance Factors Related to Process and Outcome

Because the BRT model is focused on exploring and resolving ruptures in the alliance, all of the techniques in BRT can be understood to be alliance factors. We describe these techniques in greater detail later in this chapter. At this point, we would like to underscore how our focus on ruptures is informed by research on the alliance. There is a strong consensus in the research literature that the quality of the alliance predicts outcome and that weakened alliances are correlated with unilateral termination by the client (Horvath & Bedi, 2002; Martin, Garske, & Davis, 2000). We and our colleagues have found ruptures to be highly prevalent events, occurring in 25% to 50% of sessions as reported by clients, and their resolution to be related to good outcome (Muran et al., 2009). There is also research on client-rated alliance across time that identifies V-shaped rupture–repair sequences that are related to positive outcome (Stiles et al., 2004; Strauss et al., 2006).

BRT focuses on maximizing the quality of the alliance by recognizing and addressing alliance ruptures. Several studies have found evidence that such attention to alliance ruptures may play an important role in successful treatment (Eubanks-Carter, Muran, & Safran, in press; Safran et al., 2001). Our research group has used a task analytic procedure to test a model of rupture resolution: In a series of small-scale studies, Safran and Muran (1996) confirmed that addressing alliance ruptures in a manner consistent with our model facilitated rupture resolution.

Client Characteristics Related to Process and Outcome

Research on client characteristics related to process and outcome in BRT is currently underway. On the basis of studies of interpersonal process in other treatments, we would predict that clients with significant interpersonal problems would have more difficulty developing a good alliance with the therapist in this interpersonally focused treatment. In particular, clients with a tendency toward hostile, dominant interpersonal behaviors, which are characteristic of Cluster B PDs, might have difficulty establishing a good alliance, as Muran, Segal, Samstag, and Crawford (1994) found in their study of short-term cognitive therapy. It is interesting to note that this study also found that submissive interpersonal problems, which are characteristic of the Cluster C PDs, positively predicted aspects of the alliance. As we discuss later in this chapter, research on BRT to date has been conducted primarily with clients who have Cluster C diagnoses.

Therapist Characteristics Related to Process and Outcome

Our relational model emphasizes the importance of the therapist being sensitive to the presence of ruptures and capable of managing his or her internal experience. Training in BRT specifically focuses on the development of the following therapist skills: mindfulness, emotion regulation, and interpersonal sensitivity. This emphasis is informed by research on emotional regulation in dyadic interactions (e.g., Tronick, 1989) and studies demonstrating therapist involvement in negative interpersonal process (e.g., Henry, Schacht, & Strupp, 1986).

Racial and Cultural Factors and Considerations

The process of paying close attention to the client's and the therapist's experience should bring racial and cultural identities and prejudices into awareness and clarify how both the client and the therapist define themselves and others. Safran and Muran (2000) discussed the psychotherapeutic process in terms of ongoing power plays between client and therapist toward mutual recognition. This negotiation process should be understood not only in terms of the power imbalance between client and therapist but also in terms of the power inequalities associated with race and culture (including gender and sexuality), which shape the inevitable struggle between client and therapist (Muran, 2007). The impact of race and culture on the therapeutic relationship, however, has been empirically understudied.

TECHNIQUES AND METHODS OF TREATMENT

As noted earlier, the BRT model conceptualizes change as occurring through the process of decentering, or increasing awareness, and the process of disconfirmation, whereby the client has a new interpersonal experience with the therapist that challenges the client's existing interpersonal schemas. The methods for achieving these changes are to draw the client's attention to aspects of his or her experience that he or she is avoiding or disowning while maintaining a validating and empathic stance that provides a corrective emotional experience for the client. In particular, the therapist pays close attention to ruptures in the alliance, highlighting them when they occur and encouraging the client to explore them. The therapist draws on his or her own experience of the relationship, and his or her sense of being connected to or disconnected from the client, as a guide for identifying therapeutic impasses. When the therapist feels disconnected, this is a sign that the client may be withdrawing from the interaction or may not be in contact with his or her own inner experience.

Basic Technical Principles

First introduced to the psychotherapeutic situation by Kiesler (1996), the principle of metacommunication is an approach that fits the relational formulations presented earlier especially well. In very simple terms, *metacommunication* means communicating about the communication. It is predicated on the idea that we are in constant communication—that all behavior in an interpersonal situation has message value and thus involves communication. Metacommunication describes an attempt to increase awareness of each person's role in an interaction by stepping out of the interaction and communicating directly about what is taking place between the client and therapist (Safran & Muran, 2000).

Efforts at metacommunication attempt to minimize the degree of inference and are grounded as much as possible in the therapist's immediate experience of some aspect of the therapeutic relationship—either the therapist's own feelings or an immediate perception of some aspect of the client's actions. Because it is based on a two-person psychology, and a social constructivist epistemology, the therapist's participation is considered in the frame of the lens. Therapists' understanding of themselves and their clients is always partial; evolving; and embedded in the complex, interactive, patient–therapist matrix (Hoffman, 1998; Mitchell, 1993; Stern, 1997). Metacommunication is the effort to look back at a recently unfolded relational process from a different vantage point; however, "because we are always caught in the grip of the field, the upshot for clinical purposes is that we face the endless task of trying to see the field and climb out of it—and into another one, for there is nowhere else to go" (Stern, 1997, p. 158).

The following list includes some basic principles that we have found useful in our efforts to metacommunicate with clients. (For more detailed descriptions of these and other principles, see Safran & Muran, 2000.)

- *Invite a collaborative inquiry and establish a climate of shared dilemma.* Clients often feel alone during a rupture. Frame the impasse as a shared dilemma that you and the client will explore collaboratively; acknowledge that "we are stuck together." Communicate observations in a tentative, exploratory manner that signals your openness to client input. In this way, instead of being yet one more in an endless succession of figures who do not understand the client's struggle, you can become an ally who joins the client.
- *Keep the focus on the immediate and privilege awareness over change.* The focus should be on the here and now of the therapeutic relationship rather than on events in prior sessions or even earlier in the same session. In addition, keep the focus on the concrete and specific rather than abstract, intellectualized speculation. A specific, immediate focus helps clients become more mindful of their own experience. The goal is not to change the client's experience but to increase the client's awareness of his or her experience, because awareness is the necessary precursor to lasting change.
- *Emphasize your own subjectivity and be open to exploring your own contribution.* All metacommunications should emphasize the subjectivity of the therapist's perception. This helps establish a

collaborative, egalitarian environment in which the client feels free to decide how to make use of the therapist's observation. In addition, therapists should be open to exploring their contributions to the interaction with the client in a nondefensive manner. This process can help clients become more aware of feelings that they have but are unable to clearly articulate, in part because they fear the therapist's response. Accepting responsibility for one's contributions can validate clients' experience of the interaction and help them to trust their own judgment. Increasing clients' confidence in their judgment helps to decrease their need for defensiveness, which facilitates their exploration and acknowledgment of their own contribution to the interaction.

Metacommunication is a valuable technique for exploring core relational themes. The process of metacommunication can begin with questions or observations that focus the client's attention on different aspects of the client–therapist interaction. The therapist might start by focusing the client's attention on his or her own experience with a direct question such as "What are you feeling right now?" or with an observation about the client's self-state, such as "You seem anxious to me right now. Am I reading you right?" To direct attention to the interpersonal field, the therapist might ask "What's going on here between us?" or offer an observation about the interaction, such as "It seems like we're in some kind of dance. Does that fit with your sense?" A third potential avenue for metacommunication is to focus on the therapist's experience by asking a question that encourages the client to be curious about the therapist's self-state: "Do you have any thoughts about what might be going on for me right now?" Alternatively, the therapist could make a self-disclosure about his or her internal experience, such as "I'm aware of feeling defensive right now." It is important to bear in mind that these three foci represent parallel dimensions.

Clinical Case Process of Rupture Resolution

In addition to metacommunication, a number of other interventions can be applied to problems related to the tasks and goals of therapy and the affective bond between client and therapist. In this section, we present a taxonomy of rupture resolution interventions (see Figure 6.1). The strategies in the taxonomy are organized according to whether they address the rupture in a direct manner or whether they take an indirect approach to resolving the rupture. We begin with interventions that operate at a more surface level and then proceed to interventions, including metacommunication, that focus in more depth at the level of underlying meaning.

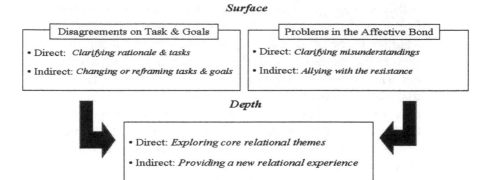

Figure 6.1. A taxonomy of rupture resolution interventions.

Surface-Level Strategies

Disagreements on Tasks and Goals

INDIRECT RESOLUTION STRATEGY: CHANGE OR REFRAME TASKS AND GOALS. The therapist may respond to the client's dissatisfaction with therapy tasks and goals by changing or reframing them, or the therapist may reframe the meaning of therapy tasks or goals by describing them in a way that is more appealing to the client. It is important that this intervention not be delivered in a manipulative way. The therapist must believe that the reframe is another valid way of understanding the task or goal, rather than a white lie. The following dialogue is a clinical case example of reframing tasks:

> *Client (C):* I tried doing that breathing exercise we practiced in session, and I really don't see the point of it. I know you said that it's important to become more aware of how I'm feeling, but I think I'm already pretty aware of the fact that I'm stressed out.

> *Therapist (T):* You know, another way to think about a mindfulness exercise is that it is a chance to take a break from all that stress. For just a minute, you can stop all that activity, all that running around, and just be.

Direct Resolution Strategy: Clarify Rationale and Tasks. The therapist also can outline or reiterate a rationale for treatment, or he or she can illustrate a therapy task. In the exchange that follows, the therapist clarifies to the client the rationale and tasks of therapy:

> *T:* As a result of learning experiences in relationships, people develop self-defeating ways of perceiving things and relating to other people. An important goal of this ther-

apy is to help you become aware of these self-defeating ways of being.

C: I don't understand how this will help me change.

T: Many of these self-defeating ways of being operate at an automatic or unconscious level. As you become more aware of these patterns, you will be able to choose to respond to situations differently.

Problems Associated With the Affective Bond

INDIRECT RESOLUTION STRATEGY: ALLY WITH THE RESISTANCE. With indirect resolutions strategies the therapist does not challenge the client's defensive behaviors but rather validates the ways in which they are adaptive and understandable. Allying with, rather than challenging, the resistance can help clients access aspects of their experience that they have been avoiding, as in the following example.

The patient starts to cry in session, and then becomes self-conscious and says that she is being melodramatic. She begins to talk about her situation in a more distant, intellectualized fashion:

T: Just be aware for a moment of whether you're in contact with your pain or more distant from it right now.

C: I'm more distant.

T: Uh huh . . . so that's OK, and perhaps it's adaptive for you to have some distance from it right now—as long as you're able to be aware of the way in which your talking about it helps you to distance from that immediate experience of a few moments back.

DIRECT RESOLUTION STRATEGY: CLARIFY MISUNDERSTANDINGS. In an open, nondefensive manner, the therapist directly addresses misunderstandings that have led to tension or strain in the relationship with the client:

C: I saw you looking at your watch. Am I that boring?

T: Oh, no, quite the contrary. Last time I was so interested in what we were talking about that I lost track of time and we ran over. I just wanted to make sure that we still had some time left, and I was happy to see that we do.

Depth-Level Strategies

INDIRECT RESOLUTION STRATEGY: PROVIDE A NEW RELATIONAL EXPERIENCE. With this indirect strategy, the therapist addresses problems in the bond by behaving in a way that disconfirms the client's maladaptive relational schema. It is important to note that the surface strategies described earlier can also serve to provide a new relational experience and thus disconfirm a patient's schema. The following is a clinical case example of providing a new relational experience:

> A patient, who was abused and neglected as a child, tells the therapist that she needs more guidance and direction. She also reports feeling uncomfortable and mistrusting because the therapist self-discloses little about himself. The therapist begins to experiment with being more active, providing advice, and being more self-disclosing because he hypothesizes that the client has been experiencing his reserve as withholding and abandoning. He observes that his efforts seem to free the client to talk more openly about herself.

DIRECT RESOLUTION STRATEGY: EXPLORE CORE RELATIONAL THEMES. Exploring strains in the bond can lead to exploration of the client's characteristic ways of experiencing and engaging in interpersonal relationships. It is important to note, however, that premature attempts to explore relational themes via transference interpretations can elicit client defensiveness and obstruct further exploration.

Our research program has particularly focused on resolving ruptures directly at a depth level by exploring core relationship themes using metacommunication as the critical intervention. Our ultimate goal is to capture the various processes involved in the resolution of ruptures, not to develop prescriptives but instead to sensitize clinicians to patterns that are likely to occur and to facilitate their abilities to respond. Figure 6.2 depicts a stage process model of rupture resolution that begins with Stage 1, in which the therapist attempts to attend to a rupture marker. The critical task here for the therapist is to recognize the rupture and try to disembed by inviting an exploration of the rupture event. Stage 2 involves exploring the rupture and unpacking nuances of client and therapist perceptions. The progression in rupture resolution typically involves moving toward clarifying the underlying wish or need (Stage 4): With withdrawal, it is a movement from qualified to clearer expressions of self-assertion; with confrontations it is a movement from exploring how the client perceives the interaction, through acknowledging feelings of hurt and disappointment, to contacting vulnerability and the wish to be nurtured. The essential task for the therapist in either case is to facilitate these movements in any way, by empathizing and validating, remaining open and nondefensive, and taking responsibility where appropriate. Throughout this progression, there are often shifts away: Stage 3 involves the exploration of such avoidances maneuvers and their function.

Resolution of Withdrawal

As noted earlier, in withdrawal ruptures the client withdraws from the therapist (withdrawal from other) or from his or her own experience

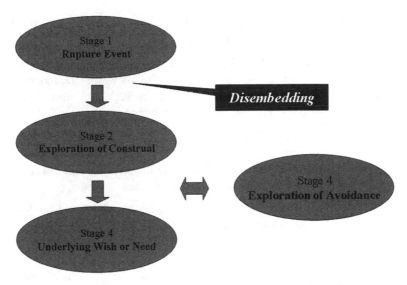

Figure 6.2. A rupture resolution model for exploring core relational themes.

(withdrawal from self). A withdrawal rupture can be very subtle; for example, the client may seem to be complying with the therapist with respect to a therapy task but behaves in an overly deferential way that suggests that the client is not in contact with his or her true feelings about the task. This kind of appeasement is indicative of a pseudoalliance rather than a truly genuine and collaborative interaction. When clients withdraw, they are prioritizing their need for relatedness at the expense of their need for agency. The process of resolving withdrawal ruptures involves exploring the interpersonal fears, expectations, and internalized criticisms that are hindering the client from directly expressing his or her negative feelings. The goal is to help clients assert their true feelings and underlying wishes.

The withdrawal resolution process we present next includes a clinical example drawn from a treatment with a client who presented with bouts of anxiety and depression and with "problems in contacting, relating, and responding to others" that had debilitated him in his marriage and his work. In this session, the therapist attempted to focus the client on a self-critical state, which emerged in an exploration of his anger toward his very critical wife. What ensued was a vicious cycle in which the client responded in cryptic ways, which frustrated and confused the therapist and led to a torturous game of cat and mouse.

In the following exchange, the client's vulnerability—his need for contact or nurturance underlying his aggression—emerges:

C: Essentially, I have such a low self-esteem that I don't even pursue something basic to my well-being like getting a new portfolio to show my work in. I mean, I feel like I've deteriorated over the years.

T: Let me ask you to try a little exercise that's sort of different from what we did last time. I'd like you to play your really critical side. What would you say to yourself right now strictly from your critical side.

C: This is difficult. When you ask me to do something like this, I feel so hopeful . . . It sort of triggers hope . . .

T: It triggers hope?

C: Not just to be obstinate perhaps, or just to be, I don't know . . . It's often . . . I don't know why, exactly.

T: What do you mean, "obstinate?"

C: It . . . Why would I say that? Because I can't figure out why I close my eyes and feel immediately hopeful rather than feeling, uh, filled with despair. I don't know why that's the case. Why am I smiling now instead of weeping now? I don't know why. I mean it's a certain, there's a certain, it's weird that I feel the opposite feeling other than what you asked me to feel . . .

The client and therapist move increasingly further away from the original task. The client continues to associate to other feelings and memories, and the therapist tries to understand what he means. Finally, the client shifts into a hopeless state regarding his life situation, and the therapist becomes aware of their cooperative movement away from the original task and disembeds from this matrix by attending to the rupture marker, refocusing attention on their immediate communication process:

C: You know, I had jokingly mentioned Dale Carnegie, or something like that, just to learn skills of presentation, might be superficial but, uh, but in conjunction perhaps with a deeper emotional restructuring of my self-esteem, some, some cosmetic, and superficial techniques might be useful as well. I just took my son to karate last night and was looking at the catalogue for the 92nd Street Y, which has courses about oh, techniques for interviews, you know. Make yourself, you know, look great. Would that be useful, do you think, I mean would that be?

T: Well, I don't mean to ignore your question, but I'm also aware that we really shifted away from what we were doing, and I'm wondering if you're aware of what happened or how that happened?

C: Trying to put a good face on things, I guess.

The client begins to explore why he needs to put "a good face on things," which leads him to reveal his negative sentiments about the usefulness of the therapist's attempts to focus him on a self-critical state, specifically, on dwelling on the negative. The therapist in turn tries to facilitate a more assertive expression of the client's objection to focusing on his self-criticism.

C: I'm not quite clear on how dwelling on this negative image is going to, and really dwelling on it, is really going to lead toward, I guess, a more positive outcome eventually.

T: So that doesn't seem very constructive to dwell on the negative.

C: I guess so.

T: So you have some misgivings about actually doing this exercise.

C: Misgivings, I guess, maybe, a little bit, you know, maybe, I guess so, that's part of it.

T: Can you express that to me in a more direct fashion?

C: I think I was a few weeks ago, a few sessions ago, talking about, oh examining, these, what were they? Negative? I forget what it is. I started to get really negative about it over the week or so. I felt very depressed over it, over that length of time. I think I was thinking a lot about my family and how that really influenced the basic way that I look at myself and the world. And just dwelling on that, on something I thought was dealt with and behind me years ago, which was quite, you know, very painful, very painful, for me until about 20 years ago when I began to be more dependent upon myself emotionally, rather than on my parents.

T: Uh-huh.

C: It was the center of the pain in my life, I think this horrible relationship between my parents. Ah, um, and don't think I covered it up really because I dealt with it and talked about it with friends a lot and so forth, and really finally felt that's their problem. I've gone beyond that now. It was a big process to get to that point, and it wasn't just swept under the rug, I don't think. I think it was, was really dealt with. I think people evolve certainly, and there's still a, no doubt, that it's a big part of my basic structure of my upbringing, life, personality, and framework, emotional framework. And it might be worth considering again. It probably is, but, but that was my reaction to it. It felt, felt like I've dealt with this before.

T: "Why am I doing this?"

C: Why am I doing it again?

T: Yeah, you don't see any benefit. You just see pain, by doing this.

C: Yeah, I feel like I'm sort of stirring up things that were painful. At that time there was, ah, some resolution by being able to feel that I was getting stronger emotionally, being on my own more emotionally, having the ability to have the courage to ask girls for dates at that time, and so forth. I felt that was, you know, really important stuff that I was doing at that time.

T: So in the same sense this exercise here doesn't seem useful to you, apparently.

C: Well, I'm not sure if it feels use . . . ah . . .

T: The costs seem to outweigh the benefits?

C: It's more, kind of, you know, talking about the reluctance or inability to get into that mode seems more like a blank wall. I mean, when I closed my eyes I didn't see black, I saw sort of, like a blank wall in front of me. I mean it was like a real, real presence. I don't know what it necessarily represents. So, ah, but there's no doubt I feel overwhelmed by these feelings.

T: I'm sort of confused, because on one hand I get the sense that there's a part of you that doesn't want to do this, but then I got kind of lost in terms of that, so I don't know. Can you clarify that?

Although he has expressed some of his negative sentiments, the client is still somewhat equivocal and unclear. He has admitted that he can still feel overwhelmed by negative feelings, suggesting a recognition that there may be a value to focusing on them. This confuses the therapist, who once more encourages a more assertive expression on the part of the client.

C: There's a part of me that doesn't want to do it. It's not an easy explanation of what that, that is. I just don't see it as useful to me. It doesn't to seem to me a helpful direction to go in.

T: How does it feel to actually say that to me?

By this question, the therapist demonstrates not only his receptivity to the assertion but also his awareness of the anxieties that made its expression so painstakingly difficult. This leads to an exploration of the client's avoidance of exploring the rupture experience:

C: Awful. [*Laughs*] I feel awful about accusing you of something like that. Suggesting to you that you didn't know what you were or whatever. And it just . . . I'm sorry I said it [*Laughing*].

T: So you're feeling apologetic and uncomfortable with saying, "I didn't find that useful?"

C: Yes, uh-huh. And I feel like sitting here for the next 10 minutes saying I'm sorry, you know [*Laughing*]. [*Long pause*] I feel so uncomfortable saying that. I could see you could see I was avoiding saying it.

T: Right, yeah.

C: [*Pause*]. And that makes me then . . . I ask myself how can I get a job when my, I'm, you know, when it's so obvious what I'm saying . . .

C: Now it sounds like you're turning self-critical. What just happened?

C: Mm-hmm. [*Long pause*] I guess I feel pathetic, and, and you must think I'm pathetic.

The preceding segment illustrates the complexity of the client's anxious world, including his fear of the condemnation of others as well as his use of self-criticism as a preemptive strike against himself. Here, the therapist facilitated the client's awareness of the anxieties that drove his avoidant operations. In this particular resolution process the avoidance stage emerged on the heels of the self-assertion stage. Although one often sees an oscillation back and forth between qualified assertion and avoidance, it is also not unusual to have a resolution process without avoidance or, in this case, to have it emerge after self-assertion. Exploring avoidance is critical for clarifying the client's underlying construal processes and understanding his or her representational world.

Resolution of Confrontation

In a confrontation rupture, the client moves against the therapist. Confrontation ruptures can be very difficult for therapists to endure because they may arouse feelings of anger, impotence, and even despair. The client may express anger or dissatisfaction by complaining about the therapist's competence or about different aspects of the therapy. In a confrontation, the client favors the need for agency over the need for relatedness. The resolution process for confrontation ruptures involves exploring the fears and self-criticisms that are interfering with the client's expression of underlying needs and helping the client to express more vulnerable feelings. Sometimes confrontations are mixed with withdrawal, and in such instances the resolution process begins much like the withdrawal resolution process, whereby the therapist's task is to get the client to stand by his or her anger. What follows is an illustration of confrontation resolution with a clinical example drawn from the same case used earlier to illustrate withdrawal rupture resolution. In this case, the client has moved against the therapist in a confrontation rupture:

> C: I was thinking about our session last week. As I've been thinking about that on and off, it just seems . . . I felt that that session was kind of—wasn't as useful to me as I had wanted it to be. I had wanted to talk about the business meeting that I attended, because I felt that it was really something important that I wanted to discuss—I thought it was really sort of emblematic of a lot of situations that I feel are difficult for me, that really hold me back from doing the things that I really need to do to make a living. But you kept bringing it back to talking about what was going on between the two of us. I mean, I guess you were trying to create some sort of confrontation here or something, I don't know what you were trying to do. So that's . . . I feel a little angry about it almost, perhaps, I don't know, a little frustrated, and so that's, I guess, one of the feelings . . . That's the sort of . . . I mean not that I've been thinking a lot about it, but I think that's something that's—that's really the only thing to pin my thoughts on, I guess, for the past week and a half. But last week was so involved with—the big thing was that I had this disagreement with my wife . . . [*Launches into an account of an argument with his wife*]

After listening to the client's story about his wife for a few minutes, the therapist gently interjects and seeks to draw the client's attention to, and help him stand by, his complaint about the therapist.

> T: Actually, I'm feeling kind of torn right now because I'm thinking—I mean I'm sort of struck by some of the similarities in the scenario you're describing, where your wife is sort of pre-empting your opinions and cutting you off, and I'm seeing some similarities to what was going on

between you and me in our last session. But I'm a little hesitant to suggest that we shift the focus onto our interaction, because I don't want to push something on you again.

C: No, you can . . . I'll continue with that if you like.

T: Well, do you sort of see similarities in that?

C: Well, sure. I think things eventually get imposed on me and then I just want to kind of stop opposing it and just sort of submit to whatever somebody else wants to do.

The therapist tries to help the client unpack his perception of the interaction, to put his experience into words through an exploration of construal processes.

T: Right. But what about in terms of what's going on between us? Was there a sense that I was imposing something on you?

C: Yes, yes. I really had a sense that you were imposing something in a situation that was sort of, in a way—well, I felt that it was taking away from the positive dynamics that had been already established in our relationship.

T: Right.

C: And I felt that the more I began to think about it, the more I felt that it was not doing any real good to go in that direction by examining something that was—it was sort of like examining something to death, I thought, that would be just examined to such a degree that it becomes—the examination sort of falsifies the experience after a while.

Even very aggressive, angry clients may experience some moments of anxiety or guilt about the powerful emotions they are expressing, and they may seek to undo the harm they have done by justifying their actions or trying to depersonalize the situation. In some situations, clients will begin to contact vulnerable feelings and will then shift back into aggression to avoid those feelings. In the following example, the client becomes anxious about his confrontational behavior.

T: How does it feel to say that to me now?

C: OK. I don't feel anything. I mean it just—I think I'm not stating it in any sort of emotional way, I'm just stating a fact, I guess, so that's the way I feel. I feel okay. What do you feel about that? I mean, you said at the very beginning that the dynamic of this patient–therapist relationship is important to progress, and talking about this dynamic is something that's probably important for you to proceed with maybe, but I don't know. What do you think?

T: Well, let me put it this way: I don't think it's so important about the contents of what we were talking about as much as what was really going on between us, where I was sort of pushing some things and you were reluctant and really wanted to pursue something else. I think that in itself was important. But I do feel like I'm imposing something on you now and you sort of, reluctantly . . .

C: Go along with it?

T: Yeah, and maybe feeling, like you said earlier in the session, angry?

C: Did I say that I was angry? I don't know. I don't know if I was angry.

T: Really? I think that is what you said. You were pretty . . .

C: Oh, I guess, maybe in the course of the week or the past couple of days, there was some kind of annoyance and frustration and so forth, and maybe there was—maybe I used the word *anger*. I guess in some instances I did feel maybe angry that my time was being wasted, that our time was being wasted, time that we could use to develop, I thought, some really important directions.

T: Is there something wrong or risky about being angry with me?

C: Hmm. [*Pause*] I guess, as we discussed, I don't like others getting angry with me . . .

T: And that would include me too.

C: Yeah.

In the following exchange, the client's vulnerability—his needs and wishes for contact or nurturance that were underlying his aggression—emerges:

T: So you felt that our time could be better spent on some important directions that had to do with the business meeting that you wanted to talk about?

C: Yes, exactly. Because I really felt that in the meeting I was really terrified. It really took me back years, like back to high school, back to grade school and so forth. I was really terrified of meeting people.

T: And you wanted to be able to talk with me about it, but I kept pushing to talk about our relationship.

C: Yes, our interaction can be explored at some later point or whatever. But the meeting was really—I was feeling anxious and really woozy and really scared. Everything becomes so confused because there is so much of this spinning of different opinions around in my mind. I don't know what's most important. So I guess, in some sense, I'm always looking for some sort of rope to hang onto or something . . .

T: Something to hang onto, some guidance and support. [*Client nods*] But when you tried to get that from me, I responded by imposing my own agenda on you.

C: Yeah. [*Long pause*]

T: What are you experiencing right now, as we talk about this?

C: I see a path of failure. I mean, if I want to do something I feel is worthwhile, but I will submit to somebody else's decision, then this is not a way to obtain any goals that I might have. That won't lead anywhere.

T: So if you turn to others for support, you end up submitting to their wishes. But if you don't ask for help . . .

C: I'm stuck out on a limb, and I could be cut off at any moment.

Here, the client becomes vulnerable and contacts a wish to be supported by the therapist. As much as it was important to assert himself with the therapist, as evidenced in the withdrawal resolution process previously described, it was also important for the client to recognize his need for support. This is a good example of how ruptures can come in both types in a single case and how the resolution process can help a client negotiate the dialectic between the need for agency and the need for communion. Learning to negotiate this dialectic more adaptively is essential to rupture resolution in particular and BRT in general.

Treatment of Comorbid Conditions

BRT was developed on the basis of work with clients with comorbid diagnoses; specifically, studies of BRT have focused on individuals with Cluster C PDs and PDs not otherwise specified (NOS), most of whom also presented with Axis I disorders. BRT therapists understand symptoms of comorbid conditions such as anxiety and depression as part of relational matrices clients continuously construct for themselves that manifest in the therapeutic relationship. Thus, the focus of the treatment generally remains on the therapeutic relationship and on increasing the client's awareness of the self in relation to the therapist as other.

Evidence suggests that this approach can be effective with clients with comorbid diagnoses. Muran, Safran, Samstag, and Winston's (2005) study, which found evidence supporting a designation of BRT as possibly efficacious for Cluster C PDs and PD NOS clients, was conducted on a highly comorbid sample in which 87% of the participants had both Axis I and II diagnoses.

SUMMARY OF EVIDENCE-BASED PRINCIPLES AND STRATEGIES

Specific Treatment Considerations

To facilitate research on the efficacy of BRT, we chose to make the treatment time limited. This decision prompted us to focus on clients with Cluster C and PD NOS diagnoses who we believed could benefit from a short-term treatment. In addition, Cluster C PDs and PD NOS are the most prevalent PD diagnoses (Mattia & Zimmerman, 2001). BRT does not target individuals with Cluster A and B diagnoses primarily because we determined that they would likely need a longer term approach.

Attachment, Relational, and Familial Factors

One would expect that personality difficulties would be related to attachment patterns, given that both personality and attachment are related to relational schemas and interpersonal functioning. There is empirical evidence of a relationship between insecure attachment and Cluster C features and diagnoses (e.g., Westen, Nakash, Thomas, & Bradley, 2006). The relation between insecure attachment and Cluster C PDs suggests that the etiology of these personality difficulties may be linked to problems in early interactions with caregivers. In fact, research on infant–mother interactions (e.g., Tronick, 1989) provides some intriguing suggestions regarding the role that emotional attunement and its absence may play in the developmental process and, by implication, in the process of working through therapeutic impasses. In a dysfunctional mother–infant dyad the mother fails to attune to the infant's emotions. Healthy mother–infant dyads also experience moments of affective miscoordination, but these are typically followed by periods of repair. The ongoing oscillation between miscoordination and repair helps the infant to develop an adaptive relational schema of the other as potentially available and of the self as capable of negotiating relatedness even in the face of interactional rupture. Similarly, in BRT, working through alliance ruptures is hypothesized to play a role in providing clients with new relational experiences through which they gradually develop new relational schemas as well as bridges to dissociated schemas.

Evidence Base for Clinical Consideration

Our research program has studied the process of change at two levels of analysis. At one level, we have examined the treatment efficacy of BRT as compared with two traditional time-limited models: (a) short-term dynamic psychotherapy (STDP) and (b) cognitive-behavior therapy (CBT). As noted earlier, Muran et al. (2005) found evidence that BRT is possibly efficacious for Cluster C and PD NOS diagnoses, according to the criteria established for empirically supported psychological therapies (Chambless & Hollon, 1998). Specifically, they found that BRT was as effective as CBT and STDP on standard statistical analyses of change. BRT was more successful than the other two treatments with respect to retention: BRT had significantly fewer dropouts than STDP (20% vs. 46%) and a difference approaching significance when compared with CBT (20% vs. 37%). This finding suggests that BRT's intensive focus on alliance ruptures may help to keep clients with PDs in treatment. There also is some preliminary evidence supporting BRT for clients with PDs who had demonstrated difficulty establishing an alliance with a previous therapist (Safran, Muran, Samstag, & Winston, 2005). Other treatment models influenced by BRT have demonstrated efficacy with depression (Constantino et al., 2008), generalized anxiety (Newman, Castonguay, Borkovec, Fisher, & Nordberg, 2008), and borderline PD (Bennett, Parry, & Ryle, 2006).

At a more microanalytic level, we have devoted considerable effort to the study of alliance rupture resolution as a critical change event. This effort has included the development of assessment strategies to identify psychotherapy sessions in which such change events occur (see Muran, 2002) as well as methods to define the interactional sequences of client states and therapist interventions in the resolution process (e.g., Safran & Muran, 1996). We have provided preliminary support for our rupture resolution model based on a series of small-scale studies (Safran & Muran, 1996;). Also, a number of studies have demonstrated the predictive relationship of rupture resolution to overall change (e.g., Muran et al., 2009; Stiles et al., 2004; Strauss et al., 2006).

CONCLUSION

BRT is a short-term approach that focuses on addressing and negotiating ruptures in the therapeutic alliance. It emphasizes a collaborative exploration of the client's and the therapist's experiences of their interaction, and it assumes that interventions can be understood only within the context of the therapeutic relationship. Through this exploration, clients become more aware of their internal processes and of how they interact with others. Interaction with the therapist also provides the client with a new interpersonal experience that challenges the client's existing, self-defeating relational schemas. In this chapter, we have presented and discussed the principle of metacommunication as well as several rupture resolution strategies. BRT has been shown to be an effective treatment for patients with Cluster C and PD NOS diagnoses, many of whom also present with Axis I diagnoses.

REFERENCES

Bennett, D., Parry, G., & Ryle, A. (2006). Resolving threats to the therapeutic alliance in cognitive analytic therapy of borderline personality disorder: A task analysis. *Psychology and Psychotherapy: Theory, Research, and Practice, 79*, 395–418.

Bordin, E. (1979). The generalizability of the psychoanalytic concept of the working alliance. *Psychotherapy: Theory, Research, and Practice, 16*, 252–260.

Brennan, K. A., & Shaver, P. R. (1998). Attachment styles and personality disorders: Their connections to each other and to parental divorce, parental death, and perceptions of parental caregiving. *Journal of Personality, 66*, 835–878.

Chambless, D. L., & Hollon, S. D. (1998). Defining empirically supported therapies. *Journal of Consulting and Clinical Psychology, 66*, 7–18.

Constantino, M. J., Marnell, M. E., Haile, A. J., Kanther-Sista, S. N., Wolman, K., Zappert, L., & Arnow, B. A. (2008). Integrative cognitive therapy for depression: A randomized pilot comparison. *Psychotherapy: Theory, Research, Practice, Training, 45*, 122–134.

Crawford, T. N., Shaver, P. R., Cohen, P., Pilkonis, P. A., Gillath, O., & Kasen, S. (2006). Self-reported attachment, interpersonal aggression, and personality disorder in a prospective community sample of adolescents and adults. *Journal of Personality Disorders, 20*, 331–351.

Eubanks-Carter, C., Muran, J. C., & Safran, J. D. (in press). Rupture & resolution. In J. C. Muran & J. P. Barber (Eds.), *Therapeutic alliance: An evidence-based approach to practice & training.* New York, NY: Guilford Press.

Greenberg, L. S., Watson, J. C., & Lietaer, G. (Eds.). (1998). *Handbook of experiential psychotherapy.* New York, NY: Guilford Press.

Harper, H. (1989a). *Coding guide I: Identification of confrontation challenges in exploratory therapy.* Unpublished manuscript, University of Sheffield, Sheffield, England.

Harper, H. (1989b). *Coding guide II: Identification of withdrawal challenges in exploratory therapy.* Unpublished manuscript, University of Sheffield, Sheffield, England.

Henry, W. P., Schacht, T. E., & Strupp, H. H. (1986). Structural analysis of social behavior: Application to a study of interpersonal process in differential psychotherapeutic outcome. *Journal of Consulting and Clinical Psychology, 54*, 27–31.

Hoffman, I. Z. (1998). *Ritual and spontaneity in the psychoanalytic process: A dialectical–constructivist view*. Hillsdale, NJ: Analytic Press.

Horvath, A. O., & Bedi, R. P. (2002). The alliance. In J. C. Norcross (Ed.), *Psychotherapy relationships that work: Therapist contributions and responsiveness to patients* (pp. 37–69). New York, NY: Oxford University Press.

Kiesler, D. J. (1996). *Contemporary interpersonal theory and research: Personality, psychopathology, and psychotherapy*. New York, NY: Wiley.

Martin, D. J., Garske, J. P., & Davis, M. K. (2000). Relation of the therapeutic alliance with outcome and other variables: A meta-analytic review. *Journal of Consulting and Clinical Psychology, 68*, 438–450.

Mattia, J. I., & Zimmerman, M. (2001). Epidemiology. In J. W. Livesley (Ed.), *Handbook of personality disorders: Theory, research, and treatment* (pp. 107–123). New York, NY: Guilford Press.

Mitchell, S. A. (1988). *Relational concepts in psychoanalysis*. Cambridge, MA: Harvard University Press.

Mitchell, S. A. (1993). *Hope and dread in psychoanalysis*. New York, NY: Basic Books.

Muran, J. C. (2002). A relational approach to understanding change: Plurality and contextualism in a psychotherapy research program. *Psychotherapy Research, 12*, 113–138.

Muran, J. C. (2007). A relational turn on thick description. In J. C. Muran (Ed.), *Dialogues on difference: Studies of diversity in the therapeutic relationship* (pp. 257–274). Washington, DC: American Psychological Association.

Muran, J. C., Safran, J. D., Gorman, B. S., Samstag, L. W., Eubanks-Carter, C., & Winston, A. (2009). The relationship of early alliance ruptures and their resolution to process and outcome in three time-limited psychotherapies for personality disorders. *Psychotherapy: Theory, Research, Practice, Training, 46*, 233–248.

Muran, J. C., Safran, J. D., Samstag, L. W., & Winston, A. (2005). Evaluating an alliance-focused treatment for personality disorders. *Psychotherapy: Theory, Research, Practice, Training, 42*, 532–545.

Muran, J. C., Segal, Z. V., Samstag, L. W., & Crawford, C. (1994). Patient pretreatment interpersonal problems and therapeutic alliance in short-term cognitive therapy. *Journal of Consulting and Clinical Psychology, 62*, 185–190.

Newman, M. G., Castonguay, L. G., Borkovec, T. D., Fisher, A. J., & Nordberg, S. S. (2008). An open trial of integrative therapy for generalized anxiety disorder. *Psychotherapy: Theory, Research, Practice, Training, 45*, 135–147.

Safran, J. D., & Muran, J. C. (1996). The resolution of ruptures in the therapeutic alliance. *Journal of Consulting and Clinical Psychology, 64*, 447–458.

Safran, J. D., & Muran, J. C. (2000). *Negotiating the therapeutic alliance: A relational treatment guide*. New York, NY: Guilford Press.

Safran, J. D., Muran, J. C., & Samstag, L. W. (1994). Resolving therapeutic alliance ruptures: A task analytic investigation. In A. O. Horvath & L. S. Greenberg

(Eds.), *The working alliance: Theory, research, and practice* (pp. 225–255). Oxford, England: Wiley.

Safran, J. D., Muran, J. C., Samstag, L. W., & Stevens, C. (2001). Repairing alliance ruptures. *Psychotherapy: Theory, Research, Practice, Training, 38*, 406–412.

Safran, J. D., Muran, J. C., Samstag, L. W., & Winston, A. (2005). Evaluating an alliance-focused intervention for potential treatment failures. *Psychotherapy, 42*, 512–531.

Safran, J. D., & Segal, Z. V. (1990). *Interpersonal process in cognitive therapy*. New York, NY: Basic Books.

Stern, D. B. (1997). *Unformulated experience*. Hillsdale, NJ: Analytic Press.

Stiles, W. B., Glick, M. J., Osatuke, K., Hardy, G. E., Shapiro, D. A., Agnew-Davies, R., . . . Barkham, M. (2004). Patterns of alliance development and the rupture–repair hypothesis: Are productive relationships U-shaped or V-shaped? *Journal of Counseling Psychology, 51*, 81–92.

Strauss, J. L., Hayes, A. M., Johnson, S. L., Newman, C. F., Brown, G. K., Barber, J. P., . . . Beck, A. T. (2006). Early alliance, alliance ruptures, and symptom change in a nonrandomized trial of cognitive therapy for avoidant and obsessive–compulsive personality disorders. *Journal of Consulting and Clinical Psychology, 74*, 337–345.

Tronick, E. (1989). Emotions and emotional communications in infants. *American Psychologist, 44*, 112–119.

West, M., Rose, S., & Sheldon-Keller, A. (1994). Assessment of patterns of insecure attachment in adults and application to dependent and schizoid personality disorders. *Journal of Personality Disorders, 8*, 249–256.

Westen, D., Nakash, O., Thomas, C., & Bradley, R. (2006). Clinical assessment of attachment patterns and personality disorder in adolescents and adults. *Journal of Consulting and Clinical Psychology, 74*, 1065–1085.

RESOURCES FOR CLINICIANS

Muran, J. C. (Ed.). (2001). *Self-relations in the psychotherapy process*. Washington, DC: American Psychological Association.

Muran, J. C. (Ed.). (2007). *Dialogues on difference: Studies of diversity in the therapeutic relationship*. Washington, DC: American Psychological Association.

Muran, J. C., & Barber, J. P. (Eds.). (in press). *Therapeutic alliance: An evidence-based approach to practice & training*. New York, NY: Guilford Press.

Safran, J. D., & Muran, J. C. (Eds.). (1998). *The therapeutic alliance in brief psychotherapy*. Washington, DC: American Psychological Association.

Safran, J. D., & Muran, J. C. (2000). *Negotiating the therapeutic alliance: A relational treatment guide*. New York, NY: Guilford Press.

7

COUPLES AND FAMILY THERAPY FOR PERSONALITY DISORDERS

JAY L. LEBOW AND AMANDA A. ULIASZEK

People with personality disorders (PDs) almost invariably have problems in family life. Most theoretical or empirical writing concerning PDs indicates that problems are inevitably found in interpersonal functioning. The *Diagnostic and Statistical Manual of Mental Disorders* (4th ed., text revision; American Psychiatric Association, 2000) lists interpersonal functioning as one of the four areas in which a person with a PD may demonstrate severe impairment. Difficulties in the other three areas—cognition, affectivity, and impulse control—can also be expressed interpersonally.

The PD criteria in the *Diagnostic and Statistical Manual of Mental Disorders* demonstrate the widespread interpersonal difficulties found in individuals with PDs (Widiger & Frances, 1985). Several of the PDs have disordered relationships as a core feature. Paranoid PD, schizoid PD, borderline PD (BPD), avoidant PD, and dependent PD all highlight problematic interpersonal relationships in various ways. The criteria for paranoid PD, schizoid PD, borderline PD (BPD), avoidant PD, and dependent PD is characterized by a pervasive distrust and suspiciousness of others, resulting in preoccupied doubts about others loyalty, a tendency to bear grudges, and a reluctance to confide in others. Schizoid PD is characterized by a persistent pattern of detachment from social relationships. A person with schizoid PD neither desires nor enjoys close relationships. Symptoms of BPD include unstable and intense interpersonal relationships and frantic efforts to avoid abandonment. Avoidant PD is characterized by extreme social inhibition, with fear and anxiety present in nearly all interpersonal interactions and relationships. Finally, symptoms of dependent PD include going to extreme lengths to obtain nurturance from others, the inability to make decisions without advice and reassurance from others, and a preoccupation with fears of being left alone.

The remaining five PDs—schizotypal, antisocial, histrionic, narcissistic, and obsessive–compulsive—have interpersonal components as well. Symptoms of schizotypal PD include excessive social anxiety and a lack of close friendships. Deceitfulness, aggressiveness, lack of remorse, and a reckless disregard for the safety of others characterize antisocial PD. Histrionic PD is often associated with stormy and ungratifying interpersonal relationships (Beck, Freeman, & Davis, 2004). People with narcissistic PD have the fundamental belief that relationships are tools; thus, they often are interpersonally exploitative in relationships (Beck et al., 2004). People with obsessive–compulsive PD tend to damage interpersonal relationships because of their rigidity regarding rules and morals. They also tend to focus on work-related tasks at the expense of social activities. Research has shown that all types of PDs are associated with impairment in social relationships above and beyond what is accounted for by depressive symptomatology (Oltmanns, Melley, & Turkheimer, 2002). Individuals with Cluster A PD traits were shown to have particularly poor social functioning in their families when compared with individuals who had Cluster B and C traits (Oltmanns et al., 2002).

Given the extent to which PDs are interpersonal conditions, one obvious hypothesis is that people with PDs would have difficulties in marital relationships. The available empirical findings support this prediction. One study that examined this question for paranoid, schizoid, antisocial, dependent, histrionic, avoidant, and obsessive–compulsive PD (Whisman, Tolejko, & Chatav, 2007) found that histrionic, dependent, and avoidant PD were all associated with a lower likelihood of marriage. All of the assessed PDs were also associated with marital disruption, which included divorce and separation (Whisman et al., 2007). Another study found that, among individuals with BPD, 29% of men and 52% of women were married at follow-up compared with an average rate of marriage of their peers of 80% to 90% (Stone, 1990).

Although there exists a sizable empirical literature on interpersonal difficulties and PDs, very few studies that have targeted these difficulties have examined couples and family therapy treatments. As described earlier, the relationships of people with PDs tend to be filled with conflict and low levels of relationship satisfaction, yet models for treating PDs have almost exclusively focused on the individual. Empirically supported couples and family therapies for PDs have yet to emerge. This is striking considering the pervasiveness of the problem across disorders. There is a small (but growing) literature on family and couples interventions for individuals with BPD (Fruzetti, Santisteban, & Hoffman, 2007; Santisteban, Muir, Mena, & Mitrani, 2003), although as yet there is little regarding other PDs.

In this chapter, we often focus on findings from studies of BPD treatment; we theorize how this research may be extrapolated to other PDs. In suggesting evidence-based guidelines for such treatment we also draw heavily from the evidence base about PD itself; the literature on the individual treatment of PDs; the research on couples and family therapy offered to individuals with relationship problems and diverse diagnoses; and broad principles of practice in couples and family therapy, in particular in problems characterized by high conflict or withdrawal.

THEORETICAL UNDERPINNINGS AND ASSUMPTIONS

Essential Theoretical Constructs

Couples and family therapy comprises four fundamental components. The first core component is the assumption that families are systems in which individuals reciprocally influence one another (Lebow, 2005). Recent advances in theory and research stress that the arcs of causal influence are not entirely equal in the circular pathways they follow, which leads to and maintains ongoing difficulties (Goldner, 1985). In today's systems theory there is a place for acknowledging the power of individual behavior and psychopathology. From this viewpoint, couples and family systems that include an individual with a PD tend to be dominated by that individual's problematic behavior in close relationships, yet reciprocal patterns readily become established. For example, withdrawal in an individual with schizoid PD might promote sequences of attack and contempt by his or her partner and further withdrawal by the individual. Emotion dysregulation in an individual with BPD may promote a sense of helplessness in his or her partner, thus leading to further emotion dysregulation by that individual.

A second core theoretical component is that family can provide a stable holding environment that can mitigate some of the difficulties associated with PDs. Individuals with PDs are exquisitely interpersonally sensitive, and the family system can be a validating environment to reduce their pain and distress (although this interpersonal sensitivity also can lead to family triggering a worsening of the PD symptoms; Linehan, 1993a). Couples and family therapy targets the relational system in which the individual lives to provide the kind of support that promotes better functioning.

A third theoretical component related to couples and family therapy for PDs is that the nature of PDs makes them too pervasive a problem to be treated with a single treatment modality. Research has shown that for people with serious and multiproblem PD symptomatology, treatments combining such diverse modalities as individual, family, couples, and group therapy are the most efficacious (Fruzzetti & Iverson, 2006; Fruzzetti et al., 2007; Linehan, 1993a; Miller, Rathus, & Linehan, 2007).

The fourth and final component is that, because of the significant interpersonal problems associated with PDs, couples and family therapy may do a better job in treating PDs than individual treatment. First, no other form of treatment can address the interpersonal and reciprocal aspects of systems in which there is a person with a PD. Research shows that individual treatment rarely has a positive impact on unsatisfying relationships (Gurman & Fraenkel, 2002), and it is unlikely that the result would be different for a person with a PD. Second, family members of individuals with PDs are a high-risk group: They share some of the same genetic, personality, and biological vulnerabilities as that individual; their actions have the ability to intensify the symptomatology of him or her; and they are at risk of developing their own symptoms as a result of the pervasive interpersonal problems experienced within their relationship with the person (e.g., Fogelson et al., 1999; Nickell, Waudby, & Trull, 2002; Skodol et al., 2002; White, Gunderson, Zanarini, & Hudson, 2003). Couples and family therapy can help partners or family members cope and manage in the face of PD and promote the relationship stability that is likely to be helpful for all members of the system. Other forms of therapy do not provide such direct help to family members.

Mechanisms of Change

The viewpoint of this chapter is that the relational system in which the individual with a PD lives has both a considerable impact on the symptomatology of that person and is significantly impacted by him or her. The relational system cannot completely alleviate the symptoms of a PD, but it can often act as an agent to increase or decrease the degree of impairment and distress in a person with a PD. The success of the family unit as a place of safety and support often ameliorates the impact of PD, whereas difficulty in relational systems promotes greater symptoms and problems. A mindful, supportive holding environment is an essential ingredient to change (Critchfield & Benjamin, 2006). Few treatments can be as potent in this way as ongoing understanding and support from the members of one's relational system. Other forms of treatment are not as likely to have a strong impact on the difficult and dissatisfied relationships of individuals with a PD; although symptoms can be alleviated with other treatment formats, specific work is needed to improve such relationships.

In this chapter, we highlight the importance of the relational system in promoting stability within the family, an increase in family support, and a strengthening of the bond between romantic partners; however, we consider a successful treatment plan to be one that combines couples and family treatment with individual PD treatment. Individual work promotes change in behavior, cognitions, affect, and dynamics in the person with a PD (foci that are largely inaccessible in family therapy); without such change, families may lose their motivation to provide the support and nurturance that are essential to the change process. We view the change process in individuals with a PD as a multi-level one that is aimed at the individual's behavior, cognitions, affect, and dynamics and at the couple/family system, without privileging one kind of work over the other. A review of the literature on the treatment of PDs indicates that such treatment is invariably an intense effort (e.g., Beck et al. 2004; Linehan, 1993a; Whitehurst, Ridolfi, & Gunderson, 2002).

Domains of Operation Within a Total Ecological System

Just as therapy can be done at the individual, couple, and family level, it is important to examine the nature of PDs from the perspective of couples and family therapy within a total ecological system. This includes the intrapsychic/biological, interpersonal, relational, and sociocultural levels.

Intrapsychic–Biological Domain

Although the literature has only recently begun to emerge, at least some research suggests that PDs have considerable biological underpinnings. For example, people with BPD (including children with BPD symptoms) have shown moderate neuropsychological impairments (Dinn et al., 2004; Judd, 2005). These deficits exist in executive functioning, specifically visuospatial learning, memory, and speed of processing (Dinn et al., 2004; Judd, 2005). This indicates difficulty with effortful processing and allocation of cognitive resources, possibly suggesting a dysfunction in the temporolimbic system (Judd, 2005). In addition to deficits in executive functioning, metacognition is also impaired in people with BPD symptoms. Metacognition encompasses the abilities to think about thinking, to understand that there can be a distinction between appearances and reality, to observe and detect errors of oneself while speaking, and to recognize the impermanence and malleability of thoughts (Flavell, 1979; Flavell, Flavell, & Green, 1983). These abilities require a high level of analytic and flexible thinking and are central to the development of empathy and functioning in mature relationships (Judd, 2005).

In addition to the previously mentioned physiological findings, individuals with BPD show an increased time to recover from a stress response. This has been shown by examining recovery cortisol levels after stressful interpersonal interaction between adolescent girls and their mothers. Although the baseline and reactivity cortisol levels between the girls with BPD and a control group did not significantly differ, the BPD group still showed an increased level of cortisol 40 minutes after the start of the interaction (Walter et al., 2008).

These findings about the individual biology of individuals with PDs are complemented by the research available on the impact of such aspects of biology in relational systems. For example, research has found that blood pressure increases dramatically when negative or hostile interactions are taking place between the members of a couple (Ewart, 1993; Kiecolt-Glaser et al., 1993). Couples who demonstrated these negative interactions showed a significant decrement in immune functioning for 24 hours after the 30-minute interaction (Kiecolt-Glaser et al., 1993). An opposite effect (a drop in blood pressure or an increase in immune functioning) has not been found in response to caring or empathic interchanges (Ewart, 1993; Kiecolt-Glaser et al., 1993). Couples that include a person with a PD clearly experience many such interactions in a typical day. This evidence suggests that it is most likely that the most effective couples/family therapy for an individual with a PD will help create a soothing environment in which members of the client's relational system are able to accept, understand, and work with the symptoms of PD and thus ameliorate such biological processes.

Intrapsychic factors also clearly play a key role in PD, and work with such processes must be integrated into effective treatment. A person with a PD clearly displays innumerable problematic behaviors, such as avoidance, cognitive distortions, childlike affective states, problematic views of his or her personal history, and massive internal conflicts, while also often having a history of trauma, comorbid disorders, and difficult early experience (Livesley, 2001). Our view is that work in each of these areas is helpful, in particular when directed by a road map developed by a skillful therapist who is knowledgeable about these problems. We leave the description of work with these levels of experience in individual therapy or individual sessions within a systemic therapy to the other authors in this volume, here emphasizing instead the work at each of these levels in the context of the relational system.

In speaking to the value of a focus on the individual in PD, we also need to highlight that many "individual" topics related to individual functioning may come into focus only when raised by family members. These topics may include certain ego syntonic behaviors whose maladaptiveness the individual, lacking insight, does not realize. Examples may include medication compliance, frequent paranoid cognitions, or an increase in parasuicidal behavior. Another example might involve an individual with a PD who mentions a history of physical or mental abuse only when prompted by his or her partner. Furthermore, because living with an individual with a PD can be just as difficult as having a PD oneself, partners and family members often are further along the stages of change than the PD client (DiClemente & Prochaska, 1998). A feeling of safety in being with one's family can also spur the exploration of these issues in couples/family therapy in clients who have great difficulty with such exploration in individual therapy.

Interpersonal–Dyadic Domain

The couple dyad in individuals with a PD can have a considerable impact on PD; research shows the beneficial effect of positive couple relationships for PD clients. Lewis (1998) reviewed a series of studies that examined the role of marriage in the adult consequences of childhood trauma. He found that a good marriage can have a healing effect on severe problem behaviors in adulthood, such as intravenous drug addiction and BPD characteristics. For example, in a sample of women raised in institutions because of adolescent behavioral problems, only 25% went on to have good outcomes; doing so was associated being in a healthy, supportive marriage (Quinton, Rutter, & Liddle, 1984). Such relationships also have been associated with stopping the parent–child abuse cycle (Egeland, Jacobvitz, & Sroufe, 1988). The presence of older, caretaking husbands can attenuate BPD symptoms in their younger wives (Paris & Braverman, 1995). In a longitudinal follow-up study of inpatients with BPD, marriage predicted better clinical outcome and improved functional status; being in a stable marital relationship appeared to dampen levels of impulsivity (Links & Heslegrave, 2000).

Research points to the importance of improving relationships in individuals with PDs similar to BPD. Gerull, Meares, Stevenson, Korner, and Newman (2008) found that BPD clients perceived their relationships with families, partners, and children to be much more difficult than did a comparison group of depressed individuals. People with a PD typically require remedial work in dealing with closeness and relational skills. As an example, after completing individual treatment with the conversational model, an empirically validated form of psychodynamic/interpersonal therapy (Meares, 2004), individuals with BPD experienced improved relationship quality with their parents and children. Communication with one's partner, dependency, submissiveness, lack of affection, and sexual dissatisfaction also were improved (Gerull et al., 2008).

Relational–Triadic Domain

Family patterns are also important in the way they affect PD symptomatology. One example of such a pattern involves *expressed emotion*, the extent to which a family member expresses critical, hostile, or emotionally overinvolved attitudes and behavior toward the family member with the disorder (Vaughn & Leff, 1976). Many studies have shown that expressed emotion is a predictor of psychotic relapse and rehospitalization in individuals with schizophrenia (e.g., Brown, Birley, & Wing, 1972; Vaughn & Leff, 1976). Family expressed emotion has also emerged as a strong predictor of poor outcome in a range of Axis I disorders, including depression, bipolar disorder, and various anxiety disorders (e.g., Hooley, Orly, & Teasdale, 1986; Miklowitz, Goldstein, Nuechterlein, Snyder, & Mintz, 1988). Treatments that target the psychoeducation of the family to reduce expressed emotion have been highly effective for individuals with severe mental illnesses, such as bipolar disorder and schizophrenia (e.g., McFarlane, 1990; McFarlane, Link, Dushay, Marchal, & Crilly, 1995; Miklowitz, 2008).

This body of research has led some researchers to explore expressed emotion in the context of PDs, specifically BPD (e.g., Hooley & Hoffman, 1999). One study of 35 BPD clients yielded results that were quite different from those of previous studies involving people with schizophrenia and other Axis I disorders (Hooley & Hoffman, 1999). This study examined the facets of criticism, hostility, emotional overinvolvement, warmth, and positive remarks as assessed by a commonly used, well-validated interview measure of expressed emotion. Only one of these constructs, emotional overinvolvement, was related—negatively—to poor outcome and rehospitalization: In other words, it appears that emotional underinvolvement is likely to lead to poor outcome and rehospitalization in BPD clients.

Hooley and Gotlib (2000) offered a potential explanation for why people with BPD are seemingly unaffected by high levels of hostility and criticism while seeming to respond well to emotional overinvolvement. They presented the *hypoarousal model*, which is based on physiological data on individuals with BPD. These data show that individuals with BPD, when compared with control participants, exhibit less physiological arousal in response to emotional stimuli (e.g., Herpertz, Kunert, Schwenger, & Sass, 1999). This may be one reason why individuals with BPD do not respond negatively to the criticism, hostility, and emotional overinvolvement of families with high expressed emotion; they may have a higher tolerance for affective stimulation within the family system and actually interpret it as a sign of care and nurturance (Hooley & Gotlib, 2000). Conversely, emotional underinvolvement may activate the fears of abandonment and being unloved that are commonly found in those with BPD.

Despite the fact that individuals with a PD have a different relationship to expressed emotion than do individuals with schizophrenia and other Axis I disorders, the treatment literature on expressed emotion still has relevance to the treatment of PDs. Psychoeducational family approaches that help members of the relational system grasp the characteristics of the target disorder and understand how to provide the best environment for the diagnosed family member may be useful in the treatment of persons with PDs (e.g., Whitehurst et al., 2002).

Sociocultural–Familial Domain

We have already spoken to the systemic patterns involved in PDs and the role couples/family therapy can play in treatment. It is likely that individuals with a PD have long histories of such patterns that extend back to early childhood. Most of the relevant research available focuses on the problematic early family histories of individuals with BPD.

Several retrospective studies that have examined the childhood of adults with BPD have found two major, seemingly contradictory, themes (Links & Monroe-Blum, 1990). The first theme concerns *underinvolvement*, including abuse, neglect, loss, and a failure of parental functioning. The second theme concerns *overinvolvement*, including overprotection and incest. Research has demonstrated that, although neither theme alone predicts BPD, the combination of the two predicts later development of the disorder (Bezirganian, Cohen, & Brook, 1993). This oscillation between over- and underinvolvement, or neglect and domination, remains consistent in the adult relationships of BPD clients (Allen & Farmer, 1996). Early childhood abuse and neglect are also related to poor outcome over the course of 2 years in adults with BPD (Gunderson et al., 2006). This family dynamic appears to parallel the rapidly shifting idealizing and devaluing in the interpersonal relationships of people with BPD.

Research has also demonstrated an association between BPD and the disorganized subtype of infant attachment style (Holmes, 2004; Levy, 2005). Judd (2005) presented a neurobiological viewpoint that integrates genetics, neuropsychology, parenting, and early attachment style. This research posits a genetic vulnerability (or early biological trauma) that results in a vulnerability to cognitive impairment. This vulnerability then interacts with a problem in the parent–child relationship, resulting in a disorganized or insecure attachment style in early childhood. A frequent problem in the parent–child relationship, consistent with the research discussed earlier in this chapter, is an invalidating, insensitive, or unpredictable caregiver (Judd, 2005). Cognitive impairment is viewed as moderating the caretaker's ability to parent and the child's ability to interpret and integrate communications from the parent, contributing to an insecure, disorganized attachment and pathological dissociation.

There is also an increasing amount of research demonstrating the relationship between BPD and insecure attachment styles in adulthood (Agrawal, Gunderson, Holmes, & Lyons-Ruth, 2004). Insecure adult attachment styles include *dismissing/avoidant* (expectation of significant others as demanding or clingy), *anxious/preoccupied* (negative self-image and feeling of unlovability), and *fearful/avoidant* (negative self-image and distrust of significant others). In a meta-analysis of 13 studies, BPD demonstrated a consistent inverse relationship with secure attachment styles (Agrawal et al., 2004). These studies examined the relationship between the participant with BPD and a target peer, parent, or significant other. Across studies, the attachment style of participants with BPD was best characterized as unresolved with preoccupied features in relation to parents and fearfulness in their romantic relationships.

Fewer studies have examined the relationship between attachment style and the other nine PDs. One such study examined all PDs in relation to adult attachment styles in a sample of more than 1,400 adolescents and young adults (Brennan & Shaver, 1998). This study not only examined the relationship between PDs and attachment but also sought to examine the similarity of the underlying structure of both sets of constructs. For individuals classified as secure, fearful, preoccupied, and dismissing, the percentages of individuals with at least one PD were 60.6%, 92.4%, 90.5%, and 79.5%, respectively. When PD symptomatology was analyzed, the results showed that most PD symptoms (with the exception of psychopathy) corresponded to the two attachment factors of insecurity and defensive emotional style. The authors suggested that PDs and insecure attachment may have some common causes (Brennan & Shaver, 1998).

Process of Therapy

We suggest that clinicians, when treating clients with PDs, combine a range of treatment modalities as well as strategies and techniques drawn from different therapies in couples/family therapy. First, therapists should use various therapeutic modalities to accomplish different goals. Individual therapy has been demonstrated to be useful for self-examination, and group therapy formats have been shown to be cost effective for individual skill development (Hoffman, Fruzzetti, & Swenson, 1999; Linehan, 1993a, 1993b; Santisteban et al., 2003). Couples/family formats uniquely deal with the creation of an environment that is conducive to improving interpersonal functioning and maintaining a soothing home environment. Therapy formats for meeting individually or in groups with partners and family members also are useful because aspects of these individuals' lives are often difficult to discuss in the presence of the PD client.

Second, the treatment literature suggests the necessity of a using a multimodal set of interventions with PD clients and their relational systems. The ideal treatment plan based on what is known about these problems incorporates psychoeducation about PDs for both the client and the members of his or her family system (e.g., Whitehurst et al., 2002), instruction on interpersonal and relationship skills (Gottman, Driver, & Tabares, 2002), behavioral skill development in such areas as communication and problem solving (Dimidjian, Martell, & Christensen, 2002), cognitive restructuring to target dysfunctional thought patterns (Beck, 1976), work on emotion (Greenberg, 2002), practicing mindfulness and various behavioral strategies (Linehan, 1993a), direct efforts to change dysfunctional aspects of family structure (Minuchin, 1974), and exploration of internal dynamics and issues extending from the client's family of origin (Stricker & Gold, 2005). Although many of these techniques can be used in individual therapy formats they take on additional meanings when presented in a couples/family context. Psychoeducation, interpersonal skill development, cognitive restructuring, mindfulness, and behavioral techniques involving distress tolerance and emotion regulation have all been found to be effective when applied in a couple or family therapeutic setting (Lebow & Gurman, 1995; Sprenkle, 2002).

There are two important caveats to such multiformat treatment. First, work in the various therapy formats must be well coordinated lest the treatment lead to splitting and disparate goals among the family members (Friedlander, Escudero, & Heatherington, 2006a). Second, there needs to be a clear understanding as to which communications of what type will be kept confidential and which will not. For example, therapy formats in which secrets about such matters as extramarital affairs are kept confidential in one part of the therapy system easily become problematic (Friedlander, Escudero, Horvath, et al., 2006).

There are many ways to approach the diverse set of problems experienced by individuals with PDs. In general, we do not envision any prescribed way for the ordering of these interventions, save that the interventions that speak to the issues of greatest concern to the couple/family are appropriately the first set of issues addressed in the beginning of treatment (Pinsof, 1995). Research and clinical experience suggest that the interpersonal difficulties that typify PDs also have great relevance in determining whether therapy will be effective. Engagement is typically difficult with PD clients, and this may be part of the reason that empirically supported treatments for Axis I disorders tend to be less efficacious with individuals with comorbid PDs (Shea & Elkin, 1996). This suggests that, regardless of the ordering of the interventions, it is essential both at the beginning of treatment and throughout treatment to focus on building and maintaining a strong therapeutic alliance with the client and members of his or her relational system.

As we have already noted, we emphasize in this chapter treatment processes in couples and family therapy, although we also view techniques applied in individual therapies (as presented in other chapters in this volume) as essential and as needing to be integrated with the systemic treatment process.

RELATIONAL CONSIDERATIONS

Alliance Factors Related to Process and Outcome

The therapeutic alliance is an important feature in all therapies, but it is even more vital to successful outcome in the treatment of PDs. In an empirically informed analysis of successful PD treatments, the therapeutic alliance emerged as important across approaches (Benjamin & Karpiak, 2001; Critchfield & Benjamin, 2006). The therapeutic alliance is strongly related to outcome in the treatment of PDs (Norcross, 2002). For example, in an examination of individual cognitive therapy for PDs, Strauss and colleagues (2006) found that a positive early alliance predicted improved symptomatology in a sample of clients with avoidant PD and obsessive-compulsive PD. Early therapeutic alliance also predicted the number of sessions completed, whereas pretreatment symptom severity did not.

One reason for the importance of a strong alliance is the high rate of therapy dropout that characterizes PD clients and their families and partners (Benjamin & Karpiak, 2001; Strauss et al., 2006). Studies have found that early treatment dropout rates for individual treatment of PDs are high as 38% to 57%, with the average estimate between 15% and 22% (Leichsenring & Leibing, 2003; Perry, Banon, & Ianni, 1999). Research has found similar rates of dropout for couples and family therapy, with rates between 15% and 55% (Allgood & Crane, 1991; Anderson, 1985; Boddington, 1995).

Although they have yet to be studied in systematic research, alliances in couples and family therapy that involve PD are likely to be complex; that is, different family members are likely to have different degrees of alliance, resulting in the possibility of split alliances whereby some family members have a strong alliance and some have a poor one (Friedlander, Escudero, & Heatherington, 2006a). A split alliance in the broader population of clients in couples and family therapy has been related to poor outcome (Friedlander, Escudero, & Heatherington, 2006b, Knobloch-Fedders, Pinsof, & Mann, 2004); therefore, the strength of the alliance should be a target early in treatment, with an eye to maintaining a positive alliance with all family members.

Client Characteristics Related to Process and Outcome

Although as yet no studies have differentiated client outcomes across different client characteristics in couples and family therapy for PDs, it is highly likely that the findings will be similar to those regarding individual therapy. As Critchfield and Benjamin (2006) described, the major factors that predict better outcome in PDs include less functional impairment, greater willingness to engage in treatment, a history of positive attachments, expectations of success, greater readiness for change, and higher social class. These factors promote easier client engagement in and willingness to receive the active ingredients of therapy.

Therapist Characteristics Related to Process and Outcome

Therapist characteristics are particularly important when dealing with PD clients. Critchfield and Benjamin (2006), in their review of evidence-based principles of practice for PDs, found that therapist comfort with long-term, emotionally intense relationships; patience; tolerance for their own feelings toward the client; specialized training; and open-mindedness and flexibility in approach are related to positive outcomes in PDs. It seems likely a similar set of therapist characteristics would be related to success in couples and family therapy. We also believe that a therapist's ability to be directive and in charge of the treatment process is essential to the treatment of these systems, even more so than in other couples and family therapy (Sprenkle, 2002), yet the therapist also must have the skills to validate and accept the client as well as to know when to push change (Linehan, 1993a).

Linehan (1993a), who studied individual dialectical behavior therapy (DBT) for BPD, and Santisteban et al. (2003), who studied family therapy for teens with BPD, both found that when dealing with clients who can be frustrating or challenging, a therapist can easily fall into the trap of blaming the client or of assuming that the intended effect of the client's behavior is to aggravate the therapist. In these cases, a therapist may become hopeless, disengaged, or hostile. These thoughts and emotions generally have a negative direct effect on the therapy in terms of missed appointments (by the therapist), siding with other family members, rigid rule setting, or avoidance of serious topics. Although these issues have been discussed almost exclusively in terms of BPD, they likely extend to all or most of the other PDs. Just as a client with BPD might tax the therapist with demands of immediate relief and late night phone calls, a client with avoidant PD might refuse to speak honestly because of fears of being judged; a client with paranoid PD might constantly question the motives of the therapist; and a client with histrionic PD may fill therapy hours with exaggerated, emotionally shallow stories and dramatic behavior. It is important for the therapist to understand that these behaviors are analogues of the interpersonal behaviors the client enacts in day-to-day life and to find ways to work with these behaviors. In this way, the therapist can also model for the family members appropriate responses to the client's problematic interpersonal behavior. This modeling can serve as a way to decrease the problematic behavior. Therapists must also cope with therapist burnout by such means as processing cases with colleagues or a consulting team so as to engage support for dealing with the most difficult behaviors these clients present.

Racial and Cultural Factors and Considerations

PDs are arguably among the most difficult mental disorders to treat. The behaviors that typify PDs are experienced as difficult in the context of almost every culture. Nonetheless, it remains vital to examine behavior in the context of culture. For example, it may be more impairing for an individual to have schizoid PD in the context of highly interdependent cultures than in those that lean toward large amounts of independence and interpersonal distance. Observation also suggests that individuals with PDs who have money and power often are treated much differently in families and the world than those who do not.

TECHNIQUES AND METHODS OF TREATMENT

Description of Methods Used

Because of the limited literature concerning empirically supported couples and family therapy for PDs, we offer not a definitive list but a working list of treatment strategies that, in our view, on the basis of what is known about PDs and about families, look most valuable in such treatments. As elsewhere, we suggest an integrative model that combines therapy formats, including individual, couples, and group therapy and an array of useful therapy techniques. We limit our description to the work done in the couples and family treatment modalities. Many of the methods we suggest are an extension and adaptation of principles validated in the individual therapy format in treatments such as DBT.

Therapeutic Approach

The creation of an engaged, but not enmeshed, family environment is a core process goal for couples and family treatment of PDs. Mindfulness exercises can prove to be a very useful pathway to producing such an environment. These exercises have the added value of an established track record of impact on different types of PDs (Robins, Schmidt, & Linehan, 2004).

Core mindfulness involves paying full attention to events as they occur, becoming aware of one's own thoughts and feelings, and not judging oneself for imperfect reactions (Stantisteban et al., 2003). Mindfulness has been adapted in conjoint therapies as *relationship mindfulness* (Fruzzetti et al., 2007). In relationship mindfulness, a person is encouraged to transfer anger into more primary emotions and practice bringing attention to everyday interactions. These mindfulness skills have the potential to reduce the negative reactivity of a person with BPD to other members of the family system, thus reducing conflicts between family members. Mindfulness is often a good skill to begin early in family or couples therapy for PDs. It provides an opportunity for the dyad or group to learn a new skill together that they can practice at home. It also serves as a type of relaxation exercise, which can calm heated emotions. It is important to adjust the mindfulness exercises to the particular needs and difficulties of the client. Clients who are prone to dissociation (a characteristic often found in schizotypal PD and BPD) should be instructed to keep their eyes open and/or focus on the physical environment around them.

The combination of validation and acceptance is a central skill in both individual and couples and family DBT and appears crucial to successful treatment with these populations. The emphasis on creating a validating environment for a person with BPD stems from a basic tenet of the etiology of BPD as described by Linehan (1993a). This tenet states that an important cause of BPD is an inherent difficulty with emotion regulation, interacting with an invalidating childhood environment. In an invalidating environment, a person learns that only extreme emotional displays (often in the form of self-harm) succeed in garnering help (Linehan, 1993a). Emotion dysregulation is reinforced, and adaptive coping mechanisms are not formed. In family DBT, the family members learn how to understand the other person, communicate that understanding genuinely, and reinforce the accurate expression of emotions (Fruzzetti & Iverson, 2004; Fruzzetti et al., 2007; Santisteban et al., 2003). The process of validation allows the person with BPD to trust his or her emotions and use more adaptive coping skills when feeling dysregulated. Validation is also an important technique to teach family members or partners of a client with any PD. Part of the client's interpersonal problems may stem from feeling (or being) misunderstood by family and partners.

Psychoeducation also has a fundamental role in couples and family approaches to PDs. Toxic transactions within the family system are strongly associated with PD symptoms. For this reason, educating the family about the specific disorder, the impact of reinforcement and punishment, expressed emotion, and a host of other variables can improve the functioning of the family, and this can lead to improvement in the client's overall distress and impairment. One study found that family members of individuals with BPD knew very little about the disorder (Hoffman, Buteau, Hooley, Fruzzetti, & Bruce, 2003); however, those who reported having more information demonstrated heightened levels of criticism, hostility, and depression and less warmth (a finding we have often seen replicated in family members who have read certain trade books about these disorders). This stands in contrast to numerous studies that have demonstrated the positive use of psychoeducation in other disorders, ranging from depression to schizophrenia (Beck et al., 2004; Whitehurst et al., 2002). This research points to the care needed in determining the content of the psychoeducation and the process for providing it. Hoffman et al. (2003) concluded that much of the family members' information was likely inaccurate and had been presented in a pessimistic style (possibly on the Internet). A small amount of unedited knowledge can lead to pejorative use of labels and a profound sense of pessimism and hopelessness. Psychoeducation should be about presenting information in a therapeutic and realistic way.

To respond to this perceived need for formalized psychoeducation for families of individuals with BPD, Hoffman and colleagues (2005) developed *Family Connections*, a 12-week, multiple-family, manualized psychoeducation program. This program covers current information and research on BPD, its developmental course, available treatments, comorbidity, individual skills to promote patient well-being, family skills to improve familial interactions, instruction in validation, and problem-solving techniques. Families in the Family Connection program decreased their levels of burden and grief while increasing their level of mastery throughout the program and at a 3-month follow-up (Hoffman et al., 2005). Similar packages need to be developed for other PDs.

The building of better interpersonal skills is also a key part of work with couples and families that include a person with a PD. Techniques such as communication training and problem solving, which are core components of behavioral couples and family therapy, have great relevance to these families (Jacobson & Follette, 1985). The interpersonal style of individuals with PDs typically includes poor skills in communication, debate, empathy, or assertiveness. Skill training can be an important part of developing needed repertoires. DBT treatment for adolescents with multiple problems and/or suicidality involves a multifamily skills group in which the adolescent and his or her parents participate in learning skills together (Miller et al., 2007). This type of group not only teaches interpersonal effectiveness but also provides a milieu in which the family members can test their newly acquired skills with the help of a therapist.

Observational learning, commonly known as *modeling*, also is an important source of change. The client and his or her significant others can learn interpersonal skills by observing the therapist enact them within the familial context (Beck et al., 2004). For example, a client might learn how to be assertive with his mother by observing the therapist be assertive with the mother and then observing her positive reaction. Other examples might involve parents learning how to validate their child, or a spouse observing the therapist using positive reinforcement. Overall, the therapist serves as someone from whom the family can learn about how to deal with the difficult feelings toward a family member with a PD and how to relate to a family member with a PD by emulating courteous and empathic responses as well as control of impulsive interpersonal behavior (Beck et al., 2004).

Behavior exchange and reinforcement also are important tools in helping family members respond to a person with a PD in the most helpful manner. Family therapy can help families view problematic behavior as a function of the interaction between the individual characteristics of the person with the PD and the familial environment (Santisteban et al., 2003) and understand when familial behaviors reinforce the problematic behaviors. For example, an adolescent might learn that she receives a great amount of attention and care after engaging in self-harm or threatening suicide. Such an examination of reinforcement not only helps identify the maintaining factors associated with PD symptomatology but also leads to targeting the specific problem. For example, in the example just given, a therapist might help the parents experiment with ignoring self-harming and threats and provide attention and care when emotions are expressed in a more adaptive manner.

Couples and families must also deal with the difficult feelings that accompany PDs. Individuals with PDs typically have strong troubled feelings, as do those around them. Here, psychoeducation can provide an entrée to work on emotion. As families become more understanding of the feelings of the person with a PD, they can learn to engage in fewer behaviors that provoke that dysregulation and learn better how to absorb it and set limits with it. In turn, the person with a PD can apply with the family what he or she is learning about how to regulate his or her own affect. In the forms of PDs that are prone to high conflict, family recognition of the rising of difficult emotion can lead to trying "fire drills" for how to contain emotion as it begins to grow. In a similar way, in families with PDs that are characterized by withdrawal, the emergence of those feelings can become the trigger for a different kind of fire drill to stay connected.

Distorted cognitions, which typically are so broad that the individual develops whole schemas about the world as being dangerous, are an essential part of PD (Beck et al., 2004); thus, understanding and working with such cognitions is yet another important strategy in couples and family therapy. Families often also end up with troubled narratives as a result of interactions with a person with a PD. One strength of couples and family therapy is that such cognitions and narratives can be discussed in the context of intimately connected others and tested as to their accuracy. These, too, can be the focus of cognitive therapy or reframing of the narrative.

Because powerful projections and projective identification are often part of much of the interpersonal interactions in PDs (Clarkin, Levy, Lenzenweger, & Kernberg, 2004), there is a powerful role for the understanding of and working with those projections, especially for clients who stay in therapy beyond the first stage. The simple insight that the PD client may be responding to early objects instead of the person who is present can prove immeasurably helpful to persons who are trying to cope with a family member who has a PD.

Integrative treatments that blend acceptance and behavior change have proven highly effective in the treatment of couples as well as families (Jacobson & Christensen, 1996). These treatments focus on changing what can be changed, building skills, changing cognitions, working with affects, and working with internal dynamics and object relations. This therapy retains a focus on acceptance by both the person with the PD and his or her family; therapists and clients examine what cannot be changed and find ways to work within these constrictions. For example, the family of an individual with paranoid PD may recognize and find a way to reduce that person's interpersonal sense of paranoia by being especially open, disclosing, and soothing.

Special Factors in Treatment

One of the special aspects of couples and family treatment of PDs is that families often seek treatment when the person with a PD does not want treatment (Friedlander, Escudero, & Heatherington, 2006b). When this is the case, the therapist's first interventions should involve reaching out to the person with a PD, both directly and through the family, to involve that person in treatment with the family. Because PDs have such pervasive effects on the relational system, one variation of family therapy focuses on learning how to cope with living with an individual with a PD (Hoffman et al., 2005). Psychoeducation about PDs and forming a behavioral plan for dealing with the PD behaviors make up the center of these treatments, which accentuate acceptance but also realistic limit-setting. One goal in almost all of these treatments is helping the PD client find the right kind of treatment.

Another special consideration in the treatment of PDs is that there are some kinds of PDs for which couples and family treatment with the client clearly appears to be contraindicated. On occasion, this may be because the client is unable to process any issue, no matter how benign, in the presence of family. For some people, such as those with BPD, some individual treatment aimed at self-soothing may be needed before they can participate in couples or family therapy without disastrous effects. In other cases, the PD itself makes for dangerous familial interactions. The clearest example is in regard to families with a member with antisocial PD. Research has shown that men with psychopathy who batter their wives show specific patterns of physiological response. Their peculiar responses caused those doing the treatment research to advise against any efforts to repair difficulties between these individuals and their partners, lest their partners be subjected to further battering that might have been avoided if the therapy had not enabled a reconciliation (Jacobson, Gottman, & Shortt, 1995).

A third special factor in couples therapy is that persons with mental disorders often marry other individuals with mental disorders (Merikangas, 1982). In such instances, the expectation that the family can assume more of a "helper" position toward the individual with PD is unjustified, and the cycles of difficult behavior often escalate. The nature of the PD and the individual's level of functioning are important. For example, the pairing of someone with narcissistic PD and someone with schizoid PD may work much of the time as long as each finds ways to soothe the other (e.g., the individual with schizoid PD may find his or her one close relationship with a partner whom he or she adores). Other pairings, such as two people with schizoid PD, may leave both parties highly satisfied because neither wants much in the way of closeness. However, there also are pairings that are challenging and sometimes inevitably destructive, such as the pairing of two people with BPD. The high levels of emotional sensitivity, emotional dysregulation, and impulsivity found in persons with BPD may interact to form quite volatile relationships.

A final special factor is that persons with PDs often have troubled relationships with their children during and after divorce; therefore, many families referred for family therapy consist of divorced parents in which at least one parent has a PD; such treatments are often mandated by the court in situations, for example, in which children become triangulated into parental conflict (Lebow & Rekart, 2007). Thus, there is a need for specialized treatments that recognize PDs when PDs are involved and that focus on limited goals to move families into better functioning. Lebow and Rekart (2007) described an approach for treating families with divorced parents who are in high conflict that centers on the goal of achieving minimal sufficient coparenting.

Compendium of Techniques

We believe the evidence strongly suggests the value of a multimodal integrative treatment approach to PDs. Because of space limitations, here we focus on only a very few techniques used in family therapy that we find particularly useful:

- *De-escalation of arguments and dysregulated affect.* Engaging in calming behaviors, slowing down the process, suggesting that affects have become too heated, and using de-escalation techniques (breathing, taking a walk, etc.) until the conversation can be resumed.
- *Reframing.* Relabeling behaviors that are viewed as negative in such a way that others will better understand them and with which they will empathize.
- *Contracting.* Negotiating an exchange that makes for a win–win solution for all parties.
- *Promoting a balance between acceptance and behavior change.* Examining what can be changed and what cannot; this then involves working toward the former and acceptance of the latter.
- *Promoting engagement and communication.* Teaching communication skills, practicing those skills, and dealing with internal blocks to communication.

Example of Clinical Process Highlighting Techniques

Jose and Susan presented for treatment after frequent fighting with complaints about difficulties morphing into violence. On hearing their stories, it became clear that although Jose and Susan engaged in symmetrical escalation, Susan also demonstrated signs of BPD. She demonstrated aspects of emotional sensitivity within her relationship; these included extreme reactivity to ambiguous responses from Jose and difficulty calming herself down after becoming upset. She had difficulties in interpersonal interactions that resulted in alternating between passivity and aggressiveness. Susan would easily become inconsolable and cope with the extreme affect by taking substances or becoming violently aggressive. Jose presented as withdrawn and indifferent. He spent the majority of the day alone in his office, avoiding interactions with Susan and his children. He also demonstrated signs of depression, including anhedonia and reduced motivation and concentration. When confronted with Susan's extreme affect, Jose would withdraw further. Eventually, he would try to remove himself from these conflicts, only to be met by physical confrontation from Susan. At this point, he would often lose control and respond with physical aggression.

The treatment plan put a primary focus on deescalating the emotion dysregulation and violence that surround many of the couple's arguments. This included practice in mindfulness, which emphasizes effective, nonjudgmental behavior, and self-soothing exercises, such as deep breathing and muscle relaxation. The treatment plan also focused on skill building. Jose and Susan and the therapist role played adaptive communication patterns, and the therapist modeled validation techniques. The combination of acceptance (including de-escalation and self-soothing) and change (improvement of skills) gave balance to the treatment for such a high-conflict couple.

In approximately the 11th session of couples therapy, the therapist began with an assessment of a recent event. An extremely volatile fight had resulted in the police being called. Susan had smashed Jose's hand with a hammer, and she was arrested for domestic battery. Susan almost immediately became flooded with affect. She raised her voice and began to cry uncontrollably. Jose angrily voiced his frustration, calling Susan "crazy" and saying that he should get a divorce. The therapist first paused the session so that each could tell his/her story separately, without using judgmental or blaming language (de-escalation of argument). During that time, Susan was helped to engage in some self-soothing skills. The therapist focused on abdominal breathing and mindfulness practice so that she could calm herself and carry on the conversation further, and therapy continued, with the rule that it would pause again if the fight escalated. The therapist reframed the issue behind the fight (Susan wanted to go on a bike ride together, but Jose wanted to be left alone to do his work) as their struggling with how to be close with one another. This notion further calmed the fight and fostered empathy between the couple. The therapist then moved to contracting about how Susan and Jose could meet each of their needs when they wanted to do different things. This included assertiveness training for both, with Susan learning how to avoid insisting on time together in an aggressive way and Jose learning how to avoid being passive–aggressive when uninterested in spending time with Susan at that moment. As both Susan and Jose became more emotionally regulated they were asked to look more directly at one another and see whether they could begin to find their better feelings for one another (promoting engagement and communication). The therapist also referred back to their discussions about what could be changed—their communication and engagement with one another—and what could not: their core wants, desires, and personality (promoting a balance between acceptance and behavior change).

Treatment of Comorbid Conditions

The ideal treatment approach to PDs involves a focus on the presenting problem rather than an overemphasis on diagnoses. In other words, we recommend focusing treatment on the problems that are most salient to the individuals involved, instead of being primarily concerned with diagnosis (Pinsof, 2005). Two special considerations are crucial in attending to other issues in clients who have a PD. First, one of the most consistent findings in psychotherapy research is the poorer outcomes achieved across problems when an individual has a PD (e.g., Ball, Kearney, Wilhelm, Dewhurst-Savellis, & Barton, 2000; Joyce et al., 2007). This means that all treatment interventions must be tailored to the individual and his or her family. Interventions typically need to be delivered more slowly to be fully absorbed, with constant attention given to how this is experienced by the client (Bienenfeld, 2007). These are inevitably treatments that require multiple sessions and, typically, multiple treatment modalities. Second, people with a PD typically have a plethora of comorbid conditions (e.g., Cassin & von Ranson, 2005; Coid, Yang, Tyrer, Roberts, & Ullrich, 2006; Widiger, 2003), and thus there is the possibility of dealing with one set of problems after another. Our approach is highly consumer oriented and looks to not only help clients primarily with the aspects of life that are most troubling but also to help them understand what will be an expeditious route to a better life.

SUMMARY OF EVIDENCE-BASED PRINCIPLES AND STRATEGIES FOR EACH CLUSTER

We do not find it especially helpful to target treatment to the various clusters of PDs. Each cluster is too heterogeneous for this to be very useful for treatment decision making. However, we do believe that some principles emerge from the research on PDs that arrives at these clusters.

First, research indicates that treatment outcome is strongly related to overall level of functioning in clients with PDs (Critchfield & Benjamin, 2006). Thus, to the extent that Cluster A PDs are more disorganized than Cluster C PDs, outcomes will be better for clients who have diagnoses in Cluster C. In psychotic individuals, the sensitivities that accompany with the psychosis must be given prime importance, and all interventions should be shaped around those difficulties. Treatment must then be simpler and less challenging.

Second, at the beginning of treatment of problems that are characterized by major affect dysregulation, as in Cluster B PDs, methods of coping with this problem, such as mindfulness practice, need to be emphasized. Couples and family therapy for clients who cannot cope with affect is at risk of being iatrogenic.

Third, antisocial personality is a special form of PD in which care should be taken not to put family members further at risk until there are signs that this PD has radically improved (Gottman, Jacobson, Rushe, & Shortt, 1995).

Fourth, Cluster C PDs call for the least adaptation of methods from more typical courses of psychotherapy and are most easily worked with in families in ways that can move these interactions into the normal range. There is less need to proceed as slowly or cautiously in this work.

CONCLUSION

Couples and family therapy are essential parts of the treatment of PDs. These therapies aim to improve relational life in a category of individuals who have vast problems in relational functioning. In this chapter, we have described an approach that combines work with couples and family with other therapy formats. The approach is integrative in that it brings together strategies of change that have been proven effective. There are many alterations in treatment approaches that need to be made in the context of these clients; most prominent are that therapies need to emphasize the building of a therapeutic alliance even more than other therapies, include some manner of soothing interventions that can help clients tolerate sessions and family environments, use psychoeducation tailored to these problems, use multiple treatment formats, and aim for a combination of acceptance and behavior change.

REFERENCES

Agrawal, H. R., Gunderson, J., Holmes, B. M., & Lyons-Ruth, K. (2004). Attachment studies with borderline patients: A review. *Harvard Review of Psychiatry, 12*, 94–104.

Allen, D. M., & Farmer, R. G. (1996). Family relationships of adults with borderline personality disorder. *Comprehensive Psychiatry, 37*, 43–51.

Allgood, S. M., & Crane, D. R (1991). Predicting marital therapy dropouts. *Journal of Marital & Family Therapy, 17*, 73–79.

American Psychiatric Association. (2000). *Diagnostic and statistical manual of mental disorders* (4th ed., text revision). Washington, DC: Author.

Anderson, S. A. (1985). Dropping out of marriage and family therapy: Intervention strategies and spouses' perceptions. *American Journal of Family Therapy, 13*, 39–54.

Ball., J., Kearney, B., Wilhelm, K., Dewhurst-Savellis, J., & Barton, B. (2000). Cognitive behavioral therapy and assertion training groups for patients with depression and comorbid personality disorders. *Behavioural and Cognitive Psychotherapy, 28*, 71–85.

Beck, A. T. (1976). *Cognitive therapy and the emotional disorders*. Oxford, England: International Universities Press.

Beck, A. T., Freeman, A., & Davis, D. D. (2004). *Cognitive therapy of personality disorders* (Vol. 2). New York, NY: Guilford Press.

Benjamin, L. S., & Karpiak, C. P. (2001). Personality disorders. *Psychotherapy, 38*, 487–491.

Bezirganian, S., Cohen, P., & Brook, S. (1993). The impact of mother–child interaction on the development of borderline personality disorder. *American Journal of Psychiatry, 150*, 1836–1842.

Bienenfeld, D. (2007). Cognitive therapy of patients with personality disorders. *Psychiatric Annals, 37*, 133–139.

Boddington, S. J. A. (1995). Factors associated with drop-out from a couples therapy clinic. *Sexual and Relationship Therapy, 10*, 321–327.

Brennan, K. A., & Shaver, P. R. (1998). Attachment styles and personality disorders: Their connections to each other and to parental divorce, parental death, and perceptions of parental caregiving. *Journal of Personality, 66*, 835–878.

Brown, G. W., Birley, J. L. T., & Wing, J. K. (1972). Influence of family life on the course of schizophrenic disorders: A replication. *British Journal of Psychiatry, 121*, 241–258.

Cassin, S. E., & von Ranson, K. M. (2005). Personality and eating disorders: A decade in review. *Clinical Psychology Review, 25*, 895–916.

Clarkin, J. F., Levy, K. N., Lenzenweger, M. F., & Kernberg, O. F. (2004). The Personality Disorders Institute/Borderline Personality Disorder Research Foundation Randomized Control Trial for Borderline Personality Disorder: Rationale, methods, and patient characteristics. *Journal of Personality Disorders, 18*, 52–72.

Coid, J., Yang, M., Tyrer, P., Roberts, A., & Ullrich, S. (2006). Prevalence and correlates of personality disorder in Great Britain. *British Journal of Psychiatry, 188*, 423–431.

Critchfield, K. L., & Benjamin, L. S. (2006). Principles for psychosocial treatment of personality disorder: Summary of the APA Division 12 Task Force/NASPR review. *Journal of Clinical Psychology, 62,* 661–674.

DiClemente, C. C., & Prochaska, J. O. (1998). Toward a comprehensive, transtheoretical model of change: Stages of change and addictive behaviors. In W. R. Miller & N. Heather (Eds.), *Treating addictive behaviors* (2nd ed., pp. 3–24). New York, NY: Plenum Press.

Dimidjian, S., Martell, C. R., & Christensen, A. (2002). Integrative behavioral couple therapy. In A. S. Gurman & N. S. Jacobson (Eds.), *Clinical handbook of couple therapy* (3rd ed., pp. 251–277). New York, NY: Guilford Press.

Dinn, W. M., Harris, C. L., Aycicegi, A., Greene, P. B., Kirkley, S. M., & Reilly, C. (2004). Neurocognitive function in borderline personality disorder. *Progress in Neuro-Psychopharmacology & Biological Psychiatry, 28,* 329–341.

Egeland, B., Jacobvitz, D., & Sroufe, L. A. (1988). Breaking the cycle of abuse. *Child Development, 59,* 1080–1088.

Ewart, C. K. (1993). Marital interaction—The context for psychosomatic research. *Psychosomatic Medicine, 55,* 410–412.

Flavell, J. H. (1979). Metacognition and cognitive monitoring: A new area of cognitive–developmental inquiry. *American Psychologist, 34,* 906–911.

Flavell, J. H., Flavell, E. R., & Green, F. L. (1983). Development of the appearance–reality distinction. *Cognitive Psychology, 15,* 95–120.

Fogelson, D. L., Nuechterlein, K. H, Asarnow, R. F., Payne, D. L., Subotnik, K. L., & Giannini, C. A. (1999). The factor structure of schizophrenia spectrum personality disorders: Signs and symptoms in relatives of psychotic patients from the UCLA Family Members Study. *Psychiatry Research, 87,* 137–146.

Friedlander, M. L., Escudero, V., & Heatherington, L. (2006a). Repairing split alliances. In *Therapeutic alliances in couple and family therapy: An empirically informed guide to practice* (pp. 161–177). Washington, DC: American Psychological Association.

Friedlander, M. L., Escudero, V., & Heatherington, L. (2006b). Therapy with unwilling and mandated clients. In *Therapeutic alliances in couple and family therapy: An empirically informed guide to practice* (pp. 197–210). Washington, DC: American Psychological Association.

Friedlander, M. L., Escudero, V., Horvath, A. O., Heatherington, L., Cabero, A., & Martens, M. P. (2006). System for Observing Family Therapy Alliances: A tool for research and practice. *Journal of Counseling Psychology, 53,* 214–225.

Fruzzetti, A. E., & Iverson, K. M. (2004). Mindfulness, acceptance, validation and "individual" psychopathology in couples. In S. C. Hayes, V. M. Follette, & M. M. Linehan (Eds.), *Mindfulness and acceptance: Expanding the cognitive–behavioral tradition* (pp. 168–191). New York, NY: Guilford Press.

Fruzzetti, A. E., & Iverson, K. M. (2006). Intervening with couples and families to treat emotion dysregulation and psychopathology. In D. K. Snyder, J. Snyder, &

J. Hughes (Eds.), *Emotion regulation in families* (pp. 249–267). Washington, DC: American Psychological Association.

Fruzzetti, A. E., Stantisteban, D. A., & Hoffman, P. D. (2007). Dialectical behavior therapy with families. In L. A. Dimeff & K. Koerner (Eds.), *Dialectical behavior therapy in clinical practice: Applications across disorders and settings* (pp. 222–244). New York, NY: Guilford Press.

Gerull, F., Meares, R., Stevenson, J., Korner, A., & Newman, L. (2008). The beneficial effect on family life in treating borderline personality. *Psychiatry, 71, 59–70.*

Goldner, V. (1985). Feminism and family therapy. *Family Process, 24, 31–47.*

Gottman, J. M., Driver, J., & Tabares, A. (2002). Building the sound marital house: An empirically derived couple therapy. In A. S. Gurman & N. S. Jacobson (Eds.), *Clinical handbook of couple therapy* (3rd ed., pp. 373–399). New York, NY: Guilford Press.

Gottman, J. M., Jacobson, N. S., Rushe, R. H., & Shortt, J. W. (1995). The relationship between heart rate reactivity, emotionally aggressive behavior, and general violence in batterers. *Journal of Family Psychology, 9, 227–248.*

Greenberg, L. S. (2002). The transforming power of affect: Facilitating access to alternate adaptive emotions and needs. In *Emotion-focused therapy: Coaching clients to work through their feelings* (pp. 193–226). Washington, DC: American Psychological Association.

Gunderson, J. G., Daversa, M. T., Grilo, C. M., McGlashan, T. H., Zanarini, M. C., Shea, M. T., . . . Stout, R. L. (2006). Predictors of 2-year outcome for patients with borderline personality disorder. *American Journal of Psychiatry, 163, 822–826.*

Gurman, A. S., & Fraenkel, P. (2002). The history of couple therapy: A millennial review. *Family Process, 41, 199–260.*

Herpertz, S. C., Kunert, H. J., Schwenger, U. B., & Sass, H. (1999). Affective responsiveness in borderline personality disorder: A psychophysiological approach. *American Journal of Psychiatry, 156, 1550–1556.*

Hoffman, P. D., Buteau, E., Hooley, J. M., Fruzzetti, A. E., & Bruce, M. L. (2003). Family members' knowledge about borderline personality disorder: Correspondence with levels of depression, burden, distress, and expressed emotion. *Family Process, 42, 469–478.*

Hoffman, P. D., Fruzzetti, A. E., Buteau, E., Neiditch, E. R., Penney, D., Bruce, M. . . . Struening, E. (2005). Family connections: A program for relatives of persons with borderline personality disorder. *Family Processes, 44, 217–225.*

Hoffman, P. D., Fruzzetti, A., & Swenson, C. (1999). Dialectical behavior therapy— Family skills training. *Family Processes, 38, 399–414.*

Holmes, J. (2004). Disorganized attachment and borderline personality disorder: A clinical perspective. *Attachment & Human Development, 6, 181–190.*

Hooley, J. M., & Goltlib, I. H. (2000). A diathesis–stress conceptualization of expressed emotion and clinical outcome. *Applied and Preventive Psychology, 9, 135–151.*

Hooley, J. M., & Hoffman, P. D. (1999). Expressed emotion and clinical outcome in borderline personality disorder. *American Journal of Psychiatry, 156,* 1557–1562.

Hooley, J. M., Orley, J., & Teasdale, J. (1986). Levels of expressed emotion and relapse in depressed patients. *British Journal of Psychiatry, 148,* 642–647.

Jacobsen, N. S., & Christensen, A. (1996). *Integrative couples therapy: Promoting acceptance and change.* New York, NY: W. W. Norton & Co.

Jacobson, N. S., & Follette, W. C. (1985). Clinical significance of improvement resulting from two behavioral marital therapy components. *Behavior Therapy, 16,* 249–262.

Jacobson, N. S., Gottman, J. M., & Shortt, J. W. (1995). The distinction between Type 1 and Type 2 batterers—Further considerations: Reply to Ornduff et al. (1995), Margolin et al. (1995), and Walker (1995). *Journal of Family Psychology, 9,* 272–279.

Joyce, P. R., McKenzie, J. M., Carter, J. D., Rae, A. M., Luty, S. E., Frampton, C. M. A., & Mulder, R. T. (2007). Temperament, character and personality disorders as predictors of response to interpersonal psychotherapy and cognitive–behavioural therapy for depression. *British Journal of Psychiatry, 190,* 503–508.

Judd, P. H. (2005). Neurocognitive impairment as a moderator in the development of borderline personality disorder. *Development and Psychopathology, 17,* 1173–1196.

Kiecolt-Glaser, J. K., Malarkey, W. B., Chee, M., Newton, T., Cacioppo, J. T., Mao, H. Y., & Glaser, R. (1993). Negative behavior during marital conflict is associated with immunological down-regulation. *Psychosomatic Medicine, 55,* 395–409.

Knobloch-Fedders, L. M., Pinsof, W. M., & Mann, B. J. (2004). The formation of the therapeutic alliance in couple therapy. *Family Process, 43,* 425–442.

Lebow, J. (2005). *Handbook of clinical family therapy.* Hoboken, NJ: Wiley.

Lebow, J. L., & Gurman, A. S. (1995). Research assessing couple and family therapy. *Annual Review of Psychology, 46,* 27–57.

Lebow, J., & Rekart, K. N. (2007). Integrative family therapy for high-conflict divorce with disputes over child custody and visitation. *Family Process, 46,* 79–91.

Leichsenring, F., & Leibing, E. (2003). The effectiveness of psychodynamic therapy and cognitive behavior therapy in the treatment of personality disorders: A meta-analysis. *American Journal of Psychiatry, 160,* 1223–1232.

Levy, K. M. (2005). The implications of attachment theory and research for understanding borderline personality disorder. *Development and Psychopathology, 17,* 59–986.

Lewis, J. M. (1998). For better or worse: Interpersonal relationships and individual outcome. *American Journal of Psychiatry, 155,* 582–589.

Linehan, M. M. (1993a). *Cognitive behavioral treatment of borderline personality disorder.* New York, NY: Guilford Press.

Linehan, M. M. (1993b). *Skills training manual for treating borderline personality disorder.* New York, NY: Guilford Press.

Links, P. S., & Heslegrave, R. J. (2000). Prospective studies of outcome: Understanding the mechanisms of change in patients with borderline personality disorder. *Psychiatric Clinics of North America, 23*, 137–150.

Links, P. S., & Munroe-Blum, H. (1990). Family environment and borderline personality disorder: Development of etiologic models. In P. S. Links (Ed.), *Family environment and borderline personality disorder* (pp. 1–24). Washington, DC: American Psychiatric Association.

Livesley, W. J. (2001). *Handbook of personality disorders: Theory, research, and treatment.* New York, NY: Guilford Press.

McFarlane, W. R. (1990). Multiple family groups and the treatment of schizophrenia. In M. I. Herz, S. J. Keith, & J. P. Docherty (Eds.), *Handbook of schizophrenia: Vol. 4. Psychosocial treatment of schizophrenia* (pp. 167–189). Amsterdam, The Netherlands: Elsevier.

McFarlane, W. R., Link, B., Dushay, R., Marchal, J., & Crilly, J. (1995). Psycho-educational multiple family groups: Four-year relapse outcome in schizophrenia. *Family Process, 34*, 127–144.

Meares, R. (2004). The conversational model: An outline. *American Journal of Psychotherapy, 58*, 51–66.

Merikangas, K. R. (1982). Assortative mating psychiatric disorders and psychological traits. *Archives of General Psychiatry, 39*, 1173–1180.

Miklowitz, D. J. (2008). *Bipolar disorder: A family-focused treatment approach* (2nd ed.). New York, NY: Guilford Press.

Miklowitz, D., Goldstein, M. J., Nuechterlein, K., Snyder, K., & Mintz, J. (1988). Family factors and the course of bipolar affective disorder. *Archives of General Psychiatry, 45*, 225–231.

Miller, A. L., Rathus, J. H., & Linehan, M. M. (2007). *Dialectical behavior therapy with suicidal adolescents.* New York, NY: Guilford Press.

Minuchin, S. (1974). *Families and family therapy.* Cambridge, MA: Harvard University Press.

Nickell, A. D., Waudby, C. J., & Trull, T. J. (2002). Attachment, parental bonding and borderline personality disorder features in young adults. *Journal of Personality Disorders, 16*, 148–159.

Norcross, J. C. (2002). Empirically supported therapy relationships. In J. C. Norcross (Ed.), *Psychotherapy relationships that work: Therapist contributions and responsiveness to patients* (pp. 3–16). London, England: Oxford University Press.

Oltmanns, T. F., Melley, A. H., & Turkheimer, E. (2002). Impaired social functioning and symptoms of personality disorders assessed by peer and self-report in a nonclinical population. *Journal of Personality Disorders, 16*, 437–452.

Paris, J., & Braverman, S. (1995). Successful and unsuccessful marriages in borderline patients. *Journal of the American Academy of Psychoanalysis, 23*, 153–166.

Perry, J. C., Banon, E., & Ianni, F. (1999). Effectiveness of psychotherapy for personality disorders. *American Journal of Psychiatry, 156*, 1312–1321.

Pinsof, W. M. (1995). *Integrative problem-centered therapy: A synthesis of family, individual, and biological therapies*. New York, NY: Basic Books.

Pinsof, W. M. (2005). Integrative problem-centered therapy. In *Handbook of psychotherapy integration* (2nd ed., pp. 382–402). New York, NY: Oxford University Press.

Quinton, D., Rutter, M., & Liddle, C. (1984). Institutional rearing, parenting difficulties and marital support. *Psychological Medicine, 14*, 107–124.

Robins, C. J., Schmidt, H., & Linehan, M. M. (2004). Dialectical behavior therapy: Synthesizing radical acceptance with skillful means. In S. C. Hayes, V. M. Follette, & M. M. Linehan (Eds.), *Mindfulness and acceptance: Expanding the cognitive–behavioral tradition* (pp. 30–44). New York, NY: Guilford Press.

Santisteban, D. A., Muir, J. A., Mena, M. P., & Mitrani, V. B. (2003). Integrative borderline adolescent family therapy: Meeting the challenges of treating adolescents with borderline personality disorder. *Psychotherapy: Theory, Research, Practice, Training, 40*, 251–264.

Shea, M., & Elkin, I. (1996). The NIMH Treatment of Depression Collaborative Research Program. In C. Mundt, P. L. Fiedler, M. J. Goldstein, & K. Hahlweg (Eds.), *Interpersonal factors in the origin and course of affective disorders* (pp. 316–328). London, England: Gaskell/Royal College of Psychiatrists.

Skodol, A. E., Siever, L. J., Livesley, W. J., Gunderson, J. G., Pfohl, B., & Widiger, T. A. (2002). The borderline personality diagnosis II: Biology, genetics, and clinical course. *Biological Psychiatry, 51*, 951–963.

Sprenkle, D. H. (Ed.). (2002). *Effectiveness research in marriage and family therapy*. Alexandria, VA: American Association for Marriage and Family Therapy.

Stone, M. H. (1990). *The fate of borderline patients*. New York, NY: Guilford Press.

Strauss, J. L., Hayes, A. M., Johnson, S. L., Newman, C. F., Brown, G. K., Barber, J. P., . . . Beck, A. T. (2006). Early alliance, alliance ruptures, and symptom change in a nonrandomized trial of cognitive therapy for avoidant and obsessive–compulsive disorders. *Journal of Consulting and Clinical Psychology, 74*, 337–345.

Stricker, G., & Gold, J. (2005). Assimilative psychodynamic psychotherapy. In J. C. Norcross & M. R. Goldfried (Eds.), *Handbook of psychotherapy integration* (2nd ed., pp. 221–240). New York, NY: Oxford University Press.

Vaughn, C. E., & Leff, J. P. (1976). The influence of family and social factors on the course of psychiatric illness. *British Journal of Psychiatry, 129*, 125–137.

Walter, M., Bureau, J., Holmes, B. J., Bertha, E. A., Hollander, M., Wheelis, J., . . . Lyons-Ruth, K. (2008). Cortisol response to interpersonal stress in young adults with borderline personality disorder: A pilot study. *European Psychiatry, 23*, 201–204.

Whisman, M. A., Tolejko, N., & Chatav, Y. (2007). Social consequences of personality disorders: Probability and timing of marriage and probability of marital dysfunction. *Journal of Personality Disorders, 21*, 690–695.

White, C. N., Gunderson, J. G., Zanarini, M. C., & Hudson, J. I. (2003). Family studies of borderline personality disorder: A review. *Harvard Review of Psychiatry*, *11*, 8–19.

Whitehurst, T., Ridolfi, M. E., & Gunderson, J. (2002). Multiple family group treatment for borderline personality disorder. In S. G. Hofmann & M. C. Tompson (Eds.), *Treating chronic and severe mental disorders: A handbook of empirically supported interventions* (pp. 343–363). New York, NY: Guilford Press.

Widiger, T. A. (2003). Personality disorder and Axis I psychopathology: The problematic boundary between Axis I and Axis II. *Journal of Personality Disorders*, *17*, 90–108.

Widiger, T. A., & Frances, A. (1985). The *DSM–III* personality disorders: Perspectives from psychology. *Archives of General Psychiatry*, *42*, 615–623.

RESOURCES FOR CLINICIANS

Gurman, A. S. (Ed.). (2008). *Clinical handbook of couple therapy* (4th ed.) New York, NY: Guilford Press.

Lebow, J. (2005). *Handbook of clinical family therapy*. Hoboken, NJ: Wiley.

8

INTEGRATED TREATMENT: COMBINING EFFECTIVE TREATMENT PRINCIPLES AND METHODS

W. JOHN LIVESLEY

In this chapter, I argue that personality disorder (PD) is best treated with an array of treatment methods, selected from different therapeutic models based as far as possible on evidence of what works, that are delivered in an integrated and coordinated way. The intent is not to offer yet another form of treatment for PD but rather to suggest a framework based on current knowledge of the nature of PD and the factors associated with positive treatment outcomes that therapists may use to tailor treatment to the needs of individual clients and the context in which they work.

The treatment of PD currently is dominated by a handful of treatments shown to be effective in reasonably sound randomized clinical trials (especially in treating borderline PD [BPD]). At first glance, these findings appear to imply that the most appropriate way to approach the treatment of PD is to select among these empirically supported treatments. There are several reasons to reject this approach. First, although studies suggest that these treatments incorporate effective methods, they do not inform clinicians about the best treatment for a given client. Under these circumstances, instead of choosing between treatments it may be more appropriate to combine effective methods from each approach. To do otherwise could lead to effective methods not being used simply because they are part of a different model. Second, outcome does not appear to differ substantially across therapies (Leichsenring & Leibing, 2003). A comparison of transference-based therapy (Clarkin, Yeomans, & Kernberg, 1999) and schema-focused therapy (Young, Klosko, & Weishaar, 2003) suggested that schema-focused therapy (SFT) was associated with reduced dropouts (a significant problem in the treatment of PD) and better outcomes (Giesson-Bloo et al., 2006). However, differences were modest, the sample size was small, and questions have been raised about the comparability of the delivery of the two treatments. Third, most cases of PD involve multiple problems and multidimensional psychopathology, ranging from symptoms such as anxiety and dysphoria to identity problems and/or self-pathology. None of the treatments currently available incorporate a sufficiently comprehensive array of interventions to cover all problem domains. Fourth, each treatment makes assumptions, often with limited empirical support, about the primary impairment associated with the disorder that determine the major focus of treatment and the methods used. With BPD, the postulated impairments include maladaptive object relationships, emotion dysregulation, mentalizing deficiencies, problems with impulse control, and maladaptive cognitive structures and processes. Despite the fact that BPD encompasses all these problems, most treatments focus primarily on a single impairment. For example, dialectical behavior therapy and mentalizing-based therapy focus on emotion dysregulation and mentalizing problems, respectively. Given that clients with BPD have difficulty with both emotion regulation and mentalizing, it seems more appropriate to use intervention strategies from both treatments instead of selecting only one approach.

OVERVIEW OF INTEGRATED TREATMENT

The framework proposed for an integrated approach reflects the idea that an evidence-informed approach should be organized around generic treatment methods common to all therapies (Castonguay & Beutler, 2006a; Critchfield & Benjamin, 2006; Livesley, 2003; Meyer & Pilkonis, 2006). More specific treatment methods drawn from different therapeutic models are added to this structure as needed to tailor treatment to the specific problems of individual clients and the domain of psychopathology that is the focus of therapeutic effort at a given moment.

Critical analyses of the empirical literature by the joint Task Force of the Society for Clinical Psychology (Division 12 of the American Psychological Association) and the North American Society for Psychotherapy Research to identify effective principles of therapeutic change point to the importance of generic mechanisms in the treatment of most mental disorders, including PD (Castonguay & Beutler, 2006a). Effective factors include a strong working alliance; repair of ruptures to the alliance in an empathic and flexible way; a therapist attitude of caring, warmth, empathy, positive regard, congruence, and authenticity; a consensus on treatment goals; and strong patient–therapist collaboration in attempting to attain treatment goals. In the case of PD, a relatively high level of therapist activity is also important (Critchfield & Benjamin, 2006).

Within the proposed framework, generic methods based on the treatment relationship are implemented by (a) maintaining a consistent treatment process based on an explicit treatment contract that includes agreement on treatment goals, (b) building a collaborative working relationship based on an empathic and validating therapeutic stance, and (c) maintaining a focus on building motivation and commitment to change. The instrumental component of general methods involves creating opportunities for new experiences and new learning and trying out new behaviors in the context of a supportive working relationship. These methods are designed to stimulate an increase in self-understanding, self-knowledge, and the capacity for self-reflection.

In an integrated treatment plan, generic treatment methods are used throughout therapy; specific interventions are introduced to treat specific problems only when there is a good working relationship and the client is motivated to change. If these conditions do not exist, the therapist should direct his or her efforts toward remedying these problems. This means that he or she needs to constantly monitor the quality of the client–therapist relationship and the client's level of motivation and be ready to address ruptures to the alliance promptly as they emerge.

The use of multiple specific interventions creates the challenge of how to coordinate their delivery and avoid treatment becoming chaotic and confusing because of an ever-changing set of interventions. Therapists can handle this problem by dividing treatment into phases based on evidence of the stability and plasticity of personality and personality pathology (Tickle, Heatherton, & Wittenberg, 2001) and the priority that needs to be given to the more symptomatic aspects of psychopathology. Five phases are recognized: (a) ensuring the safety of the client and others; (b) containment of symptoms, emotions, and impulses; (c) regulation and control of emotions and impulses, including deliberate self-harm; (d) exploration of and change to underlying psychopathological processes; and (e) integration and synthesis of a more adaptive self-structure.

With this model, the therapist tailors multifaceted interventions across time to match the flow of the client's problems and concerns and the progress being made. At first, the therapist addresses the more symptomatic component of psychopathology by stabilizing the client's symptoms and then helping him or her improve self-regulation of emotions and impulses. As self-regulation increases, attention focuses on exploring and changing maladaptive interpersonal patterns, dysfunctional cognitions, and the consequences of psychosocial adversity. In the later phase of long-term treatment, greater attention is given to helping clients forge a more integrated sense of self and develop a life they consider to be worth living.

Under ideal circumstances, with such an approach, treatment methods would be selected on the basis of evidence of what works. Unfortunately, empirical evidence on effective interventions for PD is limited. This does not, however, preclude an evidence-based approach (Sackett, Rosenberg, Gray, Haynes, & Richardson, 1996) in which the selection of treatment methods is guided by an empirically based understanding of the structure and origins of PD, the principles of behavioral change, and current studies of the effectiveness of PD treatments.

THEORETICAL FOUNDATIONS

Theoretical Underpinnings and Assumptions

The current lack of comprehensive, evidence-informed theories of PD and personality change creates the challenge of what principles to use to guide the selection and delivery of multifaceted interventions. A clear understanding of the theoretical and conceptual structure of treatment is important because outcome is enhanced when therapy is based on a "focused, theoretically coherent, consistent, and well-coordinated treatment" (Critchfield & Benjamin, 2006, p. 262). Integrated treatment is based on two conceptual frameworks: (a) a description of personality pathology based on empirical evidence of the structure, etiology, development, and stability of PD; and (b) a model of therapeutic change based on the general literature on psychotherapy outcome, outcome studies on PD, and models of behavioral change.

A Framework for Conceptualizing Personality Disorder

Three ideas about PD inform integrated treatment. First, PD involves two kinds of psychopathology: (a) the universal features that define the disorder and (b) specific features associated with the different disorders (Cloninger, 2000; Livesley, 1999). Second, personality is most appropriately conceptualized as a loosely organized set of subsystems (Livesley, 2003; Mayer, 2005). Third and last, PD is a biopsychological entity.

General and Specific Features of PD

The distinction between general and specific features of PD is implied by the decision to include in the *Diagnostic and Statistical Manual of Mental Disorders* (4th ed.; *DSM–IV*; American Psychiatric Association, 1994) criteria for general PD besides the criteria for specific diagnoses. This distinction implies the need for general interventions to treat the defining or core features of PD that could be used to treat all cases and all forms of disorder (Livesley, 2003). The clinical literature consistently conceptualizes the core or defining features of PD as the failure to establish a cohesive self-system or identity (e.g., Kernberg, 1984; Kohut, 1971) and chronic interpersonal dysfunction (e.g., Benjamin, 1993; Rutter, 1987). These features have important treatment implications: They lead to unstable relationships; difficulty setting and working toward long-term goals; and impaired interpersonal boundaries that hinder the formation of an effective working relationship, which is a prerequisite for change. Treatment methods to address these problems provide a structure to which an eclectic set of interventions could be added as appropriate to treat individual differences in problems, personality, and psychopathology. As a consequence, the model of disorder is isomorphic with the model of treatment.

Personality as a System

The personality system is primarily structured by the trait system. This consists of multiple heritable primary traits that are organized into four clusters (Widiger & Simonsen, 2005): (a) anxious–dependent or emotional dysregulation traits that resemble BPD, (b) dissocial traits that closely resemble psychopathy, (c) social withdrawal, and (d) compulsivity. Because integrated treatment is guided by empirical findings, it advocates the use of a dimensional system to describe individual differences in personality pathology rather than the categorical diagnoses of *DSM–IV*; however, the approach is compatible with both approaches to classification.

Traits influence the emergence of the self and interpersonal systems. These intertwined structures are, in essence, knowledge systems that organize information about the self and one's interpersonal world into a set of constructs or schemata that encode information, impose meaning on experience, and predict events. The self-system is formed from schemata that organize self-referential knowledge into a coherent understanding of the self that gives rise to a sense of personal unity and self-directedness. The interpersonal system consists of schemata that include representations of others, beliefs and expectations about interpersonal behavior, and behavioral strategies. These schemata function to structure one's experience of the interpersonal world and relationships with others. Adaptive self and interpersonal systems depend on the ability to understand the rules governing human behavior. These cognitive processes, referred to variously as *theory of mind* (Fonagy, Gergely, Jurist, & Target, 2002), *metacognition* (Dimaggio, Semerari, Carcione, Nicolo, & Procacci, 2007), and the *grammar of behavior* (Livesley & Bromley, 1973), are basic to self-reflective thinking, a factor that is assumed to be critical for therapeutic change.

The personality system also incorporates self-regulatory and impulse control processes that help integrate and coordinate action. Finally, the environment is also an integral part of the personality system. Each individual's environment is not totally independent of that person; instead, people select, shape, and structure their environments over time by seeking out and creating situations that are consistent with their personalities. Consequently, the environment plays an important role in maintaining behavior, and therapists must pay attention to helping clients manage the situational factors and relationships that help maintain the repetitive maladaptive patterns that characterize their disorder.

The psychopathology of PD typically encompasses all components of the personality system, giving rise to multifaceted problems. Each subsystem gives rise to a specific domain of psychopathology. At least six domains may be recognized: (a) symptoms such as dysphoria, anxiety, depression, and parasuicidal behavior; (b) impaired regulation of emotions and impulses; (c) maladaptive expressions of traits such as emotional lability, callousness, and impulsivity; (d) maladaptive interpersonal behaviors; (e) self or identity problems; and (f) environmental circumstances.

Domains differ in their stability and responsiveness to treatment (Livesley, 2003; Tickle et al., 2001). Longitudinal studies indicate that DSM–IV PD diagnoses are less stable than originally thought, although the traits that characterize each disorder are more stable than the associated diagnosis (Skodol et al., 2005). The general diagnosis of PD is also more stable than diagnoses of specific disorders (David & Pilkonis, 1996), which suggests that the core self and interpersonal features are relatively persistent. The instability of DSM–IV diagnoses probably arises in part from the inclusion of symptoms among diagnostic criteria. Symptoms are usually the most variable component of personality pathology, and many symptoms fluctuate over time. The self-control mechanisms that regulate emotions and impulses are more stable than symptoms, but evidence from cognitive–behavioral studies suggest that they can be modified by cognitive and skill-building approaches. Interpersonal patterns, maladaptive modes of thinking, characteristic expressions of traits (although not the underlying disposition), and some self-attitudes (especially self-esteem) form an intermediate level of stability. Finally, primary traits and core self and interpersonal schemata are highly stable and change slowly. This hierarchy of stability suggests that treatment goals and strategies should take into account the stability of the client's personality and the anticipated duration of treatment. Thus, the early stages of treatment and briefer treatments should focus on the more changeable components of PD. This increases the probability of achieving early changes that are useful in building the treatment relationship and motivation for change.

PD Is a Biopsychological Entity

PD has a complex biopsychological etiology, and individual differences in personality pathology have a substantial heritable component (Cloninger, 2005; Livesley & Jang, 2008). These findings have several implications for treatment. First, they provide a rationale for combining psychotherapy and medication. For example, the strategy that appears to be most optimal for treating BPD is medication used as an adjunct to psychotherapy. Second, the heritability of traits such as social withdrawal, affective lability, and sensation seeking raises questions about the nature of the changes in trait structure that may be expected from currently available methods. The heritability of these traits and their stability across the adult life span suggest that radical changes are unlikely and that a more effective strategy may be to help clients use their traits more adaptively. This may involve attempting to attenuate more extreme forms of expression, promoting more adaptive expression of basic traits, and helping clients create a personal niche that allows them to use their traits productively.

A Framework for Conceptualizing Personality Change

The second component of the theoretical foundation for integrated treatment is a framework for conceptualizing therapeutic change that is used to conceptualize the treatment process and coordinate the use of treatment methods. The framework is based on evidence of the importance of generic treatment methods common to all forms of psychotherapy, and the phases-of-change model mentioned earlier describes the process of therapy. Components of this framework are discussed in the Mechanisms of Change and Description of Methods Used sections.

Essential Theoretical Constructs

Although the heterogeneous nature of PD and the eclecticism of integrated treatment mean that the approach incorporates multiple constructs rather than a single idea, the approach suggested draws extensively on social-cognitive models of personality, especially Mischel and Shoda's (1995) cognitive–affective personality system model. Personality is assumed to involve a set of information-processing–decision-making modules that each consist of encoding, appraisal, and response initiation mechanisms that reflect the adaptive architecture of personality. This theoretical perspective implies that a major task for long-term treatment is to modify the cognitive–emotional structures and processes that underlie disordered functioning. These structures are conceptualized using the construct of *schemata* (Livesley, 2003), that is, categories that are used to organize information, interpret experience, and guide action (Segal, 1988). As used in cognitive science, schemata consist of attributes (i.e., items of knowledge) along with an explanation of how these attributes are connected (Komatsu, 1992). For example, the schema of "bird" is not just a list of features such as wings, beak, feathers, and tail but also includes an understanding of how different anatomical structures function to allow the organism to fly, although the depth of this understanding differs according to one's knowledge of birds. The different schemata dealing with a given domain are not independent but instead are organized into a hierarchical structure. Thus, schemata for specific birds, such as owls or robins, are part of the higher schema "bird," which is part of the higher order schema of "vertebrates," which in turn is part of the even higher order schema of "animal."

The self and interpersonal systems are organized similarly. The different qualities attributed to the self are low-level schemata that are organized into different images of the self. The multiple self-images most people form are linked into increasingly higher order conceptions of the self that eventually culminate in an overarching self-view or autobiographical self. Severe PD is characterized by problems with the structure of the self. Some clients may have few self-schemata and hence an impoverished understanding of the self, as is often the case with schizoid PD. In other clients, such as those with BPD, there is fragmentation of the self that is due to the failure to integrate different self-schemata into a coherent structure. This framework conceptualizes the coherence of the self in terms of the links and connections within self-knowledge. The richer and more extensive these links are, the greater the individual's sense of coherence and personal unity (Horowitz, 1998; Livesley, 2003).

The interpersonal system is organized similarly. A schema representing another person organizes information about that person's qualities, values, beliefs, and interests. With casual acquaintances, these schemata probably consist of a few salient qualities, such as whether the person is friendly, amiable, or honest. In contrast, a schema representing someone who is well known, such as a family member, is more detailed and often recognizes different facets of that individual's personality. For example, one may think of a certain person as friendly, kind, and cheerful on most occasions but irritable and disagreeable on others. An attempt is usually made to integrate these apparent discrepancies. For example, one may recognize that this person is normally friendly and cheerful but irritable when stressed. With PD it is common for the schema of another person to have impoverished or stereotyped content and for the different images of the other to remain separate rather than integrated into a global representation of that person.

Schemata are not confined to the self and interpersonal subsystems; *traits* also have a substantial cognitive component. Heritable predispositions give rise to neurobehavioral mechanisms that are shaped by experience (Livesley & Jang, 2008). These experiences lead to beliefs and expectations that mediate trait expression. For example, anxiousness, an important trait in emotional dys-regulation or the BPD constellation of traits, is based on a mechanism to manage threats. Repeated experiences of threat and appraisals of the capacity to cope with threat give rise to the trait of anxiousness. These schemata are used to evaluate threats and appraise the individual's capacity to respond to them. Over time, they influence both the activation threshold of the threat management system and the intensity of the individual's response. One strategy to treat maladaptive traits is to restructure these beliefs and expectations.

Mechanisms of Change—General and Specific

The framework for conceptualizing therapeutic change in personality pathology noted earlier incorporates mechanisms that underlie personality change and a description of the stages through which change occurs.

Meta-analyses of psychotherapy outcome and comprehensive reviews suggest that generic mechanisms appear to account for most of the outcome variance due to treatment interventions (Beutler, 1991; Castonguay & Beutler, 2006a, 2006b; Luborsky, Singer, & Luborsky, 1975), and a similar conclusion seems warranted regarding the treatment of PD (Critchfield & Benjamin, 2006; Livesley, 2003; Paris, 2005). These findings form the empirical foundation for the basic principle of integrated treatment that treatment should seek to maximize the effect of common factors (Livesley, 2001; Meyer & Pilkonis, 2006). These factors have relational and technical components (Lambert & Bergen, 1994). As noted earlier, the relationship component involves the development of a positive and collaborative treatment relationship; the use of an empathic, supportive, and validating therapeutic stance; and transparency about treatment tasks. The technical component promotes new experiences, expands self-understanding of problems and psychopathology, and provides new learning opportunities or opportunities to acquire and try out new behaviors.

Besides optimizing outcome effects, the relationship component of generic mechanisms also provides an effective way to treat core self and interpersonal pathology because therapy based on general methods provides a continuous corrective experience that helps repair core maladaptive schemata forged in the context of developmental adversity. The multiple forms of psychosocial adversity that contribute to PD outcomes (Paris, 2001; Johnson, Bromley, & McGreoch, 2005) lead to schemata involving mistrust, rejection, abandonment, the unpredictability of others' behavior, control, and powerlessness. A treatment process that emphasizes consistency, support, validation, empathy, openness, collaboration, and repair of alliance ruptures provides a milieu that continually challenges and restructures these expectations. Hence, the general process and structure of treatment are crucial components of the change process.

In addition to evidence of similar outcomes across studies (Leichsenring & Leibing, 2003), there is evidence that interventions vary in effectiveness across domains of psychopathology (Paris, 2005; Piper & Joyce, 2001). The forensic literature is especially clear on the following point: The best outcomes occur when specific behaviors are targeted with specific interventions (Lipsey, 1995). This suggests that the optimal treatment strategy is to select effective methods from different treatments based on what works and a rational consideration of the psychopathology concerned. The change mechanisms associated with specific treatment methods vary substantially with the method in question and the phase of change. As with generic interventions, change primarily results from the restructuring of cognitive–emotional structures; however, some specific methods also bring about change through the acquisition of new skills in problem solving, controlling emotions, managing social interactions, and restructuring cognitions. Especially important is the capacity for self-observation and self-reflection. Many clients with PD are painfully self-aware, but they often find it difficult to decenter and reflect on their experiences. As most therapies recognize, the acquisition of this ability is a prerequisite for most forms of change.

Process of Therapy

The course and duration of treatment vary widely. Treatment of the more reactive PDs (those involving emotional dysregulation or a BPD constellation of traits) typically takes several years. The first 6 months are usually spent dealing with symptoms and crises and engaging clients in therapy. In most instances, reasonable stability is achieved in 6 months. More attention can then be given to building emotional control, which usually takes another 6 to 12 months, although there is considerable variation. Some clients are satisfied with improved self-control and symptomatic relief and terminate treatment at this point; others, however, want to resolve the interpersonal problems that dominate their lives. This is now possible because increased control over emotions and impulses enables the client to handle the emotional arousal that usually occurs when interpersonal difficulties and the consequences of adversity are discussed in depth. This phase of treatment often spans another year. As self-understanding increases, links are forged within self-knowledge that forms the basis for work on self and identity. Most clients who stay in therapy can be helped to reduce self-harm and emotional dyscontrol and to improve the quality of their lives. It is more difficult, however, to help them to build a life they deem worth living.

With other types of disorders the outcome is less predictable and the course more variable. Highly withdrawn individuals usually respond slowly to most treatments. Engagement is long and difficult. When these clients also have emotion regulation problems and engage in self-harm, the approach is similar to that taken with the more typical BPD client. With those who are simply withdrawn or schizoid, an increased sense of well-being and improved quality of life often depend on establishing an effective relationship and focusing on helping the client tolerate and accept his or her basic personality structure and find a lifestyle that is consistent with it, especially when he or she is not motivated to make more radical changes. Finally, it is not clear whether the more severe forms of antisocial personality, especially psychopathy, respond to this approach or indeed to any other methods that are currently available.

RELATIONAL CONSIDERATIONS

The central role of generic change mechanisms means that emphasis is placed on the frame of therapy and general therapeutic strategies. The therapeutic frame is defined by the therapeutic stance and contract. These establish a context for therapeutic activity, define treatment boundaries, and create conditions for change. The therapeutic stance sets the tone of therapy and shapes intervention strategies by defining the therapeutic approach and the responsibilities and activities that form the interaction between client and therapist. The most appropriate stance is to provide support, empathy, and validation and to foster the client's participation in a collaborative, descriptive exploration of problems and more adaptive responses. A clear understanding of the nature and structure of the stance helps the therapist maintain consistency.

The *treatment contract* defines the goals, structure, and limits of treatment. Most treatments for PD agree that a structured agreement is important because it promotes stability and helps create a safe and consistent environment. The Division 12 joint task force mentioned earlier concluded that outcome is related to a goal-oriented structure to treatment in which "a treatment frame [is] established in collaboration with the patient and structured to achieve clear and explicit goals" (Critchfield & Benjamin, 2006, p. 262). A discussion of goals begins to forge the idea that treatment is a collaborative process for which client and therapist share responsibility. This discussion also needs to include the practical arrangements for therapy, including frequency and length of sessions and duration of treatment. It should also include a clear explanation of the treatment process and how treatment will address the client's problems and concerns (Critchfield & Benjamin, 2006). Critchfield and Benjamin (2006) also noted the importance of an explicit and frank discussion of the therapist's limits. This is an important part of a limit-setting process that reduces misunderstandings later in therapy because the client has a clear understanding before therapy begins of what the therapist is able to do and what is not feasible.

Generic interventions that form the basic structure of treatment can be tailored to the treatment of PD using four strategies: (a) building and maintaining a collaborative relationship, (b) maintaining a consistent treatment process, (c) promoting validation, and (d) building motivation. These place the treatment relationship at the center of the change process. Specific interventions are used only after the conditions established by general treatment strategies have been met.

Alliance Factors Related to Process and Outcome

The alliance is given priority because it provides support and predicts outcome. Unfortunately, a collaborative relationship is not easily achieved; it is often the result of treatment, not a prerequisite for treatment. For this reason, the therapist must give careful attention to building and repairing the alliance. Two ideas are useful for this purpose: (a) Luborsky's (1984) two-component description of the alliance and (b) Safran, Muran, and Samstag's (1994) work on repairing ruptures to the alliance.

Building a Collaborative Relationship

Luborsky (1984) suggested that the alliance has a *perceptual component*, in which the client sees the therapist as helpful and him- or herself as accepting help, as well as a *relationship component*, in which client and therapist work cooperatively to help the client. The former is based on the perceived credibility of therapy and the therapist. This is largely achieved through interventions that communicate hope, convey understanding and acceptance of the client's problems, support treatment goals, acknowledge areas of competence, and recognize progress toward attaining treatment goals. The relationship component is built by promoting the client's participation in a joint search for understanding, helping the client learn new skills, encouraging the client–therapist bond, and emphasizing the collaborative nature of treatment.

Any deterioration in the alliance should be dealt with promptly but supportively. Safran and colleagues (1994; Safran, Muran, Samstag, & Stevens, 2002) suggested a four-stage process to repair alliance problems:

1. Changes in the alliance, such as decreased involvement, are noted.
2. The client's attention is drawn to the event, the reasons for the rupture and the way that it was experienced are explored, and the client is encouraged to express any negative feelings about the event.
3. The therapist validates the client's account of the experience.

4. If these steps are not effective, attention focuses on how the client avoids recognizing and exploring the rupture.
5. The therapist acknowledges his or her contribution to the relationship problem and promotes joint discussion of the reasons the rupture occurred and how it may be repaired.

The value of this approach is that it uses a potentially negative event to change maladaptive schemata.

Maintaining a Consistent Treatment Process. An important factor linked to the alliance that is also a prerequisite for change is a consistent treatment process (Critchfield & Benjamin, 2006). It is noteworthy that many clients with successful outcomes mention therapist consistency as a major factor that contributed to their improvement (Livesley, 2007). *Consistency* in this context means adherence to the frame of therapy. This is the reason why therapists must pay careful attention to the treatment contract. Consistency also provides clients with the structure to contain unstable emotions and impulses, and it contributes to the formation of more adaptive representations of self and others by providing a stable experience of the self within the relationship. Maintenance of consistency is, however, a challenge, because unstable self-states, labile emotions, distrust, and difficulty with cooperation often drive recurrent attempts to alter the frame and challenge the therapist's resolve to maintain consistency. Success requires skill in setting limits without damaging one's empathic stance. This is best achieved by confronting attempts to change the frame when they first occur while also offering support and understanding. It also involves recognizing and thereby validating the reasons for violating the frame while pointing out how the violation may adversely affect therapy.

Establishing and Maintaining a Validating Treatment Process. An effective alliance is built through affirmation of the legitimacy of the client's experiences. Validation in this sense is more a function of therapist attitudes than a specific set of interventions. Validation serves multiple functions. It is inherently empathic and supportive and hence strengthens the alliance. Recognizing, acknowledging, and accepting the pain of adverse experiences also has a settling effect early in therapy when the client is searching for acceptance and understanding. Consistent validation helps to counter earlier invalidating experiences (Linehan, 1993), thereby promoting self-validation and the development of a more adaptive self-structure. The essential task is to validate experience without validating causes and consequences of experiences and responses that are invalid. This involves helping the client distinguish the experience, the reasons given for the experience, and the conclusions drawn from it.

Building and Maintaining Motivation for Change. Although motivation to change is essential for clients to seek help and work productively on their problems, low motivation and passivity are inherent to PD; thus, motivation cannot be a prerequisite for treatment, and therapists need to make extensive use of motivational interviewing techniques (Miller & Rollnick, 2002; Rosengren, 2009) to elicit and reaffirm a commitment to change. This commitment is built on expectations that treatment will be successful. The therapist creates hope through his or her approach to treatment and by reminding clients of their previous successes, no matter how small. In addition to building hope, it is useful to tap any discontentment that clients may feel about their problems to increase the discrepancy between the way things are and the way the client would like them to be. Discontent, like hope, is a powerful motivator (Baumeister, 1994).

When motivation is poor, the best course is usually to maintain a supportive stance while attempting to explore the consequences of maladaptive behavior. Although therapists are often tempted to be more confrontational at these times, this rarely works, and it usually has an adverse effect on the therapeutic alliance. As Linehan, Davison, Lynch, and Sanderson (2006) noted, motivation for treatment is enhanced when the therapist deals with low motivation and therapeutic impasses in a supportive and flexible way and acknowledges that change is difficult.

Client Characteristics Related to Process and Outcome

Three sets of enduring client characteristics influence treatment: (a) mental state related to Axis I pathology, (b) developmental factors, and (c) personality characteristics and associated level of functional impairment. The presence of substantial Axis I symptoms adversely affects the client's ability to tolerate stress and emotional arousal. Integrated treatment emphasizes an emotion regulating approach and tries to defer intense work on the effects of psychosocial adversity until emotion regulation skills are acquired and a reasonable level of symptomatic stability is achieved. The presence of a severe concurrent Axis I disorder reinforces the importance of this approach throughout treatment. For example, a client with a severe PD and bipolar disorder who becomes psychotic when stressed would be treated primarily with generic methods and structured techniques. The presence of phenomena more directly related to PD, such as dissociative and regressive behavior and quasi-psychotic symptoms that are stress induced, also suggest caution when considering interventions that are likely to evoke intense emotional reactions. The presence of neuropsychological dysfunction suggests the importance of monitoring the client's capacity to process information and to regulate affects and impulses when planning treatment.

Developmental factors, such as severe deprivation or privation and abuse, adversely affect outcome in several ways. First, severe psychosocial adversity is related to the capacity to tolerate stress and affect arousal. In general, a history of severe trauma and deprivation suggests caution in using emotion-arousing interventions, at least until the individual's capacity to manage affects and impulses is fully evaluated or his or her self-management of emotions and impulses improves. Second, adversity is associated with functional impairment in social and work relationships, including attachment relationships, which is related to outcome (Fernandez-Alvarez, Clarkin, Salguiero, & Critchfield, 2006), probably because they hinder the formation of an effective working relationship.

Several personality traits have a bearing on treatment process and outcome. Extreme levels of the major dimensions of PD, with the possible exception of compulsivity, often create problems in self-regulation, although for different reasons. Psychological-mindedness and related metacognitive processes involving the capacity to self-reflect and understand the mental states of self and others are important determinants of outcome. Although different treatments include elaborate strategies for dealing with specific psychopathology, outcome is largely determined by four broad factors: (a) the treatment alliance, (b) motivation and a commitment to change, and (c) the capacity for self-reflection coupled with (d) an active interest in mental processes. Finally, quality of object relationships is an important factor (Ogrodniczuk, Piper, & Joyce, 2001). Clients with poor object relationships seem best managed with generic interventions and a more structured approach.

Therapist Characteristics Related to Process and Outcome

Systematic analyses of therapist factors related to outcome point to the importance of the therapist being patient; adopting an open-minded, flexible, and creative approach; being comfortable with long-term, emotionally intense relationships; having tolerance for strong negative feelings about the client and treatment; and having specialized training and experience with PDs (Fernandez-Alvarez et al., 2006). Gunderson (2001) also noted the importance of being action oriented, adventurous, and good humored.

As Carl Rogers (1957) noted, therapist empathy is a major predictor of treatment outcome. Although there is little empirical confirmation of the role of empathy in the treatment of PD, clinical experience suggests that Rogers's ideas are highly relevant, and the treatment of clients with addictions (many of whom are also likely to have a PD) show that therapist empathy accounts for a substantial amount of outcome variance (Miller & Rollnick, 1991). Rogers's conceptualization of therapist empathy is highly pertinent to treating PD. For Rogers, empathy has two components: (a) an *attentiveness* component that is highly validating, engages the client and draws him or her into the therapeutic relationship, and helps create a safe and supportive environment; and (b) a *reflective* component that clarifies and amplifies the client's own material without imposing the therapist's own views onto the client and hence models openness and collaboration. The therapist's ability to ensure adequate levels of both components is critical. The actual personal qualities that correlate with this ability are less clear; however, Rogers's descriptions imply the importance of openness and personal warmth.

TECHNIQUES AND METHODS OF TREATMENT

Description of Methods Used

As noted earlier, general treatment strategies are used throughout therapy, and specific interventions are used only when there is a good alliance and the client is motivated to change. The use of specific interventions is best understood in the context of the phases-of-change model described earlier. The selection of specific treatment methods is based on a consideration of the treatment methods that are most appropriate for a given domain of psychopathology guided by the results of outcome studies. The sequence of specific interventions moves from more structured techniques to less structured methods as symptoms, including suicidality and proneness to crises, settle and emotion regulating skills are acquired.

Safety

Treatment of severe PD typically begins with a crisis presentation characterized by emotional dyscontrol and symptomatic distress and behavioral disorganization with decreased control leading to violence directed toward the self or others. In some cases, the crisis involves regressive and dissociated behaviors and cognitive dysregulation involving impaired problem solving and quasi-psychotic symptoms. In these situations, the primary goal is to ensure the safety of the client and others. This is largely achieved through structure and support that are usually delivered through outpatient treatment or crisis intervention services, although on occasion brief inpatient treatment may be needed.

Containment

The safety phase of treatment is usually brief and merges quickly with containment, which involves stabilizing symptoms, containing impulses and affects, and restoring behavioral control. Taken together, the safety and containment phases are typical of crisis management. The goals are to return the client to his or her previous level of functioning as soon as possible and to establish conditions for longer term treatment. Change is largely mediated through generic mechanisms (support, empathy, and structure) supplemented with medication as appropriate. Containment interventions are based on the recognition that the client's primary concern in a crisis is to obtain relief from distress that comes from feeling misunderstood. Thus, the therapist's task is to acknowledge the client's distress instead of confronting it, trying to change it, or interpreting it. Containment interventions are used whenever crises occur, the client dissociates, or emotional arousal reaches levels that threaten to interfere with treatment. The only specific intervention used during the containment phase is medication to target specific behaviors, such as impulsivity, affective lability, or cognitive dysregulation (Soloff, 2000).

Control and Regulation

As the presenting crisis resolves, treatment typically begins to focus on symptom reduction by increasing self-regulation of emotions and impulses. Most clients with severe PD, even those with more inhibited, socially withdrawn traits, have difficulty recognizing, tolerating, and controlling emotions because of deficiencies in their self-regulatory mechanisms arising from the interplay between genetic predispositions and psychosocial adversity. Thus, treatment should give priority to the development of skills and strategies to increase self-regulation and promote self-reflection. The intent is to reduce reactivity and encourage clients to think about their emotions and situation rather than merely experience or react to them. This usually requires an array of cognitive–behavioral interventions supplemented with medication. Emphasis is placed on cognitive–behavioral methods because of accumulating evidence of their value in treating deliberate self-harm, suicidality, and emotional dysregulation. This evidence comes from randomized clinical trials of the efficacy of general treatments, such as dialectical behavior therapy (Linehan, Armstrong, Suarez, Allmon, & Heard, 1991), and from more focused treatments, such as Systems Training for Emotional Predictability and Problem Solving (Blum et al., 2008), which is a directed therapy, as well as studies of manualized assisted cognitive therapy (Evans et al., 1999; Schmidt & Davidson, 2004) that are directed specifically toward emotional dysregulation and self-harm. These treatments offer an array of empirically supported interventions that therapists can use in a flexible and creative way to meet the needs of individual clients.

Therapists should also pay attention to maladaptive cognitive styles, such as self-invalidating and catastrophic thinking, that tend to exacerbate emotional dyscontrol. During this phase of treatment typical sessions involve a dialogue about ongoing problems and events. As these events are discussed, specific methods are introduced, and thus specific interventions are integrated into the treatment process.

The underlying model assumes that self-harm and related problem behaviors associated with crises are the end result of a sequence of events that begins with a triggering situation that activates an escalating dysphoric state that culminates with deliberate self-harm, a model that is consistent with both dialectical behavior therapy (Linehan, 1993) and transference-focused therapy (Clarkin et al., 1999; see also Swenson, 1989). Triggering situations are usually interpersonal events that activate maladaptive schemata focused on abandonment and rejection. The therapist begins treatment by explicating this sequence, because most clients do not connect the different components of this chain, and eliciting from the client a commitment to change. Explication of this sequence increases the client's awareness of the links between problem behaviors and situational factors, emotional reactions, and associated cognitions, which is an important change mechanism (Critchfield & Benjamin, 2006). The different components in the chain are subsequently targeted with specific interventions so that, over time, treatment focuses on reducing self-harm and other maladaptive crisis behaviors, increasing affect regulation, restructuring emotional experience, and restructuring perceptions of triggering situations by helping clients recognize that many of these situations may be understood differently. Underlying maladaptive schemata are discussed, but systematic attempts to explore and modify them are deferred until emotion control has increased.

As the sequence of events leading to self-harm and crises is explored, the therapist introduces the idea of delaying self-harming behaviors with the initial goal of delaying and reducing the frequency of these behaviors rather than eliminating them, because the latter is unrealistic early in treatment. By setting modest and more readily attainable goals the therapist increases the probability of early success. Any success is used to build the alliance and increase self-efficacy. Simple behavioral interventions, such as distraction, self-soothing, and response prevention, are used for this purpose. At the same time, a psychoeducational component is introduced to explain the sequence of events that leads to crises and the reasons for self-harming acts. Self-harming behavior is explained as a self-regulation strategy. This usually increases the alliance and reduces self-blame. Equally important is that the idea that self-harm is the best way the client has learned to reduce distress automatically raises the possibility of alternative ways to handle distress. This sets the stage for the therapist to introduce a variety of behavioral and cognitive–behavioral interventions to increase emotional control.

Steps to increase emotional control begin with the therapist helping the client identify emotions and recognize the nuances of their emotional experience; many clients experience relatively undifferentiated feelings. Control is possible only when feelings can be recognized accurately. Attention is also given to improving distress tolerance because many clients are remarkably phobic about negative emotions. Although many therapies promote emotion recognition and tolerance using set exercises, it is often more effective to incorporate these interventions into the process of therapy so that the therapeutic relationship and containment interventions can be used to modulate emotional arousal.

In tandem with these interventions, clients are encouraged to use self-soothing and distraction at the first signs of distress. Simple relaxation methods are introduced as ways to self-manage emotions and, as these are acquired, attention-control skills are developed to help the client refocus attention away from distressing thoughts instead of ruminating about them. Specific cognitive interventions are also used to help the client change maladaptive ways of thinking that escalate distress, such as rumination, catastrophizing, and self-invalidation.

Two other interventions are useful during this phase of treatment. First, clients often benefit from learning alternative ways to seek help in a crisis. Most clients seek help only after some form of self-harm has occurred and then present in an angry and demanding way that often alienates those to whom they turn. Clients need to be encouraged to seek help before self-harm has occurred and to do so in a more cooperative way. Second, many potential crises can be averted if clients learn to examine interpersonal situations more carefully and avoid personalizing situations so readily. For example, a client may assume that a friend's reluctance to meet is an indication that the friend does not really like him or her or wants to avoid him or her instead of recognizing that people have lives of their own and that this friend may not be available simply because of prior commitments. Encouraging clients to question their own interpretations of events often helps to restructure experiences and reduce the activation of maladaptive cognitions that lead to crises.

The duration of this phase of treatment varies considerably across different forms of disorder and cases. With less emotionally volatile forms of disorder this phase may be relatively short, although more inhibited or socially withdrawn individuals often need help managing anxiety, dysphoria, and distress. With more reactive forms of disorders involving labile emotions and/or strong tendencies to act impulsively, this phase is likely to be prolonged.

Exploration and Change

Improvement in affect regulation permits greater exploration of underlying cognitive–emotional structures and the interpersonal domain. This invariably involves dealing with more emotionally arousing events associated with adversity and trauma. Because intense emotions are destabilizing with individuals with PD, systematic attention to these issues is possible only with improved emotional control. When these problems are raised earlier in treatment, the therapist deals with them by acknowledging and validating the problems while avoiding detailed exploration.

The problems addressed during this phase include maladaptive schemata associated with self-harm and violence; dysfunctional interpersonal patterns; maladaptive traits, such as submissiveness, insecure attachment, and social avoidance; cognitive styles such as self-invalidating and catastrophic thinking; and the consequences of trauma. The common elements to these varied problems are the maladaptive cognitive structures noted in the account of the personality system. Consequently, change mechanisms are largely directed toward restructuring maladaptive schemata through continued use of cognitive interventions such as those used in schema-focused therapy, which have been shown to be effective in treating BPD (Cottraux et al., 2009; Giesson-Bloo et al., 2006). However, as the process proceeds, psychodynamic approaches are often needed to clarify and change specific maladaptive interpersonal problems and address the avoidance of critical issues that is characteristic of this stage of treatment.

Psychodynamic methods are also needed because the treatment relationship becomes a major vehicle for changing core interpersonal schemata such as distrust, rejection, abandonment, thoughts of "I am a bad person," and shame. Clients with severe PD often have difficulty using standard cognitive interventions (Layden, Newman, Freeman, & Morse, 1993); interpersonal methods are usually more effective (Young et al., 2003). The relationship with the therapist is used to explore the situational factors that activate maladaptive schemata, the feelings associated with schema activation, and the impact of these cognitive–emotional structures on interpersonal behavior.

A cognitive approach may also be used to deal with the maladaptive expressions of traits such as affective lability, submissiveness, callousness, and sensation seeking, which play an important role in maintaining maladaptive behavior and maladaptive interpersonal patterns. Although these traits are highly heritable, this does not mean that change is not possible; however, there may be limits to which trait structure can be modified with current techniques. Instead of attempting to effect major changes in trait structure, the therapist might find it more worthwhile to try to reduce the frequency and intensity of trait expression and change the actual behaviors through which a trait is expressed.

The frequency and intensity of trait expression may be attenuated by restructuring the schemata that mediate behavioral expression. For example, beliefs about personal invulnerability associated with recklessness and sensation seeking can be challenged, leading to changes in the range of situations that activate this trait. With emotional traits such as anxiousness it is often possible to combine restructuring beliefs about the threatening nature of the interpersonal world with the anxiety-control skills learned earlier to reduce the intensity of anxiety and fearfulness.

It may be possible to promote more adaptive ways to express certain traits; for example, many BPD clients are often easily bored and need excitement. These tendencies toward sensation seeking contribute to maladaptive behavior: Crises and interpersonal conflict are arousing and have exciting elements that contribute to the stability of these problems. Clients can often be helped to identify alternative ways to satisfy their need for excitement that are less harmful. They can also be encouraged to find a personal niche that is compatible with their personality, interests, and talents. Most individuals manage to create a personal niche—a personal world—that is satisfying and rewarding. Many clients with PD find this hard to do. They often seek out environments that promote maladaptive rather than adaptive behavior and find it hard to accept many of their personality characteristics because they do not understand how traits such as emotional lability and submissiveness may be used adaptively. These developments lead to the next stage: the development of a more adaptive self.

Integration and Synthesis

This final stage of treatment is rarely reached with many clients. The goal is to reformulate the individual's sense of self or identity and integrate the fragmented nature of personality and self-functioning observed in PD. This involves the synthesis of new personality structures, especially more effective interpersonal boundaries, a more coherent self, more integrated representations of others, and the capacity for self-directedness. These changes rely primarily not on analysis and resolution of maladaptive and conflicted ways of being but instead on the synthesis of new personality processes and structures. Clinical evidence suggests that such changes are more difficult to achieve and usually require long-term treatment. Although little empirical research has been reported on this aspect of treatment, an analysis of the nature of self-pathology suggests that the systematic use of general therapeutic strategies is important and that the methods of self psychology and constructionist approaches to psychotherapy may be of value.

Compendium of Techniques Consistent With the Approach and Examples of the Clinical Process

In integrated treatment, by definition, the therapist uses an eclectic array of techniques guided by a systematic conceptual structure. Within the general framework proposed, therapists are encouraged to use whatever evidence-informed methods appear appropriate and to adopt methods that fit their style and approach. The only interventions that are considered inappropriate are those that are inconsistent with the emphasis on generic mechanisms and an empathic and validating therapeutic stance. For example, a heavily confrontational stance or a challenging interpretative approach is avoided.

The following dialogue is an example of the use of validation and reframing to build the alliance and reduce self-criticism early in treatment:

Client (C):   If you want, I will sign a contract agreeing not to cut myself again and that you will stop seeing me if I do.

Therapist (T):   Have you signed a contract like that before?

C: Yes, with my last doctor

T: What happened?

C: I cut myself, and she stopped seeing me.

T: So it didn't work?

C: No, but my family doctor says I am very bad for cutting myself and if I don't stop she will take me off her list. So, if you want me to sign a contract I will, because I know I'm bad.

T: I don't think you cut yourself because you are bad but because you can't think of any other way to make yourself feel better when you are upset.

C: Nobody ever said that before.

In the next exchange, the therapist builds on modest success with a specific intervention (relaxation and desensitization) to deal with a specific aversive stimulus—men with a facial feature that was a characteristic of a perpetrator of early sexual abuse—to build the alliance and motivation. This example also illustrates the value of repeating and continually reinforcing basic ideas:

T: What was that like?

C: I really enjoyed relaxing. I didn't think I could do it.

T: You had not tried relaxing in this way before?

C: No. I didn't think I could do it. I was surprised . . . I relaxed.

T: So we have just found a way to help you do something that you hadn't thought possible? (*Emphasizing the collaborative nature of the alliance by and promoting a sense of self of self-efficacy and control*)

C: Yes . . . it was good . . . I think I'm going to try this at home.

T: If you do you will probably find that you will be able to do it more easily with practice. (*Building motivation*)

C: That would really help.

T: It also seemed that you were able to switch your mind from thinking of that kind of face. (*Reinforcing the small success*)

C: (*Surprised tone*) I was really surprised about that. I never thought it possible.

T: You were also able to control your feelings when you thought about these men.

C: I was, wasn't I? I didn't think that I would ever be able to think about him. I panic whenever I see someone like that. Now I'm talking about it without getting upset.

T: So this is a change for you. (*Helping the client recognize this small success is a change. The idea is to build hope that change is possible and hence build motivation.*)

C: Mmm-hmm! A big change! It can't be possible.

T: It seems that we found a way to help you to begin to control your feelings—something that you didn't think you could do. (*Again emphasizing and reinforcing the collaborative nature of the alliance and idea is that feelings can be controlled*)

In the next example, the therapist increases self-reflection and clarifies the way a client acts in ways that confirm her core maladaptive beliefs:

C: (*Describing how while on a walk through a park two people hit her as she walked past them*) You see! I told you everyone was against me. I can't even go for a walk! (*Activation of core schema "The world is hostile, everyone is against me, and no one gives a damn about me"*)

T: One person hitting you is understandable—by chance you just happened to pass an angry or upset person—but two is difficult to understand. (*Encouraging self-observation and self-reflection*)

C: [*Pause*] Do you think it is something I do?

T: Do you think that's possible?

C: [*Pause*] I don't know . . . perhaps I looked hostile.

T: What did you do?

C: I went for a walk because my friend said she couldn't meet me and I was mad. I think it showed.

T: Hmm!

C: I walked in a straight line and wouldn't get out of anyone's way. Then someone thumped me and another person said, "That's dreadful; that person hit you. You can't even go walk in the park safely."

T: It sounds as if you think you may have triggered it.

C: Yeah, I think I did.

T: Over the last few weeks we have talked about how you feel everyone is against you and how this affects you. It seems that you sometimes do things that cause people to act in this way.

C: You mean it's me, not them.

T: Perhaps it is sometimes. What do you think?

C: [Pause] Yeah, I think so.

T: It also seems that you don't pay as much attention to good things that happen. One person was very concerned— they were not against you. (Drawing attention to the client's tendency to ignore disconfirming information)

In the following exchange, the therapist demonstrates the task of constructing a sense of self or identity in a client in the later stages of treatment:

C: A few days ago I suddenly realized I had a future.

T: Yes?

C: Yes, I never thought about the future. I didn't think I had a future. I always thought I would suicide. Now I know I won't.

T: So these thoughts about suicide have gone away?

C: Yes, but I don't know what to do about it. I don't know what to do. I don't really know who I am or what I want. So, I don't know what to do with my life.

T: A few weeks ago we talked about your interest in the novel and how the novelist constructs the personality of the main characters. Perhaps your situation is like that of a novelist. Now you have the opportunity to write the story of the rest of your life.

C: Yes [Slowly, indicating she is thinking about the idea] . . . I might be able to.

When considering these vignettes, note that in some ways they provide a somewhat distorted view of the overall process of treating personality pathology. The features of PD change slowly, and this change often requires considerable repetition. Most of the strategies and techniques discussed in this chapter are applied over months before change becomes manifest. Consider as an example the therapeutic dialogue between client and therapist about the schema "the world is against me." This dialogue occurred only after extensive discussion over many months of the client's anger and resentment toward others and her feelings that no one cared about her and that she was continually disappointed by family and friends. This discussion gradually elaborated the details of the schema and hence set the stage for the therapeutic exchange that occurred. The session in question was followed by many more in which the therapist and client worked over the same material. In the process, it became clear that this schema was linked to an even more important schema: "I am unlovable." Similarly, the work needed to help a client with BPD who repeatedly becomes involved in abusive relationships because she is highly submissive may take many months. Even when such a client recognizes the submissive pattern, it takes time for her to recognize the many ways in which she acts in a subservient and passive way and to begin to challenge some of these behaviors. Only then can attention concentrate on helping her to find adaptive ways to use the trait, for example, by volunteering or working in situations that involves helping others. Consequently, it is important to understand specific interactions and dialogues within a broader context.

Treatment of Comorbid Conditions

The management of comorbid disorders depends on the disorders and their severity. With severe disorders that interfere with the client's ability to use psychotherapeutic interventions, therapy would be used only after the comorbid condition was treated successfully. With most clients, the comorbid disorder is usually etiologically and developmentally related to PD, for example, some mood disorders and anxiety and eating disorders. An integrated approach readily accommodates the treatment of such comorbid conditions. Under these circumstances, the methods used to treat the comorbid condition are considered specific interventions and managed in the same way as other specific interventions; that is, priority is given to the treatment relationship. This is also the case when medication is used. The benefits of medication are discussed, and the limits of medication effects are explained. The client is then asked to decide whether to take medication, which minimizes client–therapist struggles around compliance.

TREATMENT AND INDIVIDUAL DIFFERENCES IN PERSONALITY PATTERNS

Although individual differences in PD are important, integrated treatment does not adopt the *DSM–IV* approach, for two reasons. First, *DSM–IV* categorical diagnoses are global constructs that do not capture the complexity or range of psychopathology needed for treatment planning and selection of interventions. Most interventions are not designed to treat the overall disorder but instead target specific behaviors such as self-harm, impulsivity, and affective lability. Second, the *DSM–IV* classification of PDs lacks empirical support. There is, however, overwhelming evidence that individual differences in PD are best represented by a dimensional model. Dimensional systems assume that traits are organized into a hierarchy in which a large number of primary traits combine to form a few higher order traits. This arrangement allows the clinician to describe personality pathology in the detail needed to select interventions, and dimensional models are consistent with the emphasis that integrated treatment places on decomposing disorders into domains of psychopathology and defining the features of each domain that are the target for change.

CONCLUSION

In this chapter, I have argued that PD is best treated using an integrated and multifaceted approach tailored to the client's psychopathology and personality, with interventions selected, where possible, on the basis of evidence of what works. I also have argued that the core or defining features of PD involve the failure to develop an integrated self-structure and coherent personality functioning; hence, an important treatment goal is to foster more integrated personality functioning. For this reason, therapists must pay attention to delivering interventions in a systematic and coordinated way to promote integration. This is achieved by organizing treatment around the generic or nonspecific component of therapy with more specific interventions added to this structure as needed to treat specific problems. The coordinated delivery of interventions is also achieved using a phases-of-change model in which the problems that are the focus of attention change systematically during treatment.

REFERENCES

American Psychiatric Association. (1994). *Diagnostic and statistical manual of mental disorders* (4th ed.). Washington, DC: Author.

Baumeister, R. F. (1994). The crystallization of discontent in the process of major life change. In T. F. Heatherton & J. L. Weinberger (Eds.), *Can personality change?* (pp. 281–297). Washington, DC: American Psychological Association.

Benjamin, L. S. (1993). *Interpersonal diagnosis and treatment of personality disorders.* New York, NY: Guilford Press.

Beutler, L. E. (1991). Have all won and must all have prizes? Revisiting Luborsky et al.'s verdict. *Journal of Consulting and Clinical Psychology, 59,* 226–232.

Blum, N., St. John, D., Pfohl, B., Stuart, S., McCormick, B., Allen, J., . . . Black, D. W. (2008). Systems Training for Predictability and Problem Solving (STEPPS) for outpatients with borderline personality disorder: A randomized controlled trial and 1-year follow-up. *The American Journal of Psychiatry, 165*, 468–478.

Castonguay, L.G., & Beutler, L.E. (2006a). Common and unique principles of therapeutic change: What do we know and what do we need to know? In L. G. Castonguay & L. E. Beutler (Eds.), *Principles of therapeutic change that work* (pp. 353–369). New York, NY: Oxford University Press.

Castonguay, L. G., & Beutler, L. E. (Eds.). (2006b). *Principles of therapeutic change that work*. New York, NY: Oxford University Press.

Clarkin, J. F., Yeomans, F. E., & Kernberg, O. (1999). *Psychotherapy for borderline personality disorder*. New York, NY: Wiley.

Cloninger, C. R. (2000). A practical way to diagnose personality disorder: A proposal. *Journal of Personality Disorders, 14*, 99–108.

Cloninger, C. R. (2005). Genetics. In J. M. Oldham, A. S. Skodal, & D. S. Bender (Eds.), *Textbook of personality disorders* (pp. 143–154). Washington, DC: American Psychiatric Publishing.

Cottraux, J., Note, I. D., Boutitie, D., Milliery, M., Genouihlac, V., Yao, S. N., . . . Gueyffier, F. (2009). Cognitive versus Rogerian supportive theory in borderline personality disorder. *Psychotherapy and Psychosomatics, 78*, 307–316

Critchfield, K. L., & Benjamin, L. S. (2006). Integration of therapeutic factors in treating personality disorders. In L. G. Castonguay & L. E. Beutler (Eds.), *Principles of therapeutic change that work* (pp. 253–271). New York, NY: Oxford University Press.

David, J. D., & Pilkonis, P. A. (1996). The stability of personality disorder diagnoses. *Journal of Personality Disorders, 10*, 1–15.

Dimaggio, G., Semerari, A., Carcione, A., Nicolo, G., & Procacci, M. (2007). *Psychotherapy of personality disorders: Metacognition, states of mind, and interpersonal cycles*. London, England: Routledge.

Evans, K., Tyrer, P., Catalan, J., Schmidt, U., Davidson, K., Tata, P., . . . Thompson, S. (1999). Manual assisted cognitive–behavioral therapy (MACT): A randomized controlled trial of a brief intervention with bibliotherapy in the treatment of recurrent deliberate self-harm. *Psychological Medicine, 29*, 19–25.

Fernandez-Alvarez, H., Clarkin, J. F., Salguiero, M., & Critchfield, K. L. (2006). Participant factors in treating personality disorders. In L. G. Castonguay & L. E. Beutler (Eds.), *Principles of therapeutic change that work* (pp. 203–218). New York, NY: Oxford University Press.

Fonagy, P., Gergely, G., Jurist, E. L., & Target, M. (2002). *Affect regulation, mentalization, and the development of the self*. New York, NY: Other Press.

Giesson-Bloo, J., van Dyck, R., Spinhoven, P., van Tilberg, W., Dirksen, C., van Asselt, T., . . . Arntz, A. (2006). Outpatient psychotherapy for borderline personality disorder: Randomized trial of schema-focused therapy vs. transference-focused therapy. *Archives of General Psychiatry, 63*, 649–658.

Gunderson, J. G. (2001). *Borderline personality disorder: A clinical guide*. Washington, DC: American Psychiatric Association.

Horowitz, M. J. (1998). *Cognitive psychodynamics: From conflict to character*. New York, NY: Wiley.

Kernberg, O. F. (1984). *Severe personality disorders*. New Haven, CT: Yale University Press.

Kohut, H. (1971). *The analysis of the self*. New York, NY: International Universities Press.

Komatsu, L. K. (1992). Recent views of conceptual structure. *Psychological Bulletin, 42*, 500–526.

Johnson, J. G., Bromley, E., & McGreoch, P. G. (2005). Role of childhood experiences in the development of maladaptive and adaptive personality traits. In J. M. Oldham, A. S. Skodal, & D. S. Bender (Eds.), *Textbook of personality disorders* (pp. 209–221). Washington, DC: American Psychiatric Publishing.

Lambert, M. J., & Bergen, A. E. (1994). The effectiveness of psychotherapy. In A. E. Bergin & S. L. Garfield (Eds.), *Handbook of psychotherapy and behavior change* (4th ed., pp. 143–189). New York, NY: Wiley.

Layden, M. A., Newman, C. F., Freeman, A., & Morse, S. B. (1993). *Cognitive therapy of borderline personality disorder*. Needham Heights, MA: Allyn & Bacon.

Leichsenring, F., & Leibing, E. (2003). The effectiveness of psychodynamic therapy and cognitive behavior therapy in the treatment of personality disorders: A meta-analysis. *American Journal of Psychiatry, 160*, 1223–1232.

Linehan, M. M. (1993). *Cognitive–behavioral treatment of borderline personality disorder*. New York, NY: Guilford Press.

Linehan, M. M., Armstrong, H. E., Suarez, A., Allmon, D., & Heard, H. (1991). Cognitive–behavioural treatment of chronically parasuicidal borderline patients. *Archives of General Psychiatry, 48*, 1060–1064.

Linehan, M. M., Davison, G. C., Lynch, T. R., & Sanderson, C. (2006). Techniques factors in treating personality disorders. In L. G. Castonguay & L. E. Beutler (Eds.), *Principles of therapeutic change that work* (pp. 239–252). New York, NY: Oxford University Press.

Lipsey, M. W. (1995). What do we learn from 400 research studies on the effectiveness of treatment with juvenile delinquents? In J. McGuire (Ed.), *What works: Reducing reoffending. Guidelines from research and practice* (pp. 63–78). Oxford, England: Wiley.

Livesley, W. J. (1999). Suggestions for a framework for an empirically based classification of personality disorder. *Canadian Journal of Psychiatry, 43*, 137–147.

Livesley, W. J. (2001). A framework for an integrated approach to treatment. In W. J. Livesley (Ed.), *Handbook of personality disorders* (pp. 570–600). New York, NY: Guilford Press.

Livesley, W. J. (2003). *Practical management of personality disorder*. New York, NY: Guilford Press.

Livesley, W. J. (2007). Integrated therapy for complex cases of personality disorder. *Journal of Clinical Psychology, 64*, 207–221.

Livesley, W. J., & Bromley, D. B. (1973). *Person perception in childhood and adolescence.* London, England: Wiley.

Livesley, W. J., & Jang, K. L. (2008). The behavioral genetic of personality disorders. *Annual Review of Clinical Psychology, 4*, 247–274.

Luborsky, L. (1984). *Principles of psychoanalytic psychotherapy.* New York, NY: Basic Books.

Luborsky, L., Singer, B., & Luborsky, L. (1975). Comparative studies of psychotherapies. *Archives of General Psychiatry, 32*, 995–1008.

Mayer, J. D. (2005). A tale of two visions: Can a new view of personality help to integrate psychology? *American Psychologist, 60*, 294–307.

Meyer, B., & Pilkonis, P. (2006). Developing treatments that bridge personality and psychopathology. In R. F. Krueger & J. L. Trackett (Eds.), *Personality and psychopathology* (pp. 262–291). New York, NY: Guilford Press.

Miller, W. R., & Rollnick, S. (1991). *Motivational interviewing.* New York, NY: Guilford Press.

Miller, W. R., & Rollnick, S. (2002). *Motivational interviewing: Preparing for change.* New York, NY: Guilford Press.

Mischel, W., & Shoda, Y. (1995). A cognitive–affective system theory of personality: Reconceptualizing situations, dispositions, dynamics, and invariance in personality structure. *Psychological Review, 102*, 246–268.

Ogrodniczuk, J. S., Piper, W. E., & Joyce, A. S. (2001). Using DSM Axis II information to predict outcome in short-term individual psychotherapy. *Journal of Personality Disorders, 15*, 110–122.

Paris, J. (2001). Psychosocial adversity. In W. J. Livesley (Ed.,) *Handbook of personality disorders* (pp. 231–241). New York, NY: Guilford Press.

Paris, J. (2005). Treatment of borderline personality disorder. *Canadian Journal of Psychiatry, 50*, 435–441.

Piper, W. E., & Joyce, A. S. (2001). Psychosocial treatment outcome. In W. J. Livesley (Ed.), *Handbook of personality disorders* (pp. 323–343). New York, NY: Guilford Press.

Rogers, C. R. (1957). The necessary and sufficient conditions for therapeutic change. *Journal of Consulting Psychology, 21*, 95–103.

Rosengren, D. B. (2009). *Building motivational interviewing skills: A practitioner workbook.* New York, NY: Guilford Press.

Rutter, M. (1987). Temperament, personality, and personality disorder. *British Journal of Psychiatry, 150*, 443–458.

Sackett, D. L., Rosenberg, W. M. C., Gray, J. A. M., Haynes, R. B., & Richardson, W. S. (1996). Evidence based medicine: What it is and what it isn't. *British Medical Journal, 312*, 71–72.

Safran, J. D., Muran, J. C., & Samstag, L. W. (1994). Resolving therapeutic alliance ruptures: A task analytic investigation. In A. O. Horvath & L. S. Greenberg (Eds.), *The working alliance: Theory, research, and practice* (pp. 225–255). New York, NY: Wiley.

Safran, J. D., Muran, J. C., Samstag, L. W., & Stevens, C. (2002). Repairing alliance ruptures. In J. C. Norcross (Ed.), *Psychotherapy relationships that work: Therapist contributions and responsiveness to patients* (pp. 235–254). New York, NY: Oxford University Press.

Schmidt, U., & Davidson, K. (2004). *Life after self-harm.* Hove, England: Brunner-Routledge.

Segal, Z. (1988). Appraisal of the self schema construct in models of depression. *Psychological Bulletin, 103,* 147–162.

Skodol, A. E., Gunderson, J. G., Shea, M. T., McGlashan, T. H., Morey, L. C., Sanislow, C. A., . . . Stout, R. L. (2005). The Collaborative Longitudinal Personality Disorders Study (CLPS): Overview and implications. *Journal of Personality Disorders, 19,* 487–504.

Soloff, P. H. (2000). Psychopharmacology of borderline personality disorder. *Psychiatric Clinics of North America, 23,* 169–190.

Swenson, C. (1989). Kernberg and Linehan: Two approaches to the borderline patient. *Journal of Personality Disorders, 3,* 26–35.

Tickle, J. J., Heatherton, T. F., & Wittenberg, L. G. (2001). Can personality change? In W. J. Livesley (Ed.), *Handbook of personality disorders* (pp. 242–258). New York, NY: Guilford Press.

Widiger, T., & Simonsen, E. (2005). Alternative dimensional models of personality disorder: Finding a common ground. *Journal of Personality Disorders, 19,* 110–130.

Young, J. E., Klosko, J. S., & Weishaar, M. E. (2003). *Schema therapy.* New York, NY: Guilford Press.

9

METHODS, COMPONENTS, AND STRATEGIES OF UNIFIED TREATMENT: USING EVIDENCE AND PERSONALITY SYSTEMATICS TO ENHANCE OUTCOME

JEFFREY J. MAGNAVITA

Unified psychotherapy is based on a component system model of clinical science called *personality systematics* (Magnavita, 2004, 2005, 2006). Personality systematics is based on the premise that it is the unique personality system of the individual, as embedded in dyadic, triadic, family, and sociocultural processes that accounts for all forms and expressions of psychopathology and relational dysfunction. Each domain subsystem must be understood in relation to other parts of the system. Clinical science has identified many of the important component domain subsystems of human functioning, such as the neurobiological system, the attachment system, the affect–cognitive–defense system, the relational system, and others that have been presented in the various chapters in this volume. Thus, personality systematics seeks to identify and through a process of repatterning, restructure the personality system to ameliorate an individual's adaptive capacity that focuses on enhancing organization, function, and structure. Personality systematics is, in essence, personality-guided psychotherapy (Millon, Grossman, Meagher, & Millon,

I would like to thank Jacques Barber and Mark Hilsenroth for their feedback during the early phase of writing this chapter. I extend special thanks to Kenneth Critchfield, who provided extensive input and alerted me to important research that I believe strengthened this chapter.

1999; Magnavita & Carlson, 2009) in that the personality configuration and how it functions are viewed as the central operating systems toward which clinical interventions are targeted.

Psychotherapy has evolved in the 20th century from single-domain schools to increasingly integrative treatments, and today personality systematics is moving toward unification. Unified psychotherapeutics has as its foundation a systems model (von Bertalanffy, 1968) and echoes the call for unification of psychological and clinical science (Staats, 1983; Sternberg & Grigorenko, 2001):

> To the unificationist, researchers working in the many and varied subfields of psychology are united in their professional identity (they are all scientists), their goals (they seek to extend our understanding of behavior), and their empirical outlook (they all strive to collect data relevant to the research question at hand). (Forsyth & Strong, 1986, p. 115)

In personality systematics, as in technical eclecticism, the clinician uses relevant methods and techniques from all schools of psychotherapy that are evidence based. Each method or approach to treatment must be individualized and matched to the unique characteristics of the client and the features of his or her ecological system and subsystems. Personality systematics is therefore not considered a school of psychotherapy per se but rather a metatheoretical model that organizes the domains of human functioning at four levels of substrate, from the microlevel to the macrolevel. Personality systematics, while sharing some commonalities with other approaches to psychotherapy, differentiates itself from various forms of integration, including theoretical integration, assimilative integration (Stricker & Gold, 1996), common factor (Weinberger & Rasco, 2007), and technical eclecticism (Magnavita, 2008). Unified theory is viewed as a metaframe that uses multiple theoretical perspectives for understanding psychopathology, personality, and psychotherapy, and thus it is constantly evolving as new evidence emerges and theoretical constructs are formulated and refined. Although unified psychotherapy draws from various methods and techniques, unlike technical eclecticism (Lazarus, 1997, 2008), personality systematics relies on unified theoretical modeling to provide road maps for change for the clinician and client whereby all evidence-based modalities and approaches to healing are considered in developing individualized treatment packages.

Personality dysfunction is viewed as an adaptive incongruence between the goals of the individual and his or her motivational and drive systems. It is an adaptive solution to previous environmental and relational demands that have lost their adaptive value in maximizing the individual's goals for need fulfillment and goal attainment. Personality dysfunction results in repetitive patterns that comprise exaggerated adaptations that become engrained at a neurobiological and relational domain level. One of the assumptions of personality systematics is that by identifying and changing the operating system of an individual at various domain levels, the entire system can be modified and, in many cases, reach a critical threshold where a new way of operating becomes habitual (Grawe, 2007). On a neurobiological level, new neuronal circuits are organized and strengthened and reinforced by relational experience. Accumulating evidence is showing that important neurobiological circuits, such as the limbic system, are implicated in maladaptive patterns and that psychotherapy may restructure neuronal circuits (Baxter et al., 1992; Schore, 2003). Another assumption of personality systematics is that of *holism:* No part can be viewed without an understanding of its relationship to other parts. Complex systems are open, self-organizing, and must constantly be differentiating and integrating to grow and adapt to the individual's ever-changing environmental and developmental demands. According to Schore (2003), "A central tenet of dynamic systems theory holds that at particular critical moments, a flow of energy allows the components of a self-organizing system to become increasingly interconnected, and in this manner organismic form is constructed in developmental process" (p. 266). Complex systems such as the personality system always have a degree of organization as well as a level of chaos and so are never entirely predictable. When considering clinical syndromes and or personality dysfunction one must rely on the assumption that the clinical syndromes arise out of the personality configuration so that all treatment benefits from an understanding of personality systematics. The empirical evidence strongly supports the clinical observation that the more complex an individual's symptom formations or Axis I diagnoses are, the greater the likelihood that there will exist a comorbid personality disorder (PD; Dimaggio & Norcross, 2008; Magnavita, 1998). In addition, when a diagnosis of PD is made, there is a high likelihood that more than one will be diagnosed. These findings provide support for what most clinicians observe in their practices: PDs are multiple-domain phenomena. In other words, PDs, especially the more severe types, manifest dysfunction in multiple system domains, such as cognition (distorted cognitive beliefs), affect regulation (over- or underregulated), relational (issues with intimacy and closeness), attachment (low ability to establish and maintain trust), perceptual (diminished accuracy of stimulus recognition), and behavioral repertoires (self-defeating patterns). Conversely, therapists regularly report working with clients who do not meet clinical diagnostic levels of personality pathology according to the *Diagnostic and Statistical Manual of Mental Disorders* (e.g., 4th ed., text revision; American Psychiatric Association, 2000) but whom they identify as having personality issues that significantly impact their treatments (Westen & Arkowitz-Westen, 1998). It would seem, then, that any single domain approach, especially with the more severe personality dysfunction, may not have sufficient potency to address these multiple system domains. Personality systematics strives to develop an evidence-based approach that relies on convergent research from empirical findings and clinical evidence to identify the principles of treatment and treatment selection (Beutler, 2000).

In most approaches to psychotherapy with personality dysfunction, a particular domain of the client system is in the foreground, and other component systems are in the background. Personality systematics encourages the clinician to shift his or her perspective and not become stuck in one school of thought. Conducting unified psychotherapy requires a flexible stance and the ability to hold multiple and sometimes contradictory perspectives.

MECHANISMS OF CHANGE

I agree with B. E. Wampold (2007), who wrote: "The essential aspect of psychotherapy is that a new[,] more adaptive explanation is acquired by the patient" (p. 862). The mechanisms of change to achieve this restructuring and relearning can be conceptualized as those methods, techniques, and processes that create differentiation and integration within the system. *Differentiation* refers to the processes by which components of the subsystems are identified and underscored in a mutual collaboration that emphasizes mindfulness, consciousness, and awareness. For example, at the biological–intrapsychic substrate level, differentiation includes methods by which affect, cognitions, and defenses are illuminated with a variety of techniques called *restructuring methods*. At the dyadic level, differentiation includes developing awareness of self–other functions. This might include techniques that allow each member of a dyad to reclaim his or her projected relational schemata. At the relational–triadic level, differentiation would occur when techniques are used to create hierarchy in a parent–parent–child triad. At the sociocultural–familial level, differentiation would include occur when group, family, and social units are given safe boundaries to express and process feelings over societal trauma, such as at the truth and reconciliation hearings after the end of apartheid in South Africa:

> It is important to note that the process of differentiation and integration can be inherent to the developmental course of a system, so that distinctions about adaptive/maladaptive can be about pragmatics of what isn't working, but also anchored in "phase" or developmental stage considered "normal" for a given system. (K. L. Critchfield, personal communication, May 5, 2008).

Psychotherapy itself is embedded in the cultural matrix from which it derives. B. E. Wampold (2007) wrote that "one would expect psychotherapies to be embedded in and to emerge from the cultural landscape, for the explanations involved would resonate with the psychotherapy community (theorists, researchers, and clinicians) and to be acceptable to patients" (p. 864).

Integration refers to the methods and processes that allow the therapist to make connections and communication links among component domains within a subsystem. For example, once anxiety, defense, cognition, and emotion have been differentiated, integration allows one to track the interrelationships among thought, feeling, anxiety, and defensive operations.

DOMAINS OF OPERATION WITHIN THE TOTAL ECOLOGICAL SYSTEM

Within the total ecological system we can begin to view the subsystems using various lenses which progressively broaden our perspective from the micro- to the macro-level. Beginning at intrapsychic–biological matrix we are concerned with mind–brain matrix. As we continually widen our perspective we can use the lenses of the interpersonal–dyadic, relational–triadic, and sociocultural–familial to view four domain levels.

Intrapsychic–Biological

Personality systematics highlights, where appropriate, the structures and processes that occur at the biological–intrapsychic level of operation. These subdomain systems include affective–cognitive–defensive networks as well as internalized relational and attachment schemata and their neurobiological underpinnings (Grawe, 2007). In essence, this domain level encapsulates the mind–brain processes, operating systems, and structures: Each level contains the next layer. The interpersonal, attachment, and relational schemata are codified in the neurobiological networks and are enacted at the next level, the interpersonal–dyadic domain.

Interpersonal–Dyadic

The intrapsychic–biological domain is represented in interpersonal interactions. A person's unique strategies and styles are enacted in the dyadic processes. An individual whose early attachment schema is disorganized and was built on a disruptive parental style will codify a distrustful relational schema that will impair his or her ability to trust. The intrapsychic–biological matrix is represented in patterns of transaction in dyadic relationships.

Relational–Triadic

The tendency to *triangulate*, or draw a third party into a conflicted dyad, occurs with regularity in dyads in which there is a lack of differentiation that is resulting in too much dyadic tension. Triangulation is a major dynamic in this operation, especially with the more severe PDs, because of the individual's low level of self and self–other differentiation. A similar phenomenon is called *splitting*. Splitting is especially prevalent in clients who are being treated by multiple providers. For example, there may be tension between a client's psychotherapist and psychopharmacologist that is due to their different theoretical views and modes of operating. The client may pick up on this and complain to one provider that the other is incompetent or destructive. Triangulation is a kind of three-person relational molecule that contains much energy which can be potentially fragmenting when unleashed.

Sociocultural–Familial

The interrelationships among the individual personality system, the family system, and societal systems are crucial in the personality development, functioning, and adaptation modes. Many processes are involved, including the multigenerational transmission process whereby modes of conflict resolution, patenting styles, and cultural memes are carried from one generation to another. Cultural influences contextualize and shape behavioral repertoires, and clinicians must take these influences into consideration when treating any personality dysfunction.

PROCESS OF THERAPY

Unified psychotherapeutics is a metaframework that can be characterized as a flexible, responsive application of evidence-based principles to determine and apply appropriate treatment options. The wide array of methods (see Chapters 3–8, this volume), formats, and modalities (see Chapter 10, this volume) available to contemporary clinical practitioners can be incorporated into this framework. Therefore, new and evolving treatments are continually being evaluated and, where appropriate, offered in a menu of options, including transference-focused therapy (Clarkin, Yeomans, & Kernberg, 2006), schema-focused therapy (Young, Klosko, & Weishaar, 2003), mentalization-based therapy (Bateman & Fonagy, 2004), and group therapy (Piper, Rosie, & Joyce, 1996). Other types of treatment show promise. For example, the use of heart rate variability biofeedback (Lehrer, 2007), along with other stress management methods (Lehrer, Woolfolk, & Sime, 2007), is accumulating an evidence base for treatment of common disorders associated with personality dysfunction, such as anger management, depression, emotional dysregulation, and anxiety. Eye Movement Desensitization and Reprocessing (EMDR) also shows promise for complex trauma and personality disorders (Manfield & Shapiro, 2004). A clinician who follows this framework tries to always be cognizant of how to combine various methods and modalities of treatment to facilitate client growth and development. In this sense, unified psychotherapy relies on differential treatment selection (Beutler & Clarkin, 1990) and differential therapeutics (Frances, Clarkin, & Perry, 1984). The purpose of this model is to provide guidelines for determining, through careful assessment, how treatment decisions are made regarding format, type, and modality of treatment based on the most current evidence available about the efficacy of these components and empirically based therapeutic principles. The process of treatment follows a fairly standard progression, as described in the paragraphs that follow.

Assessment and Pattern Recognition

The first phase is characterized by a comprehensive assessment of the individual, couple, family, and/or network as well as their modes of operation and personality configuration within the system with which the clinician is working. A unified approach allows the clinician to use multiple theoretical perspectives. During this phase, the clinician works at conceptualizing how the symptom constellations, relational disturbances, and repetitive maladaptive patterns emerge from the personality configuration reflected at the four domain levels of the system. To provide a multidimensional assessment, he or she develops a holographic representation that includes multiple perspectives. A *holograph* is a three-dimensional image in which perspective changes with point of orientation. The *operating system*, or what keeps patterns in action, is decoded at as many of the four domain levels as reasonable. Various models of psychotherapy offer different takes on how to depict the operating system, such as cyclical dynamics, copy process, defense–anxiety, and so on. At the intrapsychic–biological level, for example, a client's operating system might react in a flight–fight–freeze response to intimacy because of early attachment disruption. I often call on a computer analogy. Some clients' or systems' larger units (dyads, triads, families, societies) may have highly functional hardware with rapid processors, strong memory capacity, and so on, but the operating system may be antiquated, so the full potential of the system is never realized. Others may have less than optimal hardware, for example, clients with neurobiological impairment. A variety of evidence-based assessment instruments and clinical psychodiagnostic methods may be selected (see Chapter 2, this volume). Specialists may be called in to provide a more detailed portrait of individuals or subsystems.

Developing a Collaborative Treatment Package and Road Map for Change

Once the clinician has completed a satisfactory assessment, a preliminary treatment package is developed on the basis of the client's resources (e.g., ego adaptive capacities, social & family support, socioeconomic status) and capacity for and motivation to change. The client must be informed about the treatment expectations, possible benefits of treatment, and any negative or adverse consequences of treatment. The treatment package includes the treatment format, methods considered most efficacious, and specific goals of treatment (see Chapter 10, this volume, for more on treatment planning and formatting as well as an in-depth review of the factors involved). This may be especially true with clients who have more severe PDs; research has demonstrated that a review of a collaborative treatment plan is related to decreased dropout from therapy and high levels of therapeutic alliance (Gregory et al., 2008; Hilsenroth, Defife, Blake, & Cromer, 2007; Yeomans et al., 1994) The clinician develops the treatment package and discusses it with the client or subsystem (couple, family, extended family, institution) engaged in treatment. Unified therapy requires clinicians to be cognizant of the efficacy of various modalities and principles of therapeutic change. Of course, one cannot be trained in every modality or approach, and in those cases the clinician should offer referrals to other professionals trained in specific styles and modalities of treatment. It is imperative that the clinician be aware of the evidence base for various treatments even if he or she has not been trained in that approach or modality. For example, if one is not trained in Dialectical Behavior Therapy (Linehan, 1993) for the treatment of parasuicidal behavior, EMDR (Shapiro, 1995) for trauma, or psychopharmacology for mood regulation, then one should at least be aware of instances in which a referral is warranted to complement treatment and to create a comprehensive treatment package. Psychoeducation should be included as part of developing treatment package. The client should be informed about the expectations for treatment and given any appropriate, relevant information regarding evidence about treatment outcomes, information about the disorder, and ideas about how his or her current difficulties will be addressed. The clinician should also make clear that the initial plan is a working plan that can be modified if it is not effective or if extenuating circumstances apply.

Engagement and Assessment Phase

Although engagement starts at the first contact, through attention to the therapeutic alliance and developing a working relationship (Hilsenroth & Cromer, 2007), in the next phase the therapist and client engage in a process of actively working at resolving the main issues and changing self-limiting behavioral repertoires that are standing in the way of more adaptive strategies and optimal functioning. This phase may take many paths. Some clients may stick with the process until they feel a satisfactory resolution has been achieved, others may disappear and reappear later for more work, and yet others may end the treatment before there is an optimal resolution. In any case, it is best to be accepting and flexible by following the client's process and wishes, unless there are clear indications of potential harm resulting. Dropouts in this phase of treatment may be an indication of initial failure on the therapist's part to collaborate or engage motivation for deeper change beyond crisis stabilization (K. L. Critchfield, personal communication, May 5, 2008).

Experimentation and Consolidation

The next phase of treatment emphasizes the use of therapeutic methods, mobilization of growth-enhancing alliance factors, and monitoring treatment impact and alliance ruptures (see Chapter 6, this volume). The clinician here is closely assessing and monitoring the outcome of various strategies to determine their impact, and he or she makes adjustments as needed. Various restructuring methods are selected and combined to optimize the differentiation and integration of component systems. Dropouts in this phase of treatment may also involve alliance ruptures but may also imply that treatment goals need to be revisited and revised and/or the contract for treatment refined (K. L. Critchfield, personal communication, May 5, 2008).

Termination, Maintenance, and Intermittent Treatment

The last phase of treatment depends on the client's developmental level (children and adolescents, as well as individuals with medical or neuropsychological impairment, may need to continue treatment); severity of disturbance (as assessed with the Global Assessment of Functioning [American Psychiatric Association, 2000]: The lower the client's score, the more likely that he or she will need ongoing or intermittent treatment); number and type of comorbid conditions, such as bipolar disorder, schizoaffective PD, and severe substance abuse; and availability and quality of social support and resources. All of these determine the need for continuation of treatment on intermittent basis or whether termination is appropriate. Many clients with personality dysfunction seem to benefit from an open-door policy, knowing that they can return when they are faced with stressful transitions or exacerbation of symptoms. The point here is that therapist flexibility and careful assessment of ego-adaptive capacities are key, and the therapist should remember that not every client with the same diagnosis will have the same needs during termination or maintenance. Some benefit from and are strengthened by the experience of termination, which gives them an opportunity to work through grief over the loss of the therapist, whereas for other clients, who need the availability of the attachment, this can be contratherapeutic or result in iatrogenic disturbance. It is often valuable to discuss the termination phase and the meaning with the client as well as predict that some regression might be inevitable (Joyce, Piper, Ogrodniczuk, & Klein, 2007).

RELATIONAL CONSIDERATIONS

Alliance Factors Related to Process and Outcome

Unified psychotherapy has at the core of its assumptions the notion that all human functioning is embedded and expressed in the relational matrix; therefore, the foundation of all effective treatment is the quality of relationship with the therapist. It will be clear to readers who have read the chapters preceding this one that relational factors are the bedrock of all contemporary treatment approaches. Herein is the challenge to clinicians when working with clients with personality dysfunction. It is clear from research that the ability to develop a collaborative trusting relationship is a strong prognostic indicator for a positive outcome (Horvath, 2001; Martin, Garske, & Davis, 2000). The dilemma, as most readers know, is that clients with PDs have disturbances in their capacity to develop collaborative attachment, often as a result of relational trauma that makes getting close to others anxiety provoking. It is apparent that the most effective clinicians are able to engage difficult people in a relationship that will provide key components for potential recovery. Chapter 6 in this volume provides an excellent summary and compendium of various technical and relational responses to alliance ruptures when they occur.

Client Characteristics Related to Process and Outcome

A number of client characteristics are related to the process and outcome of treatment, and researchers are in only the initial stages of identifying these. The client's profile includes an array of factors that alert the clinician to certain issues that might, for example, influence the stance the clinician should take (i.e., more or less directive) or the format of therapy (i.e., whether long term, brief, or intermittent), as well as the severity of presentation and obvious issues with collaboration. Critchfield and Benjamin (2006), after conducting an extensive review of the extant evidence base, summarized these factors (see Exhibit 9.1).

- Willingness and ability to engage in treatment
- History of positive attachment experiences
- Expectations of success
- Level of resistance matches type of intervention
- Pretreatment readiness for change

Note. From "Principles for Psychosocial Treatment of Personality Disorders: Summary of the APA Division 12 Task Force/NASPR Review," by K. L. Critchfield and L. S. Benjamin, 2006, *Journal of Clinical Psychology, 62,* p. 664. Copyright 2006 by the American Psychological Association.

Therapist Characteristics Related to Process and Outcome

A number of therapist and relational factors have been identified in the literature and seem to be related to therapeutic outcome and alliance (Ackerman & Hilsenroth, 2001, 2003; Hilsenroth & Cromer, 2007). Evidence suggests that, as with most skills, there is a high degree of variability in therapists' effectiveness. Although most therapists produce average results, the top and bottom quartiles of therapists produce strikingly dramatic different outcomes (M. L. Lambert, 2007). This line of research clearly underscores the importance of the therapist in determining outcome. Countertransference comprises the reactions that the therapist has to his or her clients and is another useful aspect of understanding client personality patterns. These reactions can be used to make diagnostic and therapeutic decisions (Betan, Heim, Conklin, & Westen, 2005). An important summary was provided by Critchfield and Benjamin (2006), who, after an extensive review of the literature, culled some of the important principles, which include, among others, those discussed in the following sections (see Exhibit 9.2).

- Therapist comfort with long-term and emotionally intense relationships, as well as patience and tolerance.
- The creation of a joint strong positive therapeutic alliance.
- The ability to collaborate on the goals of treatment.
- A relatively high activity level (but needs to be calibrated to the needs of patient) on the part of the psychotherapists but not necessarily directive, as well as flexibility and creativity.
- The ability to structure treatment and set appropriate limits.
- Congruence in the psychotherapist in expression of feelings and strategic self-disclosures.

Note. From "Principles for Psychosocial Treatment of Personality Disorders: Summary of the APA Division 12 Task Force/NASPR Review," by K. L. Critchfield and L. S. Benjamin, 2006, *Journal of Clinical Psychology, 62,* p. 664–665. Copyright 2006 by the American Psychological Association.

Racial and Cultural Factors and Considerations

Unified psychotherapy is concerned with all domains of human functioning and emphasizes the cultural, ethnic, and racial factors that influence both dysfunction and healing. The impact of cultural and social systems is central to issues of classification and treatment of PDs. The need for culturally competent evidence-based treatment guidelines are important issues in clinical science (Whaley & Davis, 2007). Evidence-based culturally competent treatments have not yet been established for the treatment of PDs and present a major challenge to the field of psychotherapy. The application of evidence-based treatment in a culturally appropriate and sensitive fashion requires future research. A multilevel systems approach is well suited to working with cultural and ethnic issues with sensitivity because it requires that the clinician have an awareness of how micro- and macrosystem processes interact to produce dysfunction. Some of the questions with which clinicians must contend, until there is a substantive evidence base, encompass two main issues. Culturally sensitive assessment is complicated by the "validity" of the dominant system for diagnosis and classification of mental disorders (American Psychiatric Association, 2000). This system has been primarily based on evidence from a North American European population, so therapists need to use special consideration when applying these diagnostic criteria from members of other groups. Especially with the PDs, social, ethnic, cultural, and political influence must be taken into consideration. It is incumbent on the clinician to understand the influence of these factors on the client's diagnostic presentation. Certain characteristics or behavior patterns that may be labeled pathological in North America often have adaptive value in the cultural setting from which they evolved. Solo practitioners can make a significant impact in their broader network if they use a community-based model (Dale, 2008). The notion that psychologists are embedded in the community and can effect social change in larger networks holds promise.

TECHNIQUES AND METHODS OF TREATMENT

The methods and techniques of unified psychotherapy include the full range of those that contemporary clinical science offers. Unlike in technical eclecticism, therapists do not select methods and techniques without first considering how they impact the client's system. The therapist selects the techniques and methods to use and, through collaboration with the client, determines whether they are having their desired effect. The methods and techniques of unified psychotherapy rest on empirically established principles of therapeutic change (Beutler, 2000) and theoretical models to effectively apply these.

Description of Methods Used

There are four overarching methods of unified psychotherapy that can be organized at the four domain levels of the total ecological system. At the biological–intrapsychic level, the various techniques are subsumed under *intrapsychic restructuring*, because they are aimed at reorganizing, repatterning, and restructuring internal processes and structures. At the next level, the interpersonal–dyadic level, the techniques used are termed *dyadic restructuring*, because the primary focus is the interpersonal matrix. The next set of techniques is aimed at the triadic–relational level; labeled *triadic restructuring*, these include the group of techniques that are aimed at reconfiguring triangular and family constellations. The fourth and final method is termed *mesosystem restructuring* and is aimed at techniques and operations that seek to reorganize larger interrelated sociocultural, political systems and evaluate their impact on family (Dale, 2008). For example, an individual who is struggling with sexual identity issues at the microlevel may find himself questioning his previously unexamined religious or cultural values and decide whether he will join a protest to effect change at a macrolevel. Within these four overarching categories there exist sets of methods that include various groups of techniques.

Compendium of Selected Techniques Consistent With the Approach

Presentation of a complete compendium of the techniques available to contemporary therapists is far beyond the scope of this chapter. In fact, my colleagues and I are working on mapping and organizing the techniques as part of the Unified Psychotherapy Project (© UPP; see unifiedpsychotherapy project.org). This project has important implications for the science, practice, and training of therapists. In the following sections, I present a selection of techniques to give readers a sample of some that have been particularly useful and for which there is evidence that suggests efficacy in the treatment of personality dysfunction.

Example of Clinical Process Highlighting Techniques

In the following section, selected examples of some methods of restructuring and the techniques are illustrated with client–therapist dialogue to give readers an idea of how they are used in the clinical process to enhance differentiation and, eventually, to more integration through various restructuring procedures. The first group of techniques falls under the category of *defensive restructuring*, and the target of these is the intrapsychic–biological matrix (see Exhibit 9.3).

Although the field of clinical science is not yet at the point of being able to identify methods and techniques that have empirical support, there

EXHIBIT 9.3
Selected Techniques of Defensive Restructuring

Clarification of Defense Pattern

Client (C): I never approach someone I am interested in dating. I wait for them to ask me out.

Therapist (T): So you have a pattern of avoiding situations where you may be rejected?

C: Yes; if I wait for the woman to approach me, then I don't risk feeling inadequate.

Challenge to Defense

C: I really have no idea what I should be talking about with you.

T: So you have come here to work on certain difficulties but then you say you have no idea of what you want to focus on?

Educating Client About Defensive Strategies

T: Your pattern of adaptation is to use avoidance and passivity as a way of avoiding painful feelings. I suspect that these were strategies for survival that helped you when you were younger but may no longer be adaptive.

C: I can see how, now that you point them out, how they work and I remember as a kid when my mother who was controlling told me what to do and if I sassed her she would abuse me. This might have been a better solution.

---

is some evidence that defensive restructuring can be useful for selected clients, and it has been a mainstay of short-term dynamic therapy (see Chapter 4, this volume, and Bond & Perry, 2004, 2006, cited in Leichsenring & Rabung, 2008). Defensive restructuring techniques may have their best effect on clients who are highly defended but unaware of the function and nature of their defenses.

The next selection of techniques are used for *affective restructuring* (Greenberg, Rice, & Elliott, 1993; McCullough Vaillant, 1997; see Exhibit 9.4), and these also are aimed at the intrapsychic–biological level of the personality system. These techniques have been used extensively in experiential approaches to psychotherapy and seem to benefit clients who have some tolerance of emotion.

These techniques have emerged from the Gestalt, humanistic, and experiential schools of therapy and often include emphasizing nonverbal aspects of the client's communication, such as body movements, posture, prosody, eye contact, and so on (Diener, Hilsenroth, & Weinberger, 2007; Smyth, 1998).

Clinicians should be cautious when incorporating these techniques with clients who are easily overwhelmed by emotions because they may become flooded or dissociate. They are, however, of excellent value, especially for clients with many of the Cluster C disorders or those who are more affectively constricted (Svartberg, Stiles, & Seltzer, 2004).

The next set of techniques are aimed at the interpersonal–dyadic matrix (see Chapter 5, this volume) and represent a kind of pattern recognition tool

EXHIBIT 9.4
Selected Techniques of Affective Restructuring

Amplification of Affect

Therapist (T): I notice that your hand is in a fist as you talk about your husband.
Client (C): Oh, I didn't really notice it.
    T: Can you focus your attention on the energy in your fist?
    C: [*Fist starts to move slightly, banging the chair*]
    T: Exaggerate the motion and then notice what you are feeling.
    C: There is a hot surge of anger in my abdomen and I feel like exploding.

Differentiation of Affect

    C: I really don't know what to do about school. I keep asking myself why bother, then I get mad.
    T: I wonder if you would be willing to let the part of you who wants to go to school sit in that chair and talk for a few minutes.
    C: [*Moves to chair and talks about how exciting and motivating it is to work toward goal*]
    T: Now, if you are finished, you can go to the other chair and let the part of you that doesn't want to go speak.
    C: [*Starts talking negatively about self and then wells up with tears and says that is how*]
    T: How deep does that sadness go?
    C: Deep [*crying*]. I also realize that the anger is more defensive and I am really sad that my father never believed I was smart enough to go to school.

---

used by many approaches to psychotherapy (see Exhibit 9.5). The therapist helps the client identify templates that guide relationships (see Chapter 5).

These patterns are learned in early attachment contexts and are used to navigate the relational world. There are many excellent approaches to identifying these patterns. Interpersonal, relational, and dynamic approaches emphasize the client's relationship with or transference to the therapist to help decipher the relational schema. There is a dearth of empirical evidence to support the use of various methods and techniques of psychotherapy; most outcome data compare treatment models and do not specifically isolate mechanisms of change. There are, however, some outcome data on the use of transference interpretations suggesting that clients who have a low level of object relations do not respond as well to dynamic interpretations in which the relationship with the therapist was used as a model of the repetitive maladaptive interpersonal theme (Piper, Azim, McCallum, & Joyce, 1990). Another study that investigated the use of transference interpretations did not show it to be more useful with clients who had a lifelong history of immature object relations (Hoglend et al., 2006). However, the findings of a later study, conducted by Hoglend, Johansson, Marble, Bogwald, and Amlo (2007), were more consistent with those of Piper et al. (1990), showing a positive treatment effect within samples of clients with low quality of object relations, a high level of interpersonal

EXHIBIT 9.5
Selected Techniques of Dyadic Restructuring

Expected–Transactive Restructuring

Client (C):   Coming to therapy is something I would not normally do.

Therapist (T):   You have expectations about what will occur here?

    C: Yes. I assume that you will be telling me that I am wrong about the way I am living my life.

    T: So there is an existing expectation that this experience would entail criticizing the way you are living your life.

    C: Yes, that is indeed what I expect and why I never saw a therapist before.

    T: So is likely that this expectation was a pattern or schema for viewing relationships that pre-existed coming here.

    C: Oh, certainly! I have the same experience whenever I approach any authority figure.

    T: So, I wonder if you have any notion of where this pattern was learned?

    C: That's an easy one. I learned it from my relationship with my with my mother who criticized everything about me and I guess I think everyone is going to treat me as she did.

Relational–Dyadic Restructuring

Husband: [*To wife*] I am really trying to get close to you, but you seem unresponsive, so I just stop trying.

    Wife: Whenever you offer my affection it seems as if it is contingent on being a certain way.

Husband: I really want to let you know that I value you.

    Wife: I really feel guilty when you act affectionate, because I seem to freeze.

    T: John, it seems like when you approach Jane you want your love to feel it is being received, but instead you feel rejected and withdraw, and Jane, you never seem to trust John's expression of care.

    Wife: I think my own parents never were there emotionally for me, so I expect an ulterior motive.

---

problems, severe symptoms, and a sparse social network. Hoglend et al. concluded that "less resourceful and less healthy patients show transference patterns that are easier to identify and interpret for the therapist" (p. 169). Leichsenring and Rabung (2008) suggested that less interpretive, more supportive dynamic treatments were not mediated by level of object relations, meaning that they worked better for all the people in this condition. Conversely, they suggested that healthier clients with more circumscribed problems are less likely to have their patterns emerge in such a clear fashion and that thus those problems may take longer to emerge in the client–therapist relationship. There are complex relationships among accuracy of transference interpretation, frequency, and quality of object relations that have not yet been fully untangled regarding the use of transference interpretations. W. E. Piper (personal communication, September 7, 2008) suggested that transference interpretations should be used judiciously. Until there is further research, clinicians should consider using transference interpretations in three cases: when there is (a) a strong therapeutic alliance, (b) combined with supportive interventions, and (c) after considering the quality of object relations (Ogrodniczuk & Piper, 1999).

Attachment patterns are also used to examine the dyadic configuration. There is accruing evidence that attachment patterns developed in infancy are robust indicators of adult psychopathology (Fonagy et al., 1996). All of these are schema recognition devices used by the therapist to decipher the client's relational pattern. At the first contact, the expectations are activated unconsciously and influence the action patterns (Hassin, Uleman, & Bargh, 2005).

Another set of techniques are aimed at the relational–triadic configuration (see Exhibit 9.6). These techniques were developed by structural family therapists and work toward restructuring triadic configurations (see Chapter 7).

Treatment of Comorbid Conditions

The treatment of complex disorders is necessarily challenging, in part because treatment manuals do not always inform clinicians what to do when treating clients with comorbid disorders, either multiple Axis I disorders or a combination of an Axis I disorder and a PD (Dimaggio & Norcross, 2008; Magnavita, 1998). The interrelationships among clinical syndromes, states of mind, and personality patterns are central aspects of personality systematics. "A growing body of research on Axis I and Axis II comorbidity has associated personality dysfunction with more challenging course of Axis I symptomatology and more complicated treatment for Axis I disorders" (Sheets & Craighead, 2007, p. 88). Therefore, it is essential for clinicians treating personality dysfunction to have an in-depth understanding of the ways in which comorbid or co-occurring conditions emerge from the client's unique personality configuration as well as dyadic, triadic, and family constellations. Much empirical evidence supports the likelihood that when a client has multiple Axis I disorders

EXHIBIT 9.6
Selected Techniques of Relational–Triadic Restructuring

Session participants: mother, father and 15-year-old son

Mother:	He [son] will never amount to anything. It just seems that the more I try, the less effort you put into your academics and responsibilities.
Son:	Yeah, you are never satisfied with what I do! If I get a B you say why didn't you get an A? I figure you will never be happy anyway.
Father:	[*Nonresponsive*]
Therapist (T):	So, what is your take on this situation, Dad?
Father:	I just let them go at it. This is just like it is at home.
T:	I wonder if your opinion about this should be expressed. [*To the son*] Do you mind leaving the room while the adults do some parent talk?

---

there is a co-occurring PD that needs to be addressed. The importance to clinicians of familiarizing themselves with the evidence base about comorbid conditions is that it will alert them to potential PD and help them understand why a particular client is not responding to first-line treatment interventions. One guideline is that the more chronic the condition, and the more nonresponsive it is to first-line treatments, the higher the likelihood that a PD is present. Tyrer, Gunderson, Lyons, and Tohen (1997) summarized the empirical findings and reported the following co-occurring presentations: borderline PD (BPD) and depression; depressive PD and depression; avoidant PD and generalized social phobia; Cluster B PDs and psychoactive substance abuse; Cluster B and C PDs and eating disorders and somatoform disorders: Cluster C PDs and anxiety disorders and hypochondriasis; and, finally, Cluster A PDs and schizophrenia. The important point is that certain comorbid conditions should alert the clinician to be aware of possible personality dysfunction that may require alterations to the treatment plan.

SUMMARY OF EVIDENCE-BASED PRINCIPLES AND STRATEGIES

In the following three sections we will view the extant evidence using a structural framework to organize our review. A structural framework loosely overlaps the three DSM clusters: A (psychotic), B (borderline) and C (neurotic). This structural model has clinical utility and evidence that it can be used to reliably assess personality organization (Ingenoven et al., 2009).

Psychotic Level of Personality Organization: Cluster A Personality Disorders

We will begin our review with patients who fall under the psychotic level of organization. These patients represent those with the highest level of dysfunction in their personality system.

Specific Treatment Considerations

Clinicians should be aware of multiple lines of evidence when treating psychotic-level personality dysfunction. This level comprises a spectrum of clients, mostly from Cluster A (paranoid, schizoid, schizotypal) and some from Cluster B (BPD, histrionic, narcissistic), who function at a psychotic level or, at times, usually under increased stress, show evidence of psychotic process. General treatment guidelines suggest that for this group of clients with more severe dysfunction treatment needs to be more intense and of longer duration—perhaps even lifelong—than the Cluster A PDs.

Attachment, Relational, and Familial Factors

Accumulating research indicates that many individuals at the psychotic level of personality organization suffer from extreme attachment disorders and likely have a genetic susceptibility to personality disturbance that is exacerbated by trauma and neglect, which they are also more prone to perceive in their environment. It is important for the clinician to assess the nature and viability of the client's social support system and, where there are deficits, to seek to ameliorate these (Beutler, 2000).

Extant Evidence Base for Clinical Intervention

Research shows a correlation between childhood sexual abuse and suicidal behavior. Cohen, Crawford, Johnson, and Kasen (2005) found that Cluster A symptoms were significantly higher in abused children compared with nonabused control children. They also found that psychotic and schizotypal traits increased cognitive and perceptual distortion when clients are under heightened stress, resulting in an increased suicidal risk for individuals with these profiles. The absence of social support further increases the risk of suicide (Soloff, Feske, & Fabio, 2008). Comorbid disorders, including major depressive disorder; substance use disorders; and a history of posttraumatic stress disorder, head injury, and conduct disorder, add to the risk in clients who have a history of childhood sexual abuse. A recent meta-analysis of long-term psychodynamic psychotherapy revealed a robust treatment effect on clients with multiple comorbid disorders, as is evident with this cluster. There was a strong effect size for outcome measures, which included psychiatric symptoms, personality functioning, and social functioning (Leichsenring & Rabung, 2008). The following are some of the treatment implications:

- Consider initiating a course of long-term psychotherapy with complex mental disorders if other term formats have been tried and the client is unresponsive.
- Consider adding additional modalities of treatment to make the treatment package more potent.
- Assess all children for potential abuse that may be a pathway to adult Cluster A personality dysfunction.

Borderline Level of Organization: Cluster B Personality Disorders

The borderline personality organization primarily subsumes those individuals who have unstable operating systems which capture the clinical challenge: creating more stability at all four levels of the ecosystem. Readers should be reminded that borderline organization is not the same as borderline personality disorder. In the first case we are talking about how the system operates and in the second a categorical diagnosis.

Specific Treatment Considerations

Individuals who are organized at a borderline level of functioning encompass a fairly wide spectrum of clients seen in clinical practice. Diagnostically speaking, it is often useful for the clinician to determine the level of borderline functioning by arranging borderline pathology on a continuum, with psychotic on the left and neurotic on the right. This way, after assessing the client, the clinician can place him or her on this continuum according to the client's degree of borderline dysfunction. Clients who are to the left of the center of the continuum show more severity of symptomatology, and those to the right often function at a fairly high level until they are under conditions of increased stress, at which time the borderline symptoms may be exacerbated. BPD "afflicts an estimated 1.3 percent of U.S. adults" (Conley, 2007, p. 128). Clients with BPD have a high incidence of childhood trauma, neglect (Widom, Czaja, & Paris, 2009), and family dysfunction. It is suspected that many of these individuals have a genetic predisposition to being highly sensitive. Thus, one theory is that this increased sensitivity, along with trauma and/or an invalidating environment, comprises the etiological foundation of these disorders. There is a strong association among child and adolescent substance abuse, conduct disorder, and antisocial personality disorder (Cohen et al., 2005).

There is increasing evidence for the efficacy of a number of treatments of clients with BPD. Treatments incorporating mentalization, emotional and interpersonal skill-building techniques, and dynamic techniques aimed at self–other restructuring have demonstrated value. BPD may be best treated using a team approach so that the therapist has some protection from demoralization and subsequent re-enactment of pathogenic patterns with the client. Fonagy and Bateman (2008) derived the following principles to guide treatment of clients with borderline pathology:

- Avoid allowing excessive free association, which may be more useful with clients at the neurotic level.
- Do not encourage active fantasy, because this is too distant from reality.
- Clients operate in a psychic equivalence mode, which implies they have a conviction of being right; this makes entering into Socratic debate mostly unhelpful and leads to fruitless discussions.
- Clients assume they know what their therapists are thinking, and tactful disclosure about what you are feeling can help you contrast the client's state of mind with yours.

- Explicit statements about how the therapist contributes to joint interaction further an understanding of the relationship. (pp. 15–16)

Another relevant finding for this type of client was reported by J. E. Lambert and Friedlander (2008), who investigated alliance factors and self-differentiation in brief family therapy. Their research indicated that adults who have trouble balancing thinking and feeling, along with difficulty relating to others intimately, found conjoint therapy to be more threatening. Therefore, when planning and formatting treatment it is critical to work collaboratively with the client in regard to the issue of modality selection. They suggested the following treatment principles:

- Clinicians should be attentive to alliance formation with clients who are undifferentiated.
- When using family therapy, clinicians should encourage feelings of safety and encourage connection with the therapist.
- Therapists must be vigilant about maintaining multiple alliances with family members. (p. 165)

There are complex clinical decisions that have important ethical considerations and require that a cost-benefit analysis be conducted when considering multiple alliances and modalities (Magnavita, Levy, Critchfield, & Lebow, in press). Another important treatment consideration concerns the high incidence of self-injury (nonsuicidal injury to self) that is especially evident in clients with BPD (Klonsky & Muehlenkamp, 2007, p. 1045). This is a central treatment focus with many clients and a highly stressful aspect of working with clients with a PD. Self-injury is viewed by many as a maladaptive coping strategy that has continued to be reinforced. It is used primarily to reduce intensely negative affect. When working with children, it is critical to assess for self-mutilating behavior. Research has shown that one third of clients with BPD reported that as children they had physically mutilated themselves. In addition, a childhood onset of self-harm suggests a prolonged and varied history of self-harm, with two thirds of clients reporting more than 50 acts or more over a 15-year span and 50% using four or more different forms of self-harm (Zanarini et al., 2006).

Managing chronically suicidal behavior is an inevitable part of working with BPD clients. Paris (2004) examined the value of hospitalization with these chronically suicidal individuals and reported that about one out of 10 actually commit suicide and that, over the course of a psychiatrist's or psychologist's career, he or she can anticipate one case of suicide. Prior to managed care, many of these patients were treated in the hospital, but with the current short lengths of stay can result in potential subsequent negative effects, such as reenactment of coercive patterns that possibly have their base in early traumatic relational experiences. The extant evidence suggests the following treatment guidelines:

- Clinicians should be able to tolerate the level of suicidality in this group of clients and the need to tolerate one's feelings about the client and therapy process.
- Intensive outpatient psychotherapy and day treatment should be used to manage high-risk clients. There is an accruing evidence base for the modality of day treatment (Piper et al., 1996).
- The intensity of treatment should be modulated in response to changing conditions and challenges in the client's life.
- Hospitalization should be considered when there is active psychosis or a life-threatening suicide attempt has been made, and in this case a review of the treatment approach is warranted.

The following treatment consideration also has emerged from the evidence: Early intervention should be emphasized with children who present with pre-BPD symptoms, especially an early pattern of self-mutilation.

Attachment, Relational, and Familial Factors

Empirical evidence suggests that emotional underinvolvement and invalidation by caretakers are important family and relational aspects of families with BPD members. According to Fonagy and Bateman (2008), BPD clients tend to have relationship difficulties with both parents:

> [They] see their relationships with their mothers as conflictual, distant, or overprotective; their fathers as less involved and more distant[,] suggesting that problems with both parents are more likely to be the common pathogenic influence in this group than problems with either parent alone. (p. 11)

In a review of the literature on attachment, Levy (2005) found that early instability of attachment patterns is a relatively strong feature of borderline pathology. Only 6% to 8% of the subjects from these studies were coded as having a secure attachment, and there is high likelihood of disorganized attachment patterns. Individuals with borderline pathology show high levels of aggression of various types, as well as higher levels of anxiety and avoidance in intimate relationships (Critchfield, Levy, Clarkin, & Kernberg, 2007). However, for females with BPD, even when the level of impulsivity is high there may not be a high level of concomitant aggression (Critchfield, Levy, & Clarkin, 2004). This interpersonal pattern of avoidance was associated with self-directed aggression. The researchers suggested the following considerations:

- Focus on helping patients become aware of the repetitive attachment patterns and differentiate them from early attachment patterns.
- Treatments that have shown efficacy contain components which serve to update relational templates. (p. 79)

As readers who have read the preceding chapters (see, e.g., Chapter 5) will be aware, one of the core aspects of personality dysfunction is problems in interpersonal relationships. Clients with PDs often present with marital/partner dysfunction. Methods and techniques of dyadic restructuring with couples have been developed for use in marital/couples therapy (Johnson, 2002). There is a strong evidence base supporting the high incidence of trauma for clients with PDs. Emotionally focused couples therapy, although not specifically developed for PDs, has been shown efficacious with many individuals who likely have PDs.

Another useful construct with an accumulating evidence base that can assist in formulating treatment packages is the *intergenerational* or *multigenerational transmission process*, by which families transfer patterns of behavior from one generation to the next, with important implications for personality dysfunction (Magnavita, 2000). Childhood perceptions are encoded in memory and, through a process of social learning, may be copied in three separate ways: (a) identification, (b) recapitulation, and (c) introjection (Critchfield & Benjamin, 2008). In a 20-year prospective study, researchers found that childhood behavior problems are robust predictors of partner violence and significantly increase the risk for children in these families to use violence as a means of conflict resolution (Ehrensaft et al., 2003). Maternal depression also is carried over three generations through the intergenerational transmission process, which implicates an interpersonal mechanism (Hammen, Shih, & Brennan, 2004). The findings regarding disruptive behavior, which is one pathway to adult antisocial behavior, and maternal depression, which is comorbid with many PDs, suggest that clinicians do the following:

- Intervene with the family/couple where there is indication of partner violence to stop the intergenerational transmission process.
- Actively intervene when maternal depression is evident, and look for intergenerational effects.
- Investigate the presence of premorbid PDs in children of families characterized by domestic violence and intervene.

Researchers have been ferreting out numerous interrelationships that have relevance to clinicians. Whisman, Uebelacker, and Weinstock (2004) demonstrated that depression is correlated with marital satisfaction: The greater the degree of depression, the lower the marital satisfaction. Because many clients with personality dysfunction enter treatment because of interpersonal and marital issues, this line of research suggests that therapists actively treat comorbid depression in individuals with marital and interpersonal problems and then assess the personality functioning.

Extant Evidence Base for Clinical Considerations

The presence of PDs, especially in Cluster B clients, has a moderating effect on other comorbid disorders, suggesting an increased risk of suicide in these clients (Schneider et. al, 2008). There is also reported higher rate of relational aggression (gossiping, interpersonal manipulation, and rumor spreading) in the Cluster B PDs, with an equal incidence in men and women (Schmeelk, Sylvers, & Lilenfeld, 2008). Schmeelk et al. (2009) also found relational aggression was also correlated with psychopathic traits, with an equal incidence in males and females. Another interesting line of research that has been burgeoning is in the area of facial expression of affect. Scientists who study affect have made great strides in mapping how emotions can be categorized in various facial action patterns and empirically coded for research (Ekman & Rosenberg, 2005). An interesting finding that has been often noted by clinicians is that clients with BPD seem more sensitive to perceiving facial expressions; however, they show a bias toward perceiving anger more readily with ambiguous socio-affective cues (Domes et al., 2008).

A comparison of three treatments for BPD revealed that all were generally equivalent in regard to client improvement: Dialectical behavior therapy, transference-focused psychotherapy (TFP), and dynamic supportive treatment all were effective, although somewhat differentially. TFP and dialectical behavior therapy both led to a reduction in suicidality; however, TFP and dynamic supportive therapy led to an improvement in anger (Clarkin, Levy, Lenzenweger, & Kernberg, 2007).

The therapist's activity level is an important consideration in the treatment of PDs, as has been discussed. More empirical evidence is needed to create clinical algorithms for determining the appropriate level for each client based on an individualized assessment. However, there is some evidence that more active interventions on the therapist's the part are warranted; that is, active therapists have been found to be more effective per se (Hilsenroth et al., 2007). In Hilsenroth et al.'s (2007) process and outcome study of short-term dynamic psychotherapy for comorbid depressed–borderline outpatients, the suggestion of specific activities or tasks for the client to attempt outside of sessions as well as therapists more actively initiating the therapeutic focus provided a useful framework to integrate various dynamic techniques. In addition, it is important to note that the set of interventions found in this study were provided as part of a short-term dynamic psychotherapy treatment that demonstrated large outcome effects on measures of depressive symptomatology and interpersonal functioning as well as high client ratings of therapeutic alliance. Therefore, this integrative use of cognitive, behavioral, and psychodynamic techniques might be considered especially useful in developing an integrative therapeutic approach for treating such clients in applied clinical practice.

Neurotic Level of Organization: Cluster C Personality Disorders

The neurotic level of organization is generally characterized by individuals who have a highly constricted personality system. Compared the psychotic level who tend to be fragmented or the borderline who as we discussed tend to be unstable the neurotic group tend to be more rigid.

Specific Treatment Considerations

Anecdotal as well as empirical findings suggest that clients with Cluster C disorders are more likely to be treatment seekers who wish to reduce their suffering, as opposed to clients who are treatment rejecting, primarily individuals with the Cluster A paranoid and schizoid PDs (Tyrer, Mitchard, Methuen, & Ranger, 2003). An interesting finding from van Beek and Verheul (2008) indicates that, for all categories of PD, in contrast to what is often anecdotally reported, clients were significantly more motivated for treatment than those without PDs. They suggested that the reason for this is the high level of symptomatic distress in this group. It is also important to keep in mind that even though an individual may diagnostically fit Cluster C criteria there may be an underlying psychotic process and severe suicidality, so clinicians should not be misled to believe that the Cluster C clients necessarily represent a healthier cohort. There is ample case material in the literature that describes the rapid ability of some of these Cluster C clients to deteriorate into states of paranoia and other types of psychotic process.

Attachment, Relational, and Familial Factors

Higher levels of personality dysfunction are associated with increased couple dysfunction (Gutman, McDermut, Miller, Chelminski, & Zimmerman, 2006). This association was also shown in an earlier study conducted by Miller et al. (2000). The multigenerational transmission process is a construct that has emerged from family systems theory and is beginning to accumulate empirical support. Longitudinal evidence from the Children in the Community Study "linked 'milder' forms of familial trauma/stressors—maladaptive patenting, parental conflict, power assertive punishment, even low levels of closeness with one's parents—to later personality disorders" (Clark, 2005, p. 525).

Extant Evidence Base for Clinical Consideration

Early exposure to trauma is negatively associated with personality adaptation. Rademaker, Vermetten, Geuze, Muilwijk, and Kleber's (2008) investigation of a military sample showed that exposure to emotional trauma early in life was associated with lower cooperativeness and self-directedness. There is a mixture of empirical and case study findings showing evidence of the efficacy of short-term dynamic therapy with Cluster C clients. Barber, Morse, Krakauer, Chittams, and Crits-Cristoph (1997) showed that brief dynamic therapy is effective for obsessive–compulsive and avoidant PDs. A randomized clinical trial of short-term dynamic therapy also demonstrated efficacy for Cluster C PDs (Svartberg et al., 2004).

In a randomized clinical study, clients who received psychodynamic therapy showed a greater treatment effect than clients who had comorbid panic disorder and Cluster C PDs: The presence of a Cluster C personality diagnosis enhanced treatment responsiveness and was therefore a better moderator of treatment outcome than it was for individuals without Axis II pathology (Milrod, Leon, Barber, Markowitz, & Graf, 2007). In children and adolescents, the presence of an anxiety disorder multiplies the risk of developing an adult Cluster C disorder by 4 times; if a disruptive or depressive disorder is present the risk is increased by a factor of 16: "Findings from the Children in the Community (CIC) Study make it clear that PD symptom constellations identified in adulthood have their origins in childhood and can be reliably assessed in combined youth and parent reports" (Cohen et al., 2005, p. 481).

Clinicians should consider the following recommendations that have emerged from the evidence: Child and adolescent anxiety, depressive, and disruptive disorders should be treated actively, and a client with multiple comorbid conditions should be followed over time so the clinician can intervene if he or she is on a PD course (and possibly prevent it).

SUMMARY

Unified psychotherapy draws on all sources of convergent evidence, which are far beyond the scope of this volume to present. A variety of streams of evidence support the efficacy of a unified approach. These include evidence from randomized clinical trial studies demonstrating aspects of various treatments. Unfortunately, researchers have not yet been able to identify the active ingredients of various empirically based treatments, although some of these findings have been presented in this chapter. Future research will, it is hoped, provide answers to these important questions.

We do know that there is empirical evidence to support a number of manualized treatments for personality disorders. Another evidence stream supporting a unified approach to treating PDs comes from clinical case studies and reports. Yet another line of evidence comes from meta-analytic studies suggesting that the outcome of psychotherapy among dominant schools has a high degree of equivalence. However, it has been clearly established that some clients do indeed deteriorate even with appropriate psychotherapy. Perhaps various approaches activate and restructure different elements of the personality system, which in turn affect the whole personality system in roughly and equivalent manner, whereby changes in one domain prompt changes in an other (K. L. Critchfield, personal communication, May 5, 2008). Emerging streams of evidence will allow us to build a true clinical science driven by personality systematics and a unified approach to psychotherapy.

REFERENCES

Ackerman, S., & Hilsenroth, M. (2001). A review of therapist characteristics and techniques negatively impacting the therapeutic alliance. *Psychotherapy, 38*, 171–185.

Ackerman, S., & Hilsenroth, M. (2003). A review of therapist characteristics and techniques positively impacting the therapeutic alliance. *Clinical Psychology Review, 23*, 1–33.

American Psychiatric Association. (1994). *Diagnostic and statistical manual of mental disorders* (4th ed.). Washington, DC: Author.

American Psychiatric Association. (2000). *Diagnostic and statistical manual of mental disorders* (4th ed., text revision). Washington, DC: Author.

Baldwin, S. A., Wampold, B. E., & Imel, Z. E. (2007). Untangling the alliance–outcome correlation: Exploring the relative importance of therapist and patient variability in the alliance. *Journal of Consulting and Clinical Psychology, 75*, 842–852.

Barber, J. P., Morse, J. Q., Krakauer, I. D., Chittams, J., & Crits-Christoph, P. (1997). Change in obsessive–compulsive and avoidant personality disorders following time-limited supportive–expressive therapy. *Psychotherapy, 34*, 133–143.

Bateman, A., & Fonagy, P. (2004). *Psychotherapy for borderline personality disorder: Mentalization based treatment.* Oxford, England: Oxford University Press.

Bateman, A., & Fonagy, P. (2008). 8-year follow-up of patients treated for borderline personality disorder: Mentalization-based treatment versus treatment as usual. *American Journal of Psychiatry, 165*, 631–638.

Baxter, L. R., Schwartz, J. M., Bergman, K. S., Szuba, M. P., Guze, B. H., Mazziotta, J. C., . . . Phelps, M. E. (1992). Caudate glucose metabolic rate changes in both drug and behavior therapy for obsessive-compulsive disorder. *Archives of General Psychiatry, 49*(9), 681–689.

Betan, E., Heim, A. K., Conklin, C. Z., & Westen, D. (2005). Countertransference phenomena and personality pathology in clinical practice: An empirical investigation. *American Journal of Psychiatry, 162*, 890–898.

Beutler, L. E. (2000). Empirically based decision making in clinical practice. *Prevention & Treatment, 3*(1). doi: 10.1037/1522-3736.3.1.327a

Beutler, L. E., & Clarkin, J. F. (1990). *Systematic treatment selection: Toward targeted therapeutic interventions.* New York, NY: Brunner/Mazel.

Clark, L. A. (2005). Stability and change in personality pathology: Revelations of three longitudinal studies. *Journal of Personality Disorders, 19*, 524–532.

Clarkin, J. F., Levy, K. N., Lenzenweger, M. F., & Kernberg, O. F. (2007). Evaluating three treatments for borderline disorder: A multiwave study. *American Journal of Psychiatry, 164*, 922–928.

Clarkin, J. F., Yeomans, F., & Kernberg, O. F. (2006). *Psychotherapy of borderline personality: Focusing on object relations.* Washington, DC: American Psychiatric Publishing.

Cohen, P., Crawford, T. N., Johnson, J. G., & Kasen, S. (2005). The Children in the Community Study of developmental course of personality disorder. *Journal of Personality Disorders, 19*, 466–486.

Conley, R. R. (2007). Clinical news. *Clinical Schizophrenia & Related Psychoses, 1*, 127–130.

Critchfield, K. L., & Benjamin, L. S. (2006). Principles for psychosocial treatment of personality disorders: Summary of the APA Division 12 Task Force/NASPR review. *Journal of Clinical Psychology, 62*, 661–674.

Critchfield, K. L., & Benjamin, L. S. (2008). Internalized representations of early interpersonal experience and adult relationships: A test of copy process theory in clinical and non-clinical settings. *Psychiatry, 71*, 71–92.

Critchfield, K. L., Levy, K. N., & Clarkin, J. F. (2004). The relationship between impulsivity, aggression, and impulsive aggression in borderline personality disorder: An empirical analysis. *Journal of Personality Disorders, 18*, 555–570.

Critchfield, K. L., Levy, K. N., Clarkin, J. F., & Kernberg, O. F. (2007). The relational context of aggression in borderline personality disorder: Using adult attachment style to predict forms of hostility. *Journal of Clinical Psychology, 64*, 67–82.

Dale, G. (2008). The single practitioner and community engagement: Bridging the gap between practice and social action. *American Psychologist, 63*, 791–797.

Diener, M. J., Hilsenroth, M. J., & Weinberger, J. (2007). Therapist affect focus and patient outcomes in psychodynamic psychotherapy: A meta-analysis. *American Journal of Psychiatry, 164*, 936–941.

Dimaggio, G., & Norcross, J. C. (2008). Treating patients with two or more personality disorders: An introduction. *Journal of Clinical Psychology, 64*, 127–138.

Domes, G., Czieschnek, D., Weidler, F., Berger, C., Fast, K., & Herpertz, S. C. (2008). Recognition of facial affect in borderline personality disorder. *Journal of Personality Disorders, 22*, 135–147.

Ehrensaft, M. K., Cohen, P., Brown, J., Smailes, E., Chen, H., & Johnson, J. G. (2003). Intergenerational transmission of partner violence: A 20-year prospective study. *Journal of Consulting and Clinical Psychology, 71*, 741–753.

Ekman, P., & Rosenberg, E. L. (2005). *What the face reveals: Basic and applied studies of spontaneous expression using the Facial Action Coding System* (2nd ed.). New York, NY: Oxford University Press.

Fonagy. P., Leigh, T., Steele, M., Steele, H., Kennedy, R., Mattoon, G. . . . Gerber, A. (1996). The relation of attachment status, psychiatric classification, and response to psychotherapy. *Journal of Consulting and Clinical Psychology, 64*, 22–31.

Fonagy, P., & Bateman, A. (2008). The development of borderline personality disorder—A mentalizing model. *Journal of Personality Disorders, 22*, 4–21.

Forsyth, D. R., & Strong, S. R. (1986). The scientific study of counseling and psychotherapy: A unificationist view. *American Psychologist, 41*, 113–119.

Frances, A., Clarkin, J. F., & Perry, S. (1984). *Differential therapeutics in psychiatry*. New York, NY: Brunner/Mazel.

Grawe, K. (2007). *Neuropsychotherapy: How the neurosciences inform effective psychotherapy*. Mahwah, NJ: Erlbaum.

Greenberg, L. S., Rice, L. N., & Elliott, R. (1993). *Facilitating emotional change: The moment-by-moment process*. New York, NY: Guilford Press.

Gregory, R., Chlebowski, S., Kang, D., Remen, A., Soderberg, M., Stepkovitch, J., & Virk, S. (2008). A controlled trial of psychodynamic psychotherapy for co-occurring borderline personality disorder and alcohol use disorder. *Psychotherapy, 45*, 28–41.

Gutman, J., McDermut, W., Miller, I., Chelminski, I., & Zimmerman, M. (2006). Personality pathology and its relation to couple functioning. *Journal of Clinical Psychology, 62*, 1275–1289.

Hammen, C., Shih, J. H., & Brennan, P. A. (2004). Intergenerational transmission of depression: Test of an interpersonal stress model in a community sample. *Journal of Consulting and Clinical Psychology, 72*, 511–522.

Hassin, R. R., Uleman, J. S., & Bargh, J. A. (Eds.). (2005). *The new unconscious*. New York, NY: Oxford University Press.

Hilsenroth, M. J., & Cromer, T. D. (2007). Clinical interventions related to alliance during the initial interview and psychological assessment. *Psychotherapy: Theory, Research, Practice, Training, 44*, 205–218.

Hilsenroth, M. J., Defife, J. A., Blake, M. M., & Cromer, T. D. (2007). The effects of borderline pathology on short-term dynamic psychotherapy for depression. *Psychotherapy Research, 17*, 172–184.

Hoglend, P., Amlo, S., Marble, A., Bogwald, K. P., Sorbye, O., Sjaastad, M. C., & Heyerdahl, O. (2006). Analysis of the patient–therapist relationship in dynamic psychotherapy: An experimental study of transference interpretations. *American Journal of Psychiatry, 163*, 1739–1746.

Hoglend, P., Johansson, P., Marble, A., Bogwald, K. P., & Amlo, S. (2007). Moderators of the effects of transference interpretations in brief dynamic psychotherapy. *Psychotherapy Research, 17,* 160–171.

Horvath, A. O. (2001). The alliance. *Psychotherapy, 38,* 365–372.

Johnson, S. M. (2002). *Emotionally focused couple therapy with trauma survivors: Strengthening attachment bonds.* New York, NY: Guilford Press.

Joyce, A. S., Piper, W. E., Ogrodniczuk, J. S., & Klein, R. H. (2007). *Termination in psychotherapy: A psychodynamic model of process and outcome.* Washington, DC: American Psychological Association.

Klonsky, E. D., & Muehlenkamp, J. J. (2007). Self-injury: A research review for the practitioner. *Journal of Clinical Psychology, 63,* 1045–1056.

Lambert, J. E., & Friedlander, M. (2008). Relationship of self to adult clients' perception of the alliance in brief family therapy. *Psychotherapy Research, 18,* 160–166.

Lambert, M. L. (2007). What we have learned from a decade of research aimed at improving psychotherapy outcome in routine care [Presidential address]. *Psychotherapy Research, 17,* 1–14.

Lazarus, A. A. (1997). *Brief but comprehensive psychotherapy: The multimodal way.* New York, NY: Springer.

Lazarus, A. A. (2008). Technical eclecticism and multimodal therapy. In J. L. Lebow (Ed.), *Twenty-first century psychotherapies: Contemporary approaches to theory and practice* (pp. 424–452). Hoboken, NJ: Wiley.

Lehrer, P. M. (2007). Biofeedback training to increase heart rate variability. In P. H. Lehrer, R. L. Woolfolk, & W. E. Sime (Eds.), *Principles and practice of stress management* (3rd ed., pp. 227–248). New York, NY: Guilford Press.

Lehrer, P. M., Woolfolk, R. L., & Sime, W. E. (Eds.). (2007). *Principles and practice of stress management* (3rd ed.). New York, NY: Guilford Press.

Leichsenring, F., & Leibing, E. (2003). The effectiveness of psychodynamic therapy and cognitive behavior therapy in the treatment of personality disorders: A meta-analysis. *American Journal of Psychiatry, 160,* 1223–1232.

Leichsenring, F., & Rabung, S. (2008). Effectiveness of long-term psychodynamic psychotherapy: A meta-analysis. *Journal of American Medical Association, 300,* 1551–1565.

Levy, K. N. (2005). The implications of attachment theory and research for understanding borderline personality disorder. *Development and Psychopathology, 17,* 959–986.

Linehan, M. M. (1993). *Cognitive–behavioral treatment for borderline personality disorder.* New York, NY: Guilford Press.

Magnavita, J. J. (1998). Methods of restructuring personality disorders with comorbid syndromes. *Journal of Clinical Psychology, 4,* 73–89.

Magnavita, J. J. (2000). *Relational therapy for personality disorders.* Hoboken, NJ: Wiley.

Magnavita, J. J. (Ed.). (2004). *Handbook of personality disorders: Theory and practice*. Hoboken, NJ: John Wiley & Sons.

Magnavita, J. J. (2005). *Personality-guided relational psychotherapy: A unified approach*. Washington, DC: American Psychological Association Magnavita, J. J. (2008). Toward the unification of clinical science: The next wave in the evolution of psychotherapy. *Journal of Psychotherapy Integration, 18*, 264–291.

Magnavita, J. J. (2006). In search of the unifying principles of psychotherapy: Conceptual, empirical, and clinical convergence. *American Psychologist, 61*, 882–892.

Magnavita, J. J., & Carlson, J. (Producer). (2009).*Treating personality disorder over time* [six-part DVD]. Available from http://www.apa.org/videos

Magnavita, J. J., Levy, K. N., Critchfield, K. L. & Lebow, J. (in press). Ethical considerations in the treatment of personality dysfunction: Using evidence, principles, and clinical judgment. *Professional Psychology: Research and Practice*.

Manfield, P. & Shapiro, F. (2004). Application of eye movement desensitization and reprocessing (EMDR) to personality disorders. In J. J. Magnavita (Ed.), *Handbook of personality disorders: Theory and practice* (pp. 304–328). Hoboken, NJ: Wiley.

Martin, D. J., Garske, J. P., & Davis, M. K. (2000). Relation of the therapeutic alliance with outcome and other variables: A meta-analytic review. *Journal of Consulting and Clinical Psychology, 68*, 438–450.

McCullough Vaillant, L. (1997). *Changing character: Short-term anxiety regulating therapy for restructuring defenses, affects, and attachments*. New York, NY: Basic Books.

Miller, I., McDermut, W., Gordon, K. C., Keitner, G., Ryan, C. E., & Norman, W. (2000). Personality and family functioning in families of depressed patients. *Journal of Abnormal Psychology, 109*, 539–545.

Millon, T., Grossman, S., Meagher, S., & Millon, C. (1999). *Personality-guided therapy*. Hoboken, NJ: Wiley.

Milrod, B. L., Leon, A. C., Barber, J. P., Markowitz, J. C., & Graf, E. (2007). Do comorbid personality disorders moderate panic-focused psychotherapy? An exploratory examination of the American Psychiatric Association practice guidelines. *Journal of Clinical Psychiatry, 68*, 885–891.

Ogrodniczuk, J., & Piper, W. E. (1999). Use of transference interpretations in dynamically oriented individual psychotherapy for patients with personality disorders. *Journal of Personality Disorders, 13*, 297–311.

Paris, J. (2004). Is hospitalization useful for suicidal patients with borderline personality disorder? *Journal of Personality Disorders, 18*, 240–247.

Perry, J., Banon, E., & Ianni, F. (1999). Effectiveness of psychotherapy for personality disorders. *American Journal of Psychiatry, 156*, 1312–1321.

Piper, W. E. (2008). Underutilization of short-term group therapy: Enigmatic or understandable? *Psychotherapy Research, 18*, 127–138.

Piper, W. E., Azim, H. F. A., McCallum, M., & Joyce, A. S. (1990). Patient suitability and outcome in short-term dynamic individual psychotherapy. *Journal of Clinical and Consulting Psychology, 88*, 475–481.

Piper, W. E., Rosie, J. S., & Joyce, A. S. (1996). *Time-limited day treatment for personality disorders: Integration of research and practice in a group program.* Washington, DC: American Psychological Association.

Rademaker, A. R., Vermetten, E., Geuze, E., Muilwijk, A., & Kleber, R. J. (2008). Self-reported early trauma as a predictor of adult personality: A study in a military sample. *Journal of Clinical Psychology, 64*, 863–875.

Schmeelk, K. M., Sylvers, P., & Lilenfeld, S. O. (2008). Trait correlates of relational aggression in and non-clinical sample: *DSM–IV* personality disorders and psychopathy. *Journal of Personality Disorders, 22*, 269–283.

Schneider, B., Schnabel, A., Wetterling, T., Bartusch, B., Weber, B., & Georgi, K. (2008). How do personality disorders modify suicide rates? *Journal of Personality Disorders, 22*, 233–245.

Schore, A. N. (2003). *Affect regulation and the repair of the self.* New York: W. W. Norton & Company.

Shapiro, F. (1995). *Eye movement desensitization and reprocessing: Basic principles, protocols and procedures.* New York, NY: Guilford Press.

Sheets, E., & Craighead, E. (2007). Toward an empirically based classification of personality pathology. *Clinical Psychology: Science and Practice, 14*, 77–93.

Soloff, P. H., Feske, U., & Fabio, A. (2008). Mediations of the relationship between childhood sexual abuse and suicidal behavior in borderline personality disorder. *Journal of Personality Disorders, 22*, 221–232.

Smyth, J. M. (1998). Written emotional expression: Effect sizes, outcome types, and moderating variables. *Journal of Consulting and Clinical Psychology, 66*, 174–184.

Staats, A. W. (1983). *Psychology's crisis of disunity: Philosophy and method for a unified science.* New York, NY: Praeger.

Sternberg, R. J., & Grigorenko, E. L. (2001). Unified psychology. *American Psychologist, 56*, 1069–1079.

Stricker, G., & Gold, J. (1996). Psychotherapy integration: An assimilative psychodynamic approach. *Clinical Psychology: Science and Practice, 3*, 47–58.

Svartberg, M., Stiles, T. C., & Seltzer, M. H. (2004). Randomized, controlled trial of the effectiveness of short-term dynamic therapy and cognitive therapy for Cluster C personality disorders. *American Journal of Psychiatry, 161*, 810–817.

Tyrer, P., Gunderson, J., Lyons, M., & Tohen, M. (1997). Special feature: Extent of comorbidity between mental state and personality disorders. *Journal of Personality Disorders, 11*, 242–259.

Tyrer, P., Mitchard, S., Methuen, C., & Ranger, M. (2003). Treatment rejecting and treatment seeking personality disorders: Type R and Type S. *Journal of Personality Disorders, 17*, 263–268.

van Beek, N., & Verheul, R. (2008). Motivation for treatment in patients with personality disorders. *Journal of Personality Disorders, 22*(1), 89–100.

von Bertalanffy, L. (1968) *General system theory: Foundations, development and applications.* New York, NY: Braziller.

Wampold, B. E. (2007). Psychotherapy: The humanistic (and effective) treatment. *American Psychologist, 62*, 857–873.

Weinberger, J., & Rasco, C. (2007). Empirically supported common factors. In S. Hoffmann & J. Weinberger (Eds.), *Art and science in psychotherapy* (pp. 103–131). New York, NY: Routledge.

Westen, D., & Arkowitz-Westen, L. (1998). Limitations of Axis II in diagnosing personality pathology in clinical practice. *American Journal of Psychiatry, 155*, 1767–1771.

Whaley, A. L., & Davis, K. E. (2007). Cultural competence and evidence-based practice in mental health services. *American Psychologist, 62*, 563–574.

Whisman, M. A., Uebelacker, L. A., & Weinstock, L. M. (2004). Psychopathology and marital satisfaction: The importance of evaluating both partners. *Journal of Consulting and Clinical Psychology, 72*, 830–838.

Yeomans, F., Gutfreund, J., Selzer, M., Clarkin, J., Hull, J., & Smith, T. (1994). Factors related to drop-outs by borderline patients. *Journal of Psychotherapy Practice and Research, 3*, 16–24.

Young, J. E., Klosko, J. S., & Weishaar, M. E. (2003). *Schema therapy: A practitioner's guide.* New York, NY: Guilford Press.

Zanarini, M. C., Frankenburg, F. R., Ridolfi, M. E., Jager-Hyman, S., Hennen, J., & Gunderson, J. G. (2006). Reported childhood onset of self-mutilation among borderline patients. *Journal of Personality Disorders, 20*, 9–15.

RESOURCES FOR CLINICIANS: VIDEO SERIES

Magnavita, J. J., & Carlson, J. (Producer). (2006). *Treating personality disorders* [DVD]. Available from http://www.apa.org/videos

Magnavita, J. J., & Carlson, J. (Producer). (2009). *Treating personality disorders over time* [six-part DVD]. Available from http://www.apa.org/videos

10

TREATMENT PLANNING AND FORMATTING: COMBINING SCIENCE AND ART IN IMPLEMENTING THE FRAMEWORK OF THERAPY

JEFFREY J. MAGNAVITA, KENNETH L. CRITCHFIELD,
AND LOUIS G. CASTONGUAY

Treatment planning and formatting constitute the art and science of developing and presenting to the client the essential clinical algorithms most appropriate to him or her. These include decisions about the modality, approach, length of treatment, setting, members of the system included in treatment, other members of the treatment team to be involved, and so forth. Each element of the individualized treatment plan we describe in this chapter has its own (but in most cases, small) evidence base in the literature and likely additional interactive effects with other elements included in the plan. Given the complexity of possible combinations tailored to unique client circumstances, the treatment planning and formatting process is inevitably an art that, when done well, is based on clinical expertise and knowledge and informed by empirical evidence. Science has not untangled the effect and contribution of the plethora of variables that influence the decisions clinicians make daily in their offices. Unfortunately, at the moment there is only a small and slowly accumulating evidence base to guide clinicians in treating personality dysfunction, despite the current and pressing need given the severity, chronicity, and complexity of personality disorders (PDs). Whereas the majority of the chapters in this volume examine the best available evidence to support various approaches to psychotherapy, limited attention is given to the requirements and challenges of treatment planning and formatting. This topic requires its own chapter—it probably warrants its own volume. Therefore, our goals in this chapter are, first, to describe different approaches to treatment planning and formatting and, second, to identify formatting factors available in the clinician's clinical toolbox, as well as to provide support for these factors in the literature. At the end of chapter, we briefly delineate future directions and outline some prescriptions based on empirical evidence to enhance the efficacy of treatment planning and formatting.

We believe that the best way to understand and deal with the complexity of psychotherapy, including issues related to treatment formatting and planning, is to consider empirical evidence as well as clinical observation. When we apply these guiding principles to treating personality dysfunction, we enter a process of complex decision making on a variety of issues, such as determining the most useful theoretical perspective to understand the client's problems (cognitive, psychodynamic, interpersonal, integrative, unified), as covered in previous chapters in this volume; modality of treatment (individual, group, family, couples, pharmacological, ecological); treatment format or, if more than one is offered, how these are delivered (sequential, combined, individual); intensity of treatment (number and length of sessions, intervals between sessions, balance of in-session support vs. a focus on change); and treatment setting (e.g., outpatient, inpatient).

When planning treatment—especially with complex cases, which are common in personality dysfunction—the clinician must also make a determination about how to utilize other mental health and medical specialists and how treatment will be coordinated so he or she will not be working at cross-purposes with other providers. Using a treatment team and/or facilitating optimal communication between various outside providers, especially for the more severe PDs, does seem to optimize treatment and prevent clinician burnout. Two issues are relevant. First, therapists may want to enlist support in the form of a peer consultation group or a similar arrangement to ensure adequate therapist coping and decision making with complex and high-risk cases (Critchfield & Benjamin, 2006a). The second issue involves decisions about how best to work with other providers for the same case to coordinate treatment strategies and goals, prevent splitting, and so on.

HISTORICAL BACKGROUND
AND THEORETICAL COMPONENTS

Individual psychotherapy has traditionally been the preferred modality for the treatment of PDs. Before World War II (WWII), there were only a few modalities and approaches to treatment, so the question of treatment selection was not a major consideration. Psychoanalysis was often recommended because that is what was thought to be appropriate if an individual had neurotic symptoms or characterological disturbance. The therapeutic landscape started to change dramatically after WWII. In England, therapeutic communities, using principles of group dynamics called *sociotherapy*, were developed by Maxwell Jones to treat patients with what would now be described as borderline PD (BPD) and antisocial PD (Guimon, 2002). Because psychoanalysis largely involved frequent, individual sessions, later approaches seemed to carry this tradition forward without much in the way of experimentation with the various modalities that were emerging during the 20th century.

Although clinicians have always engaged in some form of treatment planning and decision making, early in the development of psychiatry and clinical psychology there were few treatments from which to make a selection and only one that addressed character or personality dysfunction. Clinicians were of the mind that long-term psychoanalytic treatment was usually the only option for characterological disorders. Of course, there were challenges to this dominant view, such as Franz Alexander's (Alexander & French, 1946) development of short-term dynamic psychotherapy, but he was ridiculed by the analytic community. The field needed time to evolve various approaches and modalities. A major growth spurt occurred after WWII, leading to many advances. The first formal attempt to organize the available evidence on treatment planning did not take place until the early 1980s, with the publication of *Differential Therapeutics in Psychiatry* (Frances, Clarkin, & Perry, 1984). This volume laid the foundation for the treatment selection movement by presenting a theory of empirically based decision making for clinical practitioners that focuses on principles of treatment selection (Beutler, 2000). There were now enough options regarding types of therapy and modalities of treatment to consider their differential application. Another major effort to formalize the thought processes and decision making that are necessary for optimal treatment outcome was *Systematic Treatment Selection: Toward Targeted Therapeutic Interventions* (Beutler & Clarkin, 1990). These volumes represent the maturing of clinical science and an effort to articulate how treatment strategies can be tailored to the requirements of the client. Methods and techniques can be selected and delivered in an overall treatment package. The art and science of treatment selection require up-to-date information about new approaches as well as clinical judgment to know what is warranted. Clinicians now have many treatment components from which to choose. In the next section, we describe the main modalities and components clinicians can select when formulating a treatment package.

Treatment Modalities

Selection of a treatment modality involves pragmatic consideration of whether individual, group, marital, family, day treatment, and so on are available and likely to promote the necessary change. Clinician assessment of the problem is extremely important for making initial determinations not only of the likelihood for change to occur but also of the level of motivation of all parties to participate in each modality. For example, what is initially presented as a couples problem may best be addressed in individual therapy (or vice versa) depending on the formulation of the problem. Motivation and willingness to engage also are important. A particular PD client may be seen as having the potential to benefit greatly from individual work but refuses to be seen outside the context of couples work. Another client may have the potential to benefit from family therapy but for various reasons refuses to be seen with the other family members. In each case, the client's motivation for starting therapy must be considered, including the possibility that the question of modality could return as the therapeutic alliance deepens and as the client becomes more interested in the possibility of change.

Some models of therapy are explicitly structured to contain multiple modes that seek to accomplish change in multiple ways or on multiple levels. For example, dialectical behavior therapy (DBT) typically involves weekly individual sessions plus a skills training group. It is also common for one modality to be supplemented by others (e.g., individual therapy enhanced by occasional conjoint family conferences). Little is known in the empirical literature about the merits of each modality relative to specific presenting problems or diagnostic profiles. Clinicians must usually make a pragmatic choice based on the face-valid match between the client's and the clinician's own conceptualization of the problem.

One way to think about choice of modality is to consider which psychosocial attachment system, if activated, seems most likely to engage an individual's motivation and provide a meaningful context to facilitate needed change. Harlow and Harlow (1965), as well as Ainsworth (1989), have described several *affectional systems* that bear on development and are likely engaged by different treatment modalities. These include the attachment of child to parent and of parent to child as well as attachment bonds with siblings and other family members, with peers, and with romantic partners. Individual therapy provides a setting in which the therapy relationship provides a secure base analogous to that established in relation to a parent to help the client reconsider maladaptive views and behaviors related to the self and others. Group therapy may be an extremely powerful intervention to activate the peer attachment system. Marital and family therapy allow direct focus on change through the romantic and parental systems. All modalities share two things in common: (a) that a rationale for the problem and its solution are provided and (b) that a collaborative relationship is established in which support is offered, healthy change is promoted, and in which trust may be developed. In each approach there are opportunities for expanded awareness of self and others that may afford the possibility of change.

Individual Psychotherapy

As is evident from the previous chapters in this volume, the mainstay of evidence-based treatment for PDs has been delivered through an individual modality of treatment. Clearly established as a treatment modality, individual psychotherapy is often preferred for clients with personality dysfunction because of the common issues of trust many such individuals share. The anonymity afforded to the client by individual psychotherapy will continue to make this a useful way to deliver treatment. Especially in cases where there is severe attachment pathology related to early abuse or disruptions, the safety of a relationship with a trained therapist allows for the establishment of a secure base to which other modalities, such as group or couples therapy, can be added. The individual setting also allows for a more in-depth focus on unique learning history and current phenomenology when these elements are seen as necessary to motivate change. Beutler and Clarkin (1990, p. 123) summarized three distinctive advantages of using individual psychotherapy: (a) extensive self-disclosure in a private atmosphere allows the development of intimacy and trust with another, (b) it allows for the modeling of the therapist and a development of transference, and (c) it allows for individualized attention during a crises that can be tailored to the client's needs.

Group Psychotherapy

Group psychotherapy is an underutilized treatment modality with a substantive empirical base (Piper, 2008). The group environment seems ideally suited for many clients with personality dysfunction. In his senior career award paper for the Society of Psychotherapy Research, Piper (2008) wrote that "the group, which is sometimes referred to as a social microcosm, is believed to be capable of eliciting the typical maladaptive interpersonal behavior of each patient. It is also capable of mobilizing strong forces for change (e.g. peer pressure)" (p. 129). Beutler and Clarkin (1990) identified the following three advantages of a group modality: (a) it allows for identification and modeling with peers, (b) it makes use of support and advice, and (c) it allows for the practice of newly developed skills in a social environment that more closely approximates the range of reactions that will be experienced outside of the group.

Couples/Marital Psychotherapy

The use of dyadic forms of psychotherapy for the treatment of personality dysfunction has been slow to take hold, probably because of the relative isolation of systemic forms of psychotherapy from the dominant field. This seems to be due in part to the fact that early pioneers of systemic therapy eschewed the notion of diagnosis of individuals, so personality was not traditionally viewed as a relevant construct. Now, couples/marital and family therapy are used irrespective of theoretical orientations. As schools of psychotherapy have become increasingly more integrative and unified the construct of the individual personality has broadened to incorporate systems thinking (e.g., Goldfried & Castonguay, 1993; Greenberg & Johnson, 1988). Many individuals ultimately diagnosed with a formal PD or considered to be demonstrating personality dysfunction inevitably have marital distress as a component of their dysfunctioning interpersonal processes. A common way for therapy with a PD client to be initiated is when a spouse or other loved one wishes to improve the relationship, or when the loss of that relationship occurs or is threatened. This is especially the case for Cluster B disorders but is also quite common in obsessive–compulsive PD, passive–aggressive PD, and dependent PD. Disorders characterized by extreme alienation from others (paranoid PD, schizoid PD, schizotypal PD) are less likely to involve an initial couples focus. Relational processes play a central role in the development and maintenance of self-defeating interpersonal patterns, and personality is embedded in the relational matrix (Magnavita & MacFarlane, 2004; Nurse & Stanton, 2008). There is also converging evidence to suggest the use of dyadic psychotherapy with individuals whose issues comprise problematic personality patterns. It is well established that there is a link between depression and marital satisfaction, as well as between family dysfunction and conduct disorder. Beutler and Clarkin (1990, p. 123) identified four advantages of using a marital/couples modality: (a) direct observation of problematic interactions can be observed, (b) the contribution of both parties to the conflict can be witnessed, (c) mutual problem solving and conflict resolution can be practiced in vivo, and (d) support and empathy for each other can be elicited and demonstrated.

Family Psychotherapy

Another modality of treatment for personality dysfunction that has not received much attention from researchers is family psychotherapy. Family psychotherapy attempts to alter problematic relational transactions by using restructuring techniques and by incorporating advances from relational and developmental science that suggest ways to enhance communication. Although as yet little research has been done, use of conjoint family therapy has been described for PD treatment in general (e.g., Benjamin & Cushing, 2004). In addition, an approach has been recently developed to improve family functioning in BPD in the hope that this would reduce caregiver stress and in turn promote a better environment that could provide stability for the client with BPD. Empirical data are promising so far in regard to improved conditions among family members, but benefits to the individuals diagnosed with BPD remain to be assessed (Hoffman, Fruzzetti, & Buteau, 2007). Beutler and Clarkin (1990, p. 123) identified three advantages of using family psychotherapy: (a) changes in family communication and problem solving can be observed and shaped in vivo, (b) parenting skills can be strengthened and taught, and (c) multigenerational processes can be discovered that lead to problematic patterns and symptoms. In addition, as a conjoint modality, family conferences (perhaps videotaped and reviewed later) can be used to refine the individuals' understanding of problematic multigenerational patterns and help focus individual and marital modalities.

Neurobiological Approaches

The primary neurobiological treatment modality used for personality dysfunction is psychopharmacological treatment of symptom-related clusters that may have neurobiological underpinnings. Generally speaking, the pharmacological agents are used to address the comorbid conditions or Axis I disorders, such as anxiety, depression, mood lability, emotional dysregulation, and perceptual distortion, in accordance with practice guidelines suggested by the American Psychiatric Association (2001). Overall, there is a lack of extant empirical evidence for using medications with individuals with personality dysfunction, yet they are commonly used. The studies that are available have tended to focus on BPD only and have demonstrated limited effects. A recent review of pharmacological treatment research for PD was provided by Triebwasser and Siever (2007), and regarding even BPD they reached the following conclusion:

> Drugs in most medication classes have shown some efficacy for BPD, but benefits have often been limited to specific symptom areas, with rare findings of global remission: Some subjects appear to get "better," but few if any appear to become "well" in controlled medication trials. (p. 41)

A wide spectrum of pharmaceutical agents, a complete review of which is beyond the scope of this chapter, or even this volume, are used in the treatment of PD. There are also a number of psychophysiological approaches that are in experimental stages that may have application for treatment of personality dysfunction, such as heart rate variability biofeedback; neurofeedback; and other types of biofeedback, such as thermal, galvanic skin response, and muscle tension.

Psychoeducational Approaches

Some degree of explanation and teaching about client problems is inherent to most forms of therapy as part of treatment planning, contracting, and goal setting. Only one study has looked at the degree to which a purely psychoeducational intervention would help ameliorate PD: Zanarini and Frankenburg (2008) developed a 12-week psychoeducational protocol for individuals diagnosed with BPD and found significant reductions in general impulsivity and unstable relationships relative to a wait-list control group. They concluded that these particular changes were observed because behavior, in contrast to affect and cognition, is more readily changed by means of the provision of information. In addition to the professional treatment literature, a variety of resources of varying quality exist in the popular press for a number of PDs, including BPD, narcissistic PD, passive–aggressive PD, obsessive–compulsive PD, and avoidant PD; their usefulness will likely be a function of client motivation and degree of resonance with their own experience. There is some risk that treatment recommendations in books available in the lay press will conflict with the therapist's in-session approach. The fact that clients may find these, or less reputable resources, on their own amplifies the need for therapists to clearly articulate the rationale for their own treatment approach and to collaborate with clients to develop shared treatment goals.

Support Groups

There is little in the way of empirical findings for the efficacy of support groups in the treatment of personality dysfunction, although there is a trend.

Milieu Therapy and Therapeutic Communities

The use of therapeutic communities for treating PDs shows promise. Research indicates that patients diagnosed with BPD had significant symptom reductions compared with individuals in a nonhospital control group. The treatment group consisted of 137 hospitalized patients, and symptom reduction was negatively correlated with length of stay (Dolan, Warren, & Norton, 1997).

Treatment Settings

Treatment settings are critical components of treatment packages as the setting selected has major ramifications in terms of cost and potential stigma. Inpatient care is costly and should only be used when there is sufficient evidence that this is necessary. Intensive outpatient care can often be an alternative to inpatient treatment, but the empirical literature is sparse when it comes to selection. Partial programs although excellent alternatives do not exist in many communities.

Outpatient

Most PD clients are treated on an outpatient basis in community clinics and private practices, in part because of the chronicity of these disorders, coupled with waxing and waning severity over time in response to events. The outpatient practice or clinic is the primary setting in which those with personality dysfunction will be treated. At times of crises, especially when life threatening, outpatient treatment must turn to inpatient care to keep the individual safe until stabilization. In some instances outpatient care can be augmented by partial hospitalization.

Inpatient

In the last 20 years there has been a seismatic shift in the utilization of inpatient settings for treatment of severe psychiatric disorders. Lengths of stays in psychiatric hospitals were generally at least 2 months, but in many cases patients would be treated for up to a year or more. In part because of the managed care movement and efforts at cost containment, inpatient hospital stays were severely curtailed. Now, the length of stay on an inpatient unit is 3 to 5 days, which out of necessity allows only for stabilization and ensuring safety. There is little time to conduct the careful and through evaluations that used to be the mainstay of many psychiatric hospitals. There are little data on the effectiveness of these limited inpatient hospitalizations. Many individuals will be readmitted numerous times until stabilization is achieved. Some forms of treatment, such as DBT, reduce the readmission rate. Hospitalization is costly and may induce secondary trauma. There is little time to coordinate care with the outpatient clinicians, and often this is a decision that is made primarily for reasons of safety, so that the patient is, in essence, held until the crisis has passed, relieving the outpatient clinicians from managing the crisis. Of course, within the inpatient setting a plethora of factors may influence outcome. One variable that has been examined is the quality of therapeutic alliance with the inpatient psychotherapist. There is an indication that the clinicians better able to achieve a good therapeutic alliance have better outcomes (Dinger, Strack, Leichsenring, Wilmers, & Schaunburg, 2008). When considered as a whole, the literature questions the overreliance on inpatient hospitalization as perhaps not being appropriate. Inpatient care can also become a revolving door with high recidivism for more disturbed patients who go from one crisis to another.

Partial Hospitalization and Day Treatment

The use of partial hospitalization for treatment of BPD has shown to be effective in conjunction with a mentalization approach and 18 months of maintenance group therapy (Bateman & Fonagy, 2008). Partial hospitalization seems to be an underutilized but excellent setting for patients who require more intensive treatment. It also offers the option of providing other modalities such as occupational therapy and group therapy, which might not be available in outpatient settings. Psychopharmacological response can also be monitored closely. The advantage of day treatment is that it provides an ambulatory approach which can offer intensive clinical services. There is a substantial body of evidence showing efficacy for personality disorders when treated in this setting (Ogrodniczuk & Piper, 2004).

Residential Settings and Community Settings

Residential treatment and community setting such as half way houses are often the setting of choice when there is comorbid substance abuse or antisocial behavior that needs longer term care and more careful monitoring. There is little empirical evidence that demonstrates the efficacy of these settings and clearly more is needed. There has been controversy in the past decade over some forms of residential treatment especially outward bound and wilderness programs that are used for adolescents who may have PDs with substance abuse and behavioral problems.

Format

The format of treatment is a central component of treatment, but, unfortunately, clinicians have very little data to guide their treatment decisions in this regard. Knowledge of the formats and flexibility will help fine tune these decisions so they maximize treatment. Assessing clinical responsiveness and maintaining a collaborative approach are essential in being able to modify the format to the most efficient when the clinical situation calls for alteration.

The length of sessions, number of sessions per week, and length of treatment are all related to therapeutic potency, but, again, there is little data to suggest how these variables operate and interact. We are therefore left to using clinical judgment and testing our hypothesis on a case-by-case basis. Clearly assessment is critical in determining the personality profile and the likely potency needed (Magnavita, 2005b).

Length of Treatment

Treatment can be divided into four basic formats: (a) long term (more than 40 sessions), (b) short term (fewer than 40 sessions), (c) crisis intervention (1–3 sessions), and (d) intermittent treatment (distinct phases of treatment over the course of years).

Frequency of Sessions

There is no empirical evidence on the efficacy of length of time between sessions. Generally speaking, the clinical evidence from years of case reports suggests that psychotherapists—in particular, psychoanalysts—believe that the more frequent the sessions, the better the outcome. This notion has been challenged by various clinical theorists and researchers over the past century. Many pioneers in the field believed that the frequency of sessions was not set in stone and, if too frequent, could even be counterproductive and cause unnecessary dependency.

Length of Sessions

Our research group (first author) has been informally gathering information from clients regarding their satisfaction with various lengths of sessions. After we experimented with various durations, our anecdotal evidence indicates that for the majority of clients with personality dysfunction there is a clear preference for sessions that are 90 minutes in duration. Although we have not conducted formal surveys, we have interviewed more than 100 clients, many whom have been in previous treatments, who have reported that 90-minute sessions are by far preferable because they afford sufficient time to work on issues. Many have said that when in psychotherapy with the traditional 45- to 50-minute session they felt they had to leave just as they were getting warmed up and that this often caused additional frustration. Some do well with shorter sessions, typically 45 minutes, but our findings are supported by other clinical research teams who have shown that longer sessions are preferable for the majority of clients with PDs.

Developing Treatment Packages: Treatment Planning and Strategizing

Clinicians are expected and required to develop treatment packages rapidly in collaboration with the client system and deliver the treatment protocol in a way that enlists the client system, monitors the client's progress, and adjusts the various elements to provide optimal care. The contributors to this volume for the most part have underscored the importance of assessment in their chapters. Once the assessment phase is completed, the clinician offers his or her ideas about the course of treatment, including preferred modalities, treatment frames, settings, and so forth. Through this collaborative process, and once the treatment package and the specific elements have been agreed on, treatment ensues with specific goals in mind.

On the basis of the information we have provided thus far, our clinical experience, and our understanding of psychotherapy, we think that three major principles should guide clinicians in delineating and proposing to their clients the parameters that will define the framework within which therapy will be conducted: (a) comprehensive consideration of available options, (b) a cost–benefit analysis of these options, and (c) a careful attention to empirically derived guidelines pertinent to treatment planning.

Know Your Options

As we have discussed, there are multiple options clinicians need to be cognizant of when formulating a treatment package. Often clinicians stick to those that they are most familiar with, which might not be optimal. Clinicians should expand their repertoire of modalities, formats, and methods so that a greater range of treatment is available to those seeking assistance.

Furthermore, therapists should be reminded that, once contracted, the framework that they have agreed on with their client expands on as more material is gathered. For example, an individual with a narcissistic personality presented in treatment after losing his executive position with the idea of working on job transition and dealing with the injury to his self-esteem. Although he had alluded to his problem with drinking, the extent of his alcoholism did not become apparent until his wife was invited in for a conjoint session. After a discussion, the focus of treatment was expanded to include the patterns that persisted in the relationship that added to the maladaptive coping.

As the previous examples suggest, a particularly important consideration when developing appropriate treatment packages is addressing the likelihood of comorbid conditions. Clients with a PD diagnosis are likely to qualify for more than one (Dimaggio & Norcross, 2008) as well as to be more likely to have an Axis I disorder such as anxiety, depression, substance abuse, and so on. The Axis I disorders and relational disturbances typically are what motivate an individual or couple to seek treatment. There is little in the way of empirical findings to guide clinicians in making treatment decisions. Many clinical theorists believe that the clinical syndrome derives from the personality configuration. In each case, a decision has to be made whether to address the clinical syndrome first and then, if warranted, the personality system (Magnavita, 2005a).

Conducting a Cost–Benefit Analysis

As with any medical or psychological treatment, the treatment of personality dysfunction requires a consideration of both the financial and risk factors involved in offering a particular treatment package. A cost–benefit analysis must entail two major considerations. The first is to consider the potential benefit versus harm that will likely result from the delivery of a particular treatment package; in other words, when making a clinical decision one should ask the following question: "What is the worst possible outcome if this approach is followed?" For example, a highly anxious client with bipolar disorder and BPD who lived an isolated life was encouraged to enter a DBT skills building group or attend a partial hospital program. She resisted all attempts. During one stressful period, she became agitated and psychotic, and involuntary admission to an inpatient unit was considered. Having the police come to her home to take her to the hospital proved to be highly traumatic, but the danger of allowing her to be alone while decompensating seemed to be the higher risk.

The second consideration one should take into account when conducting a cost–benefit analysis centers on the question of benefits derived from adding modalities of treatment to the treatment package. This is an area where there are virtually no data to use for clinical algorithms, yet clinicians are required to consider these issues every time they revise a treatment package. For example, if a client is expected to have a 50% chance of becoming less symptomatic or making substantive changes in his or her dysfunctional personality patterns with 40 sessions of individual psychotherapy, what is the added benefit of also recommending group psychotherapy? As client complexity increases, there does seem to be a natural trend to add more modalities of treatment. Clients with personality dysfunction may be seen individually and in couples psychotherapy, as well as being treated psychopharmacologically. Sometimes, both members of the marital dyad are seeing individual therapists as well as being treated with psychotropic medication. Where cost becomes a consideration, the clinician must examine the literature and see which modality or type of treatment has the most cost-effective profile. This is an important topic for researchers and clinicians. For example, it is well documented that group psychotherapy for PDs is effective, yet there is often a lack of available programs that offer it.

Consider Empirically Based Guidelines as They May Apply in Context

A recent review conducted by a task force sponsored by Division 12 of the American Psychological Association and the North American Society for Psychotherapy Research derived treatment principles from the empirical literature, including a summary for PD (Critchfield & Benjamin, 2006a, 2006b). Their review contains many caveats emphasizing that treatment research in PD is still in its infancy and tends to focus primarily on BPD. Because PD contains a wide variety of problems and patterns—often in comorbid combination, with some bearing little similarity to BPD—the principles are necessarily tentative and require further research. The task force's conclusions were based on the small existing PD treatment literature, reasonable extensions of findings from work with other disorders, extrapolations to treatment based on the nature of PD in general, and inspection of the elements contained in treatment packages for PD that have empirical support. Task force principles were organized according to client characteristics, relationship factors, and technique factors. Although the task force's decisions about the length and frequency of sessions, modality, or setting were not directly addressed, many of the principles have bearing on treatment planning and formatting, especially the nature and process of decision making about it.

An important principle thought to predict the success of therapy in PD is the client's willingness to engage in a change process: his or her level of motivation for therapy, whatever form it ultimately takes. This implies that a match between treatment options and the client's understanding of his or her own needs is crucial for success. Technique principles that can enhance client motivation include frank and transparent discussion of the nature of his or her problems and a related rationale for treatment (after careful formulation and assessment). This principle suggests that the therapist's theoretical lens and understanding of both the pathology and the optimal treatment process should be discussed. Treatments are expected to be more successful when client and therapist both agree and the focus is clearly on the client's presenting problems and concerns. A one-size-fits-all approach is unlikely to work with PD because the diagnostic label contains a wide diversity of problems and patterns, usually involving complex combinations of multiple PD features, and Axis I disorders. We recommend that treatment parameters be tailored to individual needs and developed in a collaborative manner and with clear rationale. The collaborative nature of the process is key and may ultimately lead to the decision to pursue (or not pursue) any of the various modalities (e.g., individual, group, family, conjoint) with a specific client.

The principle with the clearest empirical support emphasizes the quality of the therapeutic relationship. One can reasonably assume that this principle applies to the early stages of assessment and treatment planning as well as to the rest of the therapy. Principles that emphasize collaboration with the client to plan and achieve treatment goals, and the need for a flexible and creative approach, also speak to the importance of the therapist's manner of arriving at and presenting treatment options.

Although the principle of achieving a strong alliance is easily stated, it can prove difficult because PD comprises a set of disorders defined in part by difficulties establishing productive relationships. Given the diversity of patterns in PD, the optimal relational process may look quite different for individual clients, and it represents an area in dire need of more research. For example, American Psychological Association Task Force principles for PD involving high therapist activity, structuring of treatment, and limit setting, were identified primarily on the basis of their presence in BPD treatment manuals (Critchfield & Benjamin, 2006a). However, this stance may not work equally well for all disorders. For example, PDs defined in part by reactivity or sensitivity to interpersonal control (e.g., passive–aggressive PD) may react negatively to structure and limit setting. Other clients may be tempted to act in the face of structure in characteristic ways that should be anticipated by a therapist with a mind toward engaging the client's will to understand and change problem patterns in affect, cognition, and behavior. It is these issues that require clinicians to apply the arts of judgment, understanding, and discernment when applying scientific findings to particular cases.

Beutler (2000), after conducting an extensive review and empirical validation, summarized the following reasonable and basic principles of treatment selection:

- *Prognosis:* The likelihood of improvement (prognosis) is a positive function of social support level and a negative function of functional impairment.
- *Level of intensity of care:* Higher levels of contact and availability may be necessary with more complex and/or severe cases of PD, especially if motivation for change is low. Some clients may need more frequent sessions; higher levels of therapist activity; and, depending on the precise nature of the pathology (e.g., potential for reactance), greater structure built into the treatment. The optimal level of care may need to be changed, increased, or decreased, depending on the perceived stressors and the client's response to stressors. This is expected to be linked also to phase of therapy, with greater intensity typically used early in treatment or to aid in handling specific crises. Judgment must be used to ensure that intensity-of-care variables are used to enhance the client's strengths and motivation for change instead of as a feature that enables acting out or other pathology.
- *Risk reduction:* Higher levels of care and direct intervention (e.g., hospitalization) are of course also necessary to ensure basic safety and preserve ability to later re-engage in productive outpatient treatment when a client is in crisis. DBT explicitly prioritizes focus on "treatment-interfering behaviors" in outpatient sessions. Benjamin (2003, Chapter 7) outlined risk management strategies tailored to a client's specific PD diagnosis, interpersonal history, motivations for acting out, and overall case formulation. Some of these interventions involve modification of treatment formatting, including increased session frequency or, in some contexts, the opposite strategy: a planned reduction of intensity in therapy, using a return to valuable work as a reinforcer for enhanced self-management.

OPTIMAL PRINCIPLES

Selected principles generated by the APA Task Force that have particular relevance to treatment formatting decisions are shown in Exhibit 10.1) (We recommend that those interested in knowing more about the principles

EXHIBIT 10.1
Selected Principles Taken From the American Psychological Association Division 12 and North American Society for Psychotherapy Research Task Force Review With Particular Relevance to Treatment Formatting Decisions in Personality Disorder

[Treatments are expected to have improved outcomes when there is:]
a) Priority of focus on presenting problems and concerns
b) Early formulation and identification of patterns (cognition, affect, and behavior) linked to problem maintenance
c) Discussion of the nature of the problem and rationale for treatment
d) A treatment frame established in collaboration with the patient and structured to achieve clear and explicit goals
e) Therapist structures treatment and sets limits on unacceptable behavior [primarily through emphasis on natural consequences of the behavior]
f) Focused, theoretically coherent, consistent, and well-coordinated treatment [including across treatment team members]
g) [Match to client's] willingness and ability to engage with treatment
h) Match between level of impairment and treatment intensity
i) Match between client's resistance level and intervention type
j) Balance focus on change/motivation for change with empathic support
k) Ongoing supervision/consultation for therapists

Note. Adapted from "Integration of therapeutic factors in treating personality disorders" by K. L. Critchfield and L. S. Benjamin, 2006a. In L. G. Castonguay and L. E. Beutler (Eds.), *Principles of therapeutic change that work* (pp. 253–271). New York, NY: Oxford University Press. Copyright 2006 by Oxford University Press. Adapted with permission.

themselves, how they were derived, and the related caveats about each read the original report: Critchfield & Benjamin 2006a) Overall, formatting principles should generally run in parallel with good decision making for treatment. The process should include collaborative planning that is based on a good assessment of problems, concerns, maladaptive patterns, and client strengths. It should involve the client directly; enlist his or her motivation for change; and target well-specified treatment goals, which will vary from client to client. They are also likely to be differently framed across theoretical perspectives, variously emphasizing behavior, affect, cognition, relating, or identity. In any case, the chosen approach should directly address the client's presenting concerns and unique pathology. It should also be accompanied by a clearly presented rationale regarding how it is expected to work and what will be required of the client. Some approaches to PD treatment (e.g., transference-focused psychotherapy) use a contracting process to formally establish the boundaries and expectations of treatment, including when and why it may end. Most well-known approaches to PD treatment involve discussions of expectations relative to specific client pathology, to a greater or lesser degree of formality. Balancing the need for clear structure and expectations in the treatment, it is also recommended that therapists working with PD clients should be flexible in their approach, including the possibility of altering the modality and formatting parameters (e.g., conjoint sessions, adjunctive therapy, increasing or decreasing frequency of sessions, hospitalization if crisis cannot be managed safely in an outpatient setting) in response to changing needs over the course of a therapy process. Any changes in response to circumstance and client need should involve clear and explicit discussion and explanation to ensure collaboration. The process of negotiating needs during a crisis may itself be a healing therapeutic element for some clients and can be used to enhance the alliance and press for change. When selecting treatment formats and parameters, therapists should expect that the process will likely be long term and that it may be quite difficult, requiring patience and tolerance (from all team members) when setbacks, impasses, and crises or acting out occur. Therapists may wish to use support and peer consultation groups to keep up their own morale as well as to receive creative and flexible input from other clinicians working with similar populations and treatment models.

SUMMARY

Treatment planning and formatting are both an art and science. A clinician who wants to optimize his or her effectiveness must be conversant with multiple literatures. This is no mean feat because the variables with which one needs to contend and the complexity of their interactions can be overwhelming even to the seasoned clinician. In this chapter, we have presented many of the important variables that should be considered and monitored along with the best guidelines clinical science has at the time to enable clinicians to make informed treatment decisions. Of course, it is essential that these treatment decisions be made in collaboration with the clients who seek assistance; otherwise, the possibility of premature termination of treatment and a less-than-optimal outcome is increased.

REFERENCES

Ainsworth, M. D. S. (1989). Attachments beyond infancy. *American Psychologist, 44,* 709–716.

Alexander, F. G., & French, T. M. (1946). *Psychoanalytic therapy: Principles and applications.* New York, NY: Ronald Press.

American Psychiatric Association. (2001). Practice guideline for the treatment of patients with borderline personality disorder. *American Journal of Psychiatry, 158*(October Suppl.), 1–52.

Bateman, A., & Fonagy, P. (2008). 8-year follow-up of patients treated for borderline personality disorder: Mentalization-based treatment versus treatment as usual. *American Journal of Psychiatry, 165,* 631–638.

Benjamin, L.S. and Cushing, G. (2004). An interpersonal family-oriented approach to personality disorder. In M. MacFarlane (Ed.), *Family Treatment of Personality Disorders: Advances in clinical practice*. New York, NY: Haworth Press, p. 41–70.

Beutler, L. E. (2000). Empirically based decision making in clinical practice. *Prevention & Treatment, 3*(1). doi: 10.1037/1522-3736.3.1.327a

Beutler, L. E., & Clarkin, J. F. (1990). *Systematic treatment selection: Toward targeted therapeutic interventions*. New York, NY: Brunner/Mazel.

Critchfield, K. L. & Benjamin, L. S. (2006a). Integration of therapeutic factors in treating personality disorders. In L. G. Castonguay & L. E. Beutler (Eds.). *Principles of therapeutic change that work*. (pp. 253–271). New York, NY: Oxford University Press.

Critchfield, K. L., & Benjamin, L. S. (2006b). Principles for psychosocial treatment of personality disorder: Summary of the Division 12 Task Force review. *Journal of Clinical Psychology, 62*, 661–674.

Dimaggio, G., & Norcross, J. C. (2008). Treating patients with two or more personality disorders. *Journal of Clinical Psychology, 64*, 127–138.

Dinger, U., Strack, M., Leichsenring, F., Wilmers, F., & Schauenburg, H. (2008). Therapist effects on outcome and alliance in inpatient psychotherapy. *Journal of Clinical Psychology, 64*, 344–354.

Dolan, B., Warren, F., & Norton, K. (1997). Change in borderline symptoms one year after therapeutic community treatment for severe personality disorder. *British Journal of Psychiatry, 171*, 274–279.

Frances, A., Clarkin, J. F., & Perry, S. (1984). *Differential therapeutics in psychiatry*. New York, NY: Brunner/Mazel.

Goldfried, M. R., & Castonguay, L. G. (1993). Behavior therapy: Redefining clinical strengths and limitations. *Behavior Therapy, 24*, 505–526.

Greenberg, L. S., & Johnson, S. M. (1988). *Emotionally focused therapy for couples*. New York, NY: Guilford Press.

Guimon, J. (2002). Groups in therapeutic communities. In J. J. Magnavita (Vol. Ed.). *Comprehensive handbook of psychotherapy: Vol. 1. Psychodynamic/object relations* (pp. 529–547). Hoboken, NJ: Wiley.

Harlow, H. F., & Harlow, M. K. (1965). The affectional systems. In A. M. Schrier, H. F. Harlow, & F. Stollnitz (Eds), *Behavior of non-human primates* (Vol 2, pp. 287–334). New York, NY: Academic Press, Inc.

Hoffman, P. D., Fruzzetti, A. E., & Buteau, E. (2007). Understanding and engaging families: An education, skills, and support program for relatives impacted by borderline personality disorder. *Journal of Mental Health, 16*(1), 69–82.

Magnavita, J. J. (1999). Challenges in treatment of personality disorders: When the disorder demands comprehensive integration *In Session: Psychotherapy in Practice, 4*(4), 5–17.

Magnavita, J. J. (2005). Using the MCMI–III for treatment planning and to enhance clinical efficacy. In R. J. Craig (Ed.), *New directions in interpreting the Millon Clinical Multiaxial Inventory—III* (pp. 165–184). Hoboken, NJ: Wiley.

Magnavita, J. J., & MacFarlane, M. (2004). Family treatment of personality disorders: Historical overview and current perspectives. In M. MacFarlane (Ed.), *Family treatment of personality disorders: Advances in clinical practice* (pp. 3–39). New York, NY: Haworth Press.

Nurse, R. A., & Stanton, M. (2008). Using the MCMI in treating couples. In T. Millon & C. Bloom (Eds.). *The Millon inventories: A practitioner's guide to personalized clinical assessment* (2nd ed., pp. 347–368). Hoboken, NJ: Wiley.

Ogrodniczuk, J. S., & Piper, W. E. (2004). Day treatment of personality disorders. In J. J. Magnavita (Ed.), *Handbook of personality disorders: Theory and practice* (pp. 356-397). Hoboken, NJ: Wiley.

Piper, W. E. (2008). Underutilization of short-term group therapy: Enigmatic or understandable? *Psychotherapy Research, 18,* 127–138.

Schimmel, P. (1997). Swimming against the tide? A review of the therapeutic community. *Australian and New Zealand Journal of Psychiatry, 31,* 120–127.

Triebwasser, J., & Siever, L. J. (2007). Pharmacotherapy of personality disorders. *Journal of Mental Health, 16(1),* 5–50.

Zanarini, M. C., & Frankenburg, F. R. (2008). A preliminary, randomized trial of psychoeducation for women with borderline personality disorder. *Journal of Personality Disorders, 22,* 284–290.

INDEX

Axis I disorders
    with Axis II symptoms, 58
    and borderline personality disorder,
        68
    dual diagnoses with, 79
    integrated treatment for, 236
    and interpersonal psychotherapy,
        150–151
    interventions for, 3
    personality disorders as, 26
    and treatment effect, 86, 203
    treatment planning to encompass,
        298
    unified treatment of, 269, 270
Axis II disorders
    borderline personality disorder, 68
    comorbidity with, 86, 151
    dual diagnoses with, 79

Bachrach, H. M., 57
Barber, J. P., 278
Bateman, A., 272, 274
Bateman, A. W., 103, 104
Beck, A. T., 71–74
Behavioral skill development, 202–203
Behavior change, 211
Behavior dyscontrol, 54
Behavior dysregulation, 53
Behavior exchange, 208
Behavior therapy, 57–58
Beier, E., 125–127
Bender, D. S., 85
Benjamin, L. S., 71, 116, 124, 125, 129,
        151, 154, 155, 204–205, 226,
        233, 262, 263, 301
Bernier, B., 125
Berscheid, E., 113
Best evidence domain, 8
Beutler, L. E., 86, 289, 291–293, 301
Bias, 33–34, 36
Binder, J., 120
Biology, 197–198, 229, 257
Biosocial theory, 50–51
Blagys, M. D., 82
Blatt, S. J., 30
Bogwald, K. P., 267
Bond, M., 86
Borderline personality disorder (BPD)
    and brief relational therapy, 189
    comorbid conditions with, 68–69

dialectical behavior therapy for
        treatment of, 50, 52–55,
        59, 72–73
expressed emotion with, 200
family therapy for treatment of, 293
interpersonal circle mapping of, 154
and interpersonal relationships,
        193–195, 197–202, 207
psychodynamic therapy for
        treatment of, 102–105
and psychoeducation, 294
settings for treatment of, 295
unified treatment for, 272–274, 276
Bordin, E., 168
Bradley, R., 123
Brief evidence-based psychodynamic
        therapy, 101–102
Brief relational therapy (BRT),
        189–190. See also Relational
        approach
    change in, 170
    development of, 167–168
    effectiveness of, 101
    relational considerations with,
        171–173
    therapy process, 171
    for treatment of comorbid
        conditions, 187–188
Buffington-Vollum, J. K., 128

Carpreol, M. J., 156
Carson, R. C., 123
Case management strategies, 60
Case studies, 10–11
CBT. See Cognitive–behavior therapy
Chambless, D. L., 6, 75
Chandler, M., 57
Change
    in couples and family therapy, 196
    in dialectical behavior therapy,
        49–52
    in integrated treatment, 231–232,
        235–236, 241–243
    in interpersonal psychotherapy,
        117–118
    in psychodynamic therapy, 81–84
    in relational approach, 169–170
Character resistance, 80
Character structures, 27–28

Norcross, J. C., 14, 121
Normality, 27
North American Society for Psycho-
    therapy Research, 224, 299

Object relations
    patients with low quality of, 93
    in psychodynamic assessment, 30
Observation, 15
Observational learning, 208
Obsessive–compulsive personality
    disorder (OPCD)
    brief dynamic therapy for treatment
        of, 278
    cognitive therapy for treatment of,
        57, 73–75
    interpersonal components of, 194
Ogrodniczuk, J. S., 90
Oldham, J. M., 4
OPCD. See Obsessive–compulsive
    personality disorder
Operant conditioning, 51–52
Operating systems (pattern recognition),
    259
Outpatient treatment settings, 294–295,
    301
Overinvolvement, 201

PAI. See Personality Assessment
    Inventory
Paivio, S. C., 125
Panic disorder, 86, 99
Panic-focused psychodynamic psycho-
    therapy (PFPP), 86
Paranoid personality disorder
    interpersonal circle mapping of, 153
    and interpersonal relationships, 193
    low communion of, 154
    maladaptive cognitive patterns in, 70
    validation/acceptance techniques
        for, 71
Parenting
    and ego strength, 30
    and family therapy, 293
Paris, J., 154, 273
Partial hospitalization, 295–296
Pathogenesis, 8
Patient right to treatment, 4–5
Pattern recognition

theoretical modeling as tool in, 8
    in unified treatment, 259
PDI-IV. See Personality Disorders
    Interview–IV
PDQ–4. See Personality Diagnostic
    Questionnaire—4
Peer consultation groups, 288
Performance-based tests, 25, 39
    administration of, 35
    and DSM–IV–TR criteria, 31
    format of, 25
    symptom-based distortions with, 32
    time commitment of, 39
Perry, J. C., 86
Perry, S., 289
Personality Assessment Inventory
    (PAI), 23–24, 38–39
Personality change, 229
Personality Diagnostic Questionnaire—
    4 (PDQ–4), 22, 38
Personality Disorders Interview–IV
    (PDI-IV), 20–21, 37
Personality disorders not otherwise
    specified (NOS)
    brief relational therapy for treatment
        of, 187–188
    psychodynamic therapy for treatment
        of, 100, 101
Personality dysfunction
    and clinicians, 5–6
    and evidence-based treatment
        movement, 5
Personality organization, 28
Personality systematics, 253–257
Personality systems
    and clinicians, 3
    and integrated treatment, 227–228
PFPP (panic-focused psychodynamic
    psychotherapy), 86
Pharmacotherapy
    in neurobiological approach, 293
    with psychotherapy, 86
Phases-of-change model, 229
Phillips, D., 75
Piper, W. E., 268–269, 291
Planning. See Treatment planning and
    formatting
Positive complementarity, 119, 126
Posttraumatic stress disorder, 70

Respondent conditioning, 51
Responsiveness
    in interpersonal psychotherapy,
        121–122
    of therapist, 14
Restructuring, 82–83, 202–203, 256,
    265–269, 275
Risk reduction, 301
Rockland, L. H., 102
Rogers, Carl, 237
Rorschach–Exner Comprehensive
    System, 24, 25, 39, 41–42
Rosenthal, R., 123
Rubin, D., 123
Rupture resolution
    defined, 167
    in relational approach, 175–179
Ruptures, 168–169, 189
Russell, J. J., 154

Safety, 238
Safran, J. D., 129, 167, 173, 188, 234
Samstag, L. W., 172, 188, 234
Samuel, D. B., 42
Sanderson, C., 236
Santisteban, D. A., 205
Schedule of Normal and Abnormal
    Personality—2 (SNAP–2),
    22, 38
Schema-Focused Therapy, 258
Schema-focused therapy (SFT), 224,
    269
Schemata, 229–231
    in interpersonal system, 227
    maladaptive, 242
Schizoid personality disorder
    criteria for diagnosis of, 26
    interpersonal circle mapping of, 153
    and interpersonal relationships,
        193–195
    low communion of, 154
    maladaptive cognitive patterns in,
        70–71
Schizophrenia, 199
Schizotypal personality disorder (STPD)
    interpersonal components of, 194
    maladaptive cognitive patterns in,
        70–71
Schmeelk, K. M., 276
Schore, A. N., 255

SCID-II. See Structured Clinical
    Interview for DSM–IV Axis II
    Personality Disorders
Scoring, of assessments, 20, 25
Segal, Z. V., 129, 172
Self-awareness, 91
Self-confirmation process, 123
Self-dysregulation, 53
Self-fulfilling prophecies, 123, 152
Self-harm, 69, 207, 209, 225, 233,
    239–241, 273
Self-regulation, 237
Self-report inventories, 21–25
    accuracy of, 36
    and DSM–IV–TR criteria, 31–32
    format of, 25
    and intervention outcomes, 35
    symptom-based distortions with, 32
    time commitment of, 38–39
Self-soothing, 241
Self-system
    formation of, 227
    organization of, 230
Semistructured interviews, 20–21
    accuracy of, 36
    defined, 25
    gender bias in, 33
    and intervention outcomes, 35
    and symptom-based distortions, 32
Settings, 294–296
Severity, of personality disorders, 31
Sexual abuse, 271
SFT (schema-focused therapy), 224
Shaping (operant conditioning), 52
Shea, M. T., 150
Sheets, E., 269
Shoda, Y., 229
Short-term dynamic psychotherapy
    (STDP), 189, 276–278, 289
SIDP-IV. See Structured Interview for
    DSM–IV Personality Disorders
Siever, L. J., 293
Skills coaching, 55
Skills training
    in couples and family therapy, 208
    in dialectical behavior therapy, 62
Skodol, A. E., 40
Sloane, R. B., 57–58
Smith, K. R., 6

in psychodynamic therapy, 86–87
in unified treatment, 263
Therapists
and difficulties with patients, 3–4
responsiveness of, 14–15, 121–122
trust with, 72
Therapy-interfering behavior, 69
Tohen, M., 270
Tracey, T. J., 124
Trait system, 227–228
Transference
for activation of unconscious
feelings, 92
in unified treatment, 267–269
Transference-based psychotherapy, 224
Transference-focused psychotherapy
(TFP), 102–104, 258, 276
Transference neurosis, 92
Trauma
childhood, 199
and dialectical behavior therapy, 54
and personality adaptation, 278
as treatment outcome factor, 236–237
Treatment contracts, 233, 293
Treatment planning and formatting,
287–303
developing packages for, 297–301
format, 296–297
historical background of, 288–289
modality selection in, 289–294
optimal principles for, 301–303
of settings, 294–296
Triadic restructuring, 265
Triangles of conflict and persons, 80–83,
92–93
Triangulation, 257–258
Triebwasser, J., 293
Trust, 72
Tyrer, P., 103, 270

Uebelacker, L. A., 275
Unconscious feelings, 92–93
Uncontrolled case studies, 10
Underinvolvement, 201
Unified Psychotherapy Project, 265
Unified treatment, 253–279
clinical process example, 265–269
with Cluster A disorders, 270–271
with Cluster B disorders, 271–277
domains of operation in, 257–258

mechanisms of change in, 256–257
methods for, 265
and personality systematics, 253–257
relational considerations with,
262–264
techniques consistent with, 265
therapy process, 258–262
for treatment of comorbid
conditions, 269
Unstructured interviews
clinician preference for, 41
format of, 20
and intervention outcomes, 35
symptom-based distortions with, 32

Vaillant, McCullough, 81, 82
Validation strategies, 59, 61
in couples and family therapy, 207
in integrated treatment, 234
Van Beek, N., 277
Vanderbilt I and II studies, 120
Verheul, R., 58, 100, 277
Vermetten, E., 278
Vicious circle, 123
Violence, 275

Walker, B. B., 13
Wampold, B. E., 256
Weinberger, J., 83
Weinstock, L. M., 275
Westen, D., 123
Whipple, K., 57–58
Whisman, M. A., 275
Widiger, T. A., 40, 42
Winston, A., 89–90, 188
Withdrawal, 178–183
Withdrawal ruptures, 169
Wolfe, B. E., 121
Woody, S. R., 121
"Working through" phase, 93
World Health Organization, 33

Yorkston, N. J., 57–58
Young, D., 125–127

Zanarini, M. C., 294
Zane, N., 122
Zen principles, 50
Zuroff, D. C., 154

ABOUT THE EDITOR

Jeffrey J. Magnavita, PhD, ABPP, FAPA, is a licensed psychologist and marriage and family therapist who has been in clinical practice for close to 30 years. He served as an adjunct professor in clinical psychology at the University of Hartford, where he taught and supervised doctoral students. Dr. Magnavita has received awards for his work in science and practice. He received the American Psychological Association's (APA's) Award for Distinguished Professional Contributions to Independent or Institutional Practice in the Private Sector for his work developing a theoretical framework for unified clinical science called personality systematics. He is the founder of the Unified Psychotherapy Project, whose mission is to catalogue the methods and techniques of unified psychotherapy. Dr. Magnavita has been featured in two APA videotapes demonstrating personality-guided therapy using a unified approach. He has published extensively and has authored *Restructuring Personality Disorders: A Short-Term Dynamic Approach* (1997), *Relational Therapy for Personality Disorders* (2000), *Personality-Guided Relational Therapy: A Unified Approach* (2005), and a textbook, *Theories of Personality: Contemporary Approaches to the Science of Personality* (2002). He also was the volume editor of *Comprehensive Handbook of Psychotherapy: Vol. 1. Psychodynamic/ Object Relations* (2002) and the *Handbook of Personality Disorders: Theory and*

Practice (2004). He serves on the editorial board of a number of leading publications and has been a guest editor of a number of special editions of journals. He was elected to serve as the president of APA's Division of Psychotherapy in 2010 and has presented his work at various conferences and symposiums. He runs ongoing seminars in psychotherapy using video recordings as the vehicle for examining the process and technical aspects of treatment. Dr. Magnavita lives in South Glastonbury, Connecticut, with his wife Anne and three daughters, Elizabeth, Emily, and Caroline.